Metamorphosis VOL.1

The March First Movement Revisited:
A Global Perspective on Decolonization and Democracy

Institute for Korean Christianity Culture HK+ Research Project,
Soongsil University

Metamorphosis VOL.1

The March First Movement Revisited:

A Global Perspective on Decolonization and Democracy

2021년 6월 17일 초판 발행

기획 및 편집
숭실대학교 한국기독교문화연구원 HK+사업단
https://kiccs.ssu.ac.kr
Tel. +82-2-820-0838

발행처
보고사(발행인 : 김흥국)
경기도 파주시 회동길 337-15
http://www.bogosabooks.co.kr
Tel. 031-955-9797

정가 23,000원
ISBN 979-11-6587-197-0 93300

First Edition, June 17, 2021.

Edited by
Institute for Korean Christianity Culture
HK+ Research Project, Soongsil University
https://kiccs.ssu.ac.kr Tel. +82-2-820-0838

Published by
Bogosa Books (Publisher : Kim Heung-guk)
337-15, Hoedong-gil, Paju-si, Gyeonggi-do, Republic of Korea
http://www.bogosabooks.co.kr
Tel. +82-31-955-9797

Price 23,000 won
ISBN 979-11-6587-197-0 93300

This work was supported by the Ministry of Education of the Republic of Korea and the National Research Foundation of Korea (NRF-2018S1A6A3A01042723)
이 저서는 2018년 대한민국 교육부와 한국연구재단의 지원을 받아 수행된 연구임(KRF-2018S1A6A3A01042723)

Statement of Purpose

Metamorphosis is a book series published by the Humanities Korea Plus (HK+) Center at Soongsil University, South Korea. It seeks to develop interdisciplinary and transnational approaches to Korean Studies from the perspective of transculturation, which encompasses a wide range of research interests from history, literature, and religion to popular culture. *Metamorphosis* includes translated versions of articles that were originally written in Korean or other languages as an attempt to expand the perspective and reach of Korean scholarship and to promote exchanges among Korean Studies scholars in different regions. Each volume focuses on a special topic that grapples with a timely, significant research subject in Korean Studies. It also comprises a general section for the topic of cultural metamorphosis, interviews with prominent Korean Studies scholars outside of South Korea, in addition to Culture Review and Book Review.

The Humanities Korea Plus (HK+) Center is a research project team affiliated with the Soongsil University Institute for Korean Christianity Culture. Funded by South Korea's National Research Foundation since 2018, the HK+ Center encourages research on translation, transculturation, and the transformation of cultures in Korea from the early modern period to the Cold War. Promoting interdisciplinary scholarship that helps draw a new outline for Korean Studies, the Soongsil University HK+ Center provides extensive research on Korean culture under the agenda of the "Metamorphosis of Culture and Knowledge in Korea's Transition to Modernity."

Metamorphosis VOL.1

The March First Movement Revisited:
A Global Perspective on Decolonization and Democracy

Contributors

Authors

Baik Young-seo	Yonsei University, South Korea
Kwon Boduerae	Korea University, South Korea
Hong Jong-wook	Seoul National University, South Korea
Youn Young-shil	Soongsil University, South Korea
Kong Im-soon	Sogang University, South Korea
Kim Jeong-in	Chuncheon National University of Education, South Korea
Sung Joo-hyun	South Korea
Nagata Akifumi	Sophia University, Japan
Jang Won-a	Seoul National University, South Korea
Jang Kyung-nam	Soongsil University, South Korea
Bhang Won-il	Soongsil University, South Korea
David W. Kim	Australian National University, Australia
Lee Yeoun-suk	Hitotsubashi University, Japan
Jooyeon Rhee	The Pennsylvania State University, U.S.
Shin Seung-hwan	University of Pittsburgh, U.S.
Lee Kee-woong	Sungkonghoe University, South Korea
Ko Sun-ho	York University, Canada
Joo Young Lee	University of Michigan, Ann Arbor, U.S.
Na Sil Heo	Yale University, U.S.
James Flynn	University of Wisconsin-Madison, U.S.

Translators

Peter Ward	University of Vienna, Austria
Rachel Min Park	University of California, Berkeley, U.S.
Park Joo-hyun	Catholic University, South Korea
Suhyun Kim	Kyoto University, Japan
Park Hyen-joo	Ewha Womans University, South Korea
Jang Han-gil	South Korea

Editor's Note

This book series title, *Metamorphosis*, encompasses abundant connotations that derive from the word's etymological, biological, and literary usages and draws on a wide range of theoretical resources such as transculturation, transnationalism, and translation studies. It can therefore provide valuable insights into cultural studies in multifaceted ways. The term metamorphosis entails perspectives that construe "a culture" as a tentative identity that always bears traces of heterogeneity and fluidity. Using this figurative concept, we aim to expand perspectives on Korean Studies beyond "national studies" (*kukhak*), which are confined to a nation-state or essentialist beliefs in national identity, as well as "area studies" that are based on western-centered points of view. While focusing on the specific "location" of Korea and its concrete historical experiences, we regard this location as an open place where diverse cultural waves constantly flow in and out. "Korea" as an object of Korean Studies is a place inexplicably related with different places in the world, and not a reservoir of self-evident identity or a homogeneous, authentic culture. In the same vein, "Korean culture" is posited as a performative construction through negotiations between differences and is always exposed to constant changes ranging from everyday fluctuations to violent upheavals such as colonial transformations or cultural paradigm shifts.

This "metamorphic" approach is reflected in the editors' choice for the special issue of the first volume of *Metamorphosis*: "The March First Movement Revisited: A Global Perspective on Decolonization and Democracy." An amount of research on the 1919 March First Movement was published in South Korea during the centennial in 2019 and many scholarly engagements clearly showed a tendency toward post-nationalistic and post-colonial perspectives. Going beyond an *a priori* presupposition of the Korean nation (*minjok*) as a suprahistorical entity and challenging national boundaries of knowledge production, scholars sought to relocate the movement in a world history of struggles for decolonization and democracy and questioned its eventual significance in terms of both global universality and regional singularity.

The first part of the special issue opens with Baik Young-seo's essay, "Interconnected East Asia and the March First Movement in Korea," which synthesizes the abovementioned research trends. He interprets the movement through the intersection of a synchronic axis of East Asian "interconnectedness" and a diachronic axis of "incremental achievements" for a "double project" — adapting to and overcoming modernity — which have continued from the Tonghak Peasant Movement (1894) through March First (1919) to the Candlelight rallies (2017). Kwon Boduerae's "Manifesto: From a Desired Reality to Its Advent" describes the historical moment of the manifesto dimensionally by repeatedly shifting focus: Kwon zooms in on individuals who voluntarily spread, transformed, and proliferated declarations of Korean independence and zooms out to a world historical landscape in which minority peoples and the colonized declared similar manifestoes across the globe. Highlighting the performativity of "declaring" independence, Kwon appreciates the significance of a "manifesto" that can "draw a future" to the present.

In "The March First Movement and Decolonization," Hong Jong-wook traces decolonization processes in colonial Korea during the interwar period. Hong keeps distance from the notion that simply identifies decolonization with political independence and instead defines it as comprehensive procedures to seek alternatives for colonial rule. He examines how three routes toward decolonization — self-governance, assimilation, and independence — converged and diverged in a complicated interplay through rivalries and negotiations between colonizer and colonized. Youn Young-shil's "National Self-Determination of Colonial Peoples and World Democracy" focuses on the eventual moment when individuals' desire for rights and the universal ideal of democracy are tied into a single knot through the motto of self-determination. Comparatively examining different usages of democracy between conflicting forces, Youn shows how colonial peoples' struggles for national self-determination not only "renewed" democracy, thereby challenging the imperial standards of a constitutional democracy, but also changed the western-centered implications of the concept of a nation itself. Kong Im-soon's essay "Yi Kwangsu's March First Movement" shows how colonial subjects became trapped within a double bind between extreme colonial violence and the colonial discourse of a "civilized/barbarian" hierarchy and thereby internalized and conformed to colonial rule. Negotiation, confrontation, and conformity, each of which is treated by Hong, Youn, and Kong respectively, consist of multifaceted relationships between colonizer and colonized, or more generally, domination and resistance.

The second set of articles aims to provide an "outline and background for the March First Movement" for foreign readers who are not familiar with Korean history. Kim Jeong-in recapitulates the main points of the movement in terms of space, resistant subjects, demonstration culture, the response of foreign countries, and revolutionary thoughts. Sung Joo-hyun's "By the Peasants, for the Peasants, the World of the Peasants" explains the outline of the Tonghak Peasant Revolution as a historical background for the March First Movement. In "The March First Movement and International Relations," on the other hand, Nagata Akifumi details the international aspects surrounding the movement with a focus on Japan-U.S. relations. From Jang Won-a's "On the 100th Anniversary of the March First Movement," readers will not only get a well-organized summary of the recent trends in research but also sharp criticism of them from an emerging scholar's perspective.

Besides articles on the March First Movement, many scholars contributed valuable material to the first issue of *Metamorphosis*. The two articles in the Cultural Metamorphosis section epitomize the research agenda of the Soongsil University HK+ (Humanities Korea Plus) Center, "Metamorphosis of Culture and Knowledge in Korea's Transition to Modernity." Jang Kyung-nam's "Two Tales of Admiral Yi Sunsin" analyzes how General Yi Sunsin's story and history have been narrated and re-narrated in a metamorphic way along with socio-political contextual changes. "Fetishism and the Encounter between Two Religions," co-authored by Bhang Won-il and David W. Kim, exemplifies an interesting case of transculturation during the encounter between shamanism and Christianity in early modern Korea.

I would like to give special thanks to Yeounsuk Lee and Jooyeon Rhee, whose interviews feature in Korean Studies Abroad, for enriching the publication with their "wise answers to stupid questions" and candid stories of experiences and considerate advice for young Koreanists. The two culture reviews, Shin

Seung-hwan's "Korea, the Land of the Living Dead" and Lee Kee-woong's "The BTS Phenomenon and Digital Cultures," also diversify the book's content with their sophisticated analyses of K-movies and K-pop, which, in themselves, are metamorphic products from cultural cross-currents, despite their K label. I am grateful to Ko Sun-ho, Joo Young Lee, Na Sil Heo, and James Flynn, all of whom are promising Koreanists, for bridging Korean Studies within and beyond Anglophone academia with their contributions to book reviews.

The publication of this book could not have been accomplished without the huge efforts of translation editors Patricia Chaudron, Lee Kyunghwa, and Jang Han-gil as well as translators such as Park Joo-hyun, Rachel Min Park, Park Hyen-joo, Suhyun Kim, Jang Han-gil, and Peter Ward. I really appreciate all of them, especially Han-gil whose role was pivotal during this whole process, and their "blood, sweat, and tears." Translation always involves quite an amount of labor that works through linguistic borders but is never exhausted by this task. However, I painfully realized that there are much more troubles and hardships in translations from Korean into English in the uneven field of knowledge production. Throughout the frustrating process of translation and repeated revisions, I was reminded of Gramsci's — or Lenin's — comment on translation: we do not know how to "translate" our language into European languages. I hope the reckless challenge of this book project and all the participants' devotion has resulted in a welcome contribution toward enhancing the collective puissance of global Korean Studies scholarship.

The romanization of words from Korean and Japanese follows the McCune-Reischauer and Hepburn systems respectively with the customary exceptions (e.g., Seoul, Pyongyang, and Rhee Syngman) or in cases when authors expressed alternate preferences.

Most essays in this book first appeared in various books and journals and were revised and translated into English for this publication. We would like to thank the editors and publishers for allowing these papers to be published elsewhere in a translated version. The original publishers are as follows:

Baik Young-seo. "Interconnected East Asia and the March First Movement in Korea: A Revolution that Continues to Be Learned." *Quarterly Changbi* 183 (2019): 37-60. [백영서, 「연동하는 동아시아와 3·1운동: 계속 학습되는 혁명」, 『창작과비평』 183, 2019]

Kwon Boduerae. "Manifesto: From a Desired Reality to Its Advent." In *The Night of March First: Dreaming of Peace in a Century of Violence*, 25-52. P'aju: Tolbegae, 2019. [권보드래, 「선언 : 현재가 된 미래」, 『3월 1일의 밤－폭력의 세기에 꾸는 평화의 꿈』, 파주: 돌베개, 2019]

Hong Jong-wook. "The March First Movement and Decolonization." In *One Hundred Years Since the March First Movement*. Vol. 3, edited by Korean History Society, 297-326. Seoul: Humanist, 2019. [홍종욱, 「3·1 운동과 비식민화」, 한국역사연구회 편, 『3·1운동 100년』 3, 서울: 휴머니스트, 2019]

Youn Yong-shil. "National Self-Determination of the Colonized and World Democracy." *The Jounal of Korean Modern Literature* 51 (2017): 53-108. [윤영실, 「식민지의 민족자결과 세계민주주의」, 『한국현대문학연구』 51, 2017]

Kong Im-soon. "Chain and Refraction of Yi Kwangsu's March First Movement." *Chunwon Research Journal* 15 (2019): 35-65. [공임순, 「이광수의 3·1운동, 「민족개조론」, 「혁명가의 아내」의 연쇄와 굴절: 이광수의 귀국 전/후와 '간도 사변'의 편재하는 폭력」, 『춘원연구학보』 15, 2019]

Kim Jeong-in. *The March First Movement Today: A New Understanding from a Democratic Perspective*. Seoul: Ch'aekkwa Hamkke, 2019 [김정인, 『오늘과 마주한 3·1 운동』, 서울: 책과함께, 2019]

Nagata Akifumi. "The March First Movement and International Relations." *Rekishi Hyōron* 827 (2019): 20-31. [長田彰文, 「三一運動と国際的背景」, 『歴史評論』 827, 2019]

Jang Won-a. "The 100th Anniversary Studies of the March 1 Movement and Current Perspectives: Democracy and Various Subjects." *Critical Studies on Modern Korean History* 129 (2019): 8-35. [장원아, 「3 · 1 운동 100주년 연구와 현재의 시선: 민주주의와 다양한 주체들」, 『역사비평』 129, 2019]

Jang Kyung-nam. "The Comparison of Representation of Yi Sunsin in South and North Korean Novels." *Journal of Korean Literary History* 66 (2018): 227-254. [장경남, 「남북한 소설의 이순신 형상화 양상 비교」, 『민족문학사연 구』 66, 2018]

Bhang Won-il. "Fetishism: The History of Idea and its Meaning in Korea." *Religion and Culture* 21 (2011): 103-119. [방원일, 「페티시즘: 개념의 역사와 선교지 한국에서의 의미」, 『종교와 문화』 21, 2011]

Contents

Special Issue

The March First Movement Revisited:
A Global Perspective on Decolonization and Democracy

Part 1. New Approach to the March First Movement

Part 2. Outline and Background of the March First Movement

Cultural Metamorphosis

Korean Studies Abroad

Culture Review

Book Review

Special Issue

The March First Movement Revisited:
A Global Perspective on Decolonization and Democracy

Part 1.

New Approach
to the March First Movement

Interconnected East Asia and the March First Movement in Korea:

A Revolution that Continues to Be Learned

Baik Young-seo

1. Revisiting the Significance of the March First Movement in World History

The spirit of the "Candlelight Revolution" in 2016–2017 seems to be shedding new light on the understanding of the March First Movement. The political space created in its aftermath, in addition to the reconciliatory efforts between North and South Korea, have prompted new ways of interpreting the March First Movement. In fact, we have witnessed the emergence of more critical approaches to the March First Movement since 2019, the year that marked its 100th anniversary. Having undergone another historical shift through the Candlelight Revolution, we have come to a fundamental reassessment of the past hundred years. As the coinage of the phrase the "March First Revolution" evinces, there is an urgent need to reexamine the existing conceptual-historical framework of the March First Movement (hereafter March First).[1]

---

[1] The special issue of the *Quarterly Changbi* (Spring, 2019) as well as Yi Kihun, ed., *The March First Movement in the Eyes of the Candlelight Revolution* (P'aju: Changbi Publishers, 2019) answer such calls for reexamining the March First Movement.

Since the 1920s, March First has been constantly redefined in a way that reflects sociopolitical changes. The movement has been remembered differently by the South and North, especially as the division became more entrenched after Korea's liberation. Moreover, there have been disputes over how March First should be remembered and defined even within South Korea. Still fresh in our memory are the debates over the historical significance of March First and the Provisional Government of Korea, entangled with the issue of "National Foundation Day" during the Park Geun-hye administration. The issues concerning commemoration of the May Fourth Movement (hereafter May Fourth) in China, where the movement's 100th anniversary was also celebrated in 2019, has similarly been a subject of debate. The problem of historical remembrance is not just a question of history, but also of reality. The new ways in which March First is being assessed — we are even witnessing proposals to replace the term March First "movement" with "revolution" — have been brought about by the latest sociopolitical changes. The question to be considered at this point thus concerns the role of historical remembrance in public life. Grappling with this question entails a meticulous assessment of the significance of March First in the context of world history as well as that of civilizational transition.

In the past decades, there have been discussions in the Korean academia around the significance of March First in the world historical context as well as the influence of March First on other national movements at the time, including China's May Fourth. Those who emphasized such influence, however, came to be accused of committing *post hoc ergo propter hoc* fallacy. An alternative view turns to the ubiquity of the national movements among the oppressed at the time when assessing the world-historical significance of March First.[2] Following this view, others claim that the relationship between March First and May Fourth is that of historical simultaneity.[3]

While I actively acknowledge the ubiquity of similar movements at the time when assessing the significance of March First in world history, I believe

---

2   Han Sŭnghun, "How the Meaning of the March First Movement in 'World history' Was Incompletely Established and Then Stuck," *Quarterly Review of Korean History* 108 (2018): 238-239.

3   Im Hyŏngt'aek, "East Asia in 1919, the March First Movement and May Fourth Movement: An Introduction to Methodologies in Reading East Asian Modernity," in *Inquiries on March First, 1919*, eds. Pak Hŏnho and Ryu Chunp'il (Seoul: Sungkyunkwan University Press, 2009), 35.

that it is also important to draw attention to the singularity of March First by means of comparative analysis. To this end, I will first reexamine March First by postulating the "interconnectedness" of East Asia. My use of the term "interconnection" simultaneously "articulates the space (i.e. structure) in which East Asian countries are intimately intertwined and interact with each other in multifaceted ways" and "signifies their autonomous acts of solidarity."[4] Additionally, it also suggests a structural relation as well as the mutual referencing between agents, the latter of which can be observed not just in (sociopolitical) movements but also throughout the broader realms of ideologies and institutions. This study pays attention to the peculiar nature of the East Asian context around the time of March First, where the three East Asian nations — Imperial Japan, semi-colonial China, and colonized Korea — occupied different places in the world hierarchy. This was due to the role of Imperial Japan, which acted as the Western powers' surrogate in East Asia, in defining the other two nations' semi-colonial and colonial status. Therefore, it is imperative that we pay special attention to such complicated relations. I do not intend to compare all the historical events in these three nations point by point. Rather, my interest lies in examining March First comparatively with May Fourth, China's anti-Japanese national movement,[5] in light of the differences between the colonial and the semi-colonial conditions.[6]

I take this approach in order to understand the complexities of (semi-) colonial modernity created by imperialism that paraded itself as "civilizing" mission, by which I wish to discover possibilities of overcoming modernity inherent in such complexities. In this context, a particularly useful methodological framework is the theory of the "double project," which articulates a simultaneous pursuit of adapting to and overcoming modernity.[7] This framework should

---

4   Baik Young-seo (Paek Yŏngsŏ), *Rethinking East Asian History from Core Locations* (P'aju: Changbi Publishers, 2013), 318.

5   See my article that compares March First and May Fourth. "East Asia on the Move in 1919: The Revolutionary Movements of March First and May Fourth," *Concepts and Communication* 23 (2019): 7-37.

6   A colony refers to a country that is under direct rule of another country and is deprived of its sovereignty. A semi-colony is not directly ruled by another, but its sovereignty is restricted by foreign powers through unequal treaties or by partitioning spheres of influence.

7   Double project theory is a creative theory that seeks to transcend the dichotomy between two

make clear the structural meaning of the similarities and differences between China's May Fourth, which occurred eight years after the successful revolution of 1911, and Korea's March First, which occurred nine years after the forced annexation by Japan in 1910.

I hope that the work of reassessing the significance of March First in the context of world history as well as civilizational transition in terms of East Asia's interconnectedness and "double-project" theory, will serve as an elucidating methodological inquiry. It is also my intention that this study contributes to conceptualizing the historical foundation of the "Candlelight Revolution" and to reassessing the history of Korea and East Asia in the last century.[8]

2. 1919, the Coming of a New Era:
The Strong Currents of Reconstruction and Liberation

The paths to modernity that Korea, China, and Japan took diverged critically from each other during the ten years between the First Sino-Japanese War

---

attitudes toward modernism: modern characteristics are either seen as positive values that must be attained (modernism) or as old legacies that should be discarded (postmodernism). This theory contributes to overcoming simplistic interpretations of "invasion vs. resistance" in our understanding of colonial history. For more information, see Paik Nak-chung (Paek Nakch'ŏng), "The Double Project of Modernity," *New Left Review* 95 (2015): 65-79 and Song Hogŭn et al., *The Programs and Challenges of Civil Society* (Seoul: Minŭmsa, 2016). Paik Nak-chung et al., *Examining the Great Shifts of Civilization* (P'aju: Changbi Publishers, 2018).

8 Marking the 70th anniversary of March First, Korean historians published the definitive book on the movement that interprets the event in accordance with the common people's views on history. See The Association For Korean Historical Studies and The Institute for Korean Historical Studies, eds., *Studies on the March First National Liberation Movement* (Seoul: Ch'ŏngnyŏnsa, 1989). However, changes have taken place in the study of the March First Movement since the 1990s as postcolonial and postmodern frames of reference dominated the field of history. This change brought about the so-called cultural historical turn, which led scholars to emphasize the individualized and polyphonic subjectivity of the populace. These scholars highlight the lived realities of the people as well as the media that represented such realities. See Hŏ Yŏngnan, "A 'Cultural Historical Turn' in the Study of the Early Modern History of Korea: The Popularization of History, Colonial Modernity, and the Historicization of the World of Experience," *Korean Cultural Studies* 53 (2010): 92-93. Although I utilize the results of these previous studies on March First that have generated a diverse understanding of the event, I am wary of the current scholarly trends' lack of structural consciousness, which might lead to overlooking colonial contradictions and making light of previous movements and thoughts.

(1894−1895) and the Russo-Japanese War (1904−1905). Defeated during the Sino-Japanese War, China fell to the status of semi-colony as the prospect of divided rule by imperial powers loomed over it. Japan had joined the world system's semi-periphery following the Korea-Japan Treaty of 1876, and ascended to the center following the Russo-Japanese War. In all of these events, Korea served as a critical geopolitical factor.

In the case of China, its semi-colonial condition allowed for a relatively autonomous space where the 1911 Xinhai Revolution could succeed. However, the superficiality of the revolution that led to the establishment of a republic in name only also gave rise to May Fourth, a movement that sought to substantialize this republican form with meaningful content.[9]

On the other hand, Korea was annexed by Japan a year before the 1911 Revolution. The colonial authorities declared that they would implement a "civilizing" policy and thus establish — legally and institutionally — the major components of modern infrastructures in the colony. Japan's self-consciousness of being under Western powers' eyes, however, caused them to take on the task hurriedly despite the lack of financial resources. This is why Japan implemented the so-called "military rule" — a series of policies that allowed the military, the police, and officials to impose violent control over all aspects of Korean lives — and as such, enforced colonial modernity in Korea.[10] Instead of respecting the unique system of local self-government during the Chosŏn Dynasty characterized by indirect rule, the colonial authorities dismantled the autonomy of rural districts and took direct control over them, thus antagonizing Koreans. The Japanese imposed new taxes on liquor, housing, cigarettes, and stamps to resolve their financial problems. They also introduced convoluted tax statement forms that were troublesome to fill in, making the everyday burdens of the colonized people heavier. Koreans suffered day-to-day discrimination on educational, administrative, and legal levels and from micro-policies of control. These mandates included the enforcement of a cemetery

---

9 See Min Tugi, *The Chinese Republican Revolution* (P'aju: Chisiksanŏpsa, 1999), particularly the first section of the conclusion. He reads the 1911 Revolution and May Fourth as the first and second Republican Revolution, i.e., as revolutions on a continuum.

10 Kwŏn T'aeŏk, "'The Civilization' Project of Japan and Koreans' Perception in the 1910s: How the March First Movement Could Become Nationwide," *Korean Culture* 61 (2013): 357-359.

order which prohibited the burying of the dead in family burying grounds, a forced order to cultivate mulberry trees, strict regulations on the slash-and-burn method in agriculture, and forced labor in reclamation projects. A deadly surge in prices and the outbreak of infectious diseases such as cholera, typhoid, and the Spanish flu aggravated colonial Koreans' dissatisfaction, which was already on the brink of explosion. The ruptures in the rationale of Japan's "civilizing mission" were beginning to show.

This is not to say, however, that March First, a nation-wide resistance movement, can simply be explained as a response to the people's growing feelings of resentment and rebelliousness. With that said, I would next like to examine the climate of the time during which 1919 was perceived as a new epoch for humanity and liberation.

What led 1919 to be interpreted in such a way was none other than World War I. Although the war itself was seen as a tragedy, the notion that its results paved the way to a "new society" of justice and humanitarianism spread throughout the world, and made "reconstruction" (kaejo) a vogue term. Having experienced the war in "near real time" through modern media such as newspapers and telegraphs, people awakened to the "worldliness of the world" and developed a sense of "contemporaneity."[11] As they went through World War I, Koreans in particular overcame, to a certain extent, the sense of inferiority they had been feeling toward the West and "civilized and enlightened countries" ever since they had been coerced to open their ports to trade. Moreover, they anticipated a fundamental reconstruction and reordering of the world system including Japanese rule, and a future in which their country would become an independent nation-state.[12] In other words, Koreans were sensing, for the first time, the coming of a new era of civilizational transition as they shared this "global moment" of history that was regarded by their international peers as groundbreaking.[13]

---

11 Ch'a Sŭnggi, "Thoughts in a Wasteland: World War I and Colonial Korea, or Regarding 'Absence-awareness'," *Literature and Society* 106 (2014): 411.

12 Yi T'aehun, "Attitudes and Perceptions about the First World War by Members of the Colonial Korean Society during the 1910s and 1920s," *The Review of Korean History* 105 (2012): 213.

13 Sebastian Conrad and Dominic Sachsenmaier, *Competing Visions of World Order: Global Moments and Movements, 1880s-1930s* (London: Palgrave Macmillan, 2007), 9, 13.

It is important to note here that although the Koreans felt this sense of "contemporaneity" with the rest of the world, they worried about missing out on the opportunities brought about by the shifting currents. The source of their anxiety lay in the question whether colonial Korea, which could not send a formal delegation to the Paris Peace Conference, unlike semi-colonial China, had a chance of playing a role during this time of global transformation. This anxiety became a major variable that influenced their thoughts and actions.[14] Two historical cases that dramatically drive the above point home come to mind. One of them concerns Yun Ch'iho, who refused to participate in the March First Movement. He was wary of the optimism that spread in response to Woodrow Wilson's talk of rights to self-determination and foresaw that the Korea problem would not even be mentioned at the Paris Peace Conference. On the other hand, Ch'oe Rin participated in the movement as he believed that it would be better for Korea to join other nations in their cry for peace despite there being no guarantee of results.[15] Presumably, the majority of Koreans stood somewhere between Yun and Ch'oe. However, it should be pointed out that the March First Movement was not led by those who took a pessimistic stance based on accurate knowledge of world politics. Rather, it was led by optimists whose hopes were grounded on their will to join the "global moment" by taking advantage of the ruptures in the changing world order. These optimists did not misunderstand the implications of these changes. On the contrary, their will to improve the situation of the Korean people accorded with the undergoing global transformations.

Such an awareness of world history was shared widely among many, including religious leaders of Christianity and Ch'ŏndogyo,[16] teachers, and students. For instance, Mun Ch'anghwan (then 24 years old), a Ch'ŏndoist farmer, told the detective interrogating him that "as the International Peace Conference is fast approaching, it seems reasonable to believe that the issue of Korea's

---

14 Ch'a Sŭnggi, "Thoughts in a Wasteland," 411.

15 Song Chiye, "Translation of 'Self-Determination' and the Feb. 8th Independence Movement," *The Review of Korean and Asian Political Thoughts* 11, no. 1 (2012): 199.

16 Ch'ŏndogyo is a 20th-century Korean religion, founded on the principles of the 19th-century Tonghak movement.

independence will be a topic at this conference and that a good conclusion will come of it." His words quite dramatically reveal the extent to which global self-awareness had spread among Koreans.[17]

As pithily expressed in the Korean Declaration of Independence, the Koreans' hopeful understanding of the times and international affairs that a "new heaven and earth" will come, as well as the angst of living under an intensely oppressive colonial government, must have been pivotal in catalyzing the mass resistance movement called March First. However, a more influential factor was the formation of "resistant subjectivity."

3. People's Mass Gathering Experiences during March First: Agents, Mediums, and Aims

In what follows, the discussion of the people's experience of mass gathering will be divided into the following terms: agents, mediums, and aims. The peculiar traits of the people's experience of March First stemmed from the co-existence of modernity and pre-modernity under the colonial condition, and from their reconstructed understanding of the two. These circumstances not only led people to become aware of the "negative sides" of the modernity of Japan's "civilizing mission," but also to use their previous experiences in resistance and intellectual resources for fueling the national movement of March First.

Let us first examine the agents of March First. The protests in 1919 erupted spontaneously across the country during March and April, but there was no national headquarters or institution overseeing them. Admittedly, the sporadic nature of the movement and the consequent lack of organization were inherent weaknesses that prevented it from overcoming Japan's violent persecution. It is, however, important to note that its very spontaneous nationwide spread of the movement, and the participants' active participation and selfless devotion to the movement's cause, are important aspects of the March First Movement.[18]

17 "The Interrogation Record of Mun Ch'anghwan," in *Sourcebook on the History of the Korean Independence Movement.* vol. 13 (Kwach'ŏn: National Institute of Korean History, 1990), 158.

18 Chŏng Yonguk, "Current Trends in Historical Studies of the March First Movement, and Where

The 33 national representatives who proclaimed the Declaration of Korean Independence in 1919 were all religious figures (fifteen Ch'ŏndoists, sixteen Christians, and two Buddhists). This grouping may have been the inevitable result of the refusal of other prominent figures to join the cause. However, it can also be said that in a colonial situation where people had no national polity to speak for them religious groups and figures stepped forward as representatives.[19] Ch'ŏndogyo, which had nearly 3 million believers, and, unlike Christianity, went by the doctrine that religion cannot be separated from politics, played an especially significant role in recruiting national representatives and financing as well as disseminating the movement in rural areas. In addition, the movement was bolstered by young students who had been brought up on nationalist education developed during the era of the Patriotic Enlightenment Movements and colonial rule. *Yangban* (aristocrat) disciples of Confucianism from Korea's local communities that managed to stay alive despite Japan's systematic efforts to dismantle them also played a major role in the movement. These groups in tandem with the spirit inherited from the Tonghak Peasant Movement and Righteous Militia Movements had a profound influence on March First.

It is commonly understood that their activities changed from peaceful urban protests to aggressive rural ones.[20] If we look at the whole picture, however, it becomes clear that these two types of protest co-existed from the beginning. Recent studies of Korea's local histories have brought to light how the participation of peasants, the driving force of the nationwide dissemination of the March First Movement, led the *manse* protests in a way that they became something akin to a rebellion.[21] There were patterns of violent protests and cases in which people resorted to violence from the outset. However, these

---

It Is Apparently Headed," *Quarterly Review of Korean History* 110 (2018): 295.

19 Chang Sŏngman, "Religion and the March First Movement," in Pak and Ryu, *Inquiries on March First, 1919*, 211.

20 Most Korean history textbooks used in high schools offer this particular narrative. Yi Chŏngŭn, *A Study on the Demonstrations in the Rural Regions during the March First Movement* (Seoul: Kukhak Charyowŏn, 2009), 340.

21 "Manse" was the rallying cry of March First; it can literally be translated as "ten thousand years" or "long live [Korea]." Pae Sŏngjun, "The Aspect of Rural Uprisings during the March First Movement," in Pak and Ryu, *Inquiries on March First, 1919*, 297.

actions were expressions of legitimate anger at injustice as well as reactions against the brutal crackdown of the movement. Moreover, the targets of this violence were restricted to colonial institutions and officers of the Japanese Empire that inflicted institutionalized violence.[22] Thus, these angry acts of resistance should be regarded as actions to achieve national self-determination, civil rights, equality, and ultimately "peace from below." These actions did not conflict with the tenet of non-violence that the March First's national representatives promoted as their strategic method of protest.[23]

The agents of March First were different from those of May Fourth. The latter was an urban-centered nationalist movement led by a coalition of people from all walks of life. The movement began with modern intellectuals and the "new youth." That is to say, it was students who led merchants and laborers into protesting through commercial boycotts and labor strikes. Students likewise catalyzed March First in Korea and merchants and laborers participated as well. Merchants in particular protested through commercial boycotts, which was a traditional means of voicing their class objections during the Chosŏn dynasty. Laborers and craftsmen went on strike, and students boycotted classes for more than three months. However, these protests were small in scale compared to their Chinese counterparts. This difference was due to the disparate circumstances in which the two countries found themselves. China as a semi-colonized nation had a government, albeit one with limited autonomy, and it did its part to adapt to modernity. Thus, when the Western powers' attention was briefly diverted away from China due to World War I, Chinese people had a little breathing room and could accomplish a boom in its national industry.

Things were different in Korea. Here, the unique characteristics of March First become quite clear in that modernity and pre-modernity coexisted and the meaning of the two was reconstructed as the movement progressed. As mentioned before, religious groups, young students, and *yangban* disciples

---

22 Kim Yŏngbŏm, "Violence during the March First Movement and Its Implications," *Korean Studies Quarterly* 41, no. 4 (2018): 86, 93.

23 For discussions on "bottom-up peace" rather than "topdown peace," see Kwon Heonik (Kwŏn Hŏnik), "Interview: 'Peace Studies' That Need to Reconsider the World Historical Significance of 1919," *Hankyoreh*, September 14, 2018.

of Confucianism were the primary agents of March First. These agents were joined by others with the shared experience and memory of the Tonghak Peasant Movements and Righteous Militia Movements. In this sense, March First can be regarded as a national movement encompassing more diverse subjects and social classes than May Fourth. One major difference was that religious groups and peasants were major driving forces of March First, and they had the potential to become catalysts for overcoming modernity.

This uniqueness is reflected in the various media that were used in the dissemination of the March First Movement. Let us examine, first, the state funeral and *manse* protests that served as mediums of mass gatherings. Anticipating that countless people would gather for the funeral ceremony of King Kojong, the March First organizers jumped at the opportunity to spread the movement. At the demonstration, a sense of mourning for the late emperor oddly mingled with a sense of joy and festivities evoked by crying "*manse*" rather incongruous with a funeral.[24] To understand this mixed response better, we must examine the meaning of the rallying cry of "*manse*."

"*Manse*" (literally "ten thousand years") and "*ch'ŏnse*" ("one thousand years") were words that expressed great joy or functioned as an exclamation of celebration much like the English word "hurrah." The terms "*manse*" and "*ch'ŏnse*" were used interchangeably during the Chosŏn Dynasty, but became unified as "*manse*" by the time that the Korean empire was established in 1897. "*Manse*," which was popularized when the Korean Independence Club (*Tongnip hyŏphoe*) and Patriotic Enlightenment Movements were active, developed into something more than a simple exclamatory word. In fact, it came to signify a political culture that Korea's modern intellectuals disseminated as they sought to enlighten the populace. And finally, at the time of March First, *manse*, "mediated by the political culture that had developed in the course of the previous peasant movements," came to "foster a sense of national unity and serve as a medium through which people's voices of protests against Japan resounded throughout the country."[25]

---

24 Kwon Boduerae (Kwŏn Podŭrae), "The Night of the March First Movement," in '*Modern*' *Experiences of East Asia*, ed. Pak Kyŏngsŏk (P'aju: Hanul, 2018), 102.

25 Cho Kyŏngdal, *The Populace and Utopia*, trans. Hŏ Yŏngnan (Koyang: Yŏksabip'yŏngsa, 2009),

The same can be said of the T'aegŭkki (the current national flag of South Korea) and other flags. It seems that the leaders of March First refrained from strategic use of the T'aegŭkki during protests because they feared that the flag, which symbolized the Korean emperor's sovereign power, would evoke memories of the lost empire. Despite their circumspection, however, the T'aegŭkki gradually came to represent national unity rather than the emperor's sovereignty.[26] In addition, there were cases in which protesters displayed their names or their membership through flags, thus following the precedent of the participants of the Tonghak Peasant Movement. Flags, in other words, had not only become a means to express an individual or collective identity, but also a modern symbol of struggle and resistance. As the slogan *manse* spread from urban to rural areas all across the country, flags, circulars, and manifestoes came to be more frequently used as expressive mediums than underground newspapers or printed declarations.[27]

Schools, religious facilities such as churches, and marketplaces also served as a public sphere of discourse. Local markets that opened at regular intervals served as an explosive intermediary space where rumors about the movement traveled through the grapevine. On a related note, "*kasa*" — a simple form of premodern verse with twinned feet of three or four syllables each — was another important medium during March First. Socio-critical *kasa* that had been sung at peasant resistance movements at the end of the 19th century and enlightenment *kasa* that became a modern means of communication through the newspapers in the 1900s had a great influence on the various patriotic songs that were heard during March First.[28] The March First participants also utilized traditional means of protest such as beacon fire protests and lamplight marches.[29] In addition to these traditional mediums, trains accelerated the

243.

26 Kwon Boduerae, "The Utopianism of 'Manse': The Restoration of Sovereignty and the Idea of a New World during the March First Movement," *The Journal of Korean Studies* 38 (2015): 204.

27 Yi Kihun, "The March First Movement and the Flag," in *The March First Movement in the Eyes of the Candlelight Revolution*, ed. Yi Kihun (P'aju: Changbi Publishers, 2019), 77-104.

28 Im Hyŏngt'aek, "Another Way to Consider the History of Korean Literature: The *Minjung* Movement, Public Sphere and Justice," *The Study of Korean Classical Literature* 54 (2018): 5-24.

29 Cho Kyŏngdal, *The Populace and Utopia*, 240. See also Pae Sŭngjun, "The Aspect of Rural Uprisings during the March First Movement," 310.

spread of modern print media as well as rumors, which can be said to be more traditional mediums of communication, and contributed to "nationalizing" March First.[30]

The multiplicity of media that were used in accordance to the March First Movement's specific needs ranged from traditional oral media to modern print media. In the case of China, traditional mediums for mass gatherings were sometimes used during the Xinhai Revolution of 1911. By May Fourth, however, capitalism had advanced further and protests in major cities mostly utilized modern print media such as newspapers, magazines, and telegrams to spread the word. This difference too, derived from the different historical circumstances surrounding colonial Korea and semi-colonial China.

Let's now examine the objective of the March First participants. The cries of "*manse*" heard at the protest sites reflected individual and national desire for liberation and hopeful anticipation for a new country. Was this "new country" envisioned as a republican polity? Despite the traditional belief that patriotism entailed loyalty to one's sovereign, the March First protesters who shouted "*manse*" at Kojong's funeral were "performing the final historical rites for both Kojong and the dynastic order."[31] Although restoration movements did occur in Korea around 1919, the forced annexation practically abolished monarchism. In other words, it was easier for the Korean people to break from the past and see republicanism as an irreversible course of history. News of the Xinhai Revolution also affected the Korean populace. What happened in Korea was, however, quite different from the course of action in China. The Chinese had made a formal break with the imperial system through the 1911 Xinhai Revolution, and then found ways to establish a republic in both form and content through May Fourth.

The phrase "national representative" was coined in the course of the March First Movement and gained special meaning especially in relation to the issue of republicanism. It showed that an awareness had emerged that people had

30 Ch'ŏn Chŏnghwan, "Rumors, Gossip, Newspapers, and Appeals: The Media at the Time of the March First Movement and the People's National Subjecthood," in Pak and Ryu, *Inquiries on March First, 1919*, 259.

31 Kim Hŭnggyu, *Beyond the Privileging of the Modern* (P'aju: Changbi Publishers, 2013), 179.

sovereign rights and that such rights were entrusted to the people's representatives during the course of constructing a new nation-state. This awareness is quite well encapsulated in the idea of "national representative." The massive protest on April 23 that occurred around Posin'gak Pavillion in Chongno — a central district in Seoul — was called a "national assembly." It was this "national assembly" that inspired the idea of the body of national representatives constituted of local representatives. The republican ideal of "representatives of the citizen body" spread rapidly among the populace, and, during the March First Movement, individuals regarded themselves as national representatives even without joining or constructing political groups or organizations.

On May Fourth, the masses held a "national assembly" at Tiananmen Square. This occasion led to the establishment of a "national congress" — an organization consisting of various political coalitions — with the "national congress movement," which continued well into the 1920s and influenced the Chinese National Party as well as the Chinese Communist Party. The people, in other words, sought ways to achieve democracy at a time when they could not elect local representatives. The notions of immediacy and representation in these movements, however, are noteworthy: The so-called representatives during March First or May Fourth were not elected through formal and/or legal elections. Thus, the legitimacy of these "representatives" can only be retrospectively assessed in terms of whether they truly represented the interest of their people by examining the mass protests that followed and their struggle against Japanese imperialism.[32] In this light, it seems that immediacy was a stronger force than representation during the March First Movement. This trend can be read as a sign of emerging experiments with a new type of democracy to overcome the representative democracy.[33]

---

32 Yi Kihun, "The Growth of Republican Discourse during the Japanese Imperial Period: with 'National Representation' as a Core Concept" (paper presented at The Notion of 'Republic' and Its Developement in Modern Korea and East Asia Conference, Institute of International Affairs, Seoul National University, November 30, 2018).

33 See Baik Young-seo, "Democracy and the National Congress Movements in the Modern History of China," *Journal of Humanities* 84, no. 10 (2002): 161-180. In this article, I argue that East Asian scholars interested in the National Congress movements start off their research by "criticizing the representative democracy that we see today, in lieu of the unique realities in which they live," and are often motivated by "their own desire for an alternative model for democracy" (169). See also

The desire for a republican system expressed in March First led to the establishment of the Provisional Government of the Republic of Korea on April 11, 1919, in Shanghai. The "Provisional Constitution of the Republic of Korea," consisting of ten articles, reflected the spirit of March First. There seems to be debates among scholars about the legitimacy of the Provisional Government in Shanghai, its political significance, and the problem of overrepresentation and overexpectation concerning the Provisional Government.[34] Rather than engaging in this debate, I instead wish to emphasize the fact that the internal logic through which March First and the Provisional Government legitimized Korean independence integrated the notion of national self-determination and the ideal of democracy in the course of pursuing freedom and equality. Put differently, the internal logic of March First has significance as a ground from which a new form of democracy could be constructed.[35] The goal of establishing a democratic republic may be superficially regarded as "pursuing a modern political model." As Yi, however, points out, "the contents of their activities reveal their will to overcome modernity"[36] in that they pursued direct democracy and equality.

I would also like to emphasize that the Koreans' yearning for a new country should not be reduced to a yearning for the establishment of a republican system. Rather, what demands our attention is the desire for utopia that erupted in March First, which, we may even say, was close to being a religious fervor. It was a desire that expressed the people's "worldly utopianism" where personal gain, national independence, and freedom on a global level converged.[37] This

---

Yu Yongt'ae, "China's Vision for Democracy in the 20th Century," *Green Review,* January & February 2018, 21-33. Yu re-examines China's democracy and suggests that the professional representative system can be regarded as more faithful to the principles of democratic republicanism as it enhances the representativeness and directness of democracy.

34 Kim Jeongin (Kim Chŏngin), "The Politicalness and Scholarliness of the March First Movement and Provisional Government Legitimacy Awareness," *Seoul and History* 99 (2018): 234. See also Kong Imsoon (Kong Imsun), "Historical Memory and the Betrayal of the March First Movement, and Ideological Politics about its Succession," *Korean Modern Literature Studies* 24 (2011): 221.

35 Kim Jeongin, *The March First Movement Today: A New Understanding from a Democratic Perspective* (Seoul: CUM Libro, 2019), 202-208.

36 Yi Namju, "The March First Movement, the Candlelight Revolution, and 'the Event of Truth'," *Quarterly Changbi* 47, no. 1 (2019): 61-78.

37 Kwon Boduerae, "The Utopianism of Manse," 212.

desire also points to the populace's awareness of their "agency as subjects of liberation" that had been "latent" and repressed but was then exploding.[38]

Hopes for a "*kaebyŏk*" (開闢, opening of a new heaven and a new earth) and the philosophy of "*taedong*" (大同, great harmony) that various folk beliefs including Tonghak had inherited gave strength to their aspiration for a new world.[39] As March First continued into April, it developed into a national struggle that brought together people of all classes, from rural and urban areas alike, turning the whole country into "a liberated zone of self-governing people."[40] Unlike in China, where the revolution occurred over two disparate phases in 1911 and 1919, in Korea the people's repressed energy erupted at once with great impact. This is why the series of events in 1919 Korea have been remembered as showing a "great leap of spirit" and serving as a "heterotopic space."[41]

The experience of liberation that people gained through March First had a great influence on the way time was conceptualized in social and personal realms. This is evident in the coinage of the phrase "post−1919" (post-*kimi*), which referred to "the never before imagined circumstances" of the time that witnessed "numerous neologisms." March First was a significant juncture in time, as it served as a yardstick for chronologizing the national movements and/or "social movements" at the time, as well as a "temporal base point" from which time was experienced and understood by individuals.[42] Intriguingly, the prevalence of such an understanding of March First made possible a positive re-evaluation of Korean national characteristics, which had been negatively defined prior to March First.[43] This positive re-evaluation brought about the

---

38 Cho Kyŏngdal, *The Populace and Utopia*, 230.

39 Some regard the significance of March First as an occasion during which Confucian universalism — which has its roots in hopes for an ideal society of great harmony — i.e., "civilizationism" and national self-determinism converged. See Miyajima Hiroshi, "Nationalism and Civilizationism: Toward a New Understanding of March First," in Pak and Ryu, *Inquiries on March First, 1919*, 67.

40 Kim Jeong-in, "The Question of a Democratic Revolution during the March First Movement" (paper presented at the March First Revolution 95th Anniversary Academic Conference, Center for Historical Truth and Justice, Seoul, 26 February, 2014), 139.

41 Kim Chinho, "March First and the T'aegŭkki Demonstrations: The Forgotten Memories of the Populace," in Yi, *The March First Movement in the Eyes of the Candlelight Revolution*, 175-200.

42 Ryu Sihyŏn, "Memories of the March First Movement in the 1920s: Time, Place, and 'Nation/Masses'," *Quarterly Review of Korean History* 74 (2009): 183-185.

"March First Generation," a generation of Korean people who experienced a great time of change, or, so to speak, "those who caught a glimpse of the heaven."[44]

4. Beyond the Success and Failure of March First: The Incremental Achievement of Movements and Thoughts

At the Washington Conference (1921–22) where unresolved issues from the Treaty of Versailles were discussed, the United States, Britain, and Japan established a collaborative system, later known as the Washington System, which initiated a "relatively stable period" during which the great powers enjoyed assured privileges in East Asia. Contrary to predictions that had been made by some of the Korean independence activists, this development led to the consolidation of Japan's political status. This turn of events in international politics around 1922 consequently dampened Koreans' hopes for independence that had been fostered by the March First Movement. As the movement subsided, the populace seemed to have returned to their everyday lives. And the social atmosphere, compared to the immediate aftermath of March First, was prominently pessimistic.

The primary cause of this state of affairs was the Japanese colonial government's violent crackdown of the 1919 national movement. However, it should also be noted that the diverse aspirations that converged into the desire for the establishment of a republic during March First ended up diverging again. The colonial situation greatly limited paths to institutionalizing the envisioned republic and led to contests over how it should be fulfilled. As a result of such contestation, those who led the nationalist movement were

---

43 "Dear Japanese Friends," (*Dong-a Ilbo*, March 4, 1921) in *Collection of Dong-a Ilbo Editorials Seized under the Japanese Colonial Rule of Korea*, ed. Dong-a Ilbo (Seoul: Dong-a Ilbo, 1978), 30. See also Ryu Sihyŏn, "Memories of the March First Movement in the 1920s," 191.

44 Paik Nak-chung, inspired by Sin Tongyŏp's poem "Who Says that He Caught a Glimpse of the Heaven" where the poet sees the Tonghak Movement and the April 19th Revolution as related events, uses the term "people who caught a glimpse of the heaven" to describe the primary agents of the Candlelight Revolution of 2016-17. Paik Nak-chung, "What to Do after Catching a Glimpse of the Heaven," *Changbi Weekly Commentary*, December 27, 2018.

divided into left and right wings. Does this split, however, mean that March First was a failure?

If we consider March First in terms of political institutionalization, i.e., building a nation-state, which is an indicator of modernity, it is difficult to deny that it failed in short term. The Koreans did not achieve immediate independence, nor did they succeed in founding an autonomous nation-state. Although the significance of the Provisional Government of the Republic of Korea should be recognized, it could not exert leadership over the entire nationalist movement in and outside of the Korean peninsula due to factionalism and internal conflicts. Obviously, the circumstances were quite different for the Koreans and the Chinese. During this time China's young students, who had experienced May Fourth in semi-colonial China and had emerged as new political subjects, developed a sense that they were "agents of social reformation." These students further matured into professional revolutionaries and participated in the anti-imperial, anti-warlord revolution led by the coalition between the Chinese Nationalist Party and the Chinese Communist Party.[45]

The March First Movement provided the momentum that Japan's Hara regime needed to revise their colonial rule. March First was an exemplary event that revealed the impact which a colony could have on the imperial mainland, and, more specifically, indicated the political and institutional effects of the movement. March First occasioned Japan to change its colonial policy from military rule to the more lenient "cultural rule," which led to the opening up of an institutional space wherein nationalist movements could unfold with vigor. This development was another pivotal achievement of March First.[46]

However, the significance of March First should not only be assessed within the narrow scope of institutionalization. March First also brought about "incremental achievements," represented by an accumulated experience of

---

[45] See Baik Young-seo, *A Study of China's Modern University Culture* (Seoul: Ilchogak, 1994). The conclusion is particularly relevant here.

[46] I must of course note that the Japanese government, which experienced World War I as a total war, gravely felt the need to establish a stable resource pipeline in the 1920s. This was a major reason Japan took to a more conciliatory approach to colonial rule. However, this does not mean that the influence that the Korean resistance had on Japan was less significant.

struggle for independence and development of ideas in its wake, which reached levels beyond the institutional.[47] Since the 1920s, Korea witnessed not only the nation-wide organization of peasants, laborers, and women as well as youth groups. Moreover, transnational groups of the anti-Japanese guerilla were organized by Korean immigrants in China. Many of them commemorated March First as the shared origin of the movements, describing it as "the Great Revolution." It was also called "the Revolutionary Movement of March First" by the Provisional Government established through the collaboration of the left and right in 1941, which was written into the "National Doctrine of the Provisional Government." The significance of March First continued to be emphasized after Korea's liberation in 1945 by both wings on the right and left. Previous studies have shed considerable light on the South Korean practice of associating March First with reunification movement during the 1950s and democratization process from the mid-1950s and onward. Hence, I will take a more in-depth look into March First's achievements from a civilizational perspective.

Above all, it is truly significant that the Koreans did locate the importance of the March First Movement in its world-historical conemporaneity. A newspaper editorial from *Dong-a Ilbo* clearly revealed that the Koreans knew about the impact of March First on China's May Fourth in the 1920s. Noting that "May Fourth in China is among all the national movements that soon followed our March First movement in 1919" (March 2, 1925), the writer referred to May Fourth as an event that was related to March First. Furthermore, the Koreans saw the 1918 "rice riots" in Japan as an "interconnected" event. These well-known "rice riots" happened due to a precipitous rise in rice prices that caused the urban poor of Japan — who had, thanks to the economic prosperity that followed World War I, gotten used to eating rice — to rise up in anger. Such riots did not occur in Korea because the Koreans, who had to consume other grains due to the increase in the quota of Korean-produced rice to be exported to Japan after the annexation, were less affected by a spike in rice prices.[48] Despite this contrast, Yŏm Sangsŏp, a Korean novelist and

47 Paik Nak-chung, "South Korea's Candlelight Revolution and the Future of the Korean Peninsula," *The Asia-Pacific Journal: Japan Focus* 16, Issue 23 no. 3 (2018), https://apjjf.org/2018/23/Paik.html

essayist, suggested that "there is no difference in the fundamental demands of the rice rioters and Korean students in Japan; their actions may seem to differ on the surface, but their actions both call for the right to survive."[49]

The realization of an "interconnected East Asia" as such is especially noteworthy as it stemmed from a new understanding of the era and the world based on a local appropriation of the "global moment." In the same vein, we must pay attention to the new perspectives on East Asia that emerged during the March First Movement. At this time, Britain and the United States sought to safeguard peace through maintaining the status quo in order to protect their vested interests. Japan, however, pushed for a new world order that went against the status quo, arguing that Eurocentrism had to be overcome and that the East Asian order had to be reconfigured with Japan at its center.[50] On the other hand, Korea, a "double periphery," criticized the contradictions of both the Anglo-American powers and Japan. It went as far as to posit that Korean independence was "an essential step for maintaining peace in the East and the world." Moreover, those who experienced March First took one step further and looked for ways to overcome modernity from such emerging perspectives.

When anti-colonial resistance was based on the standards of "advanced techniques and civilization," and adaptation to modernity was the sole measure for it, it was difficult to take a critical stance toward Japan's logic of "civilization." After March First, however, new standards emerged, grounded on the ideals of the "Reconstruction" period, or, put it differently, the global trends of justice and humanitarianism. By this standard, Japan not only had issues such as gender inequality, class inequality, and poor living conditions for workers and farmers, but also had committed "injustice" by invading Korea and China. In other words, a new frame of reference emerged with which one could

---

48 Cho Kyŏngdal, "The Siberian Expedition and the Rice Riots," *History Geography Education* 880 (2018): 6-8.

49 Yŏm Sangsŏp, "A Plea to Everyone in the Whole Nation," in *The Complete Works of Yŏm Sangsŏp's Essays*, vol. 1, *1918-1928*, eds. Han Kihyŏng and Yi Hyeryŏng (Seoul: Somyong Publishers, 2013), 48.

50 Irie Akira, *War and Peace in the 20th Century*, trans. Cho Chin'gu and Yi Chongkuk (Seoul: Yŏnam Publishers, 2016), 105, 106.

evaluate Japan critically.[51] This criticism entailed more than simply pointing out how Japan did not meet the standards of modernity. Contextualized within the colonial reality of Korea, the criticism on imperial Japan could conceive thoughts of overcoming modernity.

Let us delve further into this matter with a concrete example that suggests that colonial Koreans could find a shortcut to an alternative civilization without being overwhelmed by the need to adapt to modernity. Colonial Koreans as a colonized nation in the hierarchy of the world system were sensitive to the disparity between the time of the world and that of colonial Korea.[52] They observed that "there is not much to be said if the modern civilization was the ultimate standard ····· However, suppose there is, to our great joy, something loftier beyond modern civilization to which the entire human race could advance. The Korean people, or those in the same situations as they, ought to strive for it."[53] Although this excerpt is just one example, the argument was tied to the core thoughts of *Kaebyŏk*, a commercially successful magazine operated by Ch'ŏndogyo between June 1920 and August 1926. This idea was grounded in the tenet of Ch'ŏndogyo, which combined then widespread reconstruction theory as a critique of civilization and ills of capitalism in particular, with its own notion of "*kaebyŏk*," which means "opening of a new heaven and a new earth." As this idea reflected the lived and felt realities of the colonial Koreans suffering from the toils of life, *Kaebyŏk* became "the beloved [periodical] of the era" in the 1920s.[54]

Koreans' awareness of an alternative path to civilization that could be taken along with other oppressed peoples of the world has great significance, especially when it is read in light of the debates about Eastern and Western cultures, which was a heated issue in interconnected East Asia. In the 1920s, China, for example, saw lively "debates on Chinese and Western cultures," in which cultural conservatives argued that Western civilization was declining and that

---

51 Ryu Sihyŏn, "Memories of the March First Movement in the 1920s," 192.

52 Hŏ Su, "The Dissemination of Post-World War I Reconstruction Discourse and Korean Intellectuals," in Pak and Ryu, *Inquiries on March First, 1919*, 151.

53 "Whether the Solution of the Problem Will Be Determined by Ourselves or by Others," *Kaebyŏk*, March 1923, 6-13.

54 Ch'oe Suil, *Studies on Kaebyŏk* (Seoul: Somyong Publishing, 2008), 399-403.

Chinese culture should be regarded as its alternative. In opposition to such arguments, a group of "Westernizationists" represented by Hu Shih, joined by Marxists, opined that China still had much to learn from the West. Paek Chiun compares the above debates with the discussions on civilization featured in *Reconstruction* (*Kaizō*), one of the most influential magazines of the early 20th century in Japan, and points out that the treatment of the problem of civilization in *Reconstruction* seemed rather weak. According to Paek, *Reconstruction* did not evince the fundamental skepticism toward modern civilization that Chinese intellectuals did; rather, it stopped short at introducing new theoretical currents from the West. In contrast, the Chinese intellectuals were fundamentally critical of Western civilization, and their criticisms were often enmeshed with cultural nationalism.[55]

Examining the intellectual terrain of Korea at this time in a comparative manner, it becomes clear that Koreans came to formulate foundational grounds from where they could criticize the ruling ideologies of Japan, an imperial nation deeply obsessed with modernization. The Koreans also took comparative-critical approaches to the Japanese colonial rule by examining it through universal modern values such as liberty, equality, justice, and humanitarianism.[56] To speak in terms of "double projects," Imperial Japan veered toward adapting to, or rather, catching up with modernity. Semi-colonial China had an interest in overcoming modernity, but it ended up focusing more on adapting to modernity and sought to resolve problems through cultural nationalism by laying emphasis on the specificity of the Chinese culture. On the other hand, Korea, which had first-hand experience of the "shadows" of colonial modernity, was motivated to both adapt to and overcome modernity. The Koreans ultimately opened up a path to go beyond the boundaries of a single nation-state and form alliances with other oppressed peoples.

Examining this discourse of alternative civilization in light of the intellectual terrain at the time sheds further light on its significance. As March First waned,

55 Baik Ji-woon (Paek Chiun), "Toward a Transformation of Civilization and the Reconstruction of the World: Civilization Discourses of Kaizō Right after World War I," *The Journal of Korean Studies* 173 (2016): 156.

56 Yi T'aehun, "Attitudes and Perceptions about the First World War," 225.

those who descended from the *Kaehwa* faction, the late 19th century reformists, tended to emphasize adapting to modernity and therefore advocate colonial autonomy. In the meantime, those who championed the ideas of the late 19th century conservatives, *Wijŏngch'ŏksa* faction, characterized by their adherence to Confucian orthodoxy, repulsion to Western civilization, and wholesale refusal of modernity, devoted themselves to overseas anti-Japanese guerilla fights. In comparison, the "*Kaebyŏk* group" led by Ch'ŏndoists was more responsive to the "double project" of adapting to and overcoming modernity.[57] After the Tonghak Peasant Movement failed, its members transformed Tonghak into a religion, that is to say, Ch'ŏndogyo. While they embraced the reformist ideas as the country underwent modernization, the *Kaebyŏk* group contributed not only to the March First Movement but also to the intellectual discourse in Korea by proposing the idea of alternative civilization.[58]

The idea of an alternative civilization was not only shared by intellectual circles but also to some degree by the populace, who had returned, after March First, to their everyday lives. As some had experienced an explosive desire for liberation during March First, which still lingered in them, they continued to keep the spark alive by engaging with national religions. However, it is imperative that we discern differences between these religions, as some of them may have chosen the path of the transcendental spiritual world of enchantment to escape the colonial reality, which was becoming more and more embroiled in the global capitalism.[59]

---

57 For this three-party aspect, see Paik Nak-chung et al., *Examining the Great Shifts of Civilization*, 242. See also Cho Sŏnghwan, *The Birth of Korean Modernity: From Reform to the Great Opening* (Seoul: Mosinŭn Saramdŭl, 2018), 109-110.

58 Hŏ Su categorizes discourses about alternative civilization as a branch of cultural reformism, and points out that advocates of such discourses did not do enough to pave the way to realize an alternative civilization through preparing necessary systems and resources. However, he does suggest that such past discourses on alternative civilization can be understood as precious theoretical assets. Hŏ Su, "The Theory of Peace in Korea in the Early 20th Century," *Critical Review of History* 106 (2014): 63.

59 Cho Kyŏngdal, "Dogmas and Practices of Buddhist Society in Colonial Korea," in *War, Disasters, and Popular Religions in Modern East Asia*, ed. Takeuchi Husasi (Tokyo: Yujisha, 2014). Cho categorizes the religions of the time into four types: those involved in the great revival movement, those that reinforced apocalyptic superstitions, those that brought about the political movementalization of religion, and those that performed the simultaneous tasks of saving the inner world and enabling social contributions.

Examining Ch'ŏndogyo with the above question in mind allows us to better understand the limitations of this national religion. Its governing body was divided into "old" and "new" factions in the late 1920s and saw some of its divisions, due to its focus on adapting to modernity, gradually complying with the modernizing policies of the colonial government and ultimately turning into co-opted organizations for Japan's war efforts. On the other hand, the Society for the Study of Buddhadharma (Pulbŏb yŏn'guhoe), which later emerged as Won Buddhism in the wake of Korea's liberation, had inherited the idea of *kaebyŏk* from Tonghak, with which they combined Buddhism. This group engaged in civilizational transition movements that promoted the simultaneous pursuit of finding spiritual mindfulness and bringing social change, which, in other words, entailed achieving material and spiritual enlightenment at the same time. Such aspirations are noteworthy, as they made the Society for the Study of Buddhadharma the most suited of all religious groups to take on the "double project" of adapting to and overcoming modernity.[60] Of course, one might point out that the Society had little influence in colonial Korea and that their objectives did not directly addressed the more urgent task of establishing an independent nation-state. I, however, would like to add that Song Kyu, the second master of Won Buddhism, published *The Treatise on the National Foundation* just two months after the liberation on August 15th 1945. This publication suggests that the Society did acknowledge the urgency of political independence.[61] It is of course necessary to take a closer look at how the Society and Won Buddhist groups carried out the double project of wrestling with the colonial rule and attempting to overcome it. In addition, it is also crucial to examine how other groups at the time, ranging from other religious groups and advocates of different ideologies to leaders of different movements, engaged with such a task. These topics will be left for future research.[62]

---

60 Paik Nak-chung et al., *Examining the Great Shifts of Civilization*, 243, 245-248.

61 See Paik Nak-chung, *The Great Shift in Civilization and the Great Opening* (Seoul: Mosinŭn Saramdŭl, 2016).

62 Paik Nak-chung, "The March First Movement and Korean Nation-Building," *Quarterly Changbi* 47, no. 2 (2019): 314-317. This article proposes a transformative middle way that pursued fundamental change (Korea's independence) rather than reformation, of the Japanese colonial order/system but

The discourses I introduced above were the result of the rigorous intellectual struggles that Korean thinkers went through as they were exposed to new intellectual stimuli in the "bleak 1910s." They were also the fruits of the experiences of the populace who saw their desires for a "new world" converge and erupt in the form of the March First Movement, found a surge of confidence, but ultimately had their hopes frustrated. Korea, in this respect, experienced a "New Culture Movement" different from that of China. While experiencing the formal establishment of a republic from the 1911 Revolution and the regression to Yuan Shikai's restoration of monarchy in 1915, China ended up taking the path of westernization and anti-traditionalism.

It was due to these struggles and aspirations that the March First Movement and its underlying ideas could serve as sources for a continuous learning process. Shortly after Korea's liberation, novelist An Hoenam vowed to "bring a new March First, bigger and more powerful" than March First that occurred 28 years earlier. More recently, social and environmental activist Chang Ilsun pointed out that calls for an autonomy of the people in March First was imbued with "a spirit of non-violence," which is also originated in "the spirit of the Tonghak."[63] Their remarks suggest that March First cannot simply be regarded as a historical event to be celebrated; rather, it is a resource that continues to inspire new subjects of change.

5. A Conversation between 1919 and 2019

It seems that I must now, before concluding this paper, pose the unavoidable question: Should we revise the term March First Movement and call it the "March First Revolution"?

Truth be told, it was only after the liberation of Korea that March First began to be referred to as the March First "movement" rather than "revolution."

---

also avoided both extremes of the right and the left.

63 An Hoenam, "A Tumultuous History," in *An Outline of Modern Korean Novels.* vol. 24 (Seoul: Tonga Publishing, 1995), 527. See also Chang Ilsun, "Changing the Other and with the Other," in *I Had Not Realized, Thou Wast I*, ed. Kim Ingnok (Seoul: Sigol Saenghwal, 2012), 113.

However, we must also take a look into the past, to the times before and after March First, when press censorship and a lack of publishing spaces prevented Koreans from using the word "revolution." Even during this time, Korean youths were aware of the concept of revolution, as they had witnessed the Xinhai Revolution, which they saw as a contemporaneous event, and the cultural atmosphere of Japan's Taishō democracy. Instead of being beholden to the old notion that revolution meant dynastic changes, they interpreted revolution in a more "universal way, as the destruction of the old world."[64] As mentioned earlier, March First had been called the "Great Revolution of March First" during the colonial period, and a call for an endorsement of this term surfaced again in recent years as well.[65] That is to say, the name March First "Revolution" has its own epistemological genealogy.

Recent discussions on the issue have been stirred by the current Moon Jae-in administration and the ruling party. These were also preceded by the heated debate surrounding the National Foundation Day issue during the Park Geun-hye administration. However, we should not overlook the broader contexts where the memory of March First has been dynamically "remade" during the course of Korean democratization movements.

The significance of this issue becomes even more profound when we contextualize it in today's East Asia. Both China and Japan are striving to reinterpret the past century's history as they enter into another phase of civilizational transition wherein deepening crises of the world capitalist system have muddled the existing world order and rendered developmental models feeble. These two countries are trying to reflect back on their history and discover new developmental models. Our attempts to put the years 1919 and 2019 in conversation will ultimately lead us to the question of how we should respond to and contribute to the call of our times, which must be addressed meticulously and in depth. Before doing so, I would like to briefly address my personal opinions on whether March First should be regarded as a

---

64 Kwon Boduerae, "The Transformation of 'Revolution' in 1910 Korea," *Concept and Communication* 15 (2015): 68-69, 76.

65 Yi Chunsik, "'Movement' or 'Revolution'?: Rethinking the March First Revolution" (paper presented at The March First Revolution 95th Anniversary Academic Conference, The Center for Historical Truth and Justice, Seoul, 26 February, 2014), 42-56.

"revolution."

When dealing with this issue, we must take the liberty of going beyond the boundaries of the textbook definitions of the word "revolution." This is not to say that we should arbitrarily expand the meaning of revolution or abuse history by overrating the significance of March First. However, it is necessary to redefine the concept of "revolution" as we comparatively assess world historical events and, at the same time, in the context of Korean history. We need to balance our "eyes of the present" toward the March First Revolution and the perception of revolution in 1919, when colonial Koreans regarded a revolution "from a more universal manner, as a way to destroy the old world." I define revolution as an extensive transformation of the entire society rather than an event that ends with the subversion of an existing regime. I thus refer to revolutions of which the results reveal themselves through incremental achievements as "revolutions that continue to be learned" or "ongoing revolutions." For March First to be recognized as such a revolution, three criteria have to be met.[66]

First, we must confirm whether there is a clear continuity between the objectives of the March First Revolution and the historical challenges we have taken on today. The tasks of achieving national autonomy, integration, and democracy still remain relevant to Koreans today, who have lived through periods of the colonial rule and the Cold War. These tasks are in fact becoming more important as reconciliation processes between South and North Korea develop further, prompting aspirations to map out a new Korean peninsula.

Secondly, we must ask the question of whether March First was associated with a desire to change history on a fundamental level, i.e., a desire to change the world on a "revolutionary level." We have examined the people's radical break from monarchism, pursuit of republicanism, and recognition of a civilizational transition, all of which were evident in phrases like "destruction of the old world" or "coming of a new era," which have significance not

---

66 This notion is indebted to Paik Nak-chung who puts much emphasis on the current nature of the April 19th Revolution (1960) and thereby calls it an "Unfinished Revolution." He addresses three criteria as the basis for his argument. See Paik Nak-chung, "The Historical Meaning and Presentness of 4·19," in *Studies on the Transformation in the Division System* (Seoul: Changbi Publishers, 1994), 49-67, 53-54.

only in the history of Korea but also in global history as signs of revolutionary change. The experience of March First under the colonial condition is also significant because it now serves as historical resource for Korea's "double project of modernity." This becomes even more apparent when we examine the ways in which Korea was interconnected with Japan. "How to respond to the March First Movement" was for Japan a critical litmus test that could determine "the future of both its domestic social reform movements and its political regime."[67] During the era of Taishō Democracy (1905–1932), however, Japan failed to respond effectively to March First, either socially or institutionally. The Japanese ended up settling for a limited form of social reform while establishing constitutionalism at home and continuing to run and expand their empire abroad.[68] As such, March First can be understood as a decisive historical event through which we can reassess the last hundred years' history of interconnected East Asian countries. Japan, a country that has played a major role in it, seemed to have adapted successfully to modernity as it was empowered by its victory in the Sino-Japanese War and the Russo-Japanese War before forcibly annexing Korea in 1910. Although Japan made a slight concession after March First, in reality, it did not pay enough attention to overcoming modernity as it was fully committed to adapting to modernity, and the "national interests" it pursued in the long run were not beneficial for all the Japanese people. In contrast, China as a semi-colony supported March First and followed up with its own May Fourth, making a mark in terms of historical transition and participation in the "global moment."

Lastly, it should be confirmed whether the important legacy of March First still persists. The endeavor to revolutionize the society and reach a new world

---

67 Matsuo Takayoshi, "The Taishō Democracy Era and the March First Independence Movement," in *The March First Movement and the World Historical Significance of 1919*, eds. Geng Yunzhi et al. (Seoul: North East Asian History Foundation, 2010), 126.

68 Cho Kyŏngdal, "The Siberian Expedition and the Rice Riots," 8. It should be noted that there were activists like Yoshino Sakuzō or enlightenment clubs he led such as Reimeikai. They tried to understand the two movements of March First and May Fourth and argued for a reformation of the empire with an exceptionally international "sense of the other." Some scholars argue that their arguments for a reformed Japan and an alliance in East Asia should be appreciated. See Yonetani Masafumi, "The March First Independence Movement, May Fourth Movement and the Democracy of Imperial Japan," *Journal of History Education* 891 (2019): 28-33.

inherent in Tonghak has remained a dynamic driving force of Korea's modern history. This "incremental and accumulative achievement" of March First has been demonstrated in the struggles of April Nineteenth (1960), May Eighteenth (1980), and finally, the Candlelight Revolution (2016). These transformative events can be characterized as an incremental process of "persevering through impossibility" with constant twists and turns, which becomes evident when we compare the history of Korea to that of China or Japan.[69] The subjects of this history are the people who overcame despair under colonialism and saw the light of March First, or, "caught a glimpse of the heaven." What connects the years 1919 and 2019 is the longing for a "new world" that entails more than just the reformation of existing political institutions or systems.

It turns out that March First not only meets the criteria for a revolution but also deserves titles such as "a revolution that continues to be learned" or "an ongoing revolution." Calling it the "March First Movement" would still be acceptable if an agreement cannot be reached. We should, however, at least confirm that it was a revolutionary phenomenon with the characteristics of a revolution. •

Would the South and the North, however, be able to share this historical assessment as the reconciliation and unification efforts continue? On top of a large gap between two Koreas' assessments of the Provisional Government, a division definitely exists between the North's understanding of March First as "the People's Uprising of March First" which is based on the North's reading of history according to the "*Juche*" ideology and the South's understanding of it as "the March First Movement." The memory of March First itself is, however, valuable to both, for it offers nation (*minjok*) and democracy as a common set of concerns in the journey toward historical reconciliation between two Koreas. The journey will be a gradual one, which involves first actively taking advantage of differing historical perceptions as "productive stimulus," developing the basic framework of "coexistence of differences," and, finally,

69 Fu Ssu-nien, "The New Lessons of Korea's Independence Movement," *Xinchao* 1, no.4, April 1919. Fu Ssu-nien was the leader of the student movement at Peking University. He evaluated the March First Movement as an "epoch-making revolution," which left us three lessons: a non-violent revolution, a revolution that was realized persevering through impossibilities, and a pure student revolution.

advancing to the "shared perception."[70]

The experience of March First is a form of contemporary history that "continues to be learned." Transforming this new remembering of March First into a commons (without being swayed by legitimacy controversies associated with specific administrations) is a world-historical project that should be achieved together by historians and ordinary citizens who once again "caught a glimpse of the heaven" during the Candlelight Revolution.

Trans. by Park Joo-hyun

---

[70] See To Chinsun, "History and Memory: The Era Name, National Foundation Year, and Its Political Implications," *Critical Review of History* 126 (2019): 393-422. He notes that the March First Movement, the establishment of the Provisional Government, and the founding of the Republic of Korea are "separate issues in different dimensions" when we examine them from the "wider perspective of the entire Korean peninsula." He further notes that we must ponder ways to remember the three events from a more open and broader perspective that will enable the South and North to communicate better.

Manifesto:
From a Desired Reality to Its Advent

Kwon Boduerae

1. The Uprisings of Spring 1919 and Their Linguistic Practices

The March First Movement is one of the most significant events to have occurred on the modern Korean peninsula. With the centennial of the movement in 2019, the National Institute of Korean History constructed a database which states that from March to May 1919, there were 1,683 protests across the nation with over one million participants, along with nearly one thousand casualties at the protest sites. Considering that the investigations and reports of the colonial authorities during the March First Movement have comprised the basic research materials, these are conservative estimates and it is likely that the actual size of the protests was considerably bigger. With the colonization of Korea by the Japanese Empire in August 1910, armed struggle groups were suppressed, the majority of political and societal associations or organizations were prohibited, and modes of transportation and communication were left underdeveloped. Under these conditions, how, then, could nation-wide protests, the participation of people willing to risk their lives, and this tenacious persistence have been possible? The fact that such questions have not been sufficiently contemplated and that a convincing response has not yet been produced, demonstrates that the March First Movement still remains to be understood

33

in its entirety. Even nationalism and modernization, which have been the universal standard in interpreting the Korean peninsula's past, cannot be coherently applied to the March First Movement. Whereas the movement has been interpreted in relation to nationalism, its multiple variables, one of which was King Kojong's death, cannot be explained in terms of political and economic modernity. In the 1960s and 1970s, as research on the March First Movement was reinvigorated, materials on the uprisings were collected, organized, and reported, but these interpretations were unable to escape the framework of an ethnic-nationalistic monism.

At a certain point after the 1980s, interpretations of the March First Movement based on class theory began to emerge, but rather than fundamentally disturbing this nationalistic monism, they merely spurred partial revisions. In other words, the sub-narratives of class theory and armed resistance were mixed with the master narratives of nationalism and pacifism, resulting in some confusion regarding the March First Movement. However, while the master narratives of the movement remained at a standstill, empirical research on the regional uprisings of the March First Movement continued to accumulate. With the onset of the 2000s, there have been ongoing attempts to approach the March First Movement from the perspectives of social movements and participatory democracy. While rather obvious, this research has generally been accomplished by historians, particularly specialists of Korean history. I propose to expand on the research hitherto conducted on the March First Movement by adjusting our focus on the narrative that has taken the *minjok* (the ethnic nation) as its main subject. It is a method where one repeatedly zooms in and out, shifting our focus to the individuals that participated in the March First Movement — and not just the leaders, but ordinary people — then moving to the horizons of world history both before and after the movement, and then veering once more to the units of the individual or the village. The March First Movement is an event that is difficult to fully comprehend without referencing the vast global changes that occurred after World War I. The old empires of Austria-Hungary, Russia, and the Ottomans collapsed, and post-colonial liberation movements emerged in these former imperial territories. Revolutions successively broke out in places such as Russia, Germany, and Egypt and ushered in the establishment of the system known as socialism. *Anciens régimes* finally fell and the politics of mass utopianism commenced. The March First Movement took place within this chain of events, acted as an agent that both influenced and was influenced by these events, and expanded and transformed them. Of the many dimensions of the March First Movement, this article focuses on the linguistic practice known as the "manifesto" and approaches the subjects of the uprisings, as a part of the attempt to understand the movement within this broader chain of world historical events.

2. Seoul on March 1st, 1919:
Chungang Higher Common School Student Ch'ae Mansik

March 1, 1919. A little after two in the afternoon, Ch'ae Mansik, then a second-year student at Chungang Higher Common School (*kodŭng pot'ong hakkyo*), arrived at T'apkol Park. Having gone according to plan, the remnants of the ceremony for reciting the Korean Declaration of Independence still lingered and shouts of "*manse!*"[1] reverberated throughout the air. Students of secondary schools and colleges in Seoul were the leaders. Whereas religious organizations concentrated on distributing the Korean Declaration of Independence throughout the provinces, student networks focused on mobilizing people on the day of the declaration. However, in 1919, there were less than 2,000 students enrolled in relevant educational institutes within Seoul and the number was precisely the limit of organizational mobilization of rallying people. Though the area around the park was bustling with throngs of people, the majority of them had nearly no knowledge of the declaration's recitation and were merely visitors who had come up to Seoul to attend King Kojong's funeral planned for March 3rd.

These people would likely have been bewildered when they first saw this "disturbance." Among these old villagers who had come up to Seoul to "see

---

1   Translator's note: While "*manse*" literally means "Ten Thousand Years" or "Long Live Korea!," it has taken on connotations that far surpass its literal translation. The collective uprisings during this time are often referred to as the "*Manse* Protests" and it has come to embody a sense of the revolutionary spirit, collective uprising, and resistance to colonial rule that imbued the times. There are also instances of contemporary usage in which it is used to celebrate a collective national solidarity.

the state funeral," wearing their white *kat* hats despite rules regarding mourning dress not being publicly proclaimed, one of them asked Ch'ae Mansik: "Excuse me, student. What's going on?" Ch'ae Mansik's answer was concise: "Korea is now independent." Though this old villager's face had been full of fear, upon hearing Ch'ae Mansik's words, his "expression immediately became one of joy." As if overwhelmed by a surge of emotion, he stuttered, "R-really? I see⋯" and shortly afterwards, brandished his cane high in the air and cried, "Then I, too, will celebrate Korea's independence! *Manse!*"[2]

How would this old villager have experienced the weeks that followed? He would have likely joined the parade of protesters and strode through the city of Seoul, witnessing the colonial police[3] looking on even as tens of thousands shouted "Long Live Korean Independence" and "*Manse!*" With the forcible suppression of the protestors in Seoul only going into full effect after the student protests on March 5th, had this man gone straight back home after King Kojong's funeral on March 3rd, he may have witnessed only the "liberated Seoul." He may have even carried one or two copies of the Declaration of Independence in his hands. Perhaps he would have also encountered a copy of the *Korean Independence News* (*Chosŏn tongnip sinmun*)[4] and heard the news that "in order to realize the true intention of the 33 National Representatives, all the nation are following their words." While the police and administrative institutions of the Japanese Government-General of Korea, along with modes of transportation and communication, still appeared to be alive and well, it would have nevertheless been difficult to find proof that would have refuted this student's words that "Korea is now independent."

After returning to his hometown, he would have become one mouth among

---

2   Ch'ae Mansik, "On the Day of March First," in *The Collected Works of Ch'ae Mansik*, vol. 10 (P'aju: Changbi Publishers, 1987), 472.

3   Translator's note: Though I have chosen to use the term "colonial police," it is important to note that a distinguishing characteristic of the Japanese colonial period is the use of the military police, which acted as both a military police and secret police force. In this sense, the distinctions between the military and the police are blurrier during the colonial period.

4   Translator's note: While there were numerous Korean newspapers entitled *Tongnip sinmun*, with the most well-known being the *Independent* founded in July 1896 by Sŏ Chaep'il and published between 1896 to 1899, the *Chosŏn Tongnip Sinmun* refers to a separate newspaper founded in 1919 published through the Posŏngsa.

thousands conveying the news of "independence" and "*manse.*" How would he have explained the relationship between "independence" and "*manse*"? That people shouted "*manse*" because they were now an independent country? That they cried "*manse*" in order to assert their desire for independence? Or would he have drawn upon another explanation entirely? Given that the majority of people at the time had some knowledge of classical Chinese and would have been able to read the declaration, how would he have received the passage like "we hereby declare that Korea is an independent state and that Koreans are a self-governing people"? This grandiose passage may have invoked thousands of questions: "We hereby declare"? Did this mean that independence and self-governance were already an established fact? Or was it indicating a future that had not yet arrived? What exactly did this strange word "declaration"[5] mean?

3. The Relationship between "Independence" and "*Manse*"

Had the old villager that Ch'ae Mansik encountered participated in the protests and subsequently been arrested, he would have likely testified over the course of questioning that "I heard that we had become independent." He was not alone. Throughout the entire country, many people experienced similar vicissitudes. One rally held in Pyongyang on the afternoon of March

---

5   The word "*sŏnŏn*" (선언) in the Korean Declaration of Independence (*kimi tongnip sŏnŏnsŏ*) was translated at the time as "proclamation." English translations today generally tend to translate this word as "declaration." This differs from texts that use the word "manifesto," such as The Communist Manifesto (1848), The Fascist Manifesto (1919), and the Surrealist Manifesto (1924). Though the Korean translations of the aforementioned texts all use the word "*sŏnŏn*" in translating their titles, the foundation of a "manifesto" is the future, but the foundation for a "proclamation" or "declaration" is the present. If "manifesto" is the language of a subject in formation, the language of disclosing a goal and pursuing change, then "proclamation" or "declaration" is a word used to announce or convey the actions of a subject that already has the capacity to do so. Around the period of World War I, numerous countries presented declarations of independence (including the Korean Declaration of Independence) that claimed to be "proclamations" or "declarations," but I believe that their fundamental essence is closer to that of a "manifesto." Translator's note: Following Kwon's explanation, I have chosen to translate "*sŏnŏn*" as "manifesto" for titles or sections of this article, but have retained its translation as "declaration" when referring to actual documents which are already known by specific titles, such as the Korean Declaration of Independence or the Declaration of Independence of the Czechoslovak Nation.

1st was called "Assembly for the Celebration of Independence." To the masses that joined the rally and held a celebratory ceremony amid the onlooking colonial police, independence was already a reality. Copies of the Declaration of Independence were posted in front of government offices and the T'aegŭkki fluttered along the roads. It was to the extent that the governor himself sent an official inquiry asking "whether the rumors of the country's independence are true."[6] Though there were doubts about the veracity of this rumor, in South P'yŏngan Province, a document jointly signed by the governor and chief constable regarding Korea's independence was issued to the heads of the counties and townships.[7] There were also widespread incidents in which residents gathered at the township offices or colonial police stations and demanded that the Japanese immediately leave Korea because Korea was now independent and thus, there was no need for institutions of the Japanese Government-General.

The general public was overjoyed at the news of independence. They even developed their own reasoning and proof. Some explained that "I shouted *manse* because Korea is now independent." Others claimed that "I cried *manse* because I heard the news that countries with long histories and populations over five million people under foreign subjugation will all be liberated without exception." There were those who elaborated in detail that "the principle of national self-determination presented during the recent Paris Peace Conference clarified that countries under foreign rule will be liberated. Thus, the 33 National Representatives also declared Korea's independence in Seoul and as all the people throughout the country cried '*manse*,' so, too, did I." Thirty-one-year-old farmer Kim Sŭngsin, who participated in the *manse* protests in Sawŏn Township (*myŏn*), Pongsan County (*kun*) of Hwanghae Province, explained that "there were rumors that Korea's independence had been approved at the Paris Peace Conference and at first, even the police in this region participated in the protests,

---

6   Yun Soyŏng, ed. and trans., *Collected Articles on the Korean Independence Movement in Japanese Newspapers* (Ch'ŏnan: History of the Korean Independence Movement Research Center, The Independence Hall of Korea, 2009), 120.

7   Kim Jeong-in (Kim Chŏngin) and Yi Chŏngŭn, *The March First Movement Within Korea: The Central and Northern Regions*, vol. 1 (Ch'ŏnan: History of the Korean Independence Movement Research Center, The Independence Hall of Korea, 2009), 225.

so I thought that Korea's independence had already been decided." Sixty-eight-year-old farmer Ko Kunsam, who shouted "*manse*" alone and was subsequently arrested in Posan Township, P'yŏngsan County, testified that "I went out to visit the market and heard from people who had come down from Seoul that Korea's independence had been approved at the Paris Peace Conference. My happiness upon hearing those words was larger and more overwhelming than the mountains and oceans. All day long, I drank in celebration, raising my hands in the air and dancing, and shouted 'Long Live Korean Independence' numerous times."[8]

As a "prophetic rumor,"[9] the news of Korea's independence occasionally summoned a reality that resembled independence. In some areas of P'yŏngan Province, liberated areas were temporarily constructed, giving birth to the residents' autonomy and self-governance. In Sinch'ang Township, Sunch'ang County, after negotiations with the township head, the residents placed signs stating "Office for the Preparations of the Independence Movement of Taehan Korea" on the township office and hoisted a T'aegŭkki flag. In Unjong Township, Sŏnch'ŏn County, the residents seized the township office and carried out autonomous administration for around twenty days. In Oksang Township, Ŭiju County, self-governing citizen groups confiscated funds and equipment from the township office and for approximately ten days, performed duties in self-governance.[10] It was a reality where it was possibly to fully believe that Korea had become independent. Even governors, chief constables, and township heads were confused, and this confusion would have likely been even more prevalent among the military and administrators of the rank and file of which Koreans were in charge, such as police assistants (*sunsabo*) and township office workers. Even after the protests died down, for some time, numerous people in these organizations continued to submit their resignations

---

8   For a list of examples from each region in this section, see The Compilation Committee for the History of the Independence Movement, ed., *Collected Sources on the History of the Independence Movement*, vol. 5 (Seoul: Financial Committee for Persons of Distinguished Service to Independence, 1971), 589, 588, 719, 604 (in order of places listed).

9   Laurent Dubois, *A Colony of Citizens: Revolution and Slave Emancipation in the French Caribbean, 1787-1804* (Chapel Hill: University of North Carolina Press, 2012), 85-89.

10   The Compilation Committee, *Collected Sources on the History of the Independence Movement*, 5: 232, 258, and 262.

because of the anticipation or fear of what would happen "after independence."[11]

As the rumor that Korea was "already independent" mixed with the rumor that it would "soon be independent," stories that some regions had already become independent or that independence would be certain within a few days also began to circulate. In Imch'ŏn Township, Puyŏ County of South Ch'ung-ch'ŏng Province, seven members of the religious organization, Ch'ŏndogyo, visited the colonial police headquarters and demanded that "Seoul is already independent. Grant us the right to independence as well."[12] In the surrounding region, rumors of independence on April 10th spread like wildfire. Even after the anticipated date of independence passed, rumors that independence would be established in June spread throughout numerous regions and continued widespread until the end of the Paris Peace Conference on June 28, 1919.[13] No matter how small, the hope and anticipation for "independence" refused to be extinguished until the conference's official end, perhaps even until the end of the Washington Naval Conference in February 1922, which was understood as an extension of the Paris Peace Conference.

Nevertheless, as time passed, it became undeniable that the rumors of Korea's independence were false or that there were simply too many contradictions. Even though there were casualties as the masses clamored for Japanese administrative officials to leave Korea, the rumors persisted. Let us briefly jump forward a few decades and compare the period with the conditions of the liberation period described in novelist Kim Song's *People without Arms* (*Mugi ŏmnŭn minjok*, 1946). Expanding our perspective to encompass world history, we would do well to recall the circumstances after Germany's surrender in World War II. Even as the Supreme Commander of the Armed Forces announced their surrender, this was not immediately and instantaneously conveyed to all organizations. A time lag and resistance, even in their death throes, were inevitable. Even after May 8, 1945, there were Nazis members

---

11 Kang Tŏksang, *Materials on Modern History,* vol. 25, *Chosŏn(1): the March First Movement (1)* (Tokyo: Misuzu shobō, 1966), 429-430.

12 Kim Chinho, Pak Ijun, and Pak Ch'ŏlgyu, *The March First Movement Within Korea: The Southern Region*, vol. 2 (Ch'ŏnan: History of the Korean Independence Movement Research Center, The Independence Hall of Korea, 2009), 47.

13 Kang, *Materials on Modern History,* 25: 411, 389.

that continued to partake in the massacre of the Jewish people, and after Korea's liberation on August 15, there were Japanese soldiers who continued to execute Koreans by shooting. If this was the situation in 1945, when news of surrender could be quickly conveyed through technology such as the radio, then in 1919, despite the proclamation of "independence" and "liberation," even more time would have been required for it to be truly materialized throughout the country.

In the chasm between rumors of "already-achieved independence" and the intact reality of the past, a considerable number of Koreans drew upon such frameworks of understanding. That is, they believed that Korea had successfully achieved independence, but that Japan continued to resist. The example of Yu Haejŏng, a Confucian who lived in Pyŏllae Township, Yangju County, Kyŏnggi Province, is emblematic. Barely nineteen, he wrote a lengthy letter to the Japanese Emperor towards the end of March.[14] It was to warn the Emperor about Japan's refusal to acknowledge Korea's independence. Regarding Korea's independence as already secured internationally, Yu stated "even as all nations across the world have approved of Korea's independence, Japan still refuses to return Korea." And he attempted to warn Japan by claiming that "when the Allied Forces question you about this crime, Japan shall become a rabbit in front of a tiger."[15] If we were to further contemplate the situation at the time, it seems that he considered Korea's independence as being conclusively appraised during the ongoing Paris Peace Conference and anticipated that Korea would soon become independent in the manner of countries such as Poland and Czechoslovakia.

---

14 Yu Haejŏng wrote another letter to the Tokyo governor and enclosed the letter that was sent to the Japanese Emperor, asking it to be delivered. The letter was actually delivered to Japan in early April (though of course, it was not directly delivered to the Japanese Emperor) and afterwards, Yu was sentenced to three years in prison for the crime of treason against the emperor.

15 The Compilation Committee, *Collected Sources on the History of the Independence Movement*, 5: 308.

4. Declarations of Independence in Comparative Context

The history of the "declaration" or "manifesto," as a linguistic form that drew from a desired future that had not yet arrived, officially began in the late 18th century with the Declaration of Independence of the United States (1776) as the pioneering example. When the representatives of the thirteen colonies under British colonial rule gathered to declare their independence, the "United States" was nothing more than a kind of imaginary existence. Indeed, America's independence only became officially recognized seven years later in 1783 through international treaties. In the interim, a complicated adjustment process and a long war with Britain were required. When the 13 representatives declared that "they [these colonies] are absolved from all allegiance to the British Crown, and that all political connection between them and the State of Great Britain, is and ought to be totally dissolved; and that as Free and Independent States, they have full Power to levy War, conclude Peace, contract Alliances, establish Commerce, and to do all other Acts and Things which Independent States may of right do,"[16] their declaration was simultaneously an impossible reality while not entirely imaginary.

The gap between language and reality is an undeniable fact. In the political realm as well, all existences must first assert themselves through language. While the original classical Chinese word "sŏnŏn" (宣言)[17] does not contain this meaning, its English translations as "declaration," "proclamation," and especially "manifesto" include this idea of first proclaiming an unrealized condition through language. Apart from the United States Declaration of Independence, there is a vast array of similar examples. For instance, the Dutch Republic declared its independence in 1581, but it took around seventy years for it to be officially recognized in 1648. In contrast, on December 31, 1803,

---

16 A Korean translation can be found in *A History of the Independence of the United States of America* (Hwangsŏng sinmunsa, 1899), 91-92. Further exploration is needed on how various declarations of independence that were introduced to Korea throughout the 1900-1910s influenced the Korean Declaration of Independence.

17 "Sŏnŏn" is a word with a long history that can be found 78 times in *The Veritable Records of the Chosŏn Dynasty* (*Chosŏn wangjo sillok*) alone. Though it originally referred to the words of a king, its meaning was later expanded and was used to signify speech that was externalized publicly.

after a twelve-year-long insurrection, Haiti presented its declaration of independence and officially established an independent nation in ten months.[18] As a case that resides somewhere between these two, Vietnam declared their independence on September 2, 1945 and only realized their independence after an eight-year-long war with France. In this sense, the time lag between declaration, revolt, and independence is diverse, and in the interim, these polities faced a chasm between reality and unreality, existence and nonexistence.

The declarations of independence of various nation-states were most highly concentrated in the period between World War I and World War II. In 1918, the year World War I ended and one year prior to the March First Movement, numerous countries in Europe such as Belarus, Latvia, Armenia, Azerbaijan, Estonia, Ukraine, Georgia, and Czechoslovakia presented their own declarations of independence in quick succession. The majority of them had their independence internationally recognized the following year at the Paris Peace Conference. Around the time, Finland, Ireland, and Poland also presented their own declarations of independence. In this global context, some argue Korea must also become independent because "countries such as Poland and Iceland have become independent through national self-determination after declaring so."[19] Others insist on Korean independence because "people of all nations are becoming independent and administering their own country, as seen through the establishment of independent Ireland, Poland, and Israel," or because "India is petitioning the Paris Peace Conference for its independence."[20] The majority of these voices were the result of aptly understanding the uncertain changes taking place across the world.

As seen in the United States Declaration of Independence, which asserted the human right to pursue life, freedom, and happiness, declarations generally presented a new worldview and ideology with new words. Moreover, declarations

---

18 After independence, Haiti chose to adopt a monarchy system, and Jean-Jacques Dessalines, a military hero during the War of Independence, crowned himself the Emperor of Haiti. See C. L. R. James, *The Black Jacobins: Toussaint L'Ouverture and the San Domingo Revolution*, 2nd ed. (New York: Vintage Books, 1989), 370.

19 The Compilation Committee, *Collected Sources on the History of the Independence Movement*, 5: 862.

20 The Compilation Committee, *Collected Sources on the History of the Independence Movement*, 5: 1388.

attacked the wrongs of the old order as the U.S. Declaration of Independence disclosed the tyranny of the British monarch in detail. The declarations presented at the end of World War I were similar. The Czechoslovak Declaration of Independence, which was presented on October 1918, centered around refusing the proposal of the Habsburg Monarchy who, upon facing a crisis of collapse, suggested to the Czechoslovakian people to form a federation in order to avoid the dismantling of the empire. According to the Czechoslovak Declaration, although the Habsburgs promised "autonomy to the dissatisfied nationalities under its rule," these words "mean[t] nothing other than a deceit." It described briefly the history of Czechoslovakian nation's unity with Austria and Hungary to defend against the threat of Turkish invasion and Austria-Hungary's subsequent violation of Czechoslovakian rights and destruction of its independent constitutional government. The declaration also denounced the Hapsburg empire's mobilization and sacrifice of countless minorities in World War I for the sake of its own imperial ambitions, invasions of Belgium, France, and Serbia, as well as violent plundering of other nations.

Through the declaration of independence, the Provisional Government of Czechoslovakia attacked the Austria-Hungary empire as an "unnatural and immoral political structure, hindering every movement toward democratic and social progress." The Czechoslovak state proclaimed, in contrast, that they "shall accept and adhere to the ideals of modern democracy," incorporating the ideologies of "the principles such as liberated mankind, the actual equality of all nations and the government deriving all their just power from the consent of the governed." "The Czechoslovak State shall be a republic." By summoning a genealogy of prior declarations, the Provisional Government placed the problem of Czechoslovakian independence on the horizon of world history. Indeed, the Czechoslovakian Declaration of Independence proposed to rest upon the tradition of the "American Declaration of Independence, the principles of Lincoln, and of the Declarations of the Rights of Man and Citizen." "Our democracy shall rest on universal suffrage." Women were to enjoy the same political, social, and cultural rights as men and minorities would be assured these same rights through proportional representation. They also advanced social and economic reforms, stating that "large estates will be redeemed for home colonization" and "patents of nobility will be abolished."[21]

The international response to the Czechoslovak Declaration of Independence was favorable, to the extent that Jan Garrigue Masaryk, the architect of the declaration and later the Foreign Minister of Czechoslovak, asked himself "Are we living in a fairy-tale?"[22] Emboldened by such a response, Czechoslovakia proclaimed the founding of a republic as soon as World War I ended and on April 1919, the height of the Paris Peace Conference, declared a land confiscation policy with regards to land ownership that exceeded 150 hectares per person. It was a radical policy that did not provide any indemnity "in the case of estates of the imperial family, estates illegally acquired, and estates of the persons who during the war had been guilty of treason against the Czechoslovak nation."[23] In addition, they established a Ministry of Labor, passed an eight-hour-workday, and pushed for women's suffrage as promised in the Declaration of Independence, thus demonstrating a powerful and almost shocking momentum in passing reforms. Charles Pergler, who acted as the Commissioner of the Czechoslovak Republic in the United States at the time, introduced these policies and emphasized that though they could be seen as radical, these reforms were "diametrically opposed to Bolshevism" and that "everything is being done in an orderly and legal way."[24]

The principal actors and emphases of each country's declarations of independence slightly differed. For Finland, the main agents behind their declaration was the Finnish Parliament, which had been maintained independently while Finland was a part of Russia as an autonomous principality. For Estonia, which had been ruled by Denmark, Sweden, and Russia for three centuries before receiving autonomy, the agent of the declaration was the Estonian National Council. For Ireland, it was the National Parliament which was established outside of the British Empire's laws. Finnish Declaration of

---

21 Vladimir Nosek, *Independent Bohemia: An Account of the Czechoslovak Strategy for Liberty* (London: J. M. Dent & Sons Ltd., 1918), 178-182. An English translation of the Czechoslovakian Declaration of Independence can be found at the following website: https://en.wikisource.org/wiki/Declaration_of_Independence_of_the_Czechoslovak_Nation

22 Jan Garrigue Masaryk, "Our People Is Free and Independent!" in *The Spirit of Thomas G. Masaryk (1850-1937): An Anthology*, ed. George J. Kovtun (New York: Palgrave Macmillan, 1990), 191.

23 Charles Pergler, "An Experiment in Progressive Government: The Czechoslovak Republic," *The Annals of the American Academy of Political and Social Science* 84 (July 1919): 59.

24 Pergler, "An Experiment in Progressive Government," 59-61.

Independence (December 1917) focused on petitioning numerous countries, beginning with Russia, for approval of their independence, while Estonian Declaration (February 1918) directly mentioned "the right of self-determinations of peoples." Irish Declaration (January 1919) centered around asserting the right of representation of the Irish Republic's parliament. Furthermore, while Finland promised a "complete renewal" of their government and Estonia more concretely promised a "democratic republic," Ireland expressed a more intermediate form consisting of a "national policy based upon the people's will with equal right and equal opportunity for every citizen." The extent to which each declaration reflected idealism or universalism varied widely. Estonia was more active and practical than Finland or Ireland. The Estonian Declaration of Independence promised the creation of a constituent assembly elected by general, direct, and secret elections, proclaimed the rights of the people, and culminated with a rallying cry of "Long live the independent democratic Republic of Estonia! Long live peace among nations!"[25]

5. The Secret of the 1919 Korean Declaration of Independence

As much as there were numerous declarations of independence throughout the world, there were similarly multiple declarations within Korea as well. The "Korean Declaration of Independence" signed by the 33 national representatives was merely one of many declarations that emerged during this time period. There was the "Taehan Declaration of Independence" created by Cho Soang in early 1919[26] and the "February Eighth Declaration of Independence" written by Korean students in Tokyo right before the March

---

[25] The English translation of the Finnish Declaration of Independence can be found at the following website: https://en.wikipedia.org/wiki/Finnish_Declaration_of_Independence#Text_of_Finland's_Decl aration_of_Independence; the Estonian Declaration of Independence here: https://en.wikipedia.org/wiki /Estonian_Declaration_of_Independenceand; and the Irish Declaration of Independence here: https://w ww.difp.ie/docs/1919/Declaration-of-independence/1.htm

[26] There is continued debate as to whether the Taehan Declaration of Independence was created and presented before or after the March First Movement. See Cho Hangnae, "An Account of the Taehan Declaration of Independence's Time Period of Presentation," in *Collected Writings on the History of the Korean Independence Movement* (Seoul: T'amgudang, 1992).

First Movement. Even after the March First Movement, dozens of declarations continued to be published, including the Osaka Declaration of Independence written by Yŏm Sangsŏp and the declaration presented by the Korean National Assembly (*Taehan kungmin ŭihoe*) in Russia. Counting those published outside of Korea, approximately 30 different declarations of Korean independence were presented until the early 1920s.[27] Without any kind of systematic organization, numerous actors who had sensed the international situation and acutely seized the possibility of independence planned their "declarations" simultaneously without any connection or communication. The Korean Declaration of Independence was forged by merging three disparate strands of the declaration from Ch'ŏndoism, the petition from the Christian organizations, and the declaration from students in Seoul. Confucian scholars also released petitions that were not precisely declarations.[28] Even at the final phase of preparing the declaration, there were those who stubbornly insisted on choosing the form of a petition. Nevertheless, they reached relatively smoothly the consensus that the official document should be a form of "declaration."

"We hereby declare that Korea is an independent nation and that Koreans are a self-governing people."[29] After declaring "independence" and "self-governance" in the first sentence of the Korean Declaration of Independence, the writers validated the foundation of these claims through "the strength of five thousand years of history" and "as an expression of the devotion and loyalty of twenty million people." Going even further, the declaration claimed

---

27 For a list of the declarations of independence, see Cho Hangnae, "The Context and Ideology of the Korean Declaration of Revolution" in *Journal of Studies on Korean National Movement* 10 (December 1994): 221-229.

28 The representative examples are the petition for independence submitted to the Japanese government by Kim Yunsik and Yi Yongjik, as well as the petition recited at Posin'gak in Chongno on March 13th by Kim Paegwŏn and Mun Ilp'yŏng. The "33 National Representatives" also presented their declaration of independence and simultaneously sent a petition for independence to the Paris Peace Conference, the President of the United States, and both the House of Peers and the House of Representatives of the Japanese Diet. Like O Kisŏn of the Christian groups, who insisted on the format of a petition, there were those among the "33 National Representatives" such as Ch'oe Sŏngmo who believed they were going to present a petition rather than a declaration.

29 Translator's note: I have used the most commonly known translation of the Korean Declaration of Independence by Han-Kyo Kim in this text, which can be found in *Sources of Korean Tradition*, edited by Yŏng-ho Ch'oe, Peter H. Lee, and Wm. Theodore de Bary, vol. 2 (New York: Columbia University Press, 2000), 337-339.

it was both a "clear command of heaven, the course of our times, and a legitimate manifestation of the right of all nations to coexist and live in harmony"; it was simultaneously the will of the people and humanity's calling. In this sense, after proclaiming its legitimacy, the Korean Declaration of Independence denounced the subsequent history of colonization in which they "suffered the agony of alien suppression for a decade, becoming a victim of the policies of aggression and coercion." Yet this denunciation contains almost no traces of accusation, going on to say "we do not intend to accuse Japan of infidelity" and "we shall not blame Japan." Claiming that "our task today is to build up our own strength, not to destroy others," the Korean Declaration of Independence states that "we must remedy the unnatural and unjust conditions brought about by the leaders of Japan" — that is, the writers of the declaration assert that they merely have the noble desire to free themselves from an incorrect path. In other words, in front of the grand goals of Eastern peace, world peace, and the happiness of humanity, the writers of the declaration had no time to ruminate upon long-standing grudges. They then inserted a few lines in a tone that was close to utter joy: "Behold! A new world is before our eyes. The days of force are gone and the days of morality are here."

Drafted by Ch'oe Namsŏn, the Korean Declaration of Independence is both abstract and grave. The political, economic, and social pledges that can be found in the declarations of independence of other countries during this period are altogether absent in the Korean one. When writing for the magazine *Boys* (*Sonyŏn*), Ch'oe Namsŏn wrote in pure Korean script (*han'gŭl*), but in the Korean Declaration of Independence, he chose to write in mixed Korean and classical Chinese script and adopted a tone characteristic of classical Chinese that was difficult to understand. According to some testimonies, when the declaration was read aloud, the audience had trouble understanding and its mild tone failed to invigorate the crowd.[30] The majority of the "33 National Representatives" presumed that Ch'oe Rin wrote the Korean Declaration of Independence. This may have been because they found it difficult to believe that Ch'oe Namsŏn, who had demonstrated such a strong command of modern

---

30 Cho Tonggŏl, *The Collected Writings of 'Usa' Cho Tonggŏl*, vol. 6 (Seoul: Yŏksa konggan, 2010), 244.

writing in magazines such as *Boys* and *Youth* (*Ch'ŏngch'un*), could have written such turgid sentences in the Korean Declaration of Independence. In contrast, the sentences of "Three Open Pledges" added by Han Yongun are far more forcible and concise:

> Our action today represents the demand of our people for justice, humanity, survival, and dignity. It manifests our spirit of freedom and should not engender anti-foreign feelings.

> To the last one of us and to the last moment possible, we shall unhesitatingly publicize the views of our people, as is our right.

> All our actions should scrupulously uphold public order, and our demands and our attitudes must be honorable and upright.

The colonial authorities found the line "to the last one of us and to the last moment possible" suspicious for its possible implication of a willingness to use forcible measures and made it as grounds for interrogation. The Korean Declaration of Independence, however, clearly warns against "anti-foreign feelings" and says to "uphold public order." In comparison to the vast majority of other declarations of independence during the March First Movement, its tone is far more universalist and pacifist. The Taehan Declaration of Independence sought to "achieve independence even through bloody battles" in cases where "death of individuals is unavoidable." The February Eighth Declaration, after detailing Japan's violations of rights and freedom, also presented a warning about the possibility of an armed struggle by stating that "though we shall pursue freedom through legitimate means, in case this is not possible, we shall bleed to the last one of us with a fervent ardor and passion for freedom."

While the Taehan Declaration was signed by 39 independence activists and the February Eighth Declaration was signed by 11 representatives of the Korean Youth Independence Corps (*Chosŏn ch'ŏngnyŏn tongniptan*), the signatories of the Korean Declaration of Independence notably decided to call themselves the "National Representatives of the Chosŏn People." Despite not going through the process of officially electing general representatives, the 33 signatories designated themselves as the universal "representatives of the people" and thereby maximized the ability of the declaration to resonate with the public. Furthermore, by choosing to call themselves the "National Representatives of the Chosŏn People," they elided memories of the Korean Empire as the near past. Instead, they chose to mark the date as "Year 4252 of Chosŏn's Founding Dynasty," referring to the era in which Tan'gun established Kojosŏn. By choosing Tan'gun's Dynasty as the reign name to mark the date, the Korean Declaration of Independence invoked a history of the people (*minjok*) that spanned thousands of years and appealed to a long-standing sense of unity. The February Eighth Declaration of Independence did not include a date but the Taehan Declaration also used "Year 4252 since Tan'gun's Dynasty," thus expressing a similar consciousness. All of the declarations nonetheless remained silent on the directions and paths toward concrete political, economic, and social reforms.

6. Spreading, Transforming, and Proliferating Declarations

The Declaration of Independence carried news of independence to far-off regions from the sites of protests. The declaration provided guidance to the confused residents of the provinces, who were unsure even as to whether they were to shout "Long live the Great Korea" or "Long live Chosŏn"[31] even if they were to participate in *manse* demonstrations.[32] Transmitted orally, the Korean Declaration of Independence would have been unable to leave the site of its signing, let alone arrive at other regions,[33] but in its written form,

---

31 Translator's note: The two phrases referred to here are *"Taehan tongnip manse"* ("Long Live the Great Korea") and *"Chosŏn tongnip manse"* ("Long Live Chosŏn"). *"Taehan"* came from the Taehan Empire, which was proclaimed by Emperor Kojong in 1897, whereas Chosŏn was both the name of a Korean dynasty while also more broadly referring to the Korean people.

32 Yi Yongnak, *A Historical Record of the March First Movement* (Seoul: 3·1 tongjihoe, 1969), 945.

33 "We went to T'apkol Park ⋯⋯ someone was reciting the Declaration of Independence, but we couldn't really hear what they were saying from where we were." "The Interrogation Record of Pak Noyŏng," in *Sourcebook on the History of the Korean Independence Movement*, vol. 16, ed. National Institute of Korean History (Kwach'on: National Institute of Korean History, 1993), 303.

it could reach each and every corner of the peninsula. A portion of its distribution was organized systematically. Of the 21,000 copies of the Korean Declaration of Independence that were allegedly printed, the majority of them were distributed throughout the peninsula by Christian or Ch'ŏndoist organizations. At two in the afternoon on March First, in six cities that simultaneously hosted ceremonies for reciting the declaration of independence, Christian groups took charge of the declaration's distribution and sent out hundreds and thousands of copies through various messengers. They also sent out copies to Kunsan, Taegu, and Masan. Ch'ŏndoists sent them to Chŏnju, Ch'ŏngju, and the regions of Suan, Koksan, and Sŏhŭng in Hwanghae Province. Han Yongun, a Buddhist, tasked students of the Central Buddhist School (*Pulgyo chungang hangnim*) in Seoul to distribute 3,000 copies. The student groups managed to procure 1,500 copies of the declaration through Kang Kidŏk of Posŏng College, with Kang Kidŏk further giving 300 copies to Yi Kyuyŏng of Sŏllin School of Commerce and 200 to 300 copies to Kim Paekp'yŏng of Seoul Higher Common School (*Kyŏngsŏng kodŭng pot'ong hakkyo*). In this manner, copies of the declaration were distributed among the Seoul city residents by the morning of March First.[34] In this process, Yi Kapsŏng and Pak Hŭido of the Christian groups and Yi Chongil of Ch'ŏndogyo emerged as central figures. In Sŏnch'ŏn of North P'yŏngan Province, under the orders of Pak Hŭido, Yi Kyech'ang, an employee of Pak Tŏgyu's shoe store, distributed 300 copies. In Ch'ŏngju and Chŏnju, following the orders of Yi Chongnin, In Chongik, a worker of Ch'ŏndoist publishing company Posŏngsa, procured 3,000 copies for distribution.[35] 44.9

---

[34] "The Interrogation Record of Kang Kidŏk," in National Institute of Korean History, *Sourebook*, 11: 87; "The Interrogation Record of Yi Kyuyŏng," in *Sourcebook*, 17: 155; "The Interrogation Record of Kim Paekp'yŏng," in *Sourcebook*, 17: 245.

[35] Information on the various routes and quantities of the Korean Declaration of Independence was compiled from National Institute of Korean History, "The Distribution Routes of the Declaration of Independence," in *Sourcebook*, 3: 246 and various court records concerning the March First Movement upon which the former was based. For instance, although the Mugam pimangnok states that Yi Chongil, who had been in charge of printing and distributing the Korean Declaration of Independence, printed a total of 35,000 copies, I chose to instead use 21,000, the recorded figure that aggregated the total number of copies in circulation from court records. In a similar manner, regarding Yi Kyech'ang and In Chongik's role in distribution, Yi Kyech'ang, In Chongik, and Yi Chongil testified in their interrogation records as each possessing 200-300, 2,000, and 2,500 copies respectively, but "Tongnip sŏnŏnsŏ paep'odo" gives this figure as 300 and 3,000. However, rather than court records or "Tongnip sŏnŏnsŏ paep'odo," given the great detail of testimonies in the interrogation records,

centimeters wide and 20.1 centimeters tall, these printed declarations disseminated not only news of the March First Movement, but the movement itself.

In fact, many uprisings across the provinces were catalyzed through the Korean Declaration of Independence. However, those that had printed and distributed the declaration were merely the initial spark and did not aim to become any kind of "central headquarters."[36] There were few cases where intermediate figures only received the declaration from a central branch and distributed them in the March First Movement. Starting with the regions that hosted ceremonies on March 1st, the country as a whole did not entirely rely solely upon the Korean Declaration of Independence. Those in Sŏnch'ŏn and Ŭiju managed to procure and prepare copies of the February Eighth Declaration of Independence instead. Those in Wŏnsan worried that the declaration would arrive too late and ultimately chose to prepare 2,000 copies of the declaration on their own. In Hamhŭng, the activists obtained a copy of the declaration that had been printed in Wŏnsan and stayed up all night to print 3,000 more copies of this version. Activists in Pukch'ŏng also procured one of the Wŏnsan copies with great difficulty and prepared for the protests by transcribing 300 more copies.[37] In this manner, the Korean Declaration of Independence was rapidly proliferated and also modified. There were countless instances in which the declaration was modified, such as only printing a portion of the declaration that was written in Seoul or solely borrowing the names of the "national representatives" to be included in an entirely different document.

Still yet in Wŏnsan, declarations that had been independently written with

in cases where context was required, I prioritized using the figures from the interrogation records. For the previous paragraph on Kang Kidŏk, Yi Kyuyŏng, and Kim Paekp'yŏng, I synthesized the contents of these three people's interrogation records.

36 Apart from the colonial authorities, there were others who continued to suspect that there was a kind of central headquarters for the March First Movement. Yu Sŏgu, a missionary at the Japanese Union Church (*Nippon kumiai kyōkai*) led by Ebina Danjo, was arrested for printing notices and distributing ch'angga songs about independence, testified that he had done so not because he agreed with the March First Movement, but because he wanted to find the "headquarters" of the movement and press them to cease their activities. That is, he thought that "there must be a central headquarters for this independence movement" and that if he "had a mimeographed copy" or that he "wrote a notice and gave it to them," he would earn the confidence of the movement's headquarters.

37 The Compilation Committee, *Collected Sources*, 5: 982, 1014, 1024.

the signatures of the 33 representatives attached were scattered at ceremonies along with copies of the actual Korean Declaration of Independence. In Chinnamp'o of South P'yŏngan Province, only the introduction and the signatures of the representatives instead of the entire declaration were printed and disseminated. Those in Hamyang County of South Kyŏngsang Province chose to reduce and adapt the declaration's contents because "its sentences are too long and we cannot transcribe it onto a single page." Those in Kyŏngsŏng County of South Hamgyŏng Province wrote their own declaration of independence, the Chosŏn Declaration of Independence, under the leadership of Ch'ŏndogyo, but this document strongly displays the characteristics of an imitation written by impersonating the "33 National Representatives." As evidenced by the line, "every religious organization across the country has assembled here today to promulgate the Chosŏn Declaration of Independence on March First, with Emperor Kojong's funeral imminent," the writers of the document borrowed the voice of the "33 National Representatives" and proclaimed their own declaration.[38] Although the Korean Declaration of Independence claimed to be written by the "33 National Representatives," the document in circulation was actually a communal document of the March First Movement that included various regions' and groups' revisions and edits.

7. The Battle of Words, Print, and Voluntary Successors

As a medium published in the midst of the turmoil of the March First Movement, the *Korean Independence News* is a typical example of the processes of proliferation and transformation that publications underwent during this period. As the protests unfolded, the *Korean Independence News* occasionally played a role analogous to that of the Korean Declaration of Independence. Ten thousand copies of the publication were scattered throughout Seoul on the day of March 1st and became a rich linguistic resource equal to the Korean Declaration of Independence. The spectators of the state funeral would stuff

---

38 The Compilation Committee, *Collected Sources*, 5: 813.

copies of the declaration along with the *Korean Independence News* in their belongings and make their way home. In instances where people did not have a copy of the declaration, they recited the *Korean Independence News* in order to foster enlightenment and the protests' efficacy. On the night of March 26th in Tolma Township, Kwangju County of Kyŏnggi Province, as cheers of *manse* erupted in front of the Taewang Township Office, one person rested against the streetlight and recited the *Korean Independence News* out loud to the crowd.[39] This was perhaps why interrogators of trial proceedings frequently asked participants of the movement the question "Have you read the *Korean Independence News*?"

This highly influential newspaper was originally planned by Yi Chongil, the head of Posŏngsa. With the agreement of Yun Iksŏn, the principal of Posŏng College (now Korea University in Seoul), he resolved to release a publication in a format different from the declaration "without any publishers or a printing press." Without informing the national representatives or receiving the consent of Son Pyŏnghŭi, the leader of Ch'ŏndogyo, the newspaper began in a considerably autonomous fashion. Issue One originated from the request to "write down the Declaration of Independence that will be presented at T'aehwagwan," with 10,000 copies printed at Posŏngsa[40] and distributed throughout Seoul on March 1st. These copies were distributed by four hired laborers who were each paid 50 *jŏn*.[41] Yi Chongil was arrested that very day. After Posŏngsa was shut down, Yi Chongnin, Chang Chonggŏn, and Ch'oe Kisŏng continued the newspaper's publication at the offices of the Seoul Publishers Association (*Kyŏngsŏng sŏjŏk chohap*). It appears that Yi Chongil requested Yi Chongnin, as an employee of Posŏngsa, to continue the publication of the *Korean Independence News*. Chang Chonggŏn, then a clerk at the Seoul Publishers Association, and Ch'oe Kisŏng, a student at Kyŏngsŏng College (*Kyŏngsŏng chŏnsu hakkyo*), seem to have become involved

---

39 The Compilation Committee for the History of the Independence Movement, *The History of Independence Movements,* vol. 3 (Seoul: Financial Committee for Persons of Distinguished Service to Independence, 1971), 298.

40 Yun Iksŏn testified that it was 10,000 copies, while Yi Chongnin claimed it was 5,000.

41 "The Interrogation Record of Yun Iksŏn," in National Institute of Korean History, *Sourcebook,* 13: 4.

in the newspaper's publication through Yi Chongnin. They procured paper for publishing the newspaper from the Seoul Publishers Association and borrowed a mimeograph machine from "somewhere." While Yi Chongnin had written the newspaper's articles up until Issue Four, after his arrest, Chang Chonggŏn "thought that we should continue publishing the *Korean Independence News* on our own" and thus drew upon the aid of several students such as Ch'oe Kisŏng to successfully publish additional issues through Issue Nine.[42] With Posŏngsa shut down after March First and the impossibility of obtaining a mechanical printer, the staff used a mimeograph machine to print anywhere from between 400 to 2,000 copies of each issue.

Even after Chang Chonggŏn was arrested, the *Korean Independence News* continued to be published by a group of anonymous individuals who voluntarily chose to carry on the struggle for independence. While Issues 10 to 15 do not list the publishing staff, Paichai Higher Common School (*Paejae kobo*) student Chang Yongha and his classmates, who were residing in the same boarding house, printed and distributed 300 copies of Issue 16,[43] and Kim Yuin and Chang Ch'aegŭk took charge of publishing Issues 17 to 27. Kim Yuin and Chang Ch'aegŭk were also participants in the National Congress (*kungmin taehoe*) to establish the Hansŏng Provisional Government held on April 23, and they received the aid of the Tongyang Freight Company (*Tongyang yongdal hoesa*) to secure the paper they needed.[44]

From its very inception, the *Korean Independence News*, throughout its entire publication process, garnered much of its strength from the general public's initiative and self-determination. Though there were other newspapers that were continuously published, such as the *National News* (*Kungmin sinbo*),[45] it was the *Korean Independence News* that came to symbolize the March First

---

42 "Statement on the Decision of the Preliminary Trial," in National Institute of Korean History, *Sourcebook*, 16: 141-142.

43 National Institute of Korean History, *Collected Sources on the History of the Independence Movement*, 5: 229.

44 Ch'a Yŏngho claimed they received 16,000 sheets of paper. See National Institute of Korean History, *Collected Sources on the History of the Independence Movement*, 5: 81.

45 *The National News* (*Kungmin sinbo*) was published in Seoul, for a total of 26 issues, through figures such as Yi Ilsŏn. See National Institute of Korean History, *Collected Sources on the History of the Independence Movement*, 5: 254-255.

Movement and eventually led to the Provisional Government's official media, the *Independent*. The *Korean Independence News* did not stop at printing 10,000 copies of its inaugural issue and through a kind of "voluntary relay," it was able to continue being published for several months afterwards and thus came to symbolize the kinetic nature of the movement's proliferation and transformation.[46] It was precisely this vigor that made the heartbeat of the March First Movement.

In addition to the *Korean Independence News,* numerous newspapers, pamphlets, and announcements were published by determined individuals amid the chaos of the March First Movement without any prior planning or coordination. Yi Hŭisŭng, who stated that he personally published numerous small-scale newspapers over the course of several months, wrote that "in Seoul at the time, there were dozens of groups who produced similar newspapers." According to him, after the establishment of the Provisional Government in Shanghai, the *Independent*, which was published by the Provisional Government, became their primary source of information. They would also reference various other underground newspapers and pamphlets to prepare the contents of their own newspapers.[47] For instance, the *Newsletter of the Association for Awakening* (*Kaksŏnghoe hoebo*) was produced and published by Yang Chaesun, a sophomore at Seoul Technical College (*Kyŏngsŏng kongŏp chŏnmun hakkyo*), along with his fellow classmate Kim Chunho. The newspaper first originated after two rounds of protests in Seoul, when these two students picked up and read a notice they found in the streets and thought, "What if we also printed and distributed something like this?" With the inaugural issue published on March 8, they continued to publish and distribute the *Newsletter* through Issue Four. Yang and Kim printed between 40 to 140 or 150 copies of each issue using a mimeograph and distributed them to nearby residences. Referencing copies

---

46 For more information on the origins and circulation routes of the *Korean Independence News*, along with other underground newspapers, such as the *Newsletter of the Association for Awakening* (*Kaksŏnghoe hoebo*), the *Wooden Bell of the Peninsula* (*Pando ŭi mokt'ak*), the *Liberation* (*Chayu minbo*), and the *National News*, see Pak Ch'ansŭng, *The Activities of the Press* (Ch'ŏnan: History of the Korean Independence Movement Research Center, The Independence Hall of Korea, 2009), 49-75.

47 Yi Hŭisŭng, "The March First Movement That I Experienced," in *Collected Essays to Commemorate the 50th Anniversary of the March First Movement* (Seoul: Dong-a Ilbo, 1969), 405.

of the *Korean Independence News* and the *New People* (*Sinminbo*), along with a copy of the Korean Declaration of Independence procured from their neighbors, these two students "took the contents of whatever they could find to make a single document and turn it into a printable manuscript."[48]

In the case of Yang Chaesun and Kim Chunho, their publishing activities comprised the near entirety of their involvement in the March First Movement. Although Yang Chaesun participated in the protest on March 1st, he claimed he did not receive any prior notification for the one on March 5 at Namdaemun Station and ended up missing it. For these two, the very act of reading and editing documents to create and publish manuscripts that were distributed among their vicinity constructed their own March First Movement. A slightly more wide-reaching case in which writing and text were used for publicity is the Comets (*Hyesŏngdan*), a secret society which was active in the region of Kimch'ŏn County, North Kyŏngsang Province. With Kim Sugil, a nineteen-year-old student at Kyesŏng School, and Yi Chongsik, a twenty-five-year-old agricultural worker, as its key figures, this group prepared a diverse array of documents throughout April 1919. They published "An Expression of Sympathy" until Issue Three, and printed documents such as "Notice to Suspend Business," "Respectful Notification to Our Countrymen" and "Notification to Our Beloved Countrymen" which targeted merchants. They also wrote "Caution to Government and Public Officials" and mailed warning letters to the Japanese police chief constable and the pro-Japanese Korean leaders who organized "Self-Control Society" (*Chajehoe*).

Stating that "western reporters will come to Taegu and inspect the area," the Comets members demanded the closure of all businesses in order to express Koreans' desire for independence, and warned the public not to conduct business with Japanese merchants or believe the announcements and instructions by the Japanese Government-General or the police. Judging World War I as a sacrifice made for "freedom," they also made inflammatory remarks such as "even if there is pressure from Japan, fight with all your strength and do

---

48 National Institute of Korean History, "The Interrogation Record of Kim Chunho" (Part One) and "The Interrogation Record of Yang Chaesun" (Part 3), in National Institute of Korean History, *Sourcebook,* 13: 129-131.

not surrender." The Comets seemed to comprise mere participants in the protests on March 8 in Taegu.[49] They had the plan of "stationing headquarters in Taegu and dispatching comrades to Seoul and Manchuria" but, in reality, there was no actual instance of the group acting as leaders of the protests or dispatching members to these regions. Although they conceived resistance strategies such as boycotting Japanese products and spurring Korean merchants' closing shops and Korean public officials' resignation, the group never explored a practical course of action.[50] According to Kim Sugil's interrogation records, the Comets used "a mimeograph obtained from a nearby financial association" and "the majority were printed and published as mimeograph copies, and the rest were all transcribed by hand with all of us dividing up the labor." For those sent by mail, they wrote down "the name of the sender randomly."

8. The Power of Language, The Technology of a Movement

There were also instances in which "linguistic practice as independence activism" were manifested by individuals without any partners. One such example was Kwŏn Ojin, a twenty-one-year-old farmer residing in Yŏnch'o Township, T'ongyŏng County of South Kyŏngsang Province. On March 25, he wrote "Warning from the Independence League of Korean Citizens" and using stencil paper and pen, transcribed fifty copies and scattered them throughout the city two days later. He later added an additional document that stated, "Submit your written consent for Korea's independence to the former Taehan government by the end of April this year. If you do not, we will eradicate all the people in your country," and mailed this to Hara Takashi, the Japanese Prime Minister, and Hasegawa Yoshimichi, the Japanese Governor-General of Korea. In late April, he wrote warnings to the governor of each province telling them to resign, printed 150 copies, and then mailed them to figures such as the governor of Ch'angsŏng County. Interestingly enough, he recorded all of his activities

---

49 Kim Sugil's name can be found in a list of suspects related to the March Eighth protest in Taegu. See The Compilation Committee, *Collected Sources*, 5: 1267.

50 The Compilation Committee, *Collected Sources*, 5: 1447-1449.

in great detail in his diary.[51] For inciting rebellion through letters and language all alone, without any human connections, he was sentenced by the colonial authorities' courts to two years in prison.[52]

In Anju Township, Anju County of North P'yŏngan Province, we can find similar behavior in the case of twenty-year-old Cho Sŏngnyong. However, he was far more vigorous in his activities as his "mind had been filled with thoughts of independence and heated with passion for autonomy" after the annexation of Korean. Thus, he copied the declaration of the "33 Representatives of the Seoul Citizens' Association (*Kyŏngsŏng minhoe*)" and also printed the *Freedom News* (*Chayu sinbo*) and "Notification Regarding Our Twenty Million Countrymen." It is unclear as to whether these documents were original creations, or simply copied and reprinted from elsewhere. Yet unlike Kwŏn Ojin, Cho Sŏngnyong endeavored to expand his linguistic actions into a substantive protest. Though he was alone in obtaining and printing various documents, he later made the T'aegŭkki and Chosŏn Independence Flags and with the help of two villagers, advanced all the way into a massive marketplace, where 3,000 people had gathered. It was here that Cho Sŏngnyong gave a speech on Korean independence and distributed the materials he had printed from his mimeograph. For his activities, the courts sentenced him to two years and six months in prison.[53]

The masses of the March First Movement displayed an active molecularity by playing a role in revising and shaping the movement itself. For instance, if it were not for the notices created by several students, the student-led protest on March 5 would be likely to wither away entirely or at least greatly reduced in size. Even until the afternoon of the day right before, "neither the time nor the location had been decided" except for the actual date of the protest. Regardless of whether this was because of a lack in preparation or a mistake

---

51 The Compilation Committee, *Collected Sources*, 5: 1242.

52 Those who participated in reporting activities during the 1980 Kwangju Uprising, such as those who published the *Newsletter for Fighters' Association* (*T'usa hoebo*) or conducted broadcasts in the city, received relatively lighter sentences. This demonstrates the military dictatorship's stance at the time, which believed in the "impotence of language." See Ch'oe Chŏngun, *The Sociology of May* (P'aju: Maybooks, 2012), 45. Further research needs to be conducted on how the colonial legal authorities appraised activism conducted through language during the March First Movement.

53 The Compilation Committee, *Collected Sources*, 5: 829-830.

in communication, there were numerous rumors circulating, saying the protest would be "in front of Namdaemun, Taehanmun, or Ŭijut'ong, at 8:30 in the morning, noon, or sometime in the afternoon." Ch'ae Sunbyŏng, Kim Chonghyŏn, and Ch'ae Kangyun, students of Seoul Higher Common School who were residing in the same boarding house, stated that "because nothing would have come to fruition in this way, we decided to pick the time and location and notify everyone instead." In other words, they chose to become leaders and planners of the movement all on their own. Without any further questions or confirmations, they decided on the time and place of the protest as 8:30 a.m. in front of Namdaemun Station. They managed to procure a mimeograph machine from somewhere and printed 400 notifications, distributing them late at night to nearby areas where student boarding houses were highly concentrated.[54]

In this manner, language during the March First Movement functioned in a perlocutionary manner. "Manifesto" (sŏnŏn) was a means to draw a future to the present and also to express one's own determination to cultivate that desired future. The "33 National Representatives" agonized over deciding between a petition and a manifesto but the general masses of the March First Movement maximized the radicalness of manifesto as a "linguistic pracitce." Through people like the eighteen-year-old Ch'ae Mansik, who concisely summarized the Korean Declaration of Independence in a single sentence with "Korea is now independent," and the old villager who readily accepted his words and cried, "Then I, too, will also celebrate Korea's independence," the proclamation of the Korean Declaration of Independence incubated a reality in which independence was manifested. Indeed, the very belief that the Declaration of Independence would soon conjure the reality of independence was the secret to the March First Movement. By transforming a "desired reality" to already-advented one, by expressing, conveying, and spreading this kind of categorical imperative, the masses of the March First Movement came to comprise a part of this new reality. They earnestly accepted the Korean Declaration of Independence, in which even the "33 National Representatives" may not

---

54 "The Interrogation Record of Ch'ae Sunbyŏng," in National Institute of Korean History, *Sourcebook*, 14: 226.

have totally believed,[55] and by trusting the power of language, created a mass uprising in the spring of 1919. It was a rare moment in which the light of language seeped out underneath its eclipse.

Trans. by Rachel Min Park

---

55 This article has generally focused on the linguistic and textual performativity of declarations/manifestos and propaganda materials. For a study that focuses on oral and spoken language, see Ch'ŏn Chŏnghwan, "Rumors, Gossip, Newspapers, and Appeals: The Media at the Time of the March First Movement and the People's National Subjecthood," in *Inquiries on March First, 1919*, ed. Pak Hŏnho and Ryu Chunp'il (Seoul: Sungkyunkwan University Press, 2009)

The March First Movement and Decolonization

Hong Jong-wook

1. World War I and Decolonization

If the 19th century was the era of empires, the 20th century was that of decolonization. In 1960, the UN adopted the "Declaration on the Granting of Independence to Colonial Countries and Peoples" as Resolution 1514 (XV) of its General Assembly. This resolution stipulated that complete independence and freedom had to be granted to peoples of all Trust and Non-Self Governing Territories and territories that had yet to attain independence, in respect to the peoples' rights to self-determination and in accordance with their freely expressed will. The UN called this resolution the "Declaration on Decolonization."[1] In 1961, the UN established a special committee to implement Resolution 1514 (XV) in accordance with General Assembly Resolution 1654 (XVI), which reiterated the objectives that had formerly been noted in the "Declaration on Decolonization." The committee, formally known as "the United Nations Special Committee on the Situation with Regard to the Implementation of the Declaration on the Granting of Independence to Colonial Countries and Peoples," or simply "the Special Committee on Decolonization," continues

---

1 "United Nations and Decolonization," United Nations, accessed February 23, 2021, https://www.un.org/dppa/decolonization/en/about.

to monitor decolonization processes to this day and provides advice about methods through which the Declaration should be implemented.[2]

The UN only had 51 member states when it was initially formed in October 1945, and its size was similar to that of the League of Nations that had been assembled after World War I. Many regions in the world were still bereft of their sovereignty, but as attested by the opening of the first Asia-African Conference (Bandung Conference) of 1955, the spirit of decolonization was soaring high. As a case in point, in 1960, 17 nations declared their independence in Africa alone. The UN's declaration on decolonization was an apt reflection of such circumstances. The term "decolonization" appeared for the first time in the Oxford English Dictionary's 1972 supplementary edition. Its definition was "the action or process of a state withdrawing from a former colony, leaving it independent." Although there are very few colonies in the "classical" sense of the word in today's world, this decolonization process still continues today.

Despite the political emancipation of former colonies, colonial legacies, as well as colonialism itself, still persist. This reality is the problem and topic of postcolonialism. Recent postcolonial criticism has some commonalities with neocolonial criticism, which exposes the economic exploitation and subordination of the "new" world order. However, the central focus of post-colonialism is on the psychological and cultural influences of colonialism. As a result, the term "decolonization" has increasingly come to be understood as a liberation from spiritual and cultural colonialism. Such a trend is quite evident in academia. In *Post-Colonial Studies: The Key Concepts*, Bill Ashcroft, Gareth Griffins, and Helen Tiffin define decolonization as "the process of revealing and dismantling colonialist power in all its forms," and further explain that "this includes dismantling the hidden aspects of those institutional and cultural forces that had maintained the colonialist power and that remain even after political independence is achieved."[3]

This paper regards the world history of the interwar period as a process

2   See UN official website for more information: "Decolonization," United Nations, accessed October 31, 2018, http://www.un.org/en/decolonization/ga_resolutions.html.

3   Bill Ashcroft, Gareth Griffiths, and Helen Tiffin, *Post-Colonial Studies: The Key Concepts* (New York: Routledge, 2000), 63.

of decolonization. To this end, I will pay attention to two important points. Firstly, it is imperative that we do not overlook the significance of the abolition of political and/or institutional colonialism. As analyses of the postcolonial situation wherein colonial institutions no longer exist became paramount, the meaning of decolonization has changed to emphasize the overcoming of spiritual or cultural colonialism. Thus, using the concept of decolonization to explain the political and institutional processes through which colonial empires disintegrated can cause some confusion. Nonetheless, there is no doubt that the most critical aspect of decolonization was obtaining political independence.

Secondly, it must be noted that the dissolution and transformation of colonial empires was a process in which various forces were engaged in conflict and compromise. In this respect, it is noteworthy that the United Nations declared in 1960 that independence, self-governance, and assimilation could lead the way to decolonization. In other words, self-governance and assimilation, if they are grounded on self-determination of the colonized, could indeed be regarded as decolonization, that is, the abolition of colonial systems.

Through the concept of decolonization defined as such, this paper will attempt to illustrate the convoluted turns and twists of decolonization processes of colonial Korea during the interwar period. After World War I, both the colonizers and the colonized found difficult to avoid the epochal tide that led to the dissolution and/or transformation of colonial empires. The term decolonization in this paper refers to the epochal tide characterized by both conflict and compromise between colonizer and colonized for the abolition of colonial rule, which was reaching its limit.

Eric Hobsbawm designated the latter periods of the "long 19th century" (1875–1914) the "era of the Empire." At this tail end of the 19th century, Europe, which had a long history of Asian and African expansion spanning from the Age of Exploration, altered its expansionist policy and reinforced its territorial dominance through the establishment of political and institutional colonialism.[4] Ironically, the seeds of decolonization movements were sown in these colonial projects. In various colonies, developmental policies were

---

4 See Eric Hobsbawm, *The Age of Empire: 1875-1914* (New York: Pantheon Books, 1987), 56-57.

implemented to render processes of domination and exploitation efficient, and the development of modern industry and education led to the awakening of national consciousness of the colonized. The First World War became an all-out total war that called for the sweat and blood of not only workers and farmers but also colonized subjects. As such this war was a catalyst that led to the awakening of colonial peoples' national consciousness that erupted in the form of nationalist movements. In June 1918 when World War I was at its height, Mahatma Gandhi, who later led India's independence movement, recalled that Indian soldiers who had been recruited by the English "would go to fight for the Empire; but they would so fight because they aspire to become partners in it."[5]

Imperial powers could not ignore such decolonial currents, either. In 1917, right after the Russian Revolution, Vladimir Lenin published "The Decree on Peace," which called for an immediate truce and the establishment of peace built on the principle of self-determination unadulterated by annexations or indemnities. As is well known, British Prime Minister David Lloyd George and U.S. President Woodrow Wilson made consecutive declarations and announced the principle of national self-determination in 1918. The League of Nations, the covenant of which was submitted at the 1919 Paris Peace Conference and which was officially founded in 1920, introduced the Mandate System. Although it was a nominal measure of peace designed to redistribute the colonies of defeated Central Powers, the Mandate System did occasion the making of logical grounds on which the acquisition of new colonies could be denied.

From spring to the early summer of 1919, the time during which the Paris Peace Conference was held, nationalist movements occurred all across the globe. In March, the world saw the eruption of the March First Movement in Korea, as well as large-scale protests and unified student strikes in Cairo, Egypt. In April, a non-violent resistance movement led by Gandhi was launched in India. The May Fourth Movement, which called for the restoration of China's

---

5   Mahatma Gandhi, "Speech at Public, Bombai (June 16, 1918)," in *The Collected Works of Mahatma Gandhi,* vol. 17, 70. https://www.gandhiashramsevagram.org/gandhi-literature/mahatma-gandhi-collected-works-volume-17.pdf.

sovereignty also took place in these tumultuous times. In response to such movements, Britain and the United States emphasized that the principle of national self-determination could only be applied to colonies that had belonged to defeated Central Powers during World War I and was inapplicable to colonies of other countries.[6] Although the British and Americans stressed this latter "fact," the inherent contradictions of colonial logic had already been exposed and many colonies sought to liberate themselves from colonial rule. Yanagita Kunio, a Japanese ethnologist and member of the Permanent Mandates Commission, noted in his "The Development of the League of Nations" (1922) that "[imperial states] can no longer make explicit their intent to annex colonial territories for their interest; from now on, they must maintain, at least on the surface, the guise that their government is for the stability and happiness of the governed."[7]

Decolonization was thus gradually becoming a reality. As a result of the Irish War of Independence, Ireland became the Irish Free State, a self-governing nation among the Dominion of the British Commonwealth of Nations, in 1922. Earlier in December 1919, the Government of India Act was passed. This Act was designed to replace the extremely centralized colonial power with dispersed powers of state governments granted of considerable self-governing rights and responsibility, which resulted in an increase in Indian participation in politics. In 1922, Egypt declared its independence from Britain's protectorate. The Nine-Power Pact, which was signed at the Washington Naval Conference in 1921-1922, affirmed China's sovereignty and independence, and stipulated that the territorial control of Shantung Province had to be returned to China. The Philippines, which had been colonized by the United States, was granted the right to self-governance in 1916; and in 1934, it was agreed upon that the Philippines would become entirely independent in 10 years. Korea was a colony of Japan, which was one of the defeated country of World War II, and became decolonized in 1945. Colonies of victorious

---

6   Nagata Akifumi, *Japan's Rule Over Korea and International Relations: The Korean Independence Movement and the United States, 1910-1922* (Tokyo: Heibonsha, 2005), 78-94.

7   Yanagita Kunio, "The Development of the League of Nations," *The League of Nations* 2, no. 3 (1922): 18-23.

imperial states such as Britain or France eventually became decolonized after the 1960s. However, one can argue that the decolonization processes of all the colonized nations began right after the First World War. From where we stand now, it seems quite obvious that the 1920s and 1930s were eras of colonial rule. However, those living in those times, be they the colonizer or the colonized, were well aware of the unsustainability of 19th-century-style colonial rule, and were seeking alternatives. "Decolonization" in this article refers to the comprehensive procedures of seeking alternatives of colonial rule.

2. The March First Movement and "Cultural Rule"

Korea's colonization and decolonization should be examined in the context of the world history. Japan, which had won the Firts Sino-Japanese War and the Russo-Japanese War, signed the Korea-Japan Treaty of 1905, subjugating Korea (then Korean Empire) under military occupation. After having experimented with the form of a "protectorate" wherein the Korean government and the Japanese Residency-General of Korea co-existed, Japan annexed Korea in 1910, thus subsuming the Korean Empire under colonial territory of the "Great Japanese Empire." The term "*ilchegangjŏmgi*," which can roughly be translated into "the period of forced occupation of Korea by the Japanese Empire," is used to emphasize the coerced, and thus invalid, nature of the Annexation Treaty. This phrase has embedded within it the assessment that Japan's rule over Korea was more violent than conventional colonial rule as practiced by other imperial powers. However, Japan's colonization of Korea should also be interpreted within the context of imperialism and colonial systems of rule that ran through world history. Technically speaking, Korea was a colony forcibly occupied by Japan.

There was, however, a uniqueness to Japan's colonization of Korea. The Japanese used the colonial discourse of "*ilsŏndongjoron*," which suggested that the Japanese and Koreans shared the same ancestral roots, and stressed their racial and cultural similarities. Based on the logic, Japan argued that Japanese rule over Korea differed greatly from Western powers' colonization of non-Western peoples. In this context, it can be said that Korea-Japan relation is more comparable to that between England and Ireland rather than British-Indian or British-African relations. Another peculiarity we must consider is that Korea became a colony a few years before World War I broke out. By the end of World War I imperial powers' outspoken expansionism and acquisition of new colonies were hindered by the establishment of the League of Nations and the introduction of the Mandate System.

In this context, it can be said that Korea, which had been struggling against the global trend of colonialism since the mid-19th century, was dragged into colonialism's last strong tide in 1910 right before the currents began to turn dramatically after World War I. It is also noteworthy that the nation-building process, which usually follows the process of colonization in other regions, started in Korea prior to its annexation by Japan.

Japan, one of the victors of World War I, acquired the former German colony of Polynesia as its mandated territory. When the Hara Takashi cabinet was established as Japan's first post-war and party-based cabinet in 1918, it also had to deliberate on how to change Japan's methods of colonial rule. Hara advocated a new ruling model called the "mainland extension" principle (*naeji yŏnjang juŭi*), which aimed to extend Japanese mainland laws to its colonies such as Korea. Such a shift in policy seems to have been made in line with the global current toward decolonization. The same current occasioned Korea's March First Movement to develop into fierce protests for independence. Many Koreans' hope for independence, mingled with their condolences to the former emperor Kojong's death in January 1919, soared high around the time of the Paris Peace Conference, which emphasized national rights to self-determination. As Dane Kennedy notes in his introductory book on decolonization, "a million Koreans marched in the streets against their Japanese overlords."[8] As is quite well known, a resolution for Irish Independence was passed in the United States Congress in 1920. Much Lesser known, however, is the fact that the U.S. Congress introduced a resolution for Korea's independence that very same year. Although the resolution was voted down, with 34 yays, 46 nays, and 16 abstentions, it is worth noting that the votes supporting Korea's

---

8 Dane Kennedy, *Decolonization: A Very Short Introduction* (Oxford: Oxford University Press, 2016), 19.

independence were rather considerable in number.[9]

Startled by the March First Movement, Japan started to look critically at the military rule with which it had been controlling Korea since its annexation, and instead took to employing what was called "cultural rule." Reforms followed, such as the abolition of the law that required the Japanese Governor-General of Korea to be a military officer, the replacement of the military police system with a general police system, and the establishment of local councils. One may point out that this new policy of "cultural rule" was rather deceptive, but it undeniably changed the ways in which the Government-General reigned over Korea. In a partially open political space, Imperial Japan's government, the Japanese Government-General of Korea, Japanese residents in Korea, and various Korean entities contested the ways in which Korea had to be decolonized. "Public Sentiments" reported by the Government-General Superintendent's Office in October 1919 noted "public sentiments in Keijō (now Seoul; Kyŏngsŏng in Korean) are being formed around the middle class, who are organizing numerous groups and engaging in various actions in order to achieve their objectives." The document also distinguished these organizations into three groups: "the self-governance group," "the assimilationist group," and "the independence group."[10]

Interestingly, we can find similar groupings in the UN's efforts to ensure "complete autonomy" stipulated in "Declaration regarding Non-Self Governing Territories," the Chapter 11 of the UN Charter. Resolution 1541 XV of the UN General Assembly in 1960 stated that there are three ways for non-self-governing territories to accomplish "complete autonomy": "establishment of an independent sovereign state," "free association with an independent state," and "integration with an independent state."[11] To put them differently, non-self-governing peoples' decolonization can be accomplished through independence, self-governance, or assimilation. Keeping this similarity in mind,

---

9   Nagata, *Japan's Rule Over Korea and International Relations*, 214-220.

10 "Keijō Minjō Ihō (Kōkei 26490, 1919.10.18)," in *Materials on Modern History*, ed. Kang Tŏksang (Tokyo: Misuzu Shobō, 1966), 25: 522-523.

11 See the subsection "The United Nations and Decolonization," United Nations, accessed October 31, 2018, http://www.un.org/en/decolonization/ga_resolutions.shtml.

we must ask the following question: how were the three methods of decolonization unfolded during the Japanese "cultural rule" of Korea?

First, let us discuss assimilation. In August 1919, amidst of the aftershock of the March First Movement, Hara confirmed his mainland extensionism by conveying a document entitled "Thoughts on Ruling Korea" to Saitō Makoto and Mizuno Rentarō, who were appointed next Governor-General of Korea and Inspector General of the Political Affairs respectively. When Saitō took office in September, he gave an address saying that the ultimate goal of Japan's rule of Korea would be to "treat equally Japanese and Koreans, politically and socially, in accordance with the future development of Korean culture and Korean people."[12]

In November 1919, the Hyŏpsŏng Club, chaired by Min Wŏnsik, held a public lecture on current affairs for the first time after the Japanese annexation of Korea. In this lecture, he advocated the notion of "New Japanism," marking the beginning of so-called the "era of politics." Min Wŏnsik, the former head of Koyang County, began to argue for Koreans' right to be politically represented after he witnessed the March First Movement. The Japanese emperor's proclamation of "universal benevolence" (*ilsidongin*) and the inception of the cultural rule also encouraged him. Based on the mainland extension policy, he set the goal of obtaining Koreans' political rights equal to the Japanese. Min Wŏnsik thus founded the National Society (*Kungmin hyŏphoe*) in January 1920 and submitted a petition for the "implementation of parliamentary elections in Korea" to the Japanese Imperial Assembly in February of the same year. In this petition, Min argued that the changing tide of thoughts in postwar Japan had led "the voices of social reform to be heard everywhere." "People's political demands became increasingly high" and, he asserted, "voices pressing for general elections are resounding from every direction." The National Society filed a petition for suffrage to the Japanese Imperial Assembly every year. In the years between 1923 and 1924, when calls for a general election were especially high, 10,000 people signed the petition. Governor-General Saitō was sympathetic to the idea of granting suffrage to the Koreans. Moreover, some

12 Kang Tongjin, *Japan's Policy for Korean Invasion* (Seoul: Hangilsa, 1980), 386.

of Japanese Interior Ministry officials led by Mizuno, aforementioned Inspector General of the Political Affairs, supported the petition campaign for Korean suffrage.[13]

There were, however, also others who were more focused on rights to self-governance. *Dong-a Ilbo*, a daily newspaper founded in April 1920, showed much interest in this matter. Immediately after its foundation, the paper featured an article about Professor Suehiro Shigeo, a law professor at Kyoto Imperial University and his theories about Korean autonomy. *Dong-a Ilbo* also published articles about the "Ireland Question," focusing on the British colony's right to govern itself. Abe Mitsuie, who served as president of the *Seoul Daily* (*Kyŏngsŏng ilbo*) in the 1910s, mediated Governor-General Saitō and influential Korean figures to promote Korean self-governance. Abe criticized Mizuno and other Japanese officials of the Government-General for their supporting the suffrage movements based on assimilation policy and mainland extensionism. He instead insisted on establishing a Korean national assembly in order to achieve Korean self-governance. Abe believed that there had been a generational power shift in colonial Korea after World War I due to a heightened spirit of reform and reconstruction. He therefore thought he could convince the "new intellectuals" such as Ch'oe Namsŏn, Yi Kwangsu, and Chin Hangmun, to join forces in governing Korea. Yi Kwangsu, who had been an active member of the Provisional Government of Korea in Shanghai, returned home in 1921 and published a series of articles in *Dong-a Ilbo,* where he expressed his support for Korea's self-governance.[14]

In July 1924, Shimooka Chūji, who was amenable to the idea of a Korean national assembly, was appointed Inspector General of the Political Affairs.[15] Dropping comments about the possible establishment of a "colonial council," Shimooka tested the waters and weighed the responses. In August of the same year, Soejima Michimasa, a member of the Japanese House of Lords and a

---

13 For details on the petition movement, see Matsuda Toshihiko, *The Problem of Political Rights and Koreans in Korea under Japanese Rule,* trans. Kim Indŏk (Seoul: Kukhak Charyowŏn, 2004).

14 For details on Abe Mitsuie's activities in the early 1920s, see Yi Hyŏngsik, "A Broker of Empire, Abe Mitsuie and Cultural Rule," *Critical Studies on Modern Korean History* 37 (2017): 433-480.

15 Yi Hyŏngsik, "Abe Mitsuie's Political Career in Korea in the Mid and Late 1920s," *Korean Cultural Studies* 78 (2018): 155-194.

proponent of Korean self-governance, became the president of the *Seoul Daily*. After consulting with the Governor-General and the executives of *Dong-a Ilbo*, Soejima published an article advocating Korean self-governance in his news-paper.[16] This article was published against the background of the promulgation of the general election law in mainland Japan, the need to ameliorate U.S.-Japan relations, and a growing intent to transform Korean nationalist movements into self-governance movements.[17]

Around the same time, the Governor-General made attempts to shift ruling policy from mainland extensionism to Korean self-governance. Influential Korean figures such as Song Chinu and Ch'oe Rin responded positively to this change. In 1925, Song published an article advocating self-governance in *Dong-a Ilbo*. Like his contemporaries Song accepted decolonization as inevitable, noting that "even though Korea became a victim in the global tide of invasive imperialism which culminated from the 19th century to the beginning of the 20th century," "the world-shaking war has wrecked invasive imperialism."[18] In 1926, Song and Ch'oe tried to form the Association for the Research of Governance (*Yŏnjŏnghoe*), a political coalition pushing for Korea's self-governance, which aroused harsh criticism from colonial Koreans and failed. In the late 1920s, another attempt was made to introduce Korean self-governance with Governor-General Saitō at the helm. While compromising with mainland Japan's politicians, however, such attempts for self-governance only resulted in upgrading local advisory bodies into legislative organs.

Meanwhile, Korean independence movements also persisted. The March First Movement itself was a large-scale independence movement. At that time, the national representatives sent a document to the Japanese Governor-General, which expressed their expectation that the victory of the Allied Forces would bring about an era of "radical reconstruction on a global scale that history has never seen before." The document also warned that if Japan insisted on

---

16 Soejima Michimasa, "The Fundamentals of Korean Rule," in *Anthology of Articles on the Issue of Governing Korea*, vol. 1, ed. Imoto Kijirō (Seoul: Chikasawa Insatsu, 1929), 98-103.

17 Cho Sŏnggu, *Korea's Nationalist Movements and Soejima Michimasa* (Tokyo: Kenbun Shuppan, 1998), 152.

18 Song Chinu, "Major Currents in the World and Korea's Future (5) · (6)," *Dong-a Ilbo*, September 1-2, 1925.

dominating Korea, "peoples of the changing world would hurl harsh criticism on Japan for the outdated imperial rule."[19]Colonial Koreans, who had been deprived of the right to self-determination and channels for politics, expressed this vision through nation-wide, months-long independence protests. Although such protests could not overthrew colonial power of the Japanese Government-General, their desire for independence did lead to the establishment of the Provisional Government of the Republic of Korea in Shanghai. Driven by this fervor for Korean independence, armed activists in northeastern China kept fighting against the Japanese Empire and Koreans in the United States organized independence movements on their own.

Many Koreans on the peninsula regarded Korean independence as the most desirable route to decolonization. The Communist Party of Korea, an illegal underground organization founded in 1925, took a firm pro-independence line, even while undergoing repeated dissolution and reconstruction. In more official legal spaces, various youth coalitions, ideological organizations, and social movement groups were quite active. Even though they could not make open claims for Korean independence, they revealed their unequivocal stance for independence through aggressive criticism on political lines of assimilation and self-governance. In 1927, the socialists and nationalists founded *Sin'ganhoe* (the New Trunk Association) as a unified front against Japanese occupation and made various activities for independence on the verge of legality and illegality.

All three political lines of assimilation, self-governance, and independence shared the thought that World War I had radically and irreversibly changed the world. Recognizing that the old way of imperial rule could not be sustained in the post-war era, they all set the goal of decolonization of Korea. It seems as if the three lines were clearly distinguished from and contested one another but, in reality, things were much more complicated. The assimilationist movement was close to being utterly rejected by the Koreans. According to an analytical report by the Governor-General's Bureau of Police, "there seemed to be some understanding between advocates of independence and self-

19   Kang Tŏksang, ed., *Materials on Modern History*, vol. 26 (Tokyo: Misuzu Shobō, 1967), 51-56.

governance, but the assimilationists were in a predicament, totally shunned by others."[20] This analysis was corroborated by an event in 1921, when Min Wŏnsik, a member of the National Society, was killed by a Korean student in Tokyo. Whereas petition campaigns for suffrage were perceived as campaigns for democracy in the imperial center, they implied different connotations in colonial Korea and were often harshly criticized, which prompts us to rethink the meaning of politics in colonial situations. It should also be noted that the Japanese Government-General's policy of "cultural rule" did not necessarily mean the assimilation of Koreans. Governor-General Saitō, who was known for having created the basis of "cultural rule," stated in his famous address of instruction that Japan would "respect Korea's culture and traditions."[21] This was why Soejima called Saitō's politics "liberal."[22]

Amid the global current toward decolonization and the shock of the March First Movement, the Japanese Government-General adopted a new governance method, which included the "cultural rule," and considered assimilation or self-governance as policies that could be applied to Korea. However, this stance did not mean that the Japanese government and the Government-General unequivocally propped up decolonization. Rather, their distrust of the Koreans caused them to constantly keep in check expansion of the Koreans' rights.[23] In fact, many of the policies that scholars have identified as assimilationist as opposed to self-governance policies were, in many cases, based on older methods of colonial rule before decolonization became an unavoidable current. Both Prime Minister Hara and the Inspector General of the Political Affairs Mizuno promoted the extension of Japanese mainland law to the colonies, but objected to the immediate enfranchisement of the Koreans. Since the mid-1920s, the Japanese Government-General of Korea had considered the application of self-governance policies, but they stopped at expanding local self-government at extremely limited levels. This was due to the belief that

---

20 "Keijō Minjō Ihō," in Kang Tŏksang, *Materials on Modern History*, 25: 523.

21 *Official Gazette of the Government-General in Korea,* no. 2121, September 4, 1919.

22 Soejima Michimasa, "On the Ruling of Korea," in *Jōhōisan*, vol. 12, ed. Chōsen Jōhō Iinkai (Seoul: The Japanese Government General of Korea, 1923).

23 Matsuda, *The Problem of Political Rights and Koreans in Korea under Japanese Rule*, 153.

it was premature to allow the Koreans the right to govern themselves. The speed of the decolonizing reformation was as important as the direction in which it went, because the colonizer's assumption of "prematurity" lay at the heart of colonial discrimination.

If the Japanese Government-General had no intention to decolonize Korea, it might have not negotiated with the Koreans over the methods of assimilation or self-governance, all in the name of "cultural rule." As Kim Tongmyŏng explains, the politics between the Government-General and the Korean leaders can be seen as a form of "bargaining." According to Kim, such "bargaining" was possible due to the Koreans' strong resistance against Japan. More specifically, Saitō's policy of "cultural rule" could be materialized due to the political reality of Korea where strong resistance against the Japanese rule persisted, and the force of Korean collaborators remained weak.[24] This "resistance" meant more than opting for independence in preference to the other routes to decolonization such as self-governance or assimilation because resistance was fundamental to all forms of negotiation with Japan to some extent.

On the other hand, there was an obstinate consciousness that all forms of "bargaining" with the colonial authorities meant nothing other than giving up resistance and surrendering to imperial power. Yi Kwangsu described this resolute stance among Koreans in his 1924 article entitled "National Experience and Knowledge (*Minjokchŏk kyŏngnyun*)." In his writing, Yi identified the cause behind the Koreans' lack of "political life" was not only the Government-General's oppression but also "Korean people's strong rejection of partaking in any kinds of political acts" under the Japanese rule. Colonial Koreans, Yi explained, were reluctant to any political acts with Japan as the counterpart including "petitions for Korean enfranchisement, struggles for self-governance and even lobbying for Korean independence" because such political activities could be construed as their acknowledging Japan's sovereignty over Korea.[25]

---

24 Kim Tongmyŏng, *Rule, Resistance, and Collaboration: Japanese Imperialism and Korean Political Movements in Colonial Korea* (Seoul: Kyŏngin Munhwasa, 2006), 68.

25 Yi Kwangsu, "National Experience and Knowledge (2): Political Society and Movements," *Dong-a Ilbo*, January 3, 1924.

As Yi pointed out, such a strong sense of resistance led Koreans to refuse even to accept the reality of colonization. This refusal consequently led them to reject the notion of Japan being a force with which the Koreans had to negotiate. Colonial Koreans' rejection of colonial reality made a paradoxical parallel with Imperial Japan's refusal to acknowledge Korea as a colony. There were indeed Japanese people who promoted the idea of "common ancestry of Japanese and Korean" and thus refused to follow the epochal tide toward decolonization. Strongly aware of these extreme perspectives, advocates for assimilation, self-governance, and independence came to be intertwined in complicated ways, forming a political space in the era of decolonization. *Sin'ganhoe*, whose activities often pushed the boundaries of legal political space during the period of "cultural rule," is an apt example. In the November 1926 declaration of *Chŏnguhoe* (Righteous Friends Association) that occasioned the founding of *Sin'ganhoe*, it was noted that "we should not regard compromise and resistance struggles as entirely exclusive routes, and we should not think of reform and *** [although the word was redacted in the source text, a contextual reading of the declaration makes it possible to conjecture that this missing word was "revolution."] as incompatible."[26] Sin'ganhoe was quite openly critical of self-governance movements but it also could not avoid pondering the question of whether legitimate political activities under colonial rule were possible.

Historical interpretations of colonial Korea under Japanese rule tend to center around the extreme positions taken by both Koreans and Japanese in their refusal to recognize the fact of colonization, much less the currents of decolonization. Such readings are prone to represent the colonizers as hard-line rulers with absolute power while highlighting only uncompromising resistance of the colonized despite the multi-faceted reality of the colony. It should indeed be respected as a historical fact that the Koreans had such a sense of loyalty, but narratives focused on extremes cannot possibly give us a full picture of the complicated realities of colonial Korea. In the same vein, it should be noted that Imperial Japan also needed to "bargain with" colonial Koreans for fear of their strong resistance and its negative impact on Japan's international

---

26 "Chŏnguhoe's New Organization, Holding a Lecture, Writing a Declaration," *Chosŏn Ilbo*, November 17, 1926.

relation. A *Chosŏn Ilbo* editorial penetrated the fear of the colonizer, saying Soejima's support of Korean self-governance "revealed the concern and fear of those who reigned over Korea."[27] The concept of decolonization aptly exposes the multifaceted nature of both the colonizer and the colonized, who both often found themselves shaken up and agitated in their dealings with colonial reality.

3. Colonial Modernity and the Populace

In this section, I will introduce three intellectuals who interpreted the era of colonial modernity in the context of decolonization: Yanaihara Tadao who had optimistic vision of decolonization, and Kim Myŏngsik and Manabendra Nath Roy who maintained critical views. Indian communist Roy and Korean socialist Kim took a population perspective and criticized colonial modernity and decolonization.

Let us first examine Yanaihara Tadao's thoughts on colonial rule and policies in Korea. Yanaihara, a leading scholar of colonial policy, classified colonial policies into three categories: subordination policy, assimilation policy, and autonomy policy.[28] Subordination policy, which tethers colonial territories to the colonial mainland's interests, was imposed by European empires in their colonies from the 16th to the 18th centuries. Such a policy, Yanaihara noted, led to the annihilation of the natives and subsequent resistance against this process. Assimilation policy then emerged as a response to criticism against subordination policy. Using Algeria under French occupation and Ireland under English rule as examples, Yanaihara argued that it was impossible to apply this policy in real politics because it only incited resistance from the colonized.

What Yanaihara saw as the ideal policy for colonial rule was autonomy of colonial peoples. Based on the acknowledgment of colonial peoples' historical

---

27 "The So-Called Problem of Count Soejima's Speech (2): The Ruler's Tactics of the Disturbance Maneuver," *Chosŏn Ilbo*, December 5, 1925.

28 For details about Yanaihara's arguments and statements mentioned below, see Yanaihara Tadao, "Policy to Govern Korea," *Chūōkōron*, June 1926.

particularities and autonomous collective identity, this policy would assist their self-determined development, and, at the same time, could strengthen the whole empire through alliances and collaboration with the colonized. According to Yanaihara, Britain was able to maintain its empire by granting her colonies the right to self-govern. Policies of self-governance would never be akin to giving up colonial rule or lead to a colony's liberation because, as Yanaihara explained, the remarkable development of the modern economy had rendered the "theory of small states" implausible. Yanaihara, reflecting on the changing world order and politics in the post-World War I era, argued that the dominant global trend was to employ policies of self-governance.

As for Japanese rule over Korea, Yanaihara stated that "Japan had not implemented an explicit policy of subordination from the outset, but did intend to employ a policy of protection and correction in Korea after the events in 1919." His explications of pre-1919 policies were rather vague and abstract. On the other hand, with his comments on "a policy of protection and correction," he meant that assimilation policy had been implemented in Korea after the March First Movement. He continued to point out that Japan's "cultural rule" had brought about many advancements in colonial Korea such as the development of transportation systems and trade, the consolidation of the rule of law, reforms in education and sanitation, industrial development, and the capitalization of business management. The problem was, however, that Koreans were given very little means through which they could fulfill their heightened desire for economic gain in proportion to the abovementioned changes in their society. Another, more dire problem was that Japan did not allow for a channel through which Korean populace could express their opinions. These problems turned Japanese rule in Korea into a form of tyranny unprecedented in the world. According to Yanaihara, Koreans' demand for political rights was natural result from cultural rule, so it was imperative for Japan to think about when and how it should respond to these demands. He believed that there were two ways of doing this. One is to have Koreans represented in the mainland parliament and the other is to have them represented in an independent Korean parliament. The former would strengthen the assimilation policy, while the latter would signal a shift toward a policy of self-governance.

Some Japanese politicians seemed to lean toward a merger in a single imperial parliament but Yanaihara insisted on the establishment of a Korean parliament because, according to him, it was impossible for a single parliament to represent two distinctive societies as Japan and Korea. He also argued that implementing self-governance policies in Korea would not necessarily result in Korea's independence. If Japan acknowledged Korea's right to autonomy, Koreans would have no reason to rebel against Japan. Korean self-governance, Yanaihara argued, would make it possible for Japan and Korea to effectively exercise their combined power to pursue shared economic and military interests. Interestingly, Yanaihara saw no problem in Korean independence. If Korea were to become independent as a result of self-governance policies, he believed, Korea would maintain an amicable relationship with Japan, and therefore, there would be no problem at all. In other words, Yanaihara believed in a smooth path to decolonization through the self-governance of the colonized.

Yanaihara's view of decolonization yields interesting insights when compared to that of Kim Myŏngsik, who left a great mark on the early socialist movement in Korea. He was a noteworthy Korean intellectual who actively contributed editorials to newspapers and magazines in the 1920s and 1930s and analyzed post-March First Movement Korean society in the context of decolonization.[29] As he put it:

·····[At] the first stage of Korea's decolonization after the *Kimi* Movement [the March First Movement], there would be turn from security-first policy to industrial development policy. The second stage would entail the installment of local councils, and the third stage, in other words, the stage of complete decolonization, would see the organization of a central parliament of the Koreans.[30]

Kim believed that Korea was on its way to decolonization, judging from the establishment of a capitalist economy in Korea. He explained that "traditional relations of production had been almost destroyed"[31]and the new capitalist

---

29 Hong Jong-wook (Hong Chonguk), *Wartime Korean Converts: Integration and Cracks in the Colonial Empire* (Tokyo: Yūshisha, 2011), 106-111.

30 Kim Myŏngsik, "On the Plan to Reconstruct National Associations: Is it Disunification? Betrayal?" *Criticism,* March 1932, 3.

relations of production was established with a "shift from feudal economy to capital economy."[32] Kim pointed out that the local government system implemented in Korea was catalyzing decolonization process. As he put it, "Japan has three prefectural governments, but Korea has thirteen. The thirteen regional councils have already succeeded in decolonizing local centers as planned, and 40 or so towns are well on their way to becoming newly decolonized."

Kim's analysis of Japan's colonial rule having changed from "security-first policy" to "industry development policy" after the March First Movement is consistent with Yanaihara's analysis. His prognosis that imperialism would spur capitalism in the colony also coincides with Yanaihara's assessment of Korean society. However, unlike Yanaihara's view that decolonization was an inevitable process that had to be supported, Kim maintained a critical stance toward the outcomes of decolonization. This criticism was due to Kim's belief that industrializing the colony and permitting limited political rights to the colonized would only benefit some bourgeois groups and fail to bring any tangible advantages to the Korean population in general.

"If we could put in numbers the extent to which Korean advancements have been suppressed due to and by foreign capital [interests]," Kim argued, "the number would not be small." Moreover, it is never possible to "calculate the lived misery of people with numbers." He was also critical of the local government system in that "judging from the experiences of the regional councils, Korean representatives do not differ from Japanese representatives in their perspectives on colonial policies." He continued that "demanding the establishment of the central parliament in Korea which has already entered the third stage of decolonization would result in supporting the demands of foreign bourgeoisie. In other words, it would be actively engaging in decolonization movements and thereby colluding with anti-nationalistic forces." Even if a central parliament was established, he argued, it would only amount to serving as "an exchange center for the foreign bourgeoisie" and "only

---

31 Kim Myŏngsik, "The Problem of Korea's Manufacturing Industry," *Shindonga*, February 1935, 74.

32 Kim Myŏngsik, "A Review of the Fluctuations in Korean Economic Wealth," *Tonggwang*, July 1931, 10.

guaranteed the rights of the Korean bourgeois." What he worried about was that the decolonization as such would "obscure Korean people's consciousness of [colonial] confrontation."[33]

Kim Myŏngsik believed that Korea had to develop its industry and culture independently by protecting "immature industries and boosting self-reliance of national industry."[34] However, he was quick to point out that "in all colonies today, interests of native landowners and the bourgeoisie are at odds with workers and farmers but coincide with the interests of foreign capital."[35] By noting that "the class struggles in mainland Japan were necessarily tied up with state of affairs in colonial Korea," he emphasized the close connection between Koreans' national liberation struggles and laborers' and farmers' class struggles in the center of the empire.[36] All these analyses indicate that Kim was in favor of industrialization led by *minjung* (the populace or the subaltern people) rather than the bourgeoisie. He took a similar stance in terms of cultural development, as he identified the Korean populace as leaders of Korea's cultural development: "Korea has a class [of the subaltern people] capable of creating a culture with national uniqueness without excluding international connections, representing the whole nation of equal people, and establishing the national group *** [redacted in the original]."[37] There was indeed a rapid increase in the number of social movements in Korea in the late 1920s and early 1930s. Amid labor disputes and tenant farmers' disputes that followed each other back to back, thousands of people were annually arrested for having violated the Security Maintenance Law (*ch'ian yujibŏp*). Witnessing these events, Kim envisioned industrial and cultural development based on and spurred by the Korean populace's power.

The current of decolonization began to grow stronger around the time of World War I and had a great influence on communist anti-imperial

---

33 Kim, "On the Plan to Reconstruct National Associations," 4-7.

34 Kim, "The Problem of Korea's Manufacturing Industry," 74-75.

35 Kim Myŏngsik, "On the National Problem: An Answer to Mr. To Yuho in Berlin," *Samch'ŏlli*, February 1932, 82.

36 Kim, "A Review of the Fluctuations in Korean Economic Wealth," 14-15.

37 Kim, "On the Plan to Reconstruct National Associations," 6.

movements. During the 1920 Second Congress of the Communist International, Lenin asserted that the proletariat in colonized regions had to collaborate with bourgeois nationalists. In contrast, Indian communist Roy pointed out that the development of capitalism in colonies would only accelerate the trend of bourgeois nationalists' compromising with the colonizer.[38] Later, during the 1926 Congress of the Communist International, Roy asserted that the era of imperialism in the traditional sense had passed.[39] In a document he wrote at the behest of Nikolai Bukharin, he employed the term "decolonization" to describe India's industrialization process. Roy wrote: "the implication of [Britain's] new policy is the gradual 'decolonization' of India which would be allowed eventually to evolve out of the status of 'dependency' to Dominion Status."[40] He also argued that the "unavoidable process of gradual 'decolonization' has in it the germs of the destruction of the empire." As he saw it, this was because "such an eventuality would benefit only the native bourgeoisie and would result in exploitation for the bulk of the Indian people."

In 1928, Evgenii Samuilovich Varga, a leading economist representing the Communist International, published a thesis in which he argued that "Great Britain was now attempting to arrest industrial growth in India."[41] At the 6th Communist International Congress held in the same year, Otto Wille Kuusinen followed Varga's thesis and classified "decolonization" as a "dangerous term." Kuusinen contended that the Communist Party of India was responsible for undertaking the task of "relieving, by Communist agitation, the mass of the Indian peasantry and the proletariat of the illusion that the policy of British imperialism can make the decolonization of India a reality, or even bring it nearer."[42] The delegation of the British Communist Party argued that Kuusinen's assertion that a colony is always an "agricultural appendage" of

---

38 See Matsumoto Sachiko, "The Formation of a National Liberation Theory in the Early Comintern: Focusing on the Lenin-Roy Controversy at the Second Comintern Convention," *The Historical Science Society of Japan* 355 (1969): 12.

39 On Comintern debates on decolonization, see John Patrick Haithcox, *Communism and Nationalism in India: M. N. Roy and Comintern Policy, 1920-1939* (Princeton: Princeton University Press, 1971), 108-121.

40 Haithcox, *Communism and Nationalism in India*, 112.

41 Haithcox, *Communism and Nationalism in India*, 113.

42 Haithcox, *Communism and Nationalism in India*, 116.

the empire's industrial cities was an outdated idea based on the realities of the late-19th century. Kuusinen yielded to the British delegates' criticisms, but he berated Roy for being a "lackey of imperialism" who perceived British imperialism as that which will "lead the Indian people by hand to freedom."[43] Even in "Theses on the Revolutionary Movement in the Colonies and Semi-Colonies," the final thesis adopted by the Sixth Communist International, Kuusinen maintained that "all the chatter of the imperialists and their lackeys about the politics of decolonization reveals itself as nothing but an imperialist lie."[44]

Roy defined decolonization as a state in which industrial development, an extension of education, and participation in certain political activities are allowed in the colonies. His political assessment was geared toward exposing the native bourgeoisie who had become new accessories in colonial rule.[45] However, perhaps because "decolonization" was an unfamiliar concept, the majority of the Communist International perceived Roy's arguments as threatening. They were concerned that if the British ruling policy over India and its effects are referred to as "decolonization," it would lead to an affirmation of British imperialism. Roy did not, however, equate decolonization with the populace's liberation. What Roy really contended was that decolonization would result in the awakening of the colonial people and that class struggles intensified by such an awakening could bring about true emancipation.

The desire for industrial development and the dissemination of education dominated colonial Korea in the 1920s and 1930s. With the disintegration of the binary proposition of "agricultural colony vs. industrial metropole," discussions about the reconfiguration of the colonial territories came to the fore. This turn signaled the end of 19th-century-style colonial rule and heralded the true beginning of the era of colonial modernity. Development and the influx of foreign capital brought changes to old, conventional social relations

---

43 Haithcox, *Communism and Nationalism in India*, 119-120. Haithcox points out that Kuusinen made this attack without "considering Roy's current articles on the subject."

44 Haithcox, *Communism and Nationalism in India*, 121.

45 Matsumoto Sachiko, "M. N. Roy's Political Thought in the 1930s: Focusing on Its Decolonization Theory," *Shiron* 43 (1990): 31-50.

in Korea and occasioned the subaltern people of colonial Korea to emerge at the forefront of history. Forced mobilization and the repeated dislocation of the colonial populace awakened their political subjectivity and led to the rise of nationalistic and social movements. Colonial modernity should be redefined with regard to all these changes in Korea, including the popular movements.

Kim Myŏngsik recognized the social changes of colonial Korea after the March First Movement in relation to the global current of decolonization. He could thereby penetrate neo-colonial aspects of "decolonization" process, in which colonial peoples were allowed for limited political autonomy at the cost of economic subordination. Kim was able to keep a critical distance from neo-colonial modes of "decolonization" because he maintained the stance that decolonization had to accompany the emancipation of the colonial populace. Kim's understanding of the times is in line with Roy's. Roy's theory of decolonization has been acknowledged as an early prototype of criticism of the neocolonialism, which culminated only after World War II.[46] In contrast, after 1945 Yanaihara made a significant shift from studies on colonial policy into international relation studies built on the premise of equality of nation-states.

During the interwar period, Yanaihara also noted that the economic instability of Korea was caused by the policies of "cultural rule." However, he prospected that the situation would improve once Korean self-governance was implemented by granting political freedom to Koreans and establishing a Korean parliament. As Murakami Katsuhiko pointed out, Yanaihara's analysis was based on his belief that imperialism increases productivity, and that such advancements make the liberation of colonies inevitable.[47] In a 1937 article that sparked the "Chinese Unification Debate," Yanaihara argued that foreign capital stimulated the development of capitalism in China and that such developments led to the promotion of national unification. He asserted that such change was "a law of history."[48] Nozawa Yutaka identified the theoretical basis of

---

[46] See Nakajima Taichi, "M. N. Roy's Decolonization Theory: A Perspective on the Method of World Economy," *Hikone Ronsō* 134/135 (1969): 74-90.

[47] Murakami Katsuhiko, "Yanaihara Tadao's Colonial Theory and Policy," in *Iawanami Lecture, Modern Japan and the Colonies*, ed. Ōe Shinobu et al., (Tokyo: Iwanami Shoten, 1993), 233.

Yanaihara's argument as a theory of "decolonization."[49] According to Yanaihara's theory, colonization, which formed a "world economy" consisting of global division of labor and exchange, would also incur the destruction of capitalism and imperialism in due course.[50]

Yanaihara, Kim, and Roy all employed the frame of decolonization in their assessment of the new era of colonial modernity that had replaced the era of 19th-century colonial rule. But their understanding of the meaning of and the routes to decolonization were rather different. Yanaihara pitted himself against leftist and rightist wings that tended to belittle the potential of colonies and semi-colonies for progress. He envisioned social and national developments in China and Korea via processes of decolonization. Roy looked squarely at the era of decolonization from the perspective of the populace but was expelled from the Communist International as a result. Kim Myŏngsik's theory of decolonization received almost no attention from his contemporaries, and even today, it remains underdiscussed. However, decolonization process continued throughout the 20th century despite the twists and turns of the time and paved the way to the post-colonial era.

4. "Japan–Korea Unity" (*Naesŏnilch'e*): The Critical Point of Empire

It is generally known that Japanese rule over Korea became increasingly intense and reached its peak during the Second Sino-Japanese War. However, if we situate the post-1920 Korea in global current of decolonization, this period can be reinterpreted as the era during which the pressure for decolonization became quite extreme.[51]

The founding of Manchukuo in 1932 examplified that the Japanese Empire had adopted a new mode of governance. Instead of direct colonial rule over

---

48 Yanaihara Tadao, "Whereabouts of the China Problem," *Chūōkōron,* March 1937, 4-17.

49 Nozawa Yutaka, "For Progress in Studies of Asia's Modern History," in *Drastic Changes in Asia,* vol. 1, ed. Nozawa Yutaka (Tokyo: Azekura Shobō, 1978), 282.

50 Yonetani Masafumi, *Ajia/Nihon* (Tokyo: Iawanami Shoten, 2006), 103-104.

51 These explanations about the wartime colonial situation in Korea with a specific focus on *naesŏnilch'e* (Japan and Korea as one body or Japan-Korea Unity) come from my book, *Wartime Korean Converts.*

Manchuria, Japan made it into an independent state, albeit nominally. As the slogan "Five Races under One Union" (*Ojokhyŏphwa*) indicates, Manchukuo came to serve as a ground for propaganda that emphasized the coming of a new order in which many peoples coexisted under one union state. Pui, the last emperor of the Qing Dynasty, was the regent of Manchukuo, but this "independent state" was to be controlled by Japan's Kwantung Army. Ministers of the administration were Chinese, but it was the Japanese vice ministers who had de facto power. Such details of Japanese rule in Manchukuo are reminiscent of the vice-ministerial politics of the Japanese Resident-General before the annexation of Korea.

Peter Duss analyzed the history of the Japanese Empire after World War I as "imperialism without colonies," noting that it maintained the empire by "manipulating nationalism."[52] This transformation of the imperial order in Japan and the world during the 1920s and 1930s was related to the emergence of a new method for "fusing" nations and states. The British Commonwealth is a good example of this new method. Sakai Tetsuya analyzed this new trend as an attempt for "remodeling an empire into a 'community' of mutually dependent political entities by granting semi-autonomy, not full rights to self-determination, to colonial peoples."[53] His analysis also concerned decolonization in that decolonization means nothing but a trial for soft landing of the dissolving imperial regimes.

During the Second Sino-Japanese War, the Japanese Government-General advocated the policy of "Japan and Korea as one body" (*naesŏnilch'e*). Although some Koreans opposed such a strong assimilation policy that would lead to the ethnic extermination of Koreans, others hoped for an "escape from discrimination" through the assimilation.[54] Meanwhile, the Japanese army, which had been sending news of consecutive victories from China since the war started in July 1937, found itself at a stalemate as the Chinese government

---

52 Peter Duss, "Imperialism without Colonies: The Vision of a Greater East Asia Co-Prosperity Sphere," *Diplomacy and Statecraft* 7, no. 1 (1996): 54-72.

53 Sakai Tetsuya, "Empire and Regionalism: Interwar Japan's Theory of International Order," *The Historical Science Society of Japan* 794 (2004): 84-92.

54 Miyata Setsuko, *Korean People and Japanization Policy* (Tokyo: Miraisha, 1985), 156.

pushed back despite their defeat in Wuhan and Guangdong in October 1938. During this period, the Japanese government announced the idea of "New Order in East Asia" (*tonga sinjilsŏ*). This "New Order" acknowledged China's nationalism and proposed the formation of a federal state encompassing Japan, Manchukuo, and China. After this "New Order" idea was floated by the Japanese government, theories about an "East Asian Community" (*tonga hyŏptongch'e*) and "East Asian League" (*tonga yŏnmaeng*) became popular in Japan. Chiang Kai-shek, however, flatly noted that talk of an "East Asian Community" was merely a disguise for Japan's desire to colonize China, reminding the historical precedent of Japan's colonization of Korea with the pretext of "Japan and Korea as one body."[55]

On the other hand, Korean newspapers and magazines published many articles about an "East Asian Community" from 1939 to 1940, prospecting that the principle for the Sino-Japanese relations should be applied to Korea-Japan as well. This view was an unexpected turn of events that caught Japan off guard. As implied in Chiang Kai-shek's critical statement, the sincerity of Japan's advocate for "East Asian Community" could not help but be questioned if Japan made no changes to Korea's status as its colony. Making use of this logical predicament, Korean periodicals promoted the idea of "Cooperative Unity of Japan and Korea" (*hyŏphwajŏk naesŏnilch'e*), which meant the authentic unity of Japan and Korea could be established through mutual efforts of both parties. In other words, the Koreans were reinterpreting the "Japan and Korea as one body" campaign by merging it with Japan's other campaign of an "East Asian Community" in order to claim Korea's autonomy.

There were also fierce debates between the advocates of "Cooperative Unity of Japan and Korea," which promoted a multicultural imperialism of sorts, and the advocates of "Complete Korea-Japan Unity," that is, complete assimilation. Kim Myŏngsik was a proponent of "Cooperative Unity of Japan and Korea." Stressing the necessity of controlled economy and the economic independence of Korea, he argued that the Planning Board should be installed

---

55 Chiang Kai-shek, "Chiang Kai-shek's Memorial Week Speech in Refutation of the Konoe Statement (1938.12.26)," in *Top Secret Anti-Japanese Government Criticism on the East Asian New Order*, ed. and trans. Tōa Kenkyūjo (Tokyo: Tōa kenkyūjo, 1941), 1-20.

in Korea as in mainland Japan.[56] The Planning Board was indeed established as a branch of the Japanese Government-General of Korea in December 1939, although it never met his expectation for an "economic headquarter of Korea."[57] In terms of politics, Kim asserted that the Korean League for the Total Mobilization of the National Spirit (*Kungmin jŏngsin ch'ongdongwŏn yŏnmaeng*) had to function like the Indian National Congress led by Gandhi.[58] He also commented on the necessity of preparing for a constitutional politics and the special constitution for Korea, which would make Korea as a "special (economic and political) unit" and active participant of the "New East Asian Federation." Kim's political line can be regarded as a form of self-governance of Korea.

Yet how did Kim Myŏngsik, who had vehemently criticized the "cultural rule" as a policy of decolonization until the early 1930s, came to advocate the idea of "Cooperative Unity of Japan and Korea"? The discourse of the "East Asian Community," which was prevalent in both Japan and Korea during the Second Sino-Japanese war, was envisioned as a means to end the war by reconciling with China and to support anti-capitalist reform in mainland Japan. Discussions of the "Total War System," which Japanese scholars of modern history broached in the 1990s, suggest that the system pressed the entire society to develop in ways to maximize rationality for efficient war-waging. The system also had to implement "policies designed to turn every member of the society into bearing social functions required for the war mobilization."[59] In the same vein, Yonetani Masafumi noted that the concept of the "East Asian Community" can be understood as a type of "wartime reform" theory that envisioned a combination of social reforms and ethnic coordination.[60]

---

56 Kim, "The Problem of Korea's Manufacturing Industry," 68.

57 "Establish a Planning Board in the Government-General," *Chosŏn* 296, 1940, 119.

58 Kim Myŏngsik, "On the Problem of Controlling Korea's Economy," *Chogwang,* October 1939, 64; Kim Myŏngsik, "Continental Expansion and Koreans," *Chogwang,* April 1939, 49; Kim Myŏngsik, "The Specific Process of Realizing the Unity of Japanese and Korean Peoples," *Mining Industry of Korea,* January 1940, 62-67.

59 Yamanouchi Yasushi, "Methodological Introduction: Total War and System Integration," in *Total War and Modernization,* ed. Yamanouchi Yasushi, Victor Koschman, and Narita Ryūichi (Tokyo: Kashiwa Shobō, 1995), 12.

60 Yonetani Masafumi, "Social Thought in Japan During the Wartime Period," *Shisō,* December

It was amid this maelstrom of the total war that Kim Myŏngsik "converted" and promoted "Cooperative Unity of Japan and Korea." Taking this historical and discursive contexts into consideration, we can say that Kim's advocate for the "East Asian Community" was also a kind of "wartime reform" theory of the time, based on his judgement that it would lead to the true decolonization of the Korean people.

Changes of the ruling order during the Second Sino-Japanese War were not just rhetorical. In the Korean Federation of Patriots (*Siguk taeŭng chŏnsŏn sasang poguk yŏnmaeng*), which was founded in 1938 by a group of Korean political converts, Koreans occupied the top positions of the headquarter and branches while Japanese remained in assistant positions such as deputy manager and vice-chair.[61] The structure of the Federation was similar to the vice-ministerial politics during the rule of the Japanese Resident-General and aroused Japanese officials' protest. The local council elections of 1939 also made headlines as the Japanese dominance in the council was overturned.[62] This reality was reflected in art work of the time. For example, Mizuno Naoki's study of wartime Korean films analyzed not only the "ethnic hierarchy" but also its subversibility reflected in those films.[63]

Contestations and conflicts between the different political lines of independence, self-governance, and assimilation continued during the Second Sino-Japan War. And above all, overseas independence movements persisted. In June 1937, right before the war broke out, Korean newspapers widely reported that the Manchuria-based troops of Kim Il-sung had crossed the border into Korea to attack Poch'ŏnbo, a small border village. Meanwhile, assimilationists continued to petition for Koreans' political rights throughout the war. In a general report on the ideological movements of 1938, the Japanese army stationed in Korea noted that "the patriotic movements of the Koreans have become

1997, 69-120.

61 Hong Jong-wook, "Thought Crime Control and Yamato Juku in Wartime Korea," *The Study of Korean Culture and Society* 16 (2017): 43-67.

62 Kim Tongmyŏng, *Rule and Collaboration: Japanese Imperialism and Political Participation in Colonial Korea* (Seoul: Yŏksagonggan, 2018), 127-128.

63 Mizuno Naoki, "A Propaganda Film Subverting Ethnic Hierarchy?: Suicide Squad at the Watchtower and Colonial Korea," *Cross-Currents* 5 (2012): 63-87.

increasingly energetic especially since the war started, and consequently, issues like enfranchisement and discrimination against Koreans became remarkably pressing matters."[64] "Complete Unity of Japan and Korea," which argued for a complete Japanization of Koreans, was an assimilationist idea. On the other hand, the "Cooperative Unity of Japan and Korea" can be regarded as a self-governance discourse. Either way, the politics of "Unity of Japan and Korea" marked a critical point of colonial government in that it could lead to either the extermination of the colonized people or their elevation to autonomous political subjects. In this sense, the wartime after the Second Sino-Japanese War was a period during which "cultural politics" and colonial modernity were at their zenith.

After 1941, the Japanese government began devote itself to the complete assimilation policy, regarding the "East Asian Community" and the "East Asian League" as dangerous. The Japanese Government-General of Korea oppressed advocates for "Cooperative Unity of Japan and Korea" and forcibly implemented assimilation policies such as campaign to change Korean names to Japanese, prohibition of Korean language publication, and arrest of key members of the Korean Language Society. In 1943, the local council elections were changed into the recommendation system again. Such a move was partly made in response to the wartime emergency, but also a conscious reaction to the result of the 1939 election when the Korean members had predominance in the local council.

In 1941, the aforementioned Korean Federation of Patriots was forcibly reorganized into the School of Great Harmony (*Taehwasuk*) for mental training of the Korean, entailing the "correction" of the subverted hierarchy between the Koreans and the Japanese in the organization. Governor-General Koiso Kuniaki, who took office in May 1942, preferred the slogan of "Moral Korea" (*Doŭi josŏn*) emphasizing the imperial subjects' ethics and duties to the phrase "Unity of Japan and Korea," which might stimulate Koreans' sense of rights.[65]

---

64 General Headquarter of Japanese Army of Korea, "The State of the Korean Ideological Movement in the Second Half of 1938 (1939. 2)," in *Complete Collection of Materials on Ideological Movements under Japanese Colonialism*, vol. 3, ed. The Organization of Korean Historians (Seoul: Koryŏsŏrim, 1992), 14.

65 "Strengthen Leadership Over the Populace, and Bring About a 'Moral Korea': First Instruction to the Three Thousand Officials of Governor-General Koiso," *Maeil Sinbo*, January 19, 1942.

Startled by the spirit of decolonization that had peaked in the wartime, the Government-General turned to a forceful, coercive attitude. Japan's colonial policies in the 1940s resembled the military rule before the era of "cultural rule." In other words, political situations of colonial Korea of the 1940s were regressed to a time before the March First Movement, or put it differently, "before *manse*."[66] Attempts to decolonize Korea since the March First Movement were frustrated, at least on the surface. The only thing left for the Japanese Empire, which had refused to make a soft landing through decolonization, was a crackup. On the other hand, the Cairo Declaration of 1943 served as a turning point for colonial Koreans. Inspired by the news that the Allied Powers agreed to guarantee Korea's independence, movements for a radical decolonization of Korea, that is, movements for political independece, came to revive.

Trans. by Park Joo-hyun

---

66 "Before *Manse*" is the novel title of Yŏm Sangsŏp, a prolific writer who delved into colonial modernity of Korea. "*Manse*" literally means "Long Live!" or "Hurrah!" but it also referred to the March First Movement when colonial Koreans demonstrated for independence, crying "*manse!*" Kim Yunsik has a study that focuses on the meaning of the modern as the system of "institutional apparatus" in Yŏm's life and work. See Kim Yunsik, *Yŏm Sangsŏp Studies* (Seoul: Seoul National University Press, 1987).

National Self–Determination of Colonial Peoples and World Democracy

Youn Young-shil

1. "World Democracy," the Song of "Those Who Have No Qualification"

On May 2, 1918, toward the end of World War I, a poem entitled "World Democracy" (*Segye minjujuŭi*) was featured in the *New Korea* (*Sinhan minbo*), a newspaper run by Korean immigrants in the U.S. The poem was written by a Korean American student named Charr Easurk (Ch'a Ŭisŏk) at the time of his voluntary enlistment in the U.S. military.[1]

> People of liberty, let's go together.
> We shall bring the joy of freedom
> To those suppressed under tyranny
> And destroy the power of tyrants.
>
> The Stars and Stripes stands before me
> To advocate for freedom
> And fight for human rights.

---

1   The poem was first written in English, published in the college magazine of Parkville College and later translated into Korean for the *New Korea*. Since I could not find the original English version, I retranslated the poem into English.

Children of Belgium, Britain and France,
I shall stand side by side in your fight.
The world's destiny is in your hands
And nothing else matters anymore.

I am a defeated soldier from a perished country,
Not afraid of sacrifice.
I shall offer my humble body
For the sake of the world.

When the war ends with victory,
World peace begins here.
When the Polish and the Serbs return home,
My countrymen will also be free.

The article that accompanied the poem describes Charr's background as follows. After attending Soongsil Middle School in Pyongyang, Charr migrated to "the United States of America, his second home" in his early teens. He first worked at a sugar cane farm in Hawaii and later settled in California, where he "went through joys and sorrows with the Korean community." Charr was in his fifth year in Parkville College in Missouri when he decided to volunteer for military service in response to "Uncle Sam's call" for "justice and humanity." Although he was initially rejected due to his status as a non-citizen, Charr was eventually given permission to join the American army after making numerous appeals to the federal government.

We can find dozens of cases similar to Charr's in the *New Korea*,[2] which makes us wonder about their commonality rather than their individual backgrounds. What common cause led these men to volunteer for the war?

---

2   The *New Korea* published a number of articles on the voluntary enlistment of Korean immigrants in the U.S. between 1917 and 1919, delivering proper names such as Kim Yongsŏng, Kim Chŏngŭn, Yi Sanggu, Y Hŭibok (August 9, 1917), Kim Kilsŏk, Chŏng Ŭldon (June 6, 1918), Yi Sŏngch'ang (June 14, 1918), O Kwansŏn (June 27, 1918), Pak Ch'angsun (July 4, 1918), about 30 Koreans in Hawaii (July 25, 1918), Ch'a Chŏngok (August 15, 1918), Han Yŏngho (January 2, 1919), Im Kongsŏn, Kim Chinsŏng, Yi Tosin (July 17, 1919), etc.

Or what commonality was being constituted through stories featured in the media between the publisher, the Korean National Association (*Taehanin kungminhoe*), and its readers, colonial Koreans in America? We should remember that both the "Korean nation" and "Korean American" were precarious identities at that time, when the state called "Korea" no longer existed and Koreans did not have the right to naturalization in America, their "second home." Although they had built a tangible community across the U.S., their collective identity was neither fully articulated nor secure. Moreover, their nationality was legally classified as Japanese since Japan had colonized Korea in 1910. Hence, the case of the Koreans in the U.S. military during World War I is different from that of Korean Japanese soldiers or Japanese American soldiers during World War II. In the latter cases, a (colonial) state mobilized colonized people or immigrants from the enemy state to participate in the war, forcing them to decide between "loyalty and treason."[3] In the former case, however, there were those who volunteered for the war without state mobilization or interpellative power. Then, for what common cause did they voluntarily fight?

Of course, a simple answer comes to mind if we interpret the poem in the context of Korean nationalist independence movements, propelled by U.S. President Woodrow Wilson's idea of "national self-determination." However, instead of jumping to this familiar conclusion, I would like to emphasize two points. First, I want to locate Charr's poem "World Democracy" within the world historical moment during which various forces were fiercely opposed to and intricately enmeshed with one another. Secondly, I hope to reveal the event-ness of the moment when the identity of the "Korean nation" was just being constituted historically and performatively.

Previous studies on national self-determination in the U.S. and South Korea tend to pivot around either the question of what Wilson truly meant by the notion[4] or the matter of how (un-)successfully colonial Koreans (mis-)understood

---

3   Fujitani has analyzed this case extensively in his work. See Takashi Fujitani, *Race for Empire: Koreans as Japanese and Japanese as Americans during World War II* (Los Angeles: University of California Press, 2013).

4   For a summary of previous research, see Lloyd E. Ambrosius, "Introduction," *Wilsonian Statecraft: Theory and Practice of Liberal Internationalism during World War I* (London: SK Books, 1991); Tony Smith, *Why Wilson Matters: The Origin of American Liberal Internationalism and its Crisis*

and applied Wilson's notion.[5] Many of them have remained within the boundary of a national history or within the frame of international relations between colonial Korea, Japan, and the U.S. A more refreshing insight, however, was offered by Erez Manela's *The Wilsonian Moment*. Unlike what the title suggests, the book does not focus on Wilson's authentic intention but on how the colonial peoples of Egypt, India, China, and Korea strategically employed his rhetoric. The study also integrates events that have been confined to separate national histories into one world historical moment. As Manela reminds us, colonial peoples around the world used Wilson's words in numerous declarations, manifestos, pamphlets, and petition letters or telegrams directed at the Allied Powers in order to justify their claims of independence. Each of them sought to send delegates and secure their place at the Paris Peace Conference, while frequently appropriating Wilson's rhetoric. There are, of course, dangers that lurk within Manela viewing multiple peripheries from the center and analyzing petitions sent from the colonial peoples to the Allied Powers. Contrary to

---

Today (Princeton: Princeton University Press, 2017); Trygve Thronveit, *Power without Victory: Woodrow Wilson and the American Internationalist Experiment* (Chicago: University of Chicago Press, 2017). As to Wilson's true intention, some argue that Wilson's advocacy for self-determination was a mere cover for American imperialism, while others claim that his sincere attempt to overthrow the imperial order was thwarted by Europe and Japan. On the other hand, Tooze criticizes the existing literature that regards Wilsonian idealism as a failed project by claiming that Wilson really brought about a paradigm shift in the world order near the end of World War I. Adam Tooze, *The Deluge: The Great War, America and the Remaking of the Global Order, 1916-1931* (New York: Viking, 2014), 16.

Although I agree with the claim that there was a paradigm shift during this period, I seek to reveal that the driving force of this shift was not Wilson but the decolonization movements of the colonial peoples who appropriated Wilson's words.

5   Within the national history of Korea, some scholars assess that the Korean "nation" could find a justification of its independence movement in Wilson's ideas, whereas others argue that the colonial Koreans, unable to decipher the harsh world order, were deceived by the mere rhetoric of the great powers. See the following works on the role of Wilsonian idealism in colonial Korea: Chŏn Sangsuk, "Reorganization of International Relations after World War I and the Understanding of Korean National Leaders," *Journal of Korean Political and Diplomatic History* 26 (2004): 313-350; Chŏn Sangsuk, "Paris Peace Conference and the Issue of Independence of the People of a Small and Weak Power," *Journal of Korean Modern and Contemporary History* 50 (2009): 7-36; Song Chiye, "Translation of 'Self-Determination' and the Feb. 8th Independence Movement," *The Review of Korean and Asian Political Thoughts* 13, no. 1 (2012): 179-209; Pak Hyŏnsuk, "Paradox of Wilsonian Peace," *Daegusahak* 98 (2010): 177-212; Pak Hyŏnsuk, "Woodrow Wilson's Self-Determination and World Peace," *The Korean Journal of American History* 33 (2011): 149-190; Kim Sungbae and Kim Myŏngsŏp, "The Versailles Peace System's 'Universal Nomos' and the Different Dreams of Korea and Japan," *Korean Journal of International Relations* 52, no. 2 (2012): 37-68.

his intention of expanding the scope of U.S. history and highlighting non-Western agency,[6] Manela risks subsuming world history under American history and reducing non-Western agency to a desire to get recognition from the West. Despite such danger, this book can still evoke positive effects by reminding contemporary Korean readers of other peripheries that have been forgotten in Korean national historiography.

With this insight in mind, I will situate Charr's poem "World Democracy" in the global history of decolonization, experimenting with what Robert J. C. Young calls "postcolonial writing": the practice of restoring and re-memorizing anonymous moments of resistance forgotten or frustrated within colonial history; the practice of steering anti-colonial resistance away from the narrow framework of "Third World nationalism" and re-contextualizing it within the history of a global struggle for democracy; and the practice of grasping and overcoming the continuous oppression in the post-colonial world by reflecting upon the history of colonialism.[7] Postcolonial writing is different from a binary approach that simply endorses local, non-Western knowledges while excluding Western theories. Colonies were sites loaded with the paradox of modernity and the contradictions of capitalism and the nation-state system. It is thus necessary to grasp colonial history with the insights of theories on capital, empire, sovereignty, nation, representation, and discourse. However, theories mostly produced in the West are not interested in the "colonial differences" with which global modernity was experienced in various colonies.[8] As Dipesh Chakrabarty said, Western theories are both "indispensable and inadequate"[9] for the purpose of examining those different facets of the world that are rendered visible from the geopolitical position of colonies and the way in which they are linked to one another in the context of global modernity. This is precisely the gap that postcolonial writing has to fill by questioning the lacuna in Western

---

6   Erez Manela, *The Wilsonian Moment: Self-Determination and the International Origins of Anticolonial Nationalism* (Oxford: Oxford University Press, 2007), xi.

7   For Young's notion of "postcolonial writing," see Robert J. C. Young, *Postcolonialism: A Historical Introduction* (New York: Blackwell, 2001), 60-61.

8   Walter D. Mignolo, *Local Histories/Global Designs: Coloniality, Subaltern Knowledges, and Border Thinking* (Princeton, NJ: Princeton University Press, 2000), 50.

9   Dipesh Chakrabarty, *Provincializing Europe* (Princeton, NJ: Princeton University Press, 2000), 6.

theories and the unspeakable experiences of the colonized.

Moreover, in order to grasp the "eventual temporality" when the "Korean nation" was performatively constituted, one should move away from two layers of meaning that the word "nation" inadvertently evokes in a contemporary context. One is the stratum of nationalist narrative, solidified over time. Here, a "nation" is regarded as a given, collective identity based on shared ethnicity, language, culture, and blood. As boundaries between nations are supposed to be self-evident and clear, colonial rule is nothing but the exploitative domination of a nation by another. The only moral and political prospect for the colonized is thus political independence and the establishment of their own nation-state. All contingent events are reduced to diegetic elements of this nationalist narrative and their meaning is retrospectively defined from the moment of closure, the establishment of the nation-state. Another layer, which is rather closer to a flowing lava bed that tears down preexisting strata, consists of discourses with the prefix "post-" (post-nationalism, post-modernism, etc.). "All that is solid melts into" fluid, blurring boundaries between "imagined" nations and even between colonial violence and anti-colonial resistance. In this article, instead, I intend to emphasize how those who fought for their rights to life and self-determination constituted themselves as political subjects of "the Korean nation," rather than supposing national identity as a pre-existing entity before struggles or conflating different historical experiences indiscriminately.

For this purpose, in section 2, I analyze the semi-refugee condition of colonial Koreans around the time of World War I, and examine the meaning of their claim to the title of "nation." The question that permeates this discussion is why those who did not have "the right to have rights" anywhere in the world, to borrow from Hannah Arendt, identified themselves as members of a "colonized nation" and adopted "national self-determination" as their most viable political prospect. By arranging "the decline of nation-states" and the refugee issue in the West and colonial peoples' struggle for "national self-determination" as interconnected historical experiences in simultaneous relations, I will re-evaluate the significance of the colonized "nation" beyond Western-centered nationalism theories.

In section 3, I will reexamine the so-called Wilsonian moment as a world historical moment charged with conflicting forces over different usages of democracy, focusing on these frontlines: (a) the Allied Powers v. the Central Powers, (b) the "forerunners" of imperial powers such as the U.K. and France v. the "latecomers" such as Germany and Japan, (c) European realism v. Wilson's pragmatic idealism.

Against this background, I will return to "World Democracy" and other articles of the *New Korea* in section 4, and reassess them in the context of the confrontation between (d) the imperial order of the world and the colonized. The case of Charr and his poem remind us of the world historical moment when an individual's desire for the right to life and the universal ideal of democracy were tied into a single knot through the motto of self-determination. Highlighting this eventful moment, I would like to show how colonial peoples' struggle for national self-determination not only challenged the imperial standards of constitutional democracy and "renewed" democracy for all but also changed the Western-centered implication of the "nation" concept itself.

2. Refugees and Colonial Peoples: "The Decline of the Nation-State" and the Rise of the "Colonized Nation"

World War I came to an end when Germany surrendered on November 11, 1918, four years from the beginning of the war in July 1914 and about a year and a half after the United States' participation in the war in April 1917. Unlike the U.K. or France, which had to pay dearly for the long waging war, the U.S. paid a minimum cost yet became a major player in postwar planning. President Wilson began to lead the reconfiguration of the postwar order by presenting his Fourteen Points speech at a joint meeting of the House and the Senate on January 8, 1918. The Fourteen Points not only laid out general principles, such as the prohibition of secret diplomacy, freedom of the seas, removal of economic barriers, reduction of armaments, and the establishment of a world organization, but also included several specific proposals pertaining to the reconfiguration of the political order in Europe. Among these, Point V stated that "the interest of the population concerned" must be weighed equally with that of the government when determining the matter of sovereignty.[10]

The expression "interest of the population concerned" was later changed to "the consent of the governed" and mixed with "national self-determination," and was appropriated as a basis for colonial peoples to demand independence.

Among Korean publications at the time, the *New Korea* was the quickest and the most eager news outlet to report Wilson's speech.[11] In an article that introduced several principles (Points I, V, XI, XII, and XIV) of the Fourteen Points, the journalist summarized Point V as follows: "The competing demands pertaining to colonies are to be negotiated in a fair manner based on the principle that the people have equal rights as any government has."[12] Right after the speech was delivered, the *New Korea* did not regard Wilson's speech with much significance, reporting from time to time that Japan and Germany objected to it.[13] Expectations for the Fourteen Points and Wilson rose rapidly only after the end of the war, ten months after the news was first delivered. This change was clearly visible in the article entitled "A Letter of Congratulations to President Wilson" on November 21, 1918. The article was a Korean translation

---

10 Point V reads "a free, open-minded, and absolutely impartial adjustment of all colonial claims, based upon a strict observance of the principle that in determining all such questions of sovereignty the interests of the populations concerned must have equal weight with the equitable claims of the government whose title is to be determined."

11 Nagata Akifumi, *Japan's Rule of Korea and International Relations: The Korean Independence Movement and the United States 1910-1922*, trans. Pak Hwanmu (Seoul: Ilchogak, 2008), 98-123. According to Nagata, the earliest response to Wilson's proclamation by Koreans in Japan was made at the welcoming event for Jole Kensen, the former head of the Korean YMCA in Tokyo, on June 27, 1918. In China, the Sinhan Youth Party (*Sinhan ch'ŏngnyŏndang*) was the first organization that proclaimed nationalism, democracy, and international peace in response to Wilsonianism on August 20, 1918, asking Charles R. Crane — Wilson's friend — on November 26 of the same year for his assistance for having Korean delegates at the Paris Peace Conference. In colonial Korea, *Daily News* (*Maeil sinbo*) was the first news outlet that reported on Wilson's The Fourteen Points with the article "Telegrams from the West" in January 1918. Due to their geographical proximity, the Koreans in the U.S. were able to respond to Wilson's idea the quickest, and the message eventually reached colonial Korea via China and Japan. There is also the possibility that the Koreans in Russian territories were exposed to Lenin's notion of national self-determination prior to Wilson's, which is in need of further research.

12 "American Stance on Peace Treaty Talks," *New Korea*, January 17, 1918.

13 "Japan's opposition to American Stance on Peace Treaty Talk," *New Korea*, January 24, 1918; "German Prime Minister's Speech on Peace Treaty," *New Korea*, January 31, 1918. These articles reported that Japan was opposed to Wilson's proposal for fair commercial interest, arms control, and elections in the colonial territories and that the German chancellor only agreed with four of Wilson's The Fourteen Points, problematizing the notion of national self-determination for the population in the colonial territories.

of the congratulatory letter sent to Wilson by the Korean National Association, which celebrated the Allied Powers' victory as "the success of [Wilson's] democracy" and hoped that "owing to Mr. President's success, the people of the world will gain freedom and equality, which will give rise to a new era of democracy."

Charr's poem came from this background. Sharing the same context as the *New Korea* articles, the poem envisioned the realization of the universal ideal of world democracy directly connected to the liberation of their country, that is, self-determination of the colonized "nation." But what made this outlook so convincing to the colonized? Charr as an individual could have had diverse political prospects: the elimination of racial discrimination and acquisition of citizenship in the U.S., a resolution of the colonial differences in the Japanese Empire and "becoming Japanese,"[14] the foundation of an independent Korean nation-state, proletarian internationalism and a working class-revolution, or an anarchist refusal of the nation-state system, etc. In the following century, these various possibilities were actually attempted, frustrated, or are still ongoing as unfinished projects. Around 1917–1919, however, when Lenin and Wilson each advocated for national self-determination, and when both the colonial peoples and minorities in Europe demanded their right to self-determination, these various possibilities were not fully differentiated but were rather condensed in the slogan of national self-determination among Koreans. The implications of "national self-determination," the shared origin of all these political lines, therefore, need to be examined against the background of that era. Why was the outlook of national self-determination met with such enthusiastic response from not only colonial Koreans but also oppressed peoples all across the world?

With this question, let us go back to Charr's biography and his poem "World Democracy." According to the *New Korea*, Charr migrated to Hawaii in his early teens and worked at a sugar plantation between 1903 and 1905. He was one of the 7,266 first-generation Korean immigrants in the U.S. Their population remained rather stable during the following couple of decades since Imperial Japan did not allow colonial Koreans to migrate to America. American

---

14 Leo T. S. Ching, *Becoming Japanese: Colonial Taiwan and the Politics of Identity Formation* (Berkeley: University of California Press, 2001).

immigration policy since the Chinese Exclusion Act in 1882 also blocked Koreans' immigration. The 1917 Immigration Act (The Asiatic Barred Zone Act) banned Asian peoples' immigration except for the Japanese and Filipinos. Furthermore, Asian immigrants were prevented from becoming American citizens by naturalization laws and this barrier was maintained until the 1940s. In these circumstances, the United States military was reluctant to allow Asian immigrants' enlistment for fear of them making claims to citizenship. Although U.S. eventually accepted several thousands of non-citizen "colored" people to serve in the American military, this amounted to no more than temporary measures during the war emergency.[15] Some of these soldiers were able to acquire U.S. citizenship later, but nothing was guaranteed at the time of their enlistment and their naturalization became a reality only after going through numerous legal obstacles.

In short, Charr and other Korean immigrants in the U.S. did not initially belong to the category of "American citizens" recruited by "Uncle Sam." Nonetheless, the speaker of Charr's poem celebrates "the Stars and Stripes" as the protector of freedom and human rights and deliberately leaves out mention of racial discrimination in the United States. Instead, he proclaims universal ideals such as freedom, human rights, peace, and "world democracy." Neither does he speak as an individual "world citizen." Likewise, the brothers he will "fight together" with are called "children of Belgium, Britain, and France" rather than individual proper names, say, Hercule Poirot, Edward, or André. That is, he performs as a member of the Korean nation toward members of other nations as if membership to a nation is necessary for their political acts and speeches.

This situation is what Arendt analyzed as "the paradox of human rights." According to Arendt, ever since "the rights of man" became linked to national sovereignty in "The Declaration of the Rights of Man and of the Citizen,"[16]

---

15 "Military History of Asian Americans," *World Heritage Encyclopedia*, http://self.gutenberg.org/articles/Military_history_of_Asian_Americans.

16 Article I of the Declaration reads: "Men are born and remain free and equal in rights. Social distinctions can be founded only on the common good." The aforementioned "rights of man" then become grounded in the "Nation" in Article III: "The principle of any sovereignty resides essentially in the Nation. No body, no individual can exert authority which does not emanate expressly from it."

human rights have never been granted to individuals per se or human beings in general. Instead, these "universal" human rights have been protected and enforced only as national rights. In other words, human rights can only be secured by belonging to a specific nation under international law and the system of modern sovereignty.[17] In this world composed of a "family of nations," there is no place for a world citizen who does not belong to a nation-state first. Membership to a nation is a prerequisite not only for citizenship and the enjoyment of "universal" human rights but also for fighting for such rights in the public sphere or on real battlefields. Conversely, the "denationalization" (i.e. denaturalization) of "stateless peoples" or ethnic "minorities" in Europe during the interwar period deprived them of the very right to have rights, degrading them to "refugees" vulnerable to extreme violence and mass killings like the Holocaust. Through this analysis, Arendt revealed the blind spot of the notion of human rights and pointed to the fundamental contradictions embedded in the nation-state system.

Compared to "denationalized" refugees in Arendt's analysis, the legal status of colonial peoples was more ambivalent. If "nationality" means that someone belongs to a specific nation-state in terms of the legal order, Charr had Japanese nationality since Imperial Japan had stipulated that "those who had been subjects of the Korean Empire would acquire the Japanese nationality for foreign countries"[18] after the 1910 Japanese annexation of Korea. However, he did not belong to the Japanese nation (*kokumin*) within the domestic political order of Imperial Japan. Colonial Koreans were only subject to the Japanese constitution "in principle" but, in practice, they were subject to the provisional decree of the Japanese Government-General of Korea.[19] They were categorized and identified pejoratively as *chōsenjin* (the Korean people) vis-à-vis the mainland Japanese (the Japanese nation). They were torn between exclusion and inclusion,

---

17 Hannah Arendt, *The Origin of Totalitarianism* (New York: Harcourt Brace & Company, 1973), 230.

18 According to international law expert Yamada Saburo, any Korean "including the ones who became naturalized in foreign countries and therefore hold dual citizenship" was to be regarded as a Japanese subject. Yi Sŭngil, *Legislative Policy of the Government-General of Colonial Korea* (Seoul: Yŏksabip'yŏngsa, 2008), 94.

19 Yi, *Legislative Policy of the Government-General of Colonial Korea*, 93.

their actual status and their status on paper.[20] In this respect, the "state of exception," Giorgio Agamben's term for refugees, seems to be more appropriate to describe the legal status of the colonized as "semi-refugees," who were governed by the imperial state but excluded from the imperial nation.

The speaker in Charr's poem, who describes himself as "a defeated soldier from a perished country," identifies himself with the colonial "Korean" as a semi-refugee. Trying to fight for world democracy alongside the peoples of "Belgium, Britain, and France," he sings as a "Korean," not as an American or Japanese, nor as an individual world citizen. For him, the pursuit of universal ideals such as freedom and human rights is linked to the hope that "when the Polish and the Serbs return home, my countrymen will also be free." Such aspirations lead him to envision Korean people's "national self-determination" in order to secure freedom, equality, and human rights that could not be guaranteed in the U.S., the country of his residence, or in Japan, the country of his legal nationality. In this vein, individuals' struggle for rights became interconnected with the collective "national claim" of the Korean people, because "a nation" was not only a prerequisite for an individual to have rights but also a qualification to be recognized in the international order led by a few great powers.

Korean historiographies have long described these struggles as an anti-colonial movement for national self-determination. However, such familiar explanations have faced fierce challenges in the last couple of decades because such a view took for granted that the Korean nation was a given, self-evident identity, although in fact it was an "imagined community," as Benedict Anderson defined it. Post-nationalist criticism on the nation-state and nationalism has strengthened the tendency to critically reassess national self-determination, which used to be regarded as the practical and theoretical ground for decolonizing struggles. Especially, third-world nationalism has even been regarded as a "regressive" idea that goes against the notion of universal human rights or

---

20 For analyses on colonial governmentality based on Agamben's "state of exception," see Nasser Hussain, *The Jurisprudence of Emergency: Colonialism and the Rule of Law* (Ann Arbor: University of Michigan Press, 2003) and Simone Bignall and Marcelo Svirsky, eds., *Agamben and Colonialism* (Edinburgh: Edinburgh University Press, 2012).

democracy embedded within Western nationalism.

In fact, the adverse effects of national self-determination was already noticeable from the end of World War I. Wilson's self-determination was basically a plan to dismantle the old empires of Central and Eastern Europe, and divide them into several nation-states. The problem was that there were many different ethnic peoples that had inhabited these regions for multiple generations, which made it impossible to establish "pure" nation-states based on the trinity of territory, ethnicity, and state. The League of Nations, led by the great powers, tried to solve this problem through institutional supplementary measures without modifying the basic framework of the nation-state system. The Peace Treaties, according to Arendt, "lumped together many peoples in single states, called some of them 'state people' and entrusted them with the government"[21] while seeking to secure minority peoples' rights with "Minority Treaties." However, the ruling state people perceived this international intervention as a violation of their national sovereignty, whereas the "minorities" began to yearn for their own nation-state(s), resulting in the exacerbation of national conflicts between them. Under the premise that a "nation" is identified with pure ethnicity and that a state should be monopolized by one nation, many ethnic minorities, deprived of their nationality (denationalized), turned into refugees. The most terrible consequence of the conflicts was ethnic cleansing, which characterized the Holocaust. Due to the failure of Wilsonian idealism in Central and Eastern Europe, the interwar period in European history is remembered as a time when the "evil specter of nationalism" was invoked.

In this respect, contemplation on national self-determination of the colonized "intersects" with emerging political philosophy on the refugee issue. This is not for "applying" cutting-edge European theories on refugees in an anachronistic way to the history of non-Western regions. Such "intersection" is legitimized by the fact that refugees and the "colonized nation" as political subjects emerged simultaneously during and after the First World War. So far, the former has been connected to an apocalyptic narrative about the "decline of the nation-state

21 Arendt, *The Origin of Totalitarianism*, 270.

and the end of the rights of man."[22] The latter, on the contrary, has been linked to an Exodus narrative of the colonized who resisted the imperial order by demanding "national self-determination" and human rights. However, it is noteworthy that those two narratives, which have been handed down in the history of Europe and in the history of former colonies, actually pertain to a single historical moment.

It is problematic that these narratives of birth and decline seem to be twisted into one as in a Möbius strip. On the one hand, struggles for national self-determination in colonies were a project of liberation in order to defend the rights of those who were excluded from the world that had been divided into imperial nation-states. On the other hand, the "refugee" issue seemed like a dystopian future that the colonized would inevitably encounter when they were liberated "into" a nation-state. Thus, considering refugees and colonized nations as Western/non-Western historical experiences situated within simultaneous relations raises ominous questions: Was the colonized "nation," "born" as a political subject during the era of the "decline" of European nation-states, predetermined to fail by repeating European history? How should we understand the relationship between Western nations and colonized nations?

Western theories on nationalism do not provide a satisfactory answer to these questions. A well-known version of nationalism theories makes a distinction between civic nation and ethnic nation. This dichotomy, which finds its origins in the "nation" of the French Revolution and the "Volk" of Germany respectively, defines the former as a rational and democratic political community and the latter as a cultural and ethnic community. In this binary approach, it is obviously the latter that often becomes subject to criticism, which targets the fictional nature of cultural and ethnic identity and exemplifies the dangers of exclusivity and homogeneity of ethnic nationalism with numerous historical cases.

A problem arises when civic nation and ethnic nation are presented as different historical entities, even though they have never existed in purely separate forms. The worst, although not so rare, result, is to postulate two nations as Western normality versus non-Western deviation: Western nationalism (Britain, France, and the U.S.) that had inherited the tradition of universalism

---

22 See especially Chapter 9 in Arendt, *The Origin of Totalitarianism.*

and democracy of the French Revolution versus non-Western nationalism (including Nazi Germany) that was enthralled with the myth of ethnic purity and cultural homogeneity. Many critics of Korean nationalism also implicitly or explicitly presuppose such a dichotomy. In this binary, the "disease" of nationalism is regarded as endemic only in the non-West. While its historical causes remain unquestioned, the "disease" is explained as if it stems from certain non-Western attributes, which should be "cured" by the "Enlightenment" of Western rationality. The notion of "national character" that had been dismissed for being mythic and fictional is thus reintroduced to put forth a claim that the source of all evil lies in non-Western national character.

It is surprising that contemporary criticism of nationalism blindly repeats the colonial discourse of the colonial period. To overcome this view, it is necessary to re-emphasize colonial violence as a prior cause. Colonial violence was inflicted on the colonized along with international "law," which only guaranteed human rights and equality to those within "the family of nations." Under this legal order, the colonized were subject to the colonial government of imperial states but were excluded from the imperial "nations." As a result, the anti-colonial resistance of the colonized naturally took the direction of claiming that they were a "nation" and "the subject of human rights."

What matters here is to grasp the difference between the imperial nation and the national claims of the colonized. When the focus is only put on congealed forms of representation, colonial peoples' national claims just seem to repeat imperial nations as a mirror image, trapped in what Naoki Sakai calls "the scheme of co-figuration."[23] However, the political practice of colonial peoples resisting imperial rule did not remain in the realm of static, objectified representations. Colonized "nations," constituted as political subjects in the practice of resistance, did not just repeat the "nation" of empires, but "renewed" it. This process of renewal unfolded in a way that was opposite to what the civic/ethnic nation dichotomy explains. Colonized nations "extorted" the imperial concept of the nation that had exhausted the possibilities of revolution and democracy, and put it back on track toward revolution and democracy.

---

[23] Naoki Sakai, *Translation and Subjectivity: On "Japan" and Cultural Nationalism* (Minneapolis: University of Minnesota Press, 1997), 40-71.

3. World War I and the Conflicting Usages of Democracy

Alain Badiou argues that the word democracy is "the dominant emblem of contemporary political society" and the "untouchable" core in the symbolic system of the modern world. All forms of political and social conflict pivot around this emblem and unfold in a way that appropriates its symbolic significance.[24] Any participant in politics must start from the emblem of democracy, on which their self-justification as well as criticism of their enemies should be based. Indeed, in every important phase of modern world history there have been fierce conflicts over the usage of democracy. World War I was one of those eventful moments. There were numerous conflicting claims to democracy during this period between (a) the Allied Powers v. the Central Powers, (b) the "forerunners" of imperial powers such as the U.K., France v. the "latecomers" such as Germany and Japan, (c) European realism v. American pragmatic idealism, and (d) the imperial order of the world v. the anti-colonial struggles of the colonized.

The Allied Powers understood World War I as a transition from absolutism to democracy. Wilson claimed to be the savior of democracy when the U.S. declared war against Germany.[25] Some German and Austrian socialists also justified their participation in the war by claiming to protect freedom and democracy from the Tsarist autocracy of Russia.[26] However, more weight was put on the Allied Powers' claim when the Tsarist Empire became dismantled due to the Russian Revolution. Around 1918, the confrontation of war seemed to lie between the "democratic" countries of the Allied Powers and the absolutist countries of the Central powers except Japan. The term "democracy" here refers to a republic or a constitutional monarchy that represents the will of the people. Wilson often employed the phrase "self-determination of the

---

24 Alain Badiou, "The Democratic Emblem," in *Democracy in What State?* ed. Georgio Agamben et al. (New York: Columbia University Press, 2010), 6-7.

25 Manela, *The Wilsonian Moment*, 35. Wilson claimed that the Kaiser's regime was illegitimate because it lacked the consent of the German people, justifying U.S. participation in WWI as an act of making the world "safe for democracy."

26 Hwang Tongha, "'Wars of National Self-Defence': The German Social Democratic Party and Rosa Luxemburg," *Marxism 21* 11, no. 3 (2014): 12-39.

governed" in order to indicate an institutional democracy. Wilson's Fourteen Points contained the idea of dismantling the old empires in Europe and dividing them into several democratic nation-states, which was realized to a certain degree with the dissolution of the Ottoman Empire and the Austro-Hungarian Empire after the war.

Recent studies, however, have pointed out that World War I was basically triggered by the fierce competition between the imperial powers regardless of their constitutions.[27] Along this line of confrontation, Germany and Japan, two imperial "latecomers," were on the same side, challenging the hegemony of the "forerunners" and revealing the deception of their claim to democracy. In particular, Japan, one of the Allied Powers, kept running into conflicts with the U.S. with regard to the racist U.S. immigration laws, Japan's intervention in Siberia, and the handover of Shandong. Rumors circulated that Japan would secretly align with Germany[28] and several fictions about the U.S.-Japan war were published.[29] The U.S. criticized Japan's militarism and promoted anti-Japanese sentiments about the "yellow peril" while Japanese intellectuals viciously exposed the hypocrisy of the U.S. promotion of democracy.[30]

For example, historian Ōrui Noboru argued that the Allied Powers' claim of "a war of liberalism against absolutism" was nothing but propaganda. He instead sympathized with German scholar Erich Marcks, who analyzed the war as a clash between old and new imperialism. However, he disagreed with

---

27 For analyses of WWI based on "the power transition theory" in the context of political science, see Kim Chunsŏk, "The Lessons of the First World War and Implications for International Relations of East Asia," *Critical Review of History* 108 (2014): 154-187.

28 For example, the *New Korea* on March 21, 1918, ran several articles on U.S.-Japan conflicts and an alleged Japan-Germany alliance such as "American Views on Japan's Dispatch of Troops," "Russia and Japan's Dispatch of Troops," "Opposing Japan's Dispatch of Troops with the Lesson from the Precedent Case of Korea," "Japan Finally Dispatched Troops," "German Journalism Suddenly Turned Pro-Japanese," "Secret Treaties on the Division of Russian Territory between Germany and Japan," and so on.

29 Homer Lea, *The Valor of Ignorance* (New York: Harper and Brothers, 1909). There was also a book titled *The Next Great War*, written by an unknown navy officer and published by Kanao Bun'endō in Tokyo in 1914. On these novels, see Yamamuro Shin'ichi et al., *World War I: The Starting Point of Contemporary* (Tokyo: Iwanami Shoten, 2014), 19-22.

30 The *New Korea* reported on anti-Japanese sentiments in the U.S., citing the American journal *Examiner* and senator James Hamilton Lewis. "Japan Is a Wolf in Sheep's Clothing," *New Korea*, April 11, 1918; "U.S.-Japan War Shall Break Out Soon," *New Korea*, April 25, 1918.

Marcks's characterization of new imperialism as defensive and limited, as opposed to the aggressive and expansive old imperialism. In Ōrui's view, the competition between the great powers was not a matter of who was just, but who was strong. What drew his attention even more was Marcks's conception of "federal imperialism." Marcks suggested that Germany create a federal-state system with other peoples in the Central European cultural sphere in order to confront the old empires of Western Europe. This project was contradictory as it included conflicting ideas of federal solidarity and imperial expansion. Nonetheless, Ōrui expected that this idea would be "the trend of the new world" when the acquisition of overseas colonies reached its limit, and that it was the most viable vision for the Japanese Empire.[31] Within less than a couple of decades, his prospects were realized in the form of Nazi Pan-Germanism and Japan's Greater East Asia Co-Prosperity Sphere. One of the causal links between the two Great Wars was the recognition of latecomer empires that Wilsonian democracy was just "a billboard that deceives the world and conceals the real motive of national interest."[32]

U.S.-Japan conflicts over racial issues escalated Japan's criticism of Wilson's promotion of democracy. Law scholar Ninagawa Arata argued that Japan had faithfully followed the path to civilization with the United States' guidance ever since the beginning of Japan-U.S. relations in the 1850s, so anti-Japanism in the U.S. was like inviting a guest and then kicking him out. He went as far as to warn that Japan-U.S. relations would be threatened if the U.S. kept violating the principles of equality with racist sentiments against Japan, which also contradicted Wilson's idealism of "permanent peace." Behind this remark was the confidence that Japan was no longer a small country that at best had been treated as an "unexpectedly civilized country" by the United States.[33]

International political scholar Kamikawa Hikomatsu also warned that Wilson had better amend the racist American laws first before promoting lofty

31 Ōrui Noburu, "Erich Marcks' Imperialism and the World War," *Revue Diplomatique* (*Gaikō Jihō*), June 1, 1918. Here, Ōrui seems to be referring to Erich Marcks's *Der Imperialismus und der Weltkrieg* (1916).

32 "The Object of the War (1)," *Daily News*, January 30, 1918.

33 Ninagawa Arata, "Anti-Japanese Sentiment in the United States and Peace," *Revue Diplomatique*, March 1, 1918, 16-20.

humanitarianism. He insisted the racist immigration policies of the U.S. could cause armed conflicts between the two countries, insinuating that Japan, which was suffering from a serious population problem, would resort to any means possible for the sake of its national interest.[34]

Japan, which was struggling with rapid population growth, was discontent with the U.S. policy of blocking both the gateway of militaristic territorial acquisition and peaceful migration.[35] In this light, Tanaka Suiichirō pointed out that the object of the League of Nations and the notion of national self-determination were contradictory in principle.[36] According to him, the postwar order envisioned by the League of Nations was to maintain borders and territories around 1919, whereas nationalism boosted by national self-determination had a tendency to dismantle existing territorial boundaries between states. Land is static and limited in nature but nations are dynamic entities that always progress and decline over time. If territorial issues are therefore only determined by the will of the residents according to the principle of "national self-determination," it would necessarily lead to conflicts over national borders, betraying the aim of the League of Nations to maintain peace by fixing borders.

Tanaka argued that the idea of national self-determination was so outdated that it had already been crossed out from international law since the Bismarck era, when "might is right" was declared as the principle of realpolitik. However, he also suggested his own solution for reconciling nationalism with the aim of the League of Nations: guaranteeing both free trade and free immigration. Tanaka did not deny the core proposition of Wilson's idealism that free trade would ultimately bring about world peace but he, at the same time, pointed out that free trade should go hand in hand with open immigration. Criticizing American racism with the very language of Wilson's idealism, as Tanaka did,

---

34 Kamikawa Hikomatsu, "Urgent Need to Resolve Racism," *Revue Diplomatique,* January 1919, 32-40.

35 The population of Japan, which was estimated to be around 30 million during the early Meiji era, rose to 56 million in 1920, escalating a sense of crisis that had a strong impact on Japan-U.S. relations, especially in terms of U.S. immigration policy.

36 Tanaka Suiichirō, "The League of Nations and Nationalism," *Revue Diplomatique,* December 1918, 1251-1269.

was the most viable compromise for Japan, which could not completely oppose the order of the League of Nations yet.

In the light of today's world where laborers' migration is still controlled along racial and ethnic lines but goods and capital can move freely across borders, Tanaka's criticism divulged the internal paradox of liberalism from which Wilsonian idealism derived. In fact, exposing the deception of Western-centered ideology was a unique function of Japan as a location of enunciation in world history during the past century. The discourse on "overcoming modernity" in the 1940s or even Japan's recent right-wing ideology of "normal statehood" contains a grain of truth that ruptures the West-centered world order. This may be the reason why the confrontation between Japan and the West is still recalled as a dramatic moment in the postcolonial tradition of the tri-continents (Asia, Africa, and Latin America).[37] However, Japan's path to another empire that just sought to replace the hegemony of the West cannot be a real alternative to the colonial world order. In this vein, former colonies under Japanese rule and their experiences may serve as important historical resources for rethinking decolonization, and revealing the limitations of both Western centrism and Japan-centric Pan-Asianism.

In this context, it is worth paying attention to the ground on which Japan demanded racial equality from the United States. It was the national confidence that Japan had achieved a civilization comparable to that of the whites in America. Japan argued that discrimination simply based on skin color was unjust when the degree of civilization was similar. To make this claim more persuasive, however, Japan had to repeatedly proved that it could meet Western

---

37 Most postcolonial analyses of Japan's Asianism fail to fully account for its limits as another form of expansionism. For example, Robert J. C. Young describes the Japanese victory against Russia in 1905 as the first successful attempt at confronting European imperialism from outside the West, which leads him to claim the year 1905 as decisive for the ideological development of all national movements. In regard to the so-called "The Greater East Asian War," Young, citing Abdel-Malek, argues that the most significant aspect of this war for the colonized people was the fact that the Western imperial powers in Southeast Asia were defeated by Japan, a non-white Asian regional power, regardless of the final outcome of the war. (Young, *Postcolonialism*, 100, 162). However, I argue that these Japanese "achievements" can hardly be regarded as "postcolonial" in its true sense because it kept the colonial order intact and merely replaced white with Japanese or secured Japan's place in the Western world order. This assessment should be applied to national self-determination movements by the colonized as well: Were they merely trying to secure their place in the existing world order or disrupt it altogether? This question will be addressed again in Section 4.

"civilized standards." One of these requirements was the implementation of an institutional democracy. Some worried that Japan's fight for democracy in all sincerity might contradict the "Japanese national body," the emperor system.[38] Nonetheless, Japan was forced to expand its democratic system to a certain extent as the world witnessed the fall of numerous totalitarian regimes during and after World War I. It was in this space of possibility that the Taishō Democracy emerged. Ozaki Yukio, once a militarist, was reborn as "the father of parliamentary politics" after witnessing the brutality of the war while Yoshino Sakuzō ardently promoted his ideas on a "government for the people" (minponshugi) in the Central Review (Chūōkōron).[39] On September 29, 1918, the full-fledged party cabinet was established for the first time in Japan.

However, this space of possibility that was founded on civilized standards was also the limit of its discursive horizon. A civilized standard was a structural cause for Japan, the only Eastern empire, "to represent the interests of colored peoples all over the world" by proclaiming racial equality; but, at the same time, they used this principle to oppress Korean independence movements and impose the Twenty-One Demands on China under the pretext of civilizational hierarchy.[40] Imperial Japan's anti-racism was not elevated to radical anti-colonialism but only justified its own colonial rule over other Asian peoples while priding itself as the representative of the "yellow" (Asian) race.

This duality of invasion and solidarity that recurred in Japan's Asianism — invading other Asian countries in the name of a civilization mission while proclaiming solidarity — resulted from the violence of modernity itself.[41] This paradox was not unique to Japan and similarly repeated in the British colonization of India, Ireland, and Egypt and French interventions in Vietnam and Algeria, thus revealing the very limit of civilized standards. The United States also cracked down on Filipino liberation movements while presenting itself as a supporter of democracy.

---

38 "The Object of the War (1)," Daily News, January 30, 1918.

39 See Narita Ryūichi, Taishō Democracy, trans. Yi Kyusu (Seoul: Ŏmunhaksa, 2012).

40 Kamikawa, "Urgent Need to Resolve Racism," 38.

41 Yonetani Masafumi, Asia/Japan, trans. Cho Ŭnmi (Seoul: Greenbee, 2010).

Wilson's notion of self-determination similarly functioned within this fundamental limit. Early on, Japanese experts had examined the Fourteen Points, especially Point V pertaining to colonial territories, and understood its implications in terms of real politics. According to Tachi Sakutaro, an international law scholar, drawing national borders based on "the consent of the population concerned" had two completely different meanings. Lenin's idea was an attempt to fundamentally redefine the existing geopolitical order by literally taking into consideration the interests of the population in any given territory. The other was a suggestion that the population concerned should be taken into consideration in postwar negotiations with defeated states over their occupied territories. Tachi evaluated Lenin's idea as "a preposterous suggestion" unprecedented in the history of international law but Wilson's concept of self-determination would never exceed the scope of the latter which Japan had no reason to oppose.[42] Generally speaking, this was an accurate judgment and provided the ground for Japan to warn colonial Koreans not to misunderstand Wilson's notion of national self-determination. A people's qualification for self-determination would not be determined by the will of the people concerned but by the international legal order. Moreover, the great powers that had set up the international legal order would never endorse the independence of their colonies. It was this strong realist idea that prevailed in the world of the time.

However, the blind spot that clever realists can never see is that reality itself is always open to change. Wilson's idea of self-determination was indeed within the imperialist order but, at the same time, marked ruptures within that order. Behind Wilson's Fourteen Points Speech was The Inquiry, a project group consisting of 150 or so progressive scholars. The group was deeply involved in Wilson's policy making and its core members accompanied Wilson to the Paris Peace Conference. Hence, Wilson's vision of a postwar world order cannot simply be reduced to an individual's sheer idealism or to another realism that adhered to the old order. In addition to the confrontation between old imperialism versus new imperialism, there was another political rupture

---

42 Tachi Sakutaro, "Treating Territorial Issues and the Interests of the Population Concerned," *Revue Diplomatique*, March 1918, 1-13.

that contemporary historians refer to as "European realism" versus "American idealism."[43]

Henri Lambert's paper entitled "National Self-Determination," published in May 1918, exemplifies American idealism that challenged the imperialist world order.[44] Lambert, a Belgian liberal intellectual, stayed in the U.S. for two and a half years during World War I. At this time, he interacted with Colonel Edward M. House, the leader of The Inquiry, and influenced Wilson's policy making. In particular, Lambert is known to have influenced the formation of Point III on free trade. His ideas are well condensed in the title of his book *Pax Economica* and its lengthy subheading: "Freedom of International Exchange, the Sole Method for the Permanent and Universal Abolition of War."[45] As the subtitle shows, American idealism was a product of a crisis in which the existing world order could no longer be sustained. In this sense, American idealism was pragmatic idealism in nature.

The First World War, which caused devastating damage, was regarded as a sign of the collapse or serious crisis in Western "civilization." The intense scramble for colonies between the great powers throughout "the age of empire (1875–1913)" had almost reached its limits. As Lenin described, "for the first time the world was completely divided up, so that in the future only redivision is possible, i.e., territories can only pass from one 'owner' to another, instead of passing as ownerless territory to an owner."[46] The only possibility left in such a world would be an endless repetition of territorial battles between imperial states. Such an acknowledgement prevailed among the U.S. and the other European powers and served as a strong motivation for the foundation of

---

43 On scholars who tend to analyze and assess Wilson's notion within the framework of realism v. idealism, see the introduction in Lloyd E. Ambrosius, *Wilsonian Statecraft: Theory and Practice of Liberal Internationalism during World War I* (Wilmington: SR Books, 1991).

44 Henry Lambert, "National Self-Determination," *The North American Review* 207, no. 749 (1918): 541-548. Lambert's writing was translated into Japanese and featured in the *Revue Diplomatique* 329 (July 1918): 206-216.

45 Henry Lambert, *Pax Economica* (New York: John C. Rankin Company, 1917). Point III of Wilson's The Fourteen Points reads as follows: "The removal, so far as possible, of all economic barriers and the establishment of an equality of trade conditions among all the nations consenting to the peace and associating themselves for its maintenance."

46 Vladimir Lenin, *Imperialism: the Highest Stage of Capitalism* (New Delhi: General Press, 2021), loc. 1587 of 2806, Kindle.

the League of Nations and the pursuit of a new world order.

There was another crisis, however, which these western powers were more reluctant to acknowledge. The values by which they justified colonial rule had ironically become corrupted in the very process of colonization. There was a pervasive sense of unease that the insane violence, exploitation, and human rights abuses perpetrated in the colonial territories were tearing down the proud heritage of Western civilization, including freedom, equality, human rights, and rationality. Such anxiety about the fall of Western civilization was a haunting theme in the literature of the British empire from Jane Austen's *Mansfield Park* (1814) to Joseph Conrad's *The Heart of Darkness* (1899).[47] The brutal cruelty of slavery practiced in the Belgian territory of Congo came as a shock to even the Europeans. There was also anxiety about a crisis of white supremacy that had supported colonial rule over colored peoples. In *The Great Gatsby* (1925), set in 1922, F. Scott Fitzgerald conveyed a sense of crisis in his time with a novel character Tom Buchanan's saying that "the white race will be utterly submerged."[48] In that scene, Tom refers to Lothrop Stoddard's *The Rising Tide of Color: The Threat against White World-Supremacy* (1920), which warned that the exponential population growth of the colored peoples could bring about the fall of the white empire. There even appeared physiological and statistical predictions that the countless casualties and disabled from the First World War, which was cast as a "civil war" between white peoples, would accelerate the impending fall of the white race.[49]

Anxiety about the collapse of the white dominant world also stemmed from the increasingly fierce resistance of the colonized ranging from the 1913 anti-France protests in Angola, the 1914 uprising in Kenya, the 1916 Easter Rising in Ireland, the Barue uprising against Portuguese rule in Mozambique in 1917, and anti-Japan resistance in colonial Korea.[50] Anti-colonial resistance

---

47 Through his "contrapuntal reading" of the canons in English literature, Edward W. Said has analyzed the traces of colonialism that are buried deep within the "civilizations" of the imperial metropole. See Edward W. Said, *Culture and Imperialism* (London: Chatto & Windus, 1993).

48 Scott F. Fitzgerald, *The Great Gatsby* (London: Harper Press, 2010), 18.

49 "Racial Issues after the War," *New Korea*, July 4, 1918.

50 While Robert J. C. Young constructs an expansive archive of the histories and theories of postcolonial resistance in the tri-continents, the histories of East Asian uprisings are mostly omitted. See Young,

had existed even before the advent of modern Western concepts such as human rights, freedom, equality, and national self-determination. However, once the colonized began to appropriate those concepts to criticize Western imperialism, these words became powerful weapons for the decolonizing struggles of the colonized, who had been excluded from abstract universality. The cost of defending colonial territories from not only other imperial powers but also the anti-colonial resistance of the colonized kept rising, which led to questioning the efficiency of colonial domination and, in its extreme form, insisting on abandoning colonial territories.

Russia's socialist revolution, which took place during World War I, was another important factor in the search for a new world order. Socialists continued to criticize imperialism since advocating for socialist internationalism at the First International in 1864. At the Second International in 1896, the right to self-determination of the oppressed peoples was approved for the first time, and three years later, in 1899, the Brünn Congress endorsed the position of nationalist internationalism. Of course, there were always ruptures and ambiguity in Marxist positions on colonial and national issues. The paradox of colonial modernity was deeply rooted in Marxism as well, leaving it uncertain whether to fully criticize colonialism or to approve of it as an essential step toward modernization. In addition, the socialist position as to what extent the Marxist movement would be in solidarity with anti-colonial nationalist movements continued to fluctuate with time, because from a Marxist perspective they inherently have bourgeois limits.

However, Lenin's theory of imperialism and self-determination became a major turning point in regard to the Marxist view of colonial questions. By identifying imperialism as the highest stage of capitalism — or "state monopoly capitalism" — Lenin was able to lay the theoretical grounds that necessitated solidarity between socialist class struggles and anti-colonial resistance. Furthermore, opposing European socialists who criticized national self-determination with the cause of proletarian internationalism, he insisted that the principle of national self-determination had to be consistently applied to

Postcolonialism, 159-334. The shared history of East Asia, most of which is kept in the national history of each country, needs to be rewritten as part of the global history of decolonization.

all ethnic minorities and colonial peoples.[51] Initially, Lenin's radical idea of self-determination originated from opposition against czarist Russian imperialism. Under the censorship of the czarist regime, Lenin raised the colonial issue by changing the Russian Empire to Japan and the Russian colonies to colonial Korea.[52]

> Let us suppose that a Japanese condemns the annexation of the Philippines by the Americans. The question is: will many believe that he does so because he has a horror of annexations as such, and not because he himself has a desire to annex the Philippines? And shall we not be constrained to admit that the "fight" the Japanese is waging against annexations can be regarded as being sincere and politically honest only if he fights against the annexation of Korea by Japan, and urges freedom for Korea to secede from Japan?[53]

To contemporary South Korean readers, the significance of the above passage is twofold. First, Lenin criticized Japan with the same logic that Japan would use to criticize Wilson by indicating the hypocritical contradiction of promoting the self-determination of oppressed peoples in other countries and not recognizing the self-determination of its own colonies. However, whereas Japan, criticizing the contradiction of Wilsonian idealism, arrived at the realistic conclusion that "might is right," Lenin went into the opposite direction. He applied the same logic to his own country, Russia, and proceeded toward a radical idealism that fully recognized the right to self-determination of all oppressed peoples. This principle was maintained until the Russian Revolution, culminating in his party's platform in March 1917 that proclaimed the right of minority peoples in Russia to form independent states.

Secondly, Lenin's radical notion of national self-determination was inspired

---

51 Lenin had written a number of works regarding this issue, including *The Right of Nations to Self-Determination* (1914), "The Discussion on Self-Determination Summed Up" (1916), "The Socialist Revolution and the Right of Nations to Self-Determination" (1916), and more.

52 In the preface to the 1917 edition, Lenin confessed that he had to write the book under Tsarist censorship and urged his readers to pay "special attention" to this specific passage, where Japan needed to be replaced with Russia and Korea with Russia's colonies such as Poland and Finland to get his true message across. Lenin, *Imperialism, loc.* 89 of 2806, Kindle.

53 Lenin, *Imperialism*, loc. 2562 of 2806, Kindle.

by various uprisings in colonial territories, including colonial Korea, to which Lenin referred in his above-mentioned 1916 writing.[54] Having a deep appreciation of the puissance of the oppressed peoples to fight against imperialism, Lenin assigned a dual mission to the Russian proletariat. One was to fully recognize the right to self-determination of all "nations" in opposition to "Great Russian nationalism," and the second was to keep the unity of this resistance and integrate it into an international organization in opposition to the "nationalism of all nations." Lenin's dual mission was based on the distinction between the national self-determination of oppressed nations and the nationalism of oppressing nations. A revolution, according to this dual logic, starts from crushing the oppressors' nationalism by supporting the self-determination of oppressed nations, and is achieved by coalescing these liberated nations into international solidarity and preventing them from lapsing into another form of oppressive nationalism.[55] Contrary to European socialists, who insisted that the proletarian revolution of the developed countries should lead the liberation of backward colonial peoples, Lenin's theory of national self-determination opened up the possibility of driving change in the center through the liberation of the periphery.

The post-revolutionary civil war and Stalin's rise to power precluded the realization of Lenin's radical version of self-determination. However, it is evident that Lenin's idea exerted strong pressure on the Allied Powers' postwar planning. Leon Trotsky fiercely denounced the hypocrisy of the Allied Powers that "demand self-determination for the peoples that are comprised within the borders of enemy states and to refuse self-determination to the peoples of their own state or of their own colonies."[56] Toward the end of World War I, British Prime Minister David Lloyd George, redefining British war objectives, adopted Bolshevik rhetoric in order to appeal to the leftists in the U.K. During this course, he bundled the Bolshevik term "self-determination" with Wilson's

---

54 Whereas the existing literature disproportionately examines the impact of the theories and ideas from the "center" on resistance movements taking place in the peripheries, the opposite — how resistance movements in the peripheries inspired the theories and ideas of the center — must also be examined. Just as the Irish resistance transformed Marx's take on colonialism, decolonizing resistance in Eastern Europe and the so-called "Far East" must have had a strong impact on Lenin's thought.

55 Vladimir Lenin, *The Right of Nations to Self-Determination* (Moscow: Foreign Languages Publishing House, 1947), 74. The original Russian version was published in 1914.

56 Manela, *The Wilsonian Moment*, 38.

"consent of the governed," which led to casually obfuscating the differences between them.[57] In this respect, it was not unreasonable for the Third International of 1919 to deride the League of Nations as having been designed to counteract revolutionary internationalism.

In short, Wilsonian idealism was a trial to overcome the overall crises by (1) containing the expansion of "latecomer" imperialism, (2) preventing Western civilization from collapsing from within, (3) appeasing anti-colonial resistance, (4) competing against socialist class struggles and Lenin's paradigm of national self-determination, and (5) optimizing the system of the market economy. This Wilsonian solution was by no means unprecedented. Rather, it had deep roots within the liberal anti-colonialism of the 18th century. Adam Smith's *The Wealth of Nations* (1776), as an example of this tradition, pointed out the economic inefficiency of a monopoly maintained by the political and military domination of colonial territories.[58] Smith believed that free trade would ultimately bring about greater benefit to imperial powers and equal rights for non-Europeans in the future despite the temporary tragedy of colonial rule. Smith's liberal anti-colonialism was inherited by the Manchester economists of the mid-19th century, such as Richard Cobden and John Bright, replaced by liberal imperialism in the late-19th-century "age of empire," and revived with Wilson's "pragmatic idealism" during the crisis of the great war.

Lambert's paper "National Self-Determination" exemplifies liberal thoughts deeply embedded within Wilson's pragmatic idealism. Reminding readers of war-ravaged Europe, he remarked that a pacifism that naively appeals to justice is nothing more than empty rhetoric. Detecting the real cause behind national conflicts as economic interests, he argued that peace could only be achieved with the economic development of all nations, which could only be guaranteed by free trade. Without this guarantee of free trade, strong nations were bound to form a bigger political economic bloc by expanding their territory as much as possible, which would inevitably result in the sacrifice of weaker nations. On the other hand, if the freedom of exchange was fully guaranteed, all countries

---

57 Manela, *The Wilsonian Moment*, 39.

58 Adam Smith, *An Inquiry into the Nature and Causes of the Wealth of Nations*, ed. Edwin M. Cannan (Chicago: University of Chicago Press, 1976), 130-131.

would be able to enjoy greater benefits without territorial expansion or colonial conquest. According to this logic, "national self-determination" was not the goal, but a side effect of economic world peace, *Pax Economica*, that free trade would realize. Carefully distinguishing the usage of "nation" and "nationality" and only confining the word "nation" to citizens of sovereign states, he wrote:

> National self-government is not an unquestionable principle, is not a truth that stands by itself as natural and immanent; it is a political contingency depending on such a progress of morality and progress as will be marked by international security. Freedom of nationalities cannot be the origin and *cause* of this security and peace; it can only be the natural, gradual, logical *consequence* of these.
>
> International security and peace must fundamentally manifest themselves in the economic life and relations of the nations. In proposing, as the third of his fourteen articles, "the removal, as far as possible, of all economic barriers and an equality of trade conditions for all nations," the President of the United States has enunciated the moral condition and, we may hope, has laid the moral foundation of a new and better world order, in which national collectivities will gradually find the necessary opportunities for the material and spiritual welfare and happiness of their members. Such will be the result, the blessed fruit, of a *Pax Economica*.[59]

According to Lambert, a democratic form of government is not the universal solution for all nationalities. Any hasty separation of the oppressed peoples from imperial rule before the firm establishment of a free economic system and international security would only bring about poverty, developmental stagnation, and security threats. Moreover, democratic electoral or parliamentary systems are not suitable for "young, uneducated and turbulent peoples." Pursuing the unconditional self-government of all nationalities by misunderstanding national self-determination would only lead to the dissolution of nation-states, a chaotic state of anarchy, and incessant wars. In order to qualify for self-determination, the nations first had to be "enlightened." Until sufficiently

---

[59] Lambert, "National Self-Determination," 548.

enlightened, each nationality had to remain stable within a larger political unit, an imperial state, and had to gradually progress from colonial rule to self-governance and from partial autonomy to independence.[60]

Lambert's writing made explicit Wilson's attitude toward the colonial question in general. As is well known, Wilson's stance was far from the position of the colonized who demanded immediate liberation. For Wilson, the right to self-determination and even democracy needed certain "qualification[s]," which would only be granted to "civilized" nations. However, colonial peoples, whose democratic potential had been denied by imperial powers and colonial discourse, radically transformed the usage of "democracy" in their struggles for liberation by appropriating Wilson's words.

4. The Resistance of the Colonized and A Renewal of Democracy

Michael Hardt and Antonio Negri assessed Wilson's solution to the crisis of imperialism as a form of "lucid foresight" and characterized him as an "efficient promoter of the passage" from imperialism to Empire.[61] Although Wilson's project was not realized during his era, it portrayed the image of "Empire" in a kind of future perfect tense. The "Wilsonian moment" therefore serves as a privileged reference point for a better understanding of today's postcolonial world in relation to the colonial past. From monopolistic capital that circulated within the economic blocs of imperial powers to transnational capital that flows throughout the world; from the formal subjugation of colonial labor to capital, which often took the form of modern slavery, to the real subjugation of immigrant labor "voluntarily" flowing from former colonies; from the territorial, political, and military rule of imperial powers to economic domination through multi-layered networks of power; from a colonial state

---

60 Lambert, "National Self-Determination," 545. The U.S., in fact, realized this idea in the Philippines, where a congressional election was introduced in 1907 and bicameral legislature in 1916. With the passing of the Philippines Independence Act in the U.S. Congress in 1934, the Philippines underwent a decade-long transition period and finally achieved political independence in 1946. At the same time, however, the U.S. military massacred around 600,000 Filipinos during the resistance movement led by Emilio Aguinaldo between 1899 and 1901.

61 Michael Hardt and Antonio Negri, *Empire* (Cambridge: Harvard University Pres, 2000), 176.

of exception in which the colonized were governed by arbitrary decrees to a state of exception that strips refugees of their rights by suspending normal legal order; from colonial racism to modern "racism without race."[62] This transition is not a simple replacement but a "different repetition" in the Deleuzian sense of the word.

Similarly, one could draw connections between the Wilsonian ideal of *Pax Economica* and the domination of *Homo Economicus* since the 1960s — when most of the former colonies achieved political independence — which was identified by Michel Foucault as neo-liberal governmentality.[63] While analyzing technologies of government based on economic rationality, Foucault highlighted the voluntary subjectivation of the governed instead of the sovereign power wielded by acts of domination or coercion by the state. Likewise, the liberated peoples from colonial rule were so driven by the desire for modernization and economic development that they voluntarily got themselves wrapped up in Empire's power network. Wilson's promise to grant the right to "self-determination" to colonial peoples someday has been paradoxically realized in this postcolonial world, where former colonies "voluntarily" choose subjection to the power network of "Empire."

Because of the ironic result of postcolonial history and the seemingly exhausted possibility of a transformation of the world, there is a widespread lament that democracy is "dead" on the one hand, and rampant distrust and hatred of democracy on the other hand. In the face of such a conundrum, how is it possible to reinvent political subjectivity without lapsing into blind faith in democracy or abandonment of it? Interestingly, contemporary political thinkers trying to answer this question derive their insights from Arendt's "paradox of human rights." Human rights were declared to be universal rights for anyone but were subject to nation(-ality) so that those who are not solidly incorporated into a nation-state find themselves in a condition of rightlessness.[64]

62 Etienne Balibar, "Is There a 'Neo-Racism?'" in *Race, Nation, Class: Ambiguous Identities*, trans. Chris Turner (London: Verso, 1991), 21-23.

63 Michel Foucault, *The Birth of Biopolitics: Lectures at the College de France, 1978-79*, trans. Graham Burchell (New York: Palgrave Macmillan, 2008), 225-227.

64 For surveys on the debates in political philosophy where Arendt's take on the contradiction of human rights is expanded on or criticized, see Ch'oe Wŏn, "The Issues of the Division of Korea

As a result, human rights amounted to nothing but the tautology of citizenship (the "rights of those who have rights") or just an empty abstract word (the "rights of those who have no rights.") This paradox reveals how the Holocaust, which was far from an exceptional deviation in human history, was structurally related to the nation-state system. The refugee issue was also not a specific problem during the interwar period but is a recurrent, contemporary one. In this context, Agamben suggested that the "refugee" is the only thinkable figure that allows the people of our time to critically reflect on the nation-state system, redefine existing categories such as human, citizen, sovereignty, etc., and build a new form of political thought and communities. Moreover, while seeking a way to go "outside" all sovereign laws/rights, Agamben went as far as to claim that the only right that we ought to pursue is having no rights at all.[65]

On the other hand, Jacques Rancière criticizes Agamben's argument for inducing a "depoliticization" of the people, and defines human rights anew as "the rights of those who have not the rights that they have and have the rights they have not."[66] The phrase "those who have not the rights that they have" entails that there are those who are deprived of the universal rights inscribed in "The Declaration of the Rights of Man and of the Citizen" (1789). To "have the rights they have not" means "those who have no share" can actually obtain and realize such rights in the process of claiming and struggling for universal rights. In short, human rights is the very process of struggle for actualizing universal rights which were declared but have not yet been realized.

Such a notion of human rights is linked to Rancière's idea of democracy. He uniquely defines the "police" (Fr. *la police*) as the dominant order that assigns hierarchical places and functions for each member of the community

---

and Its Reunification Seen from the Perspective of the Politics of Human Rights," *Humanities for Unification* 61 (2015): 119-151; and Chin T'aewŏn, "Right to Have Rights," *Webzin Minyŏn* 26 (June 2013). http://rikszine.korea.ac.kr/front/article/humanList.minyeon?selectArticle_id=384.

65 Giorgio Agamben, *Means without End: Notes on Politics*, trans. Vincenzo Binetti and Cesare Casarino (Minneapolis, MN: University of Minnesota Press, 2000), 15-25.

66 Jacques Rancière, "Who is the Subject of the Rights of Man?" *South Atlantic Quarterly* 103 (2004): 302.

and "politics" (Fr. *la politique*) as practices that oppose and interrupt the "police" order. For Rancière, democracy is not the sum of institutions such as rule of law, rule of majority, or parliamentary systems of consensus. Democracy instead can be measured by the possibility of "disagreement" by those who are excluded from the existing police order. It is a dynamic process where those without share push into the community from which they have been excluded, making claims to rights and equality. In this sense, democracy is paradoxically defined as "the power of those who have no qualification for exercising power."[67]

Rancière's perspective provides an important clue for reassessing the struggle of the colonized for national self-determination and its significance in relation to competing usages of democracy.[68] The colonized refused to just sit and wait for liberation as promised by Wilson. They opposed colonial discourse which advised the colonized to be guided by "good shepherds"[69] and enlightened with Western civilization in order to qualify for democracy. Instead, they insisted on the self-determination of all peoples with such recklessness that it must have been regarded as "democratic surplus" by the imperial powers. They appropriated the term "nation," which was not allowed to colonized peoples, and demanded their own rights under that name. They constituted themselves as political subjects challenging the international "police" order that divided the world with exclusive qualifications and thresholds.

It is necessary, however, to discern such voices carefully. For instance, let us look at the previous quotes again from "A Letter of Congratulations to President Wilson."

To His Excellency, Woodrow Wilson, the President of the United States

---

67 Jacques Rancière, *Dissensus: On Politics and Aesthetics* (London: Bloomsbury Publishing, 2015), 78.

68 These terms, which describe the resistance of the colonized, are derived from the following works by Rancière. While he originally used those terms to analyze domestic politics within a single nation-state, I "displaced" them onto a transnational level. Jacques Rancière, *On the Shores of Politics*, trans. Liz Heron (New York: Verso, 2007); Jacque Rancière, *The Names of History*, trans. Hassan Melehy (Minneapolis, MN: University of Minnesota Press, 1994).

69 Jacques Rancière, *Hatred of Democracy*, trans. Steve Corcoran (New York: Verso, 2009), 37.

The North American General Assembly of the Korean National Association
is posting a tribute to you for the great victory of the Allies and the United
States. We eagerly think that the Allied Powers won the war this time through
the participation of the United States, which is the success of your democracy.
The nations of the world will all gain equal freedom through your success, so
we believe that all races around the world will establish a new era of democracy.

At first glance, this excerpt seems to reflect the powerlessness of the colonized,
who had been deceived by Wilson's empty promise and naively expected him
to take them into "a new era of democracy." In fact, such a diplomatic tone
was prevalent in colonial Koreans' numerous writings, such as petitions, appeals,
and requests sent to the American President, Congress, and delegations of
the Paris Peace Conference as well as articles and reports informing the Western
audience of the brutal situation in colonial Korea. They praised Western
civilization for its achievement of democracy, criticized the exceptional savagery
of Japan's colonial rule and its oppression of Christianity, and asked the U.S.
to save them from Japan's evil in order to defend democracy. Some of them
went as far as to petition for placing Korea under the mandate of the League
of Nations instead of demanding immediate independence.[70]

However, we can hear a very different voice in the writings directed toward

70 There are competing views on the Korean leaders' petition for mandate after the First World
War. (1) A critical view regards it as an anti-national attempt mostly led by Rhee Syngman and
Chŏng Hankyŏng (Henry Chung). (2) However, O Yŏngsŏp argues that it was the only realistic
diplomatic solution at the time, which allegedly was shared widely by not only Rhee Syngman but
also by Kim Kyusik and Ahn Changho (An Ch'angho) and came to fruition with the U.S. occupation
and the establishment of South Korea after the defeat of Japan in World War II. (3) Meanwhile,
Kim Tohyŏng points out that while nationalist leaders like Ahn and Kim indeed had agreed with
the attempt at one point, they changed their attitude after witnessing the March First Movement.
Based on the editorials and the tone of the articles in *the New Korea* — Ahn was the chairman
of the General Assembly of the Korean National Association, the publisher of the newspaper —
at the time, I think Ahn's take on the matter can be summarized as follows: While Ahn did not
entirely rule out the realist option of appealing to Wilson and the League of Nations, he also acknowledged
that the ultimate goal of the colonized people was to achieve independence on their own. This view
aligns with Kim Tohyŏng's analysis that Ahn began to support the immediate and unconditional
liberation from Japanese rule after the March First Movement. See O Yŏngsŏp, "Disputes over the
Petition for Mandate in the Early Stages of the Provisional Government of the Republic of Korea,"
Journal of Korean Independence Movement Studies 41 (2012): 81-156; Kim Tohyŏng, "A Survey on
the Related Materials for the Petition to the Mandate," *Journal of Korean Modern and Contemporary
History* 68 (2014): 104-139.

Koreans as the implied readers. Let me take an example from "The Triumph of Democracy," which was published on the same day and the same page as the abovementioned "A Letter of Congratulations to President Wilson."

> Some argue that the general trend of the international order necessarily depends on a few great powers. The great powers are bound to make treaties with one another for the expansion of their commerce and protection of their colonial territories. Therefore, banning secret treaties is unrealistic no matter how one tries. And promoting democracy will be partial at best and cannot spread all over the world. At the Paris Peace Conference there will be trickeries and schemes just like at the Congress of Vienna after the Napoleonic War. Such an argument had a point in its own way but it only concerns visible power, not the inner spirit.
>
> Behold! What does so-called power mean in today's world where the idea of equality is rising explosively among all peoples? After America first removed bondage from Britain, France succeeded in revolution. Soon afterward, the Greeks rebelled against Turkey for independence, Belgium separated itself from Holland, and Hungary obtained the constitution for self-governing. Romania, Serbia, and Montenegro raised their heads against oppression. The rest are also demanding freedom, risking death: Ireland from Britain; Poland from Germany, Russia, and Austria; the Balkans from Turkey; India from Britain; and even the Philippines from America. For what? It is because their spirit became so full of aspiration for democracy and freedom that it exploded from the inside. These peoples resisted oppression even a century or a half century ago. Then who would enjoy subordinating themselves to others in today's world where nationalism is flourishing? ⋯⋯ The fate of a nation cannot be decided with a couple of words. Reluctance to being bound by others makes us struggle for freedom. Whether it succeeds or not only depends on our own power.[71]

Nothing in this text suggests that the writer was fooled by Wilson's deceptive slogan of national self-determination or was earnestly asking for recognition by the great powers. The writer seems to be fully aware that "the international

---

71 "The Triumph of Democracy," *New Korea*, November 21, 1918.

order" was up to a few great powers who sought "expansion of their commerce and protection of their colonial territories" and that postwar peace treaties would be greatly affected by the secret "trickeries and schemes" between them. However, it is not in "visible power" but in the "inner spirit" where the writer finds hope. It is the spirit "of equality among all peoples" which "is rising explosively" and the spirit that is "so full of aspiration for democracy and freedom." Here, this "spirit" is not a static speculation or ideology, but a collective puissance that "exploded from the inside" with an irrepressible force.

This spirit was ignited by the independence of the United States and the French Revolution, but when the First World War ended, it not only drove the minority peoples of the Central Powers, such as the Polish or the Balkans, but also the colonial peoples of the Allied Powers, such as the Indians, the Irish, and the Filipinos, to demand independence and freedom. The author of the article seems to be clearly conscious of the global anti-colonial resistance as a massive power. Thus, a frontline was drawn not just between imperial Japan and colonial Korea but between the whole imperial order and the colonized from all over the world. What was quickly transmitted from the metropoles to the periphery through the telegraph network built for imperial domination were not only Wilson's words but also the news of other colonial peoples that were uprising using Wilson's words as weapons. Colonial peoples heard the news and encouraged each other's resistance, strengthening their collective puissance. Korean diasporas scattered around the globe were also triggered and inspired by each other's messages. Just as the news of the Korean-Americans' self-determination movement was delivered to colonial Korea and became a catalyst for a new movement, news of the March First Movement in colonial Korea elevated and radicalized the Korean-Americans' independence movement. Ahn Changho (An Ch'angho) and Kim Kyusik, who once considered petitioning for a League of Nations mandate as a realistic diplomatic strategy, turned to a more radical independence movement after the March First Movement.[72]

---

[72] The news of the March First Movement was delivered to Ahn Changho around 11 AM on March 9, 1919, which was a turning point for Ahn to shift his view from a petition for a mandate of the League of Nations to the more active independence movement. See Kim Tohyŏng, "The March First Movement and Koreans' Activities and Responses in America," *Journal of Korean Modern and Contemporary History* 50 (2009): 80.

The writer of the *New Korea* also anchored his hope for "the triumph of democracy" in the puissance of the colonized. He did not entrust "the fate of a nation" to "a couple of words" from a British Prime Minister or American President. What was at stake was the "struggle for freedom" of the oppressed, whose success relied on their "own power." After skimming off the diplomatic rhetoric of petitions directed at the great powers, only a clear acknowledgement of power struggle and a will to confrontation remained. That does not mean that demanding independence and self-determination was merely fruitless rhetoric or posturing. The tension between these two layers is rather the starting point for dismantling the extant order. At first glance, a colonial people's demand for rights to the great powers as the Other only seems to confirm the latter's authority as to whether to approve the demand. However, the very act of demanding what is not allowed by the Other, which Judith Butler calls a "performative contradiction,"[73] is a practice to rebel against the law and order of the Other. From this crack opened up by contradictions, new possibilities appear that has been precluded by the existing law and order. Even though the demand cannot be immediately realized, it draws the future to the present and inscribes new meaning onto existing concepts. Here we find a new usage of democracy that empires did not teach to colonial peoples.

So-called national self-determination is a provisional term invented by the Allied and American politicians to win support of the people in each country during the war. With the fog of war cleared and the smell of gunpowder vanished, the term is no longer of use to them. Thus, they seek to remove this word from their dictionary. However, the word has already been imprinted in the dictionaries of all nations. Some peoples, engraving the word on their heart, gained independence from despotism. Others, with this word carved in their bone, obtained freedom from oppression and declared independence. Thus, how pathetic the politicians of the great powers are! The word they coined to deceive the peoples has now become a big obstacle to their road ahead.

In the 20th century, every nation loves democracy and speaks the new word,

---

[73] Judith Butler and Gayatri Spivak, *Who Sings Nation-State?: Language, Politics, Belonging* (Chicago: Seagull Books, 2007), 63.

"national self-determination," to protect their proper rights as human beings. Lloyd George and Orlando hope to obtain patent and monopoly rights of this noun at the peace conference. Because the peace treaty is a league of their own, they may be able to do as they please. However, how long do they think they can maintain the patent and monopoly right of the word?[74]

The colonizers say that the colonized should first be enlightened in order to qualify for democracy. The colonizers teach the colonized to remain in the waiting room of history until they have been fully assimilated into the civilization of the empire, perhaps waiting forever. The great powers divide the world into several imperial nation-states, and only allocate a "place in the world" to those who belong to a nation-state. They assign superior/inferior qualities to each people of empires/colonies and grant/deprive them of the "right to have rights," and allot ranks and shares to each people from civilization to barbarism according to their similarity with Western culture. Proclaiming the "*nomos* of the earth" (international law) founded on imperial violence and immersing themselves in the "police" according to the law, they forgot "politics" and democracy long ago. They pretentiously teach democracy to the colonized, but "do not know" democracy.

The colonized declare independence and insist on equality with inscriptions, newspapers, leaflets, pleas, petitions, proposals, letters, in short, all forms of utterances. Above all, with the shouts of the masses who cry for national independence, they confront the imperial knowledge and colonial discourses that deny the democratic capacity of the colonized. They do not claim to return to their authentic innocence by isolating themselves from the "world" they were forcibly driven into by imperial violence. The colonized as those who are displaced, those who are not counted, those who do not have a share, demand that this common world be shared together. They become "political," shaking up the boundaries divided by the imperial "police" and claiming "the share of those who have no share." Facing the gap between the word of national self-determination and its reality, they fight with a belief that the word should

---

74 "On National Self-Determination," *New Korea*, January 23, 1919.

be truly realized, rather than adhering to clever realism or nihilism saying "that's the way it is." They extort the "patent and monopoly rights" of the word from those who made it up but do not want the word to become a reality, and fight with the word as a weapon. Now that "every nation loves democracy," they engrave the new word, national self-determination, into their hearts and bones, protest against the empires that are trying to erase it from their dictionaries, and fight for freedom, independence, and human rights.

As such, the colonized "know" democracy. They learned democracy from the "ignorant schoolmaster,"[75] subverted the intellectual hierarchy between the colonizer and the colonized, and validated themselves as equal political subjects. This self-validation should be distinguished from the claim that they meet the standards of Western civilization, which is often found in, for example, colonial peoples' petitions for independence to the great powers. These petitions to the imperial audience, ornamented with rhetorical words with which the colonized merely ask for "a place" in the world, did not shake the imperial order of the world. If a colonial people had wanted only "a place" in "their own league," say, the League of Nations, it would have been impossible for them to stand with other colonial peoples. They would, just applying the imperial standards of civilization to themselves, have proven how different they were from others without a share. On the other hand, the colonized who "know" and "love" democracy shall always shout for "world democracy" and national self-determination for everyone who is "not qualified," as did the unknown writers of the *New Korea*.

---

[75] Here, I altered Rancière's term a bit. In order to affirm the equal intelligence of all people, Rancière uses the example of Joseph Jacotot, who, knowing no Flemish, could still teach French to Flemish students who knew no French. With this example, Rancière foregrounds "the ignorant schoolmaster" as a model of an emancipatory teacher who strengthens students' will and self-confidence and enables them to learn independently beyond unilateral teaching and the hierarchical relationship between teacher and student. On the contrary, colonizers as the "ignorant schoolmaster" in this article do not mean emancipatory schoolmasters. Nonetheless, I adopted the figurative expression "ignorant schoolmaster" to refer to the colonizer because the colonized could learn a new usage of the term democracy and emancipate themselves in the process of their decolonizing movements against the colonizer who did not actually know democracy.

5. In Lieu of a Conclusion: The Politics of *Demos* under the Name of Nation (*minjok*)

> I pondered all these things, and how men fight and lose the battle,
> and the thing that they fought for comes about in spite of their defeat,
> and when it comes turns out not to be what they meant,
> and other men have to fight for what they meant under another name.
> — William Morris

Ch'oe Namsŏn, a Korean nationalist who had been imprisoned for drafting the Korean Declaration of Independence during the March First Movement, evaluated the significance of the movement in the editorial "On the Korean Nation of the People" (*Chosŏn minshiron*) in 1922. The historical significance of the March First Movement, according to him, lay in the proclamation of the "will to live" (*Wille zum Leben*) of the Koreans by promoting the "nation" (*minjok*) in the fullest sense of the word. What mattered most for him was that this awareness of the nation did not only sprout from a few intellectuals but from the voluntary activities of the subaltern people themselves. The further task would be to "complete the nation" which had been "discovered" as such.[76] His way of undertaking this task was the practice of Korean studies (*chosŏnhak*), ranging widely from history, mythology, folklore, and philology to literature. His production of knowledge on Korea amounted, in a sense, to "inventing" the Korean nation (*Chosŏn minjok*) as a solid entity that had existed long before it was "discovered."

What should be noted here is that the "invented (or imagined) nation" through Ch'oe's work had the real foundation of a "discovered nation" during the historical event of the March First Movement. What was the nation that was found during the March First Movement? It was the emergence of a *demos*, a mass of people who recognized themselves as a political unit with the right to self-determination "under the name of a nation." In this sense, the "nation" discovered during the March First Movement was a nation as

---

76 Ch'oe Namsŏn, "On the Korean Nation of the People (1): From Groping to Discovery," *Tongmyŏng*, September 1922, 4.

a political subject.

The "nation" discovered during the March First Movement also marked a distinct break in the conceptual history of the Korean word, "*minjok*." Since the introduction of modern Western concepts during the Enlightenment period, "*minjok*" (民族) had been understood as an ethnic cultural community while "*kungmin*" (*kuk-min*, 國民) was viewed as the political community of a sovereign state.[77] This binary configuration of concepts originated from J. C. Bluntschli's distinction between "people" (Ger. Nation) and "nation" (Ger. Volk).[78] With this distinction, Bluntschli intended to confine the usage of the word "nation" to refer to civilized peoples who were qualified for self-government and sovereignty. The terms were translated in East Asia around the turn of the 19th century, and, in Korean, "*minjok*" became a translation for "people" whereas "*kungmin*" was equivalent to "nation." In the face of the imminent perishing of the state around 1908, "*minjok*" began to have the more political implication of a "spiritual state." However, it was not until the March First Movement that the word came to be clearly related to the people as a political subject. "*Minjok*" was intentionally counter-translated into "nation" in English, thus appropriating Wilson's concept of national self-determination and changing the meaning of nation itself.[79]

Unlike the national discourse during the Korean enlightenment era, which was driven by the desire to become a strong imperial nation, the national discourse connected to national self-determination generally promoted both anti-imperial national liberation and the universal ideal of democracy. In the February Eighth Declaration of Independence in 1919, Korean students in Tokyo demanded to "apply the principle of national self-determination" to

---

[77] Song Kue-jin, "The Introduction of the Concept of 'Nation' into Korean Society and the Adaptation of Its Usage, *International Journal of Korean History* 13 (2009): 125-151.

[78] See J. C. Bluntschli, *The Theory of the State*, trans. D. G. Ritchie, P. E. Matheson, and R. Lodge, (Oxford: The Clarendon Press, 1885), 82-88.

[79] How to interpret "national self-determination" also poses a problem of how to translate and define the word "nation." Wilson's concept of nation was close to "citizen" in the Hegelian sense while Japan tried to confine its meaning to extant nation-states. Colonial or minority peoples like the Koreans broadened its implication to the extent that it could embrace a stateless population, demanding their right to self-determination. The interpretative conflicts over national self-determination and the concept of a nation constituted an important political moment after World War I, which is in need of further research.

the Korean nation while presenting "democracy based on justice and freedom" as the political prospect of a new nation-state of Koreans. Likewise, in the Korean Declaration of Independence, the commitment to "human equality" was aligned with the demand for "the right of the national autonomy" of colonial Korea.

The Korean nation (*minjok*), which emerged as a political subject in and beyond the mourning of the dead King Kojong, provided the ground for establishing the Provisional Government of the Republic of Korea. Since then, however, various kinds of political imaginations have coexisted under the name of "nation." Especially during the colonial period of Korea, the name of "nation" not only became associated with nationalism in its narrow sense but also socialism, anarchism, and other political projects.

Meanwhile, Rhee Syngman claimed to "represent" the Korean nation and promoted the League of Nations' mandate of Korea. Rhee's view corresponded to Wilson's solution to the colonial issue, which suggested a gradual process of decolonization from protection (mandate) and enlightenment by civilized nations through economic development and free trade to "granting" independence to the colonies. In fact, Rhee Syngman wrote his doctoral dissertation at Princeton when Wilson served as the president of the university. Rhee's thesis topic was the American influence on the development of wartime neutrality law, which was related to Wilson's practical idealism of *Pax Economica*, world peace through free trade.[80]

Although Rhee's petition for this mandate was criticized and dismissed in the elevated atmosphere of post-March First movements, it was partially realized with the U.S. decision to enact trusteeship of Korea after its liberation from Japan in 1945 and culminated in South Korea's integration into the capitalist order led by the U.S. In this process of national "liberation" and the construction of the nation-state, what Negri called the "regressive aspects of subaltern nationalism" became manifest with "all of the oppressive functions of modern sovereignty."[81]

---

80 See Rhee Syngman, *Neutrality as Influenced by the United States*, trans. Chŏng Insŏp (Nanam Press: 2000).

81 Hardt and Negri, *Empire*, 107-109.

133

Nevertheless, it is noteworthy that various forms of political practices against the division system and developmental dictatorship in South Korea have long been waged "under the name of nation." Furthermore, the term was constantly renewed by the revolutionary potential of the *demos* from the April 19th Revolution (1960) to the June Democratic Struggle (1987). In that revolutionary tradition, the concept of "nation" has rarely been trapped within the myth of ethnic homogeneity, aiming to be an "open nation," a "democratic nation," a "third-world nation," "a nation of the subaltern people (*minjung*)," and so on. It was more a performatively constructed identity that was always accompanied by the question of "who are a nation" than a given category in the primordial and essentialist sense. Thus, if the name of nation exhausted its democratic potential after the 1990s, it is necessary to accurately settle accounts with it by carefully examining under what conditions and historical experiences its potential was erupted or exhausted. This is because even if we now have to fight "under another name," the thing we have to fight for may not be different from what predecessors fought for "under the name of nation."

Yi Kwangsu's March First Movement: Colonial Violence and the "Civilizing Mission"

Kong Im-soon

1. Diverging Paths: Yi Kwangsu, before and after His Return to Korea

This article is about one of the leading Korean novelists and intellectuals of the colonial period, Yi Kwangsu. It seeks to examine how he changed as a result of the March First Movement and what happened after his secret return to colonial Korea from the Provisional Government of Korea in Shanghai. Yi Kwangsu is so important in the modern literary and cultural history of Korea that he has been called the pioneer of the modern Korean literature. His novel *The Heartless* (*Mujŏng*), which was serialized in a newspaper in 1917 and published as a book in 1918, captivated many young readers at the time and is appreciated as the start of modern Korean fiction.

Following the end of World War I, U.S. President Woodrow Wilson and Russian Bolshevik leader Vladimir Lenin's calls for national self-determination inspired independence movements across the world, including colonial Korea. At first, Yi Kwangsu was optimistic about the possibility of Korea's independence from Japan. While studying at Waseda University in Tokyo, he took a leave and came to Korea, intending to meet other Korean intellectuals and help lead the Korean independence movement. He returned to Tokyo in November 1918, and penned the "February Eighth Declaration of Independence," which played a pivotal role in catalyzing the March First Movement. This declaration was delivered at the heart of the empire, Tokyo, on February 8, 1919, causing embarrassment to the authorities.

Yi's fellow Korean students studying in Tokyo urged him to go into hiding because they feared for his safety. Yi indeed fled to the French Concession in Shanghai before the movement erupted. The March First Movement led to the formation of the Provisional Government of the Republic of Korea (or the Shanghai Provisional Government) by Korean independence activists who exiled themselves after or even before the March First Movement. Yi, as one of the pivotal figures of this government, was in charge of running its newspaper, the *Independent* (*Tongnip sinmun*). He was, figuratively speaking, the face of the Shanghai Provisional Government.

Since Yi held such an important position, not many had expected his sudden secret return to Korea with his wife, Hŏ Yŏngsuk, which was bound to have repercussions. His return in March 1921, two years after the March First Movement, amounted to him turning his back on the Provisional Government. Even Pak Chonghwa, one of the leading writers of historical fiction and one of Yi's close friends who had co-founded the literary magazine *Swan* (*Paekcho*) with him, did not know about Yi's return at all. Yi was a leading figure in the Provisional Government who was wanted by the colonial authorities and thus his safe return to Korea was sufficient to provoke a scandal. A *Chosun Ilbo* article on Yi's return soon followed, provoking further controversy.[1]

The controversy was described in the unpublished diary of Pak Chonghwa as follows:

> Everyone knows about Yi's relationship with Doctor Hŏ [Hŏ Yŏngsuk], to whom he is married. What they do not know, and are curious to find out, concerns the following question: how could Yi, a famous writer of our time and leader

---

1 "A Certificate of Defection in Hand, Yi Kwangsu Arrives in Ŭiju," *Chosun Ilbo*, April 3, 1921. By "a certificate of defection" the writer implied that Yi's return meant none other than his surrender to the colonial authorities. Such a sensational title on the public media heightened people's suspicions about Yi. Since Yi's return drew suspicion over his defection, his speeches and writings that followed suffered the same fate. This also signaled the divide-and-rule policy by the colonial authorities following the March First Movement.

in the independence movement from early on, safely returned to Kyŏngsŏng [Seoul]? ····· Hŏ, for some reason, convinced Yi to return to Korea, by telling him that if she went with him, they would be protected ····· by the Japanese Governor-General. If they have difficulties in making ends meet, they will receive support from the authorities and don't have to worry.

Hŏ safely made it to Shanghai and met Yi secretly. She suggested they both return to Korea ····· And so Yi followed Hŏ back to Korea, and has been living there since, in safety ····· This is the other side of their loftiness, the true colors of those who call themselves intellectuals. Alas! This disgusting vice. He gave into pleasure of the flesh! The rottenness of the flesh! Yi Kwangsu, a man thrust by a pitiful fate! What a pathetic man!"[2]

Pak Chonghwa's unpublished diary gives us some ideas about how Yi's act was interpreted. Yi's decision to return to Korea, in Pak's account, was out of his love for Hŏ. This account mainly came from Pak's antipathy to "free love." As was well known, Pak criticized Yi for having previously "written stories about the triumph of free love and publishing articles that emphasized the idea of the New Woman (sinyŏsŏng), which had corrupted innocent young men and women in Korea."[3] Nevertheless, Pak also expressed sympathy to Yi for what he brands as "pitiful."[4]

Pak's reaction to and view of the situation was not limited to him alone. Yi's shocking return led to all kinds of conjecture, speculation, and spiteful suggestions. Pak's account of Yi's return as a runaway love story thus seems to have simplified what was likely far more complicated. In reality, Yi's return was fundamentally linked to issues raised by the March First Movement and

---

2 Pak Chonghwa, "Unpublished Diary, August 1-September 9," quoted in *The Life and Literature of Pak Chonghwa*, ed. Yun Pyŏngno (Seoul: Korean Studies Service, 2001), 54-56.

3 Pak Chonghwa, "A Record of My Youth," in *With the Moon, with the Clouds, and with Ideas* (Seoul: Mimun Publishers, 1965), 113-115.

4 As Pak's private diary shows, he blamed Yi's inappropriate relationship with Hŏ for all the controversies surrounding Yi's actions, which was out of Pak's own repulsion to free love. Yi's endorsement of free love was seen as the sin of permitting indulgence and even adultery amongst Korea's immature youth. Yi's return was thus interpreted as an extension of his attachment to free love. As such, Pak could not grasp the essential point of what was actually happening, or the gravity of the choice that Yi had made.

its aftermath. Yi's return touched upon these core, hidden concerns and thus provoked such deep and broad repurcussion in colonial Korean society.

For the same reason, Yi's case remains controversial to this day. As Michael Shin noted, "the debate on Yi continues to this day as scholars are still obsessed with explaining how someone so seemingly nationalistic turned into a pro-Japanese collaborator." Shin added "research on Yi often has the drama of a detective story: a search of his writings for clues to a shocking and unforgivable real-life crime."[5]

In this article, I gladly take on the role of a detective novelist in unearthing clues in Yi Kwangsu's writing that would illuminate the circumstances surrounding his return to Korea. There is a clear divide in the reception of Yi's works and activities, which takes his return as a turning point. Before his return, Yi was synonymous with the *Independent*, the Shanghai Provisional Government's official newspaper, whereas, after his return, he came to be associated with his writing "National Reconstruction" (*Minjok kaejoron*), which became subject to outrage and criticism from the Korean people. Yi's return, criticized as "defection" and leaving him deep stigma and disgrace of treachery exceeding his expectation, also revealed the deep cleavage of the colonial Korean society. It was the discrepancy between the cultural movement and the radical armed struggle or conflicts over how to balance between legality and illegality under the "cultural rule" after the March First Movement.

This gulf between before and after Yi's return polarized arguments about Yi's personal life and his times. Moreover, Yi's entanglements with the public sphere of colonial Korea and its inherent contradictions make Yi's case a

---

5 Michael D. Shin, "Interior Landscapes: Yi Kwangsu's 'The Heartless' and the Origins of Modern Literature," in *Colonial Modernity in Korea*, eds. Gi-wook Shin and Michael Robinson (Cambridge: Harvard University Press 1999), 249. As Shin traces the idea of "modern literature as translation," he examines closely the paradoxes and contradictions of modernity that are inherent to Yi's "conversion." He takes a critical view of how Yi's story is presented as being that of a "pro-Japanese collaborator." This "drama" is inescapable if one does not grasp the duality of "translational modernism." While I am open to Shin's views, I employ his metaphor of being a "detective novelist" in my attempt to make sense of Yi's migrations, changing views, and his struggles. The wounds that his name encompasses are part of dramatic change of Korean national history, ranging from pro-Japanese collaboration to anti-Communism. They are also historical traces of an intellectual's abandonment of his own principles. Here I echo the sentiments of Edward Said in his 1993 Reith Lectures on the responsibility of the intellectual.

"complex" affair in which private and public significances were inexplicably entangled.[6] Thus, it is all the more important to examine what drove Yi to return to Korea when the aftermath of the March First Movement was still lingering in the colonial Korean society. With the eyes of a detective novelist, I will examine Yi's words disseminated in his texts to make sense of his return and its deep and wide repercussion in colonial Korea.

2. The Shanghai Provisional Government and the Kando Massacre

Yi wrote numerous texts about his life in China. However, he kept his silence about the reasons for and circumstances surrounding his return to Korea. His silence is likely related to the intense censorship by the colonial authorities. The harsh censorship system entailing deletion of phrases, confiscation of manuscripts, prohibition of sale, and even forcible suspension of publication resulted in the distortion of texts and self-censorship of the colonial subjects, who had to voluntarily subjugate themselves and conformed to the colonial authorities in order to sustain their colonial everyday life. In this way, the censorship system functioned a key pillar that supported colonial rule.[7]

The arbitrary line between what was permitted or forbidden became the official and everyday reality, defining the boundary of legality. Within that boundary, Yi depicted his life in China and his trips to northern Russia, where the October Revolution took place. Even if we just take a quick look at his life, we see that the only part that is absent from his writings is the time

---

6 Bringing the public and private aspects of this complex affair together in this manner allows us to see the various ways in which imperial Japan, semi-colonial China, and colonial Korea came in contact with and got involved with one another. Therefore, the context surrounding Yi's return was inseparable from the rise of those who advocated armed independence struggle, empowered by the Battle of Chŏngsalli. See Kong Im-soon, "Remembering and Forgetting the Battle of Ch'ŏngsalli," *Korean Language and Literature in International Context* 76 (2018): 55-98.

7 The transition from violent repression under military rule to cultural rule following the March First Movement brought with it the institutionalization of surveillance. Amidst rapid changes in the media environment, colonial censorship exerted both a covert and overt influence on the colonial public sphere that it sought to regulate. See Han Mansu, *Permitted Sedition* (Seoul: Somyong Publishing, 2015) on how censorship mediated the distorted public sphere in colonial Korea.

he spent in Shanghai immediately before returning to Korea. We can infer some of the reasons for his silence in the following passage from "The Troublesome Path of Half a Life" (*Tananhan pansaengŭi tojŏng*), published in *Chogwang* as a series from April to June 1936:

> Meanwhile, my health declined still further, and with one year left until graduation I returned to Korea. However, I did not afford to take a rest and returned to Tokyo to continue my studies. But I escaped to Shanghai the year after World War I ended. (I am not at liberty to write about the circumstances of this period, so I have omitted them). I returned to Korea from Shanghai in the spring of the year I turned 30 (I am now 45). My close friends were very critical of my return. First, they attacked me for returning without facing imprisonment, second for getting divorced. Even with such accusations, I had many kind friends. I will never forget them and how they looked after me even as the rest of the world was attacking me.[8]

Yi here records how he moved from Tokyo to Shanghai, and then from Shanghai to Korea, but he gives no details as to what he experienced or what he did in each place. He seems to have been conscious of the censorship, judging from his remarks "I am not at liberty to write." The most important part of the narrative is thus missing and leaves us guessing.

The seal of repression was broken only after Korea's liberation from colonial rule, and Yi's book, *My Confession (Naŭi kobaek)* significantly allowed Yi to say what he could not express publicly during the colonial rule, supplementing "The Troublesome Path of Half a Life."

As Yi explains in the introduction, the book is effectively an autobiography that narrates his life from the beginning in order to explain the "reason why I have been mistaken for a Japanese collaborator." Yi claims his personal life has been aligned with the "path trodden by our national movement." Thus, his life story begins when his "national consciousness started to grow within"

---

8   Yi Kwangsu, "The Troublesome Path of Half a Life," *The Complete Works of Yi Kwangsu*, vol. 8 (Seoul: Usinsa, 1979), 453-454. The original title of the piece, which was published in *Chogwang* in 1936, is "Looking Back at the 30 Years in the Literary World."

him and encompasses all the historical moments "from annexation [of Korea by Japan], the March First Movement, and the Second World War right up to just before liberation," focusing on his own experiences, the events he "was part of and saw," and people he "came into contact with."[9]

Following liberation from Japanese colonial rule, the southern half of the Korean peninsula went through a period of American military occupation before the establishment of the Republic of Korea in August 1948. In September that year, a law on the punishment of anti-national activities was implemented and the Special Investigation Committee of Anti-National Activities (SICANA) was formed. Yi was arrested in February 1949 as the second person to be investigated by the committee. People expected him to reflect and atone for his actions but Yi instead wrote and published *My Confession* in December 1948, in which he sought to excuse and defend his actions.

Written immediately before his arrest by the SICANA, *My Confession*, especially the chapter titled "The Year of 1919 and I" (*Kiminyŏn'gwa na*) included parts that were not written in "The Troublesome Path of Half a Life." These parts had been left out due to colonial censorship, and it was only after liberation that Yi was finally able to write about his time in the Shanghai Provisional Government.

"The Year of 1919 and I" provides Yi's version of events regarding the writing of the "February Eighth Declaration of Independence," his escape to Shanghai and his interactions and friendships with exiled independence activists, and his roles with respect to the formation and operation of the Provisional Government, as well as the *Independent* and his work with the Provisional Historical Materials Compilation Committee. Though much of the contents could have been guessed or anticipated without reading "The Year of 1919 and I," it is noteworthy that he singles out the Kando Massacre as a major "motivator and [source of] anger."[10] The Kando Massacre refers to the first and second Hunch'un (Húnchūn in Chinese) incidents and the Kyŏngsin

---

9 Yi Kwangsu, "Preface to *My Confession*," in *The Complete Works of Yi Kwangsu*, vol. 10 (Seoul: Usinsa, 1979), 539.

10 Yi Kwangsu, "*My Confession*," in *The Complete Works of Yi Kwangsu*, vol. 7 (Seoul: Usinsa, 1979), 262-263.

incident.[11] Yi describes these incidents as "the massacre of our compatriots at the hands of Japanese forces in Hunch'un." What he calls "The Hunch'un incident" in *My Confession*, or the Kando Massacre, was considered to be of great importance in his writings for the *Independent*.

Based on Kim Chonguk and Kim Chuhyŏn's analyses on the editorials and literary works that Yi published in the *Independent* and the compilation of Yi's writings of the time by Kim Sayŏp and Kim Wŏnmo, most works published in the newspaper were about the Kando Massacre.[12] This provides clear evidence that the Kando Massacre, which was a consequence of the Japanese advance into Siberia, deeply affected Yi. He stressed that the incident further deepened factional strife within the Provisional Government. The massacre intensified ideological divisions and strategic differences between those who wanted to immediately fight back and those who thought it best to prepare for a future showdown. Yi notes that severe conflicts and antagonism vitiated the significance of the Provisional Government and served as a partial reason for his return to Korea, along with his participation in Ahn Changho's Young Korean Academy (*Hŭngsadan*).

---

11 On the Kando Massacre, see Cho Tonggŏl, "The Truth about the Kando Massacre in 1920," *History Critique* 45 (1998): 47-57; Ch'ae Yŏngguk, "Trends in the Independence Army before and after the 1920 Hunch'un Incident," *Korean Independence Movement History Research* 5 (1991): 273-294; Sŏ Jungsŏk, *Sinhŭng Military School and Exiles* (Seoul: Yŏksabip'yŏngsa, 2001). The colonial authorities took a completely different view of the huge damage and brutality inflicted upon the Korean migrants in Kando by the Japanese Army. *Osaka Asahi Shinbun* reported on the events as if they were the result of the rebelliousness of the Koreans, and sought to justify the intervention of the Japanese forces as an effort to keep the peace. See for instance, Ōsaka Asahi Shinbun Research Team, ed., *Articles about Korea in the Ōsaka Asahi Shinbun*, vol. 1 (Ch'ŏnan: History of the Korean Independence Movement Research Center, The Independence Hall of Korea, 2016), 393.

12 See Kim Chonguk, "The Anti-Japanese Editorials of Yi Kwangsu Prior to His Conversion," *Square* 160 (1986): 222-243; Kim Sayŏp, ed., *The Independent: Yi Kwangsu's Patriotic Writing* (Seoul: Munhak Saenghwalsa, 1988); Kim Wŏnmo, *Yi Kwangsu's Theory of Liberation: The Independent* (Seoul: Dankook University Press, 2009).

Figure 1) An image of the Japanese military massacre of Koreans at the Kando Massacre

Figure 2) Yi Kwangsu's editorial "The Kando Massacre and the Future of the Independence Movement" and his poem "Three Thousand Victimized Souls"

Yi departed for Shanghai before the March First Movement began. Hence, he could not participate in the demonstrations, where the masses enjoyed shared feeling of excitement and delight of liberation. Nor did he witness the mass arrests and brutal massacres by the Japanese colonial authorities. All he was able to see were "fragments" of news smuggled across the border hidden "under their clothes or in shoes." The Kando Massacre apparently made Yi aware of his distance from the events and he started to feel the violence of Japanese colonialism in a way he had not experienced before. Such sudden consciousness of colonial violence, along with his painful love triangle, economic difficulties and health problem, drove him to return to Korea.

Yi did not see his return as an act of surrender or defection, but as an act based of the great ambition and hope to follow "India's Gandhi" and "save the nation." The Kando Massacre led Yi to believe that the appropriate course of independence movement was not the radicalism he saw in China, but something equivalent to Gandhi's movement. Originally, Yi had supported the Shanghai Provisional Government and its line of mounting a war of independence starting in 1920. He, however, turned against this idea. He not only opposed organizing an independence army in North Kando and the Soviet Maritime Province (Yŏnhaeju) but also criticized lobbying foreign governments for Korean independence as "hoping for luck and the help of others [i.e. foreign powers]." Instead, he claimed that Gandhi's "non-violent resistance" should be prioritized as a means to legally cultivate the power of the nation in colonial

143

Korea, where the Korean people carried on with their everyday life.[13]

Yi's position was thus one of gradualism (*chunbiron*), aiming at "cultivating the national power" within the boundary of legality. Advocates for gradualism came into conflict with those who insisted on armed struggles against Imperial Japan. The confrontation between these two positions within the Provisional Government, which was evident in the changing editorial line of the *Independent*, was further exacerbated by the Kando Massacre. In late 1920, amidst social turbulence, Yi clarified his position in a series of editorials titled "The Kando Massacre and the Future of the Independence Movement." Kim Chuhyŏn's meticulous study revealed that these editorials were the same thing that Yi called "business, education and conscription of all the people" in *My Confession*. In *My Confession*, Yi states that this is his last editorial published in the *Independent* before returning to Korea.[14]

The first part of "The Kando Massacre and the Future of the Independence Movement" was published in the *Independent* on December 18, 1920. This particular issue of the *Independent* is especially noteworthy because it was the first one published after the paper shut down for six months following Japan's issuing of complaint directed at the Shanghai French Concession in regard to the paper's content. Yi's column on the Kando Massacre was printed on the front page.[15] He also published three poems, including "Three Thousand Victimized Souls" (*Samch'ŏnŭi wŏnhon*), which occupied the center of the

---

13 Evidence that Yi Kwangsu appropriated Gandhi's ideas as the basis for his own actions can be found in the five-part series he published in *Dong-a Ilbo* (August 16-21, 1922) under the title "An Inquiry Concerning Gandhi's Ideas." These writings, appearing under the penname "a Y," were not included in *The Complete Works of Yi Kwangsu*, and thus have not received much attention. Yi had a high opinion of Gandhi's "idealistic non-resistance," which he contrasts with the violent socialism of Russia. He claims that Gandhi's ideas inhabit a "higher dimension." However, Yi's interpretation of satyagraha as "non-resistance" differs from what it actually meant – i.e. non-violent disobedience and non-cooperation. It would be more accurate to say that Yi was using Gandhi to justify his compromise and involvement in the legal cultural movement in colonial Korea.

14 Kim Chuhyŏn, "Unearthing and Understanding Yi Kwangsu's Editorials in the Shanghai 'Independent'," *Korean Language and Literature* 176 (2016): 575-626.

15 On the publication history of the *Independent*, see the thorough work of Ch'oe Kiyŏng, *The National Intellect and the Cultural Movement during the Colonial Period* (P'aju: Hanul, 2003). After the publication of the paper on June 24, 1920 (issue no. 86), the Japanese intervention resulted in the ownership of the printing equipment being transferred to foreigners. The paper resumed publication with its December 18, 1920 edition (issue no. 87).

first page (Figure 2), "The Sound of That Wind" (*Chŏ param sori*) printed on page 2, and "Disaster upon Kando Compatriots" (*Kando tongp'oŭi ch'amsang*) on page 3. These poems added further weight to the tragedy described in the editorial. It seems quite likely that Yi wrote all the poems while he could not publish the *Independent* because of its shut down for six months.

The three poems give voice to the terrible pain and sacrifices endured by overseas Koreans during the Kando Massacre.[16] In a manner arousing sympathy and compassion, Yi poured everything he had wished to express thus far into "The Kando Massacre and the Future of the Independence Movement." Having decided to give up all his activities related to the Shanghai Provisional Government, Yi frankly gave his views about what the Kando Massacre had exposed as the problems of the overseas independence movement.

3. Yi's "National Reconstruction" and the Negative Portrayal of the So-called "Radical Socialists"

Yi begins the first column in "The Kando Massacre and the Future of the Independence Movement" series with the description that Kando had been completely demolished by the Japanese Army. Foregrounding the event as a "horror unseen since the Imjin War,"[17] he described with painful tone the tragedy of three thousand innocent overseas Koreans being slaughtered. These were people who had no relation to the Independent Army or the battles that it had fought. Yi thus argued against the prevailing line within the Provisional Government, which favored armed struggle as a response to such indiscriminate mass killing. Yi's view was that these radicals were actually only radical in their words, and were neither prepared nor preparing for any actual action.

---

16 The compilation of selected writings that Yi had written for the *Independent* fails to deliver a sense of the shock and despair that Yi felt toward the Kando Massacre, which is expressed more fully in the December 18, 1920 edition of the paper. The affective register of his writing is amplified by the lyrics of the song printed on page four in the article headlined "Speech Meeting to Aid Compatriots."

17 Yi Kwangsu, "The Kando Massacre and the Future of the Independence Movement (Part 1)," *Independent,* December 18, 1920.

He further criticized that a large number of organizations made after the annexation of Korea and even in the wake of the March First Movement were only weighting towards hollow and frothy slogans without solid preparation.

According to Yi, ill-conceived calls for military action led to the incredible suffering and tragedy as in the case of the Kando Massacre. Poorly prepared armed struggle was therefore dangerous. Such views were extremely unwelcome to those advocating for armed struggle but also reminiscent of Yun Ch'iho's realistic view that "the only people who are hurt by armed struggle are Koreans."[18] Yi believed a crude attempt of armed struggles had only offered excuse for violent suppression of colonial power. Instead, he called for focusing on education and business to cultivate Korean people's capacity, financial power, and unity. Under Yi's thoughts of gradualism or preparation theory were his lurking fears and horrors about "naked life" exposed to an unconditional threat of death.

Aimé Césaire realized "at the borders of the Western world there begins the shadowy realm of primitive thinking." According to him, colonial violence in the name of "civilization" was founded on the distinction between the "civilized who knew how to think" and the "barbarous" who were driven by "primitive thoughts" and incomplete notion of "participation, incapable of logic."[19] Along this line of distinction people were divided into two groups: those with rights and those without rights. Those who are deemed barbarous were left outside the law and without any rights. What Yi Kwangsu found, while witnessing the Kando Massacre, was those who were stigmatized as "barbarians," thus expelled outside the law, and driven to death. Yi was overwhelmed by fear

---

18 Yun Ch'iho, *Yun Ch'iho's English Diary*, vol. 19 (Kwach'ŏn: National Institute of Korean History, 1969), http://db.history.go.kr/item/level.do?itemId=sa&levelId=sa_031_0010_0110_0180&types=o. Yun also wrote: "The Japanese seem to have decided to stamp out the independence movement by [the] German method of terrorism. Wherever and whenever a pretext is found, they will wipe out villages and lives without mercy." Yun appears to have been of the same view as Yi about armed struggle.

19 Aimé Césaire, *Discourse on Colonialism*, trans. Robert D.G. Kelley (New York: Monthly Review Press, 2000), 69. Césaire observes that the "thought, preparation and education" of the "civilized" were counterposed by the "instincts, emotions, and nature" of the "barbarians" in a dichotomous hierarchy. The paradox of civilization entails the inevitability of an endless vicious cycle of seeking to overcome these irreconcilable differences. Yi Kwangsu is the quintessential intellectual from a colony who has been entrapped in this paradox.

about the horrible misery that colonial Koreans were prone to experience only because "they were born in a collapsed country and inherited karma from their poor forefathers."[20] The Kando Massacre made Yi realize not only the brutal essence of colonial rule but also the solidity of the ruling power. The injustice of colonial rule was not something that could simply be immediately avenged, but had to be responded to with ambitious plans and long preparation.

The problem was that most Koreans were just pursuing lucky chance, temporary ease and extraordinary success without preparation. Yi thought even the Provisional Government, which should lead organizations within the independence movement, only focused on "stopgap measures" and "petty issues" and "failed to cultivate the necessary capacity to maintain the independence movement." Only with "people who were interested in fortune and temporary measures" and "leaders who just flattered the feelings of the immature nation," colonial Koreans could not overcome the conditions that gave rise to the Kando Massacre. As Yi put it: "if today's leaders and the people do not turn their back on old customs and take a new path, the darkness that lies in front of our nation will continue, and a bright future will never come." This pessimistic prospect was the reason why Yi sought to stoke the sense of crisis among Koreans.

Yi thus articulated a view that was different from that of the mainstream in the Shanghai Provisional Government. It was a long-term and comprehensive project to transform the Korean people into "civilized people who knew how to think." This "civilizing" project was difficult to reconcile with the radicalism of the Provisional Government, which supported immediate engagement in armed struggle.

Yi knew very well that the mainstream in the Provisional Government would be highly reluctant to accept his views. He believed that extraordinary crisis of the nation required extraordinary methods to overcome it, but those embroiled in their own small interests and emotions would not understand such an approach. Yi's views led him to return to Korea, even rejecting the advice of the prominent independence activist Ahn Changho. Against the

---

20 Yi Kwangsu, "The Sound of That Wind," *Independent*, December 18, 1920.

advocates of immediate armed struggle, Yi called for national integration and long-term preparation for independence, based on a developmentalist concept of time and the epochal tide of "reconstruction" after World War I.

As Yi stated in *My Confession*, "The Kando Massacre and the Future of the Independence Movement" was his final written work before leaving Shanghai, which could also be seen as his attempt to offer up something like an alibi for his return to Korea. This writing is also illuminating in regard to the continuities and discontinuities between "Reconstruction" (*Sŏnjŏn kaejo*), a series of eighteen articles that Yi published in the *Independent* between August and October 1919, and "National Reconstruction," which he published, despite severe criticism from his contemporaries, in the magazine *Kaebyŏk* in 1922. While the topic of these two writings is the same, there is a definite sense of disconnect between them.

With "presentiments of violence" in Tomiyama Ichiro's term, Yi prescribed "preparation" for future as a "preventive measure" of even more colonial violence. "National Reconstruction," therefore, was not just a simple repetition or extension of his work written during his time in Shanghai but a redesign for a long-term project that could resist all forms of radicalism.

Following his return, and in spite of the doubts it gave rise to, Yi wrote to the then Governor-General Saitō Makoto, which was not released at the time. The piece was entitled "The Letter of Suggestions Concerning Koreans Living Abroad." This secret document, which has only recently been discovered, was written in Japanese and constitutes a vow on Yi's part to pursue legal activities after having returned to Korea. He proposed something of a plan and solutions to prevent all forms of radicalism against the colonial authorities. He also offered the direction and outlines of a cultural movement that could occupy the post-March First Movement space. If this document had been made public at the time, many problematic things he wrote in it would have left no doubt that he had surrendered to Japanese colonialism. For instance:

> There are over two thousand people with a secondary education or higher living itinerant lives in China and Siberia following the eruption of the Korean independence movement in 1919. Further, these people cannot or have no plans to return to Korea. They lack food and clothing and struggle in the winter. They

have three paths forward:

1. Declare membership in the independence movement, take up arms and enter Korea secretly.
2. Become a radical socialist in Russia.
3. Become a confidence trickster, burglar or robber.

These two thousand people form a class of intellectuals and are respected as patriots especially among overseas Koreans. And they have considerable power to stir up popular opinion. They run a number of organizations for independecne movements with plans and activities being carried out by their hand. They are also leaning toward radical ideas. The Soviet government has put in place plans to use the underprivileged young intellectuals of Korea as disseminators of radical ideology in the East, and they are training them in Shanghai and other places. If this situation is left as it is, this group of at least 2,000 will be radicalized.[21]

As the above text implies, Yi was primarily focused on Korean intellectuals living abroad in nearby countries. He stresses the potential threat they could pose: "though they may appear small in number, they cannot be taken lightly in terms of the national defense and social cohesion of the Japanese society." He sought to focus interest and attention on them as a result. He pointed to their radicalism and the involvement of the Soviet government in this process, and associated their independence movement with radical ideology. He also said that "their radicalism deceives and incites about a million Koreans living in Kando and West Kando who are regressing to the point of being Manchurian savages with no politics, no law, no religion, no education or art." Yi believed they constituted a threat to Japanese national security. At the same time, Yi also implied that these people were prone to become what the Japanese authorities called "criminal Koreans" (Pullyŏng sŏnin) and, broadly speaking, could bring harm to the stability of the colonial order.

Yi saw the edification of the two thousand intellectuals and the "development of the million people" through education and cultural movements as urgent.

---

21 Yi's letter to Saitō Makoto, Japanese Governor-General of Korea, was discovered in Saitō's files by Hatano Setsuko, who explained the context in which it was written. Yi Kwangsu, "Letter of Suggestions Concerning Koreans Living Abroad," *The Modern Bibliography Review* (2013): 391-403.

Yi asked for confidentiality with regards to his letter containing such proposals, and this meant that its existence and contents were known to very few people. Given that Yi's harshest critics never commented on it, it seemed that this request was respected.

Yi's appeals to colonial power and the colonial Korean society continued after his return. Writing under various pen names, he wrote pieces of editorials such as "The Leading Class and the Society," "Koreans' View of Life Based on Fatalism," "To Boys," "Art and Life," and "To Those Who Set Their Heart on Literature." And, finally, in May 1922, Yi wrote the essay entitled "National Reconstruction" under his own name. This 54-page essay sought to offer a systematic argument for long-term preparation for independence as opposed to active, radical resistance to colonialism.[22]

To justify his views, Yi depreciated the March First Movement, calling it the acts of "barbarians." Despite the rapid change in Korean national consciousness following the movement, Yi regarded it as "ignorant and irrational drift of a barbaric race without self-awareness" brought about through natural instinct and chance.[23] Such assertions are clearly highly problematic. The writer of the "February Eighth Declaration of Independence," who had participated in the formation of the Provisional Government, reduced not only the collective action undertaken by his people but also his own political activities to that of the "barbarian movement" driven by "primitive thoughts."

Yi called for a spiritual regeneration through the "reconstruction" of the Korean mindset. Contrasting the civilized with the barbaric, he described the former as being goal-oriented, flexible, self-aware, and not driven by instinct and impulse. His view of "National Reconstruction" was built on a depoliticized

---

22 "National Reconstruction" was written with the intent of attracting supporters to Yi's point of view, yet the text also underlined a logic of exclusion. This idea was close to the concept of order as distinct from the declarative politics that Jacques Rancière describes in his book *Disagreement*. Those who were in accordance with certain norms of conduct and social order were included, while so-called deviants and vagrants were excluded. The underlying logic of all this was deferring the present, which is exemplified by the idea of developmental modernization. It was for this reason that "National Reconstruction" was of use under the dictatorship of Park Chung-hee, who endorsed developmentalism and ruled Korea with an iron fist for 18 years.

23 Yi Kwangsu, "National Reconstruction," *The Complete Works of Yi Kwangsu*, vol. 10 (Seoul: Usinsa, 1979), 116.

notion of culture, premised upon ethics and the cultivation of the mind and body. He insisted that focus on self-discipline and gradualist reform was the "only path of survival." Yi also took a dim view of revolutionaries and patriots: "Their reputation is built upon emptiness. Of course, not all of them are like this. But it seems that their reputations come only from the noise they make, their time in prison and their wanderings abroad. I would like to talk in more detail about this here, but due to a number of circumstances I am not at liberty to do so."

These views were further echoed in the article "From a World of Struggle to a World of Support" published soon after "National Reconstruction" came out. This article also stresses the "anachronistic fallacy" inherent in armed struggle.[24] Yi argues that "Gandhi's non-resistance method of organizing" is far closer to the ideals of humanity than "Lenin's organizing through violence and politics." He advocated for the unity of the "civilized" and the establishment of a "culture of love and conscience."

Yi's rejection of all radicalism in the wake of the March First Movement led him to regard radicalists as antagonists. In his fictional works written after his return, which have been criticized for being primarily focused on this political message and failing to abide by the form of the novel,[25] radicals were portrayed as merely the violent "other" who only aimed to overthrow everyday life.

4. Internalizing Colonial Violence

In the final parts of *My Confession*, Yi defends his pro-Japanese activities: "The Japanese authorities were said to have made a list of nationalist Korean intellectuals, numbering between 30,000 and 37,000. There was a rumor that the Governor-General, the Prosecutor's Office, and the Yongsan Garrison were considering preemptive arrest and execution of those Korean nationalists with

24 Yi Kwangsu, "From a World of Struggle to a World of Support," *The Complete Works of Yi Kwangsu,* vol. 10 (Seoul: Usinsa, 1979), 172.
25 For instance, see Kim Tongin, "Yi Kwangsu Research (5)," *Samchŏlli,* June 1935, 262.

the declaration of martial law." Although this rumor cannot be verified, Yi claims to have believed it, and to have "substantiated" it through his book. It would nevertheless be unreasonable to just accept his claims at face value.

My Confession mixed fact with fiction and exaggeration alongside hearsay. Yi aimed to present himself as living constantly under the threat of indiscriminate violence at the hands of colonial authorities. The appendix to the book, entitled "The Words of a Japanese Collaborator" (*Ch'inilp'aŭi pyŏn*), also seeks to cement his status as a victim: "Strictly speaking, being alive is collaboration [with the Japanese]. Why? Because if you did not collaborate, you would die or be sent to prison." Here, Yi was echoing the rumor of the coming massacre of Korean intellectuals, justifying his collaboration as sparing the nation a further sacrifice.

Such was the self-defense Yi offered, but it was also his deep-rooted fear of exclusion and extermination associated with his memory of the Kando Massacre that played a major role in shaping his views. For Yi, indiscriminate colonial violence was the damage and scars that radicalism could bring. The radicalism Yi had rejected reemerged, however, during the Korean War fought between the left and right as part of the global Cold War.

Up to now, studies on Yi Kwangsu tended to pay little attention to the Kando Massacre, which occurred while he was still deeply involved with the Provisional Government. This article has raised the need to reexamine the impact of the massacre on Yi. What happened in Kando was a wanton act of mass killing of Korean migrants by the Japanese army with the tacit support of the Chinese government. Yi sought to overcome the pain and sacrifices of a powerless colonial subject by advocating a pro-colonial line of building a "more civilized nation." This article examined Yi's post-return writings to prove that his fear of colonial violence and exclusion was an important factor for his return.

The questions surrounding Yi's return are closely related to largely unresolved issue of pro-Japanese collaboration in Korean society today. His activities after return and his voluntary collaboration during the Second Sino-Japanese War and the Second World War, which he later described as a "compromise for the sake of the nation," left a deep scar on Korean history. Even as his other contemporaries fought to the end, Yi, a pioneer of modern Korean literature, turned collaborator and left us with the task of assessing his place in history. In the anti-communist South Korea, some sympathized with the argument he made in "The Words of a Japanese Collaborator." To defend his work, they extrapolated that one would be seen as a collaborator even by virtue of being alive under Japanese colonial rule. Others, however, were far more critical. These two contrasting sets of views existed throughout Cold War period of post-colonial South Korea and continue to shape how we view Yi Kwangsu and his legacy.

Trans. by Peter Ward

Part 2.

Outline and Background
of the March First Movement

The March First Movement: A Memory of A Hundred Years Ago

Kim Jeong-in

1. The March First Movement Seen from Today

In 2019, the March First Movement celebrated its 100th anniversary. In the past 100 years, the March First Movement has always been remembered among South Koreans as a historical achievement that established the legitimacy of the Republic of Korea. However, such popular notion that has accumulated over the past century is apt to confine the meaning of the March First Movement, merely repeating the past interpretations of the movement. Now it is time to look back and see whether such a repetition has limited our understanding of history.

This article attempts to reconstruct the memories of the March First Movement by focusing on the concepts of space, people, culture, world, and ideology and expand the historical significance of the March First Movement. This is not a simple record of memories that have accumulated from the past, but a narrative of the March First Movement seen from today, because no present is free from the past, and no past is free from the present.

2. The March First Movement's Space: Starting from the Northern Region, Spreading from Urban to Rural Areas

It is commonly believed that the March First Movement demonstrations took place only in Seoul on March 1, 1919. Seoul was indeed the place where the leading figures of the movement gathered and proclaimed Korea's independence. However, when the Declaration of Independence was read in Seoul, similar demonstrations took place in six other cities on the same day. These six cities were Pyongyang (P'yŏngyang), Chinnamp'o, Anju, Ŭiju, Sŏnch'ŏn, and Wŏnsan, all located in what is now North Korea. State censorship during the Cold War left most South Koreans ignorant about what happened in the other six cities on March 1, 1919. Following the initial rallies, demonstrations for national independence spread throughout the northern regions of Korea in the next 15 days, and reached the central and southern regions after mid-March. The peak of these national independence demonstrations was in early April. The March First Movement was the first case in modern Korean history in which mass protests in cities spread to rural areas.

1) The Demonstrations on March 1, 1919: Seoul, Pyongyang, Chinnamp'o, Sŏnch'ŏn, Ŭiju, Wŏnsan, and Anju

When we think of the independence demonstration on March 1, 1919, the demonstration that began at T'apkol Park in Seoul normally comes to mind. It is true that Seoul was the birthplace of the March First Movement but Ch'ŏndoist and Christian groups in Seoul functioned as national representatives together with local religious leaders, and students from all corners of the country.

By early morning of March 1st, students had distributed copies of the Declaration of Independence all across the city. In the morning, a ceremony was held in Tŏksu Palace to read condolences as part of the funeral procedures for the deceased Emperor Kojong. The city was full of people from all over the country who had gathered to attend the funeral. Students who had left their school gates around noon distributed the Declaration of Independence as they marched to T'apkol Park. 29 of the 33 national representatives gathered at T'aehwagwan, and at 2 p.m., they held a ceremony for the declaration of independence. The representatives were then arrested by the police who had heard about the gathering. Meanwhile, about 200 students had gathered in T'apkol Park at 2 p.m. Chŏng Chaeyong, a Christian leader from Haeju, went up to the P'algakchŏng Pavilion and read the Declaration of Independence. When the reading of the document was over, the protesters shouted *manse* (long live Korea!) for independence as they marched out of T'apkol Park in the direction of Tongdaemun and Chongno. The group protesters departing from T'apkol Park were initially around 200 in number, but soon reached thousands as they circled Seoul throughout the afternoon. The protesters divided into several groups and gathered at Ponjŏng (current Ch'ungmuro) around 4 p.m. in order to march to the building of Japanese Government-General at the foot of Namsan Mountain. Surprised by this protest, the Government-General of Korea requested the commander of the Chosŏn army (Japanese occupation forces in colonial Korea) to send troops. Soldiers laid a defensive line on the 2nd street at Ponjŏng at around 5 p.m. and broke up the protest.

Meanwhile, demonstrations for independence took place simultaneously in the northern regions. The independence demonstration on March 1st in Pyongyang, the second largest city in Korea after Seoul during the Japanese colonial period, was prepared by Christians and Ch'ŏndoists. Although the demonstrations were prepared separately by each religious group, they joined hands in solidarity. At 1 p.m. that day, the Presbyterian Church, the Methodist Church, and Ch'ŏndoists each held a memorial service for King Kojong, who had died on January 21 and was to be buried on March 3. They then gathered in the city and held a demonstration together. The Presbyterian protesters, who had earlier gathered at the Sungdŏk School, joined the Ch'ŏndoist protesters, who marched after a rally at the Ch'ŏndoist Church. As the two groups arrived in front of Pyongyang police station, the police and the military police blocked their way. Soon after, the Methodist protesters came from the Namsanhyŏn Church and joined the group. Although soldiers dispersed the protests in Pyongyang at around 7 p.m., the students marched through the streets, shouting *manse* with a marching band late into the night.

Chinnamp'o was an emerging port city in South P'yŏngan Province. The demonstration on March 1, 1919, in Chinnamp'o was led by Hong Kihwang, the Samsung School principal and a Methodist. At 2 p.m. that day, after the memorial service for King Kojong, 500 people gathered at Sinhŭng Methodist Church, including 100 students from Samsung School. Hong Kihwang read the Declaration of Independence, and at around 3 p.m., the crowd held a demonstration in the city carrying flags with "*tongnip manse*" (long live independence) and a large T'aegŭkki (Korean national flag).

In Sŏnch'ŏn, a transportation hub located in North P'yŏngan Province, an independence demonstration was prepared by pastor Yang Chŏnbaek, one of the 33 national representatives who had signed the Declaration of Independence. Teachers and students who attended the daily prayer meeting at Sinsŏng School on March 1st held a ceremony for the declaration of independence and started a street march with a large T'aegŭkki in front of them. Ch'ŏndoists also participated in the independence demonstration by distributing mimeographs of the Declaration of Independence.

The independence demonstration in Wŏnsan, a trading port located in South Hamgyŏng Province, was organized by Chŏng Ch'unsu, a pastor of the South Methodist Church and one of the national representatives. The independence demonstration began at 2 p.m. at Wŏnsan Market, with Methodists and Presbyterians walking side by side.

In Ŭiju, North P'yŏngan Province, the gateway to China, at 2:30 p.m., national representative Yu Yŏdae personally held a ceremony for the declaration of independence at a vacant ground near West Church. Afterwards, they went to the streets and held an independence demonstration with Ch'ŏndoists. In Anju, a commercial city located on the plains of South P'yŏngan Province, an independence demonstration was held at 5 p.m., led by pastor Kim Ch'ansŏng.

On March 1st, all seven demonstrations for national independence took place in cities. These demonstrations displayed solidarity between religious circles and between religious circles and students. Except in Seoul and Pyongyang, most of these protests were organized by Christians. It is noteworthy that the Declaration of Independence was read aloud in all seven places during the demonstrations for national independence. This coordination means that Ch'ŏndoist and Christian leaders had printed the Declaration of Independence on February 27th and successfully distributed it nationwide by February 28th the next day.

2) The Birthplace of the Independence Demonstration and the Northern Regions

Of the seven demonstrations for national independence on March 1st, six took place in the northern region, Seoul being the sole exception. This region, subject to regional discrimination throughout the Chosŏn Dynasty, became even more alienated from the political center after the Hong Kyŏngnae Uprising in 1811. As a result, people in the northern regions were more open to accepting Western civilization. They expressed a strong interest in pursuing a career-oriented Western education and were fascinated with Christianity.

In the northern region, the indigenous religion of Ch'ŏndogyo and the foreign religion of Christianity took root at the same time from the end of the 19th century. Christianity spread mainly among businessmen and intellectuals in the city while Tonghak and Ch'ŏndogyo were popular among landowners, farmers, and intellectuals in the rural areas. The early adopters of Christianity were from the commercial and industrial classes. They accepted Christianity more quickly than others because they had been excluded from the benefits of the Confucian tradition. However, as soon as colonial rule began, the Japanese Government-General of Korea used the attempted assassination of Governor-General Terauchi in 1911 as a pretext for repression and arrested Christian leaders in the north.

Northern rural intellectuals, in contrast, chose Tonghak, with its tradition of anti-government struggles, to heal the scars incurred from political discrimination. Intellectuals discovered a possibility for self-innovation and political power through enlightenment in Tonghak. People in rural areas, who had difficulty accepting a foreign religion like Christianity, embraced Tonghak, an indigenous religion. After Son Pyŏnghŭi established Ch'ŏndogyo succeeding to Tonghak in 1905, the number of Ch'ŏndoists in the northern region continued to increase. By 1919, nearly 80% of 1 million Ch'ŏndoists lived in the northern regions. For the people of the north who dreamed of overcoming political alienation and gaining power based on Western civilization, Japan's aggression and forced rule aroused both pain and despair.

The March First independence demonstration spread from the six northern cities to the surrounding areas the very next day. For a week after March 1st, 147 demonstrations for national independence took place in 81 towns across the country, mainly in P'yŏngan Province, Hwanghae Province, and South Hamgyŏng Province. Fifty eight of the towns were part of P'yŏngan Province. Of the 276 national independence demonstrations that were held from March 1 to 14, more than 70% took place in the northern region, with 71 protests in South P'yŏngan Province, 45 in North P'yŏngan Province, 28 in Hwanghae Province, 41 in South Hamgyŏng Province, and 12 protests in North Hamgyŏng Province.

3) Expansion from Urban to Rural Areas

The March First Movement was triggered in cities and later spread to rural areas, creating the notion that cities were the centers of protests and assemblies. The June 10th Independence Movement in 1926 and the Kwangju Student Movement in 1929 were also national movements that started in cities. Along with modernization, the space of resistance changed into cities and the March First Movement was a turning point in that change.

The urban and rural protest scenes were different. The protests in Seoul, the heart of modernization, began with a recitation of the Declaration of Independence at T'apkol Park. This was a modern public park made during the Korean Empire as part of its urban improvement project on Chongno street, which was always busy with people. After reciting the Declaration of Independence and shouting *manse* three times, protesters comprising students and citizens marched on Chongno street. In cities, protesting subjects and methods were new and varied. Students who benefited from modern education emerged for the first time as the driving force of protests. The labor class that had grown along with capitalization went on strike, while merchants closed their stores in order to participate in the protests.

In the rural protests, on the other hand, traditional and modern elements were mixed. In many cases, demonstrations for independence in rural areas took place in marketplaces on market days when large crowds gathered. Specific market days had been set in each region, so when that day came, the merchants

gathered and waited for someone to lead the protest by shouting *manse*, while
the military police and the police monitored and patrolled the crowd. Finally,
some leaders would give a speech at a scheduled time on a crowded spot,
read the Declaration of Independence, and then shout *manse* for independence
with the crowd. They would then start to march waving the T'aegŭkki and
other flags. Farmers' bands, performing music or blowing traditional trumpets,
inspired people to join the demonstration. When the atmosphere heated up,
the protesters marched to county offices or police stations, shouting the slogan
"Japanese, go away!" The military police and the police then appeared and
threatened protesters with firearms, forcibly disbanding and arresting them.
Infuriated by the violent suppression, the farmers armed with pebbles, clubs,
bamboo spears, spades, shovels, hoes, axes, and sickles, would barge in to
destroy military police stations or county offices. The protesters would demand
the release of the arrested, and if the officials did not comply, they exerted
violence. Protests broke up only after casualties arose due to the violent
suppression by the police.

3. The March First Movement and the People: The Emergence of New Modern Subjects

Through the March First Movement, new modern subjects emerged. Religious
groups played a key role in planning and spreading the movement. As a group,
Ch'ŏndogyo became the main agent within the March First Movement camp.
Students also played a decisive role in the spread of independence demonstrations.
Moreover, the appearance of female students who took the lead in independence
demonstrations pointed to a change of times. Finally, laborers and peasants
participated in demonstrations and were able to gain status as agents of the
movement.

1) Ch'ŏndogyo Becomes Mainstream

Ch'ŏndogyo was a new religion founded in 1905 by Son Pyŏnghŭi, who
led the Tonghak Peasant Revolution as the third leader of Tonghak. In 1910

when the Korean Empire fell and colonial rule started, the Japanese Government-General of Korea dissolved all political and social organizations. During this era of forced rule, only religious groups were able to maintain their autonomy. As a result, people who felt suffocated by Japanese oppression flocked to religion. Ch'ŏndogyo, in particular, emerged as the country's largest religion, boasting 1 million members.

Ch'ŏndogyo systematically participated in the March First Movement. Of the 33 national representatives who signed the Declaration of Independence, 15 were Ch'ŏndoist leaders and key executives. Son Pyŏnghŭi participated as the head of the Ch'ŏndogyo, Kwŏn Pyŏngdŏk as the head of the Ch'ŏndoist Central Assembly, Ch'oe Rin as the head of the Ch'ŏndogyo-affiliated school Posŏng Higher Common School, and Yi Chongil as the editor-in-chief of the *Monthly Ch'ŏndogyo*. In addition, Ch'ŏndogyo contributed to the nationwide spread of the protests by printing and distributing the Declaration of Independence and the *Korean Independence News*. Yi Chongil printed 21,000 copies of the Declaration of Independence at Posŏngsa, a printing house in Seoul, and distributed them throughout the country through Ch'ŏndoist and Christian leaders.

During the March First Movement, Ch'ŏndoist leadership did not mobilize all their members at once. However, news of the protests in Seoul and other regions quickly spread to Ch'ŏndoists in remote mountain villages through the administrative networks of central headquarters, archdioceses, parishes, missionaries, and the personal networks between Ch'ŏndoists called *yŏnwŏn*, which soon led to organized protests. During the March First Movement, as mentioned above, Ch'ŏndoists' role was remarkable especially in the northern regions, which were densely populated with Ch'ŏndogyo believers. Moreover, the ample finances of Ch'ŏndogyo, which was the largest Korean new religion in terms of influence, supplied funds to the March First Movement. Son Pyŏnghŭi, for example, generously provided 5,000 won to Christian leader Yi Sŭnghun on spot when Yi requestes for a living stipend for the families of arrested Christian leaders.

During the March First Movement, which lasted for more than two months, Son Pyŏnghŭi made great contributions to the uprising and was revered as a national leader. When efforts to establish a provisional government took place in midst of the March First Movement, Son was elected president. Although Ch'ŏndogyo was severely damaged due to its devotion to the independence movement, its involvement elevated its political status and social influence even further.

2) Students Appear in History

Students first appeared on the streets in the March First Movement, enraged by ethnic discrimination. Students' contribution to the movement was incredible from the early stages of preparation. It is well known that the February Eighth Declaration of Independence announced by Korean students studying in Tokyo triggered the March First Movement. While preparing for the February Eighth Declaration of Independence, they discreetly sent Song Kyebaek, a student at Waseda University, to colonial Korea with plans for a nationwide demonstration.

Meanwhile, college (*chŏnmunhakkyo*) students in downtown Seoul conferred about the independence movement from the end of January 1919. On January 26th, Kim Wŏnbyŏk of Yŏnhŭi College, Kang Kidŏk of Posŏng Law and Commerce College, and Han Wigŏn of Kyŏngsŏng Medical College had a meeting with Posŏng College graduate Chu Ik and Pak Hŭido, a secretary of the Christian Youth Association, to prepare for the independence movement. In February, they established a plan to have Chu Ik draft a declaration of independence and mobilize college students for a demonstration. On February 20th, they selected representatives from each college as well as deputies that would take charge of the protests in case any of the representatives is arrested. At 2 p.m. on March 1st, the college representatives heard the news that a religious circle-led declaration of independence would be held at T'apkol Park and mobilized secondary school students to join the demonstration. They also established a plan to have a student-only demonstration on March 5th. Owing to these organized activities, students could play a main role in the process of the demonstration.

On March 1st, student representatives from each school gave a speech saying, "since Korean representatives are participating in the Paris Peace Conference, we must cry for our independence today in order to inform the world of our aspirations," and marched with about 200 students to T'apkol

Park. At 2 p.m., after reading the Declaration of Independence and shouting *manse* three times, they staged a protest march. On March 5th, which was the scheduled date for the student-only demonstration, thousands of students gathered at Namdaemun Station Square at 9 a.m. and held a rally for independence. Those who came to Namdaemun Station to go back to their hometown after attending the funeral of King Kojong joined the demonstration, quickly increasing the size of the protest up to 10,000. The protesters waved the Korean national flag and marched on the street.

On March 10th, the Government-General issued an order to temporarily close the secondary schools and colleges in Seoul, fearing an expansion of student protests. Ironically, however, the school closure measure contributed to the spread of the March First Movement as students returned to their hometowns with copies of the declaration and started independence demonstrations there. For example, Yu Kwansun participated in the demonstration on March 1st and March 5th as a student of Ewha Women's College. When school closed, she returned home on March 13th with a copy of the Declaration of Independence. On April 1st, she started an independence demonstration on a market day at Pyŏngch'ŏn Aunae marketplace.

The appearance of female students garnered great attention at the time. *Ōsaka Daily Newspaper* featured articles about the March First Movement, highlighting the participation of female students. The appearance of female students who were arrested, imprisoned, and put on trial for their participation in the independence movement aroused shock and anger among Koreans. Media outlets reported that "the appearance of female students being transferred from the police station to detention centers aroused intense feelings of hatred and anger in the hearts of Koreans."

3) Laborers and Peasants Appear in the Independence Demonstrations

As the March First Movement continued, the subaltern people, with a clear awakening of national aspirations, gradually came to the forefront of the protests. The most noticeable change was the participation of laborers. In Seoul, on March 2nd, laborers participated in a demonstration alongside the students, after which more and more laborers refused to go to work in order to join independence demonstrations. After March 10th, only 10% of workers went to work, leaving factories out of operation. By late March, many people had been arrested and the independence demonstration in Seoul waned, but laborers continued their protests. On March 22nd, about 300 to 400 workers participated in a demonstration, and a workers' conference was held to urge laborers to join the movement. They walked around the city holding flags that read "Workers' Convention" and "Long Live Korean Independence."

In rural areas, farmers were the main driving force of the independence demonstrations. In the 1910s, new laws on land and forestry registration projects enforced by the military police brought many changes to Korean farmers' daily lives. Although these projects aimed to establish modern systems of ownership, the farmers had a hard time accepting forced changes that did not recognize their rights and customary notions of land ownership. Farmers, therefore, did not just participate in demonstrations for national independence but also for their economic survival. They rejected enforced crop variety improvement, compulsory labor and tax payment, boycotted Japanese products, and refused to sell food and fuel to the Japanese.

By the end of March, workers and peasants were at the forefront of the protests. At the same time, violent struggles increased in frequency. This violence was essentially a defensive measure following ruthless repression of the protests. However, there were also cases in which protesters actively took over colonial authorities or intentionally used violence. On April 1st, 1919, protesters in Wŏn'gok County, Kyŏnggi Province, followed the guidance of leadership that had urged them to "[d]estroy the police posts, county offices, and post offices in Wŏn'gok and Yangsŏng Counties. Drive out the Japanese. Everyone should fight with a club or stones in your hands." The protesters flocked to Yangsŏng County, set fire to the police substation, and destroyed post offices, Japanese shops and moneylenders' homes. They raided the county office again and burned documents, furniture, and Japanese flags.

What fueled these people's struggle was their will to liberate themselves from the powers imprisoning their lives. Farmers suffered from land extortion, unilateral and forceful agricultural administration, heavy taxes, and compulsory labor. Workers were victims of starvation, discriminatory wages, and brutal working conditions. For these groups, national independence was a promising alternative to the suffering in their lives.

4. The March First Movement and Culture: The Origin of Demonstration Culture

On March 1st, 1919, all seven demonstrations followed the same format. After reciting the Declaration of Independence, the protesters shouted *manse* together for Korean independence, and then marched on the streets waving the Korean national flag. The setup of the independence demonstrations in the seven places on the first day spread immediately and ensuing demonstrations followed the common procedure. These are the characteristics which first appeared during the March First Movement and became the origin of contemporary Koreans' demonstration culture: a combination of rallies and marches, various handouts scattered at protest sites, flags and songs symbolizing and inspiring resistance, solidarity formed in the process of protest.

1) *Manse* Demonstration Is Invented

Manse demonstration was an invention of the March First Movement. *Manse* was a crowd cheer that had been invented in Meiji Japan. During the period of the Korean Empire, the cheer was used in combination with "*manse* (long live) the Korean Empire," "*manse* the Great Emperor," and "*manse* the Crown Prince." The practice was revived in the way of calling for "hurrah for Korea's independence (*Taehan tongnip manse* or *Chosŏn tongnip manse*) during the March First Movement.

Flags and songs as national emblems made participants keenly feel the pain of the loss of national sovereignty and inspired the will to struggle for independence. Though various flags appeared on the protest scene, the most frequently used flag was the T'aegŭkki. Throughout the March First Movement, the T'aegŭkki became a symbol of the Korean nation and awakened people's will to independence. Afterward, the T'aegŭkki was used at various commemoration ceremonies of the March First Movement and all the events of the Provisional Government of Korea began ceremonies with a salute to the

T'aegŭkki. The T'aegŭkki also appeared during the June 10th Independence Movement in 1926 and the Kwangju Student Movement in 1929 as well. Through this process, the T'aegŭkki became the national flag of the Korean people.

New songs also appeared during the protests, including "Song of Fatherland," "Song of Sword," "Song of Liberation," "Revenge Song," "Blood Song," "Song for Korean Independence," and "Boys, Move Forward." One of the most popular songs in the repertoire was "Patriotic Song" (*Aegukka*) which had been sung since the time of the Korean Empire (1887–1910). Its melody was borrowed from the western folk song "Auld Lang Syne." The lyrics began with the phrase "until the day when the East Sea's waters and Mt. Baekdu are dry and worn away, God protect and save us. Long live our nation!" which was the same as the first verse of the current South Korean national anthem. During the March First Movement, the song spread throughout the country and eventually became the national anthem of the provisional government of Korea.

2) Print Media Encourage the March First Movement

A key factor for the quick spread of protests, according to colonial authorities, was the distribution of printed materials of propaganda which provoked public sentiment. Print media, such as underground newspapers, handouts, and inscriptions, facilitated the nationwide spread of the March First Movement. After the Japanese Government-General of Korea was established in 1910, the only newspaper published in Korean was the *Daily News* (*Maeil sinbo*), which was the colonial government mouthpiece. As there was no freedom of speech, religious circles and students who prepared for the independence demonstration produced many leaflets and papers on their own. The first underground newspaper was the *Korean Independence News*, which was first published on March 1, 1919 and continued up to its 27th issue. It was the brainchild of Yi Chongil, the editor-in-chief of the *Monthly Ch'ŏndogyo* and was published under the name of Yun Iksŏn, who was the principal of the Posŏng College and president of Posŏngsa, a Ch'ŏndogyo-run printing company. Yi Chongnin, an executive of the *Monthly Ch'ŏndogyo*, wrote the manuscript and printed 10,000 copies at Posŏngsa. The *Korean Independence News* continued to be published until the end of April, changing

167

its chief publishers in a relay manner because they were arrested one after another. It inspired the rise of various underground newspapers throughout the country: *Kungmin hoebo, Chŏnminbo, Ch'ungbuk chayubo, Taedongbo, Chayubo, Pandoŭi mokt'ak, Kungmin Sinbo, Kaksŏnghoe hoebo,* and *Tongnim sinmun (The Independent)*.

People were brought to the streets by leaflets, graffiti, and posters with simple slogans, along with underground newspapers, inscriptions and round robins informing people of protest plans and the policy of the struggle. Some leaflets included warnings or intimidation demanding the resignation of Korean officials or the eviction of the Japanese. Sometimes those propaganda materials were written and produced in each region, but most of them were imported from Seoul or China and reprinted with a mimeograph machine. The "Declaration of the Provisional Government," "Provisional Government Decree," and "New Korean Government Declaration" were produced in Shanghai, brought into Korea via Beijing and Tianjin by rail, and distributed near railway stations. The documents were distributed further either by mail or by delivering them directly to each house.

Print media was a great propaganda tool during the March First Movement. Thanks to newspapers and handouts, news about protests and struggles as well as brutal repression by soldiers and the police taking place all corners of the country easily spread, which continuously fueled demonstrations for two months. The mimeograph machine, which was widely used since the 1910s, reproduced these print media. Most of the mimeographs were printed by machines at Christian and Ch'ŏndogyo churches or schools, as well as county offices, temples, and private homes.

3) The Culture of Solidarity Is Established

The March First Movement played a pioneering role in many aspects of the independence movement. Even in terms of a struggle for solidarity, the March First Movement opened up a new world of experience. Depending on each other as a colonized people, Ch'ŏndogyo followers and Christians, students and workers, and people from neighboring villages joined demonstrations for national independence in cities and rural areas. A culture of solidarity between leaders, religious people, and students was naturally created while preparing for independence demonstrations under the rigorous military rule.

On February 24th, 1919 a pact of solidarity was established between Ch'ŏndogyo and Christianity during the preparations for the March First Movement. The two sides decided to hold a ceremony for the declaration of independence at T'apkol Park on March 1st at 2 p.m. in Seoul. They also decided to cooperate with Buddhists. Ch'oe Rin, who was in charge of preparing for the March First Movement as a leader of Ch'ŏndogyo, met Han Yongun, the chief monk at Sinhŭngsa Temple that night, and determined to stage a joint struggle. After estabishing solidarity between Ch'ŏndogyo, Christianity, and Buddhism, student leaders also decided to join the independence movement despite their original plan for a student-only independence movement.

February 27th and 28th marked two important solidarity activities : selecting national representatives and printing and distributing the Declaration of Independence. On February 27th, the religious community selected their national representatives. 15 top-ranked executives including *dosa* (preachers) and elders participated from Ch'ŏndogyo. From the Christianity 6 Presbyterians and 10 Methodists participated and two Buddhists joined. On that day, national representatives sent their seals to Ch'oe Rin to stamp on the Declaration of Independence.

The distribution of the Declaration of Independence on February 28 was also a coordinated act of solidarity between the religious communities and students. Yi Chongil, the editor-in-chief of the *Monthly Ch'ŏndogyo*, took the mission of distributing copies of the declaration. Among Christian figures, Yi Kapsŏng and Ham T'aeyŏng led the distribution. In the Buddhist circle, Han Yongun ordered students to distribute 1,500 copies in Seoul and the rest in southern regions.

As the March First Movement spread across the country, solidarity demonstrations between religious groups and students took place in various parts of the country. Since then, joint struggles in which various forces prepare and lead mass demonstration in solidarity with one another have become familiar phenomena.

5. The March First Movement and the World: Different Viewpoints on the Colonial Resistance

How did foreigners interpret the March First Movement? Was the world moved by the Koreans' struggle for independence and did they show their support? As long as the world was divided into imperial states and colonies during the first half of the 20th century, such things did not happen. Western powers, such as the United States and the United Kingdom, regarded the March First Movement as a rebellion rather than as a legitimate struggle for independence. Colonized peoples and weak countries in danger of colonization, in contrast, highly appreciated the March First Movement as a struggle for Korean independence. There were quite different viewpoints of the March First Movement according to each country's position on the colonial problem.

1) The Cheamri Massacre Becomes Known to Western Powers

After March 1st, 1919, as the independence demonstrations continued, Westerners living in colonial Korea heard of the inhumane repression by Japanese soldiers and the police. They demanded their home countries to protest against Japan. Each country tried to figure out the situations through their consulates in Seoul. L. A. Berghlz, U.S. Consul General in Seoul, instructed Consul R. S. Curtice to investigate Such'on Village (Changan Township, Suwŏn County) as rumors spread that the Japanese police demolished the village and slaughtered its residents. On April 16th, 1919, on the way to Such'on Consul Curtice and his staff stopped for lunch in Hyangnam Township. They noticed smoke rising from behind a small hill about a kilometer away. After questioning, they learned that smoke had billowed from Cheam Village since the afternoon of April 15th. On that day, Japanese soldiers came to Cheam Village, gathered all men over 15 years old at the Cheam Church and shot them, leaving 29 people dead. Then they burned the church down to cover up the mass-killing. Consul Curtice and his staff thus accidentally discovered the terrible scene of the Cheamri massacre.

On April 21st, the day after the Cheamri massacre, Consul Curtice submitted a report to Consul General Bergholz. Two days later, on April 23rd, Consul

General Bergholz submitted a report entitled "Japanese Troops Slaughter 37 Koreans in a Church" to the U.S. Secretary of State. On May 12th, another report was submitted entitled "The Massacre of 37 Koreans and the Destruction of Villages by Japanese Forces in Cheamri," containing more details from further investigation. With these reports, the U.S. State Department became aware of Japanese repression. However, it did not take official diplomatic steps to protest these human rights abuses by Japan. After these massacres were disclosed by Consul Curtice, the British and French consulates also undertook on-site investigations. They reported the mass-killings to their governments and asked them to protest against Japan. However, both U.K. and France, which were imperial states like Japan, did not take any diplomatic measures against Japan.

While their governments remained passive, British and French missionaries sent reports to the mission headquarters in their home countries, and tried to reveal the truth to the public. F.W. Schofield, a Presbyterian missionary, who took photos of the protests from the first day of the March First Movement, heard about the news of the Cheamri massacre on April 17th. The next day he went to the village, took pictures of the scene and wrote the "Report on the Cheamri Massacre" and the "Report on the Massacre in Such'onri." He sent these reports to mission headquarters and contributed anonymously to an English newspaper on the violent suppression. On May 27th the *Shanghai Gazette* featured two long articles entitled the "Suwŏn Cheamri Massacre" and "Such'onri Turned to Ashes," the contents of which were identical to Schofield's reports.

The Paris Peace Conference was held from January to June 1919 for the international settlement after World War I. Criticism on Japan's cruel suppression during the March First Movement, albeit not a meeting agenda, put pressure on the Japanese representative at the negotiation table. For the Western powers, however, the March First Movement was not a legitimate resistance of the oppressed but an illegal mob violence in a colonial territory. Although many Koreans hoped that the story of the Japanese colonial violence would awaken the conscience of the western powers and bring about their intervention, this did not happen.

2) The March First Movement Becomes a Stimulant for the May Fourth Movement

China watched the March First Movement more closely than any other country. Around the time when the Paris Peace Conference started on January 18th, 1919, China was on the verge of losing Shandong Province to Japan. On July 28th, 1914, when Austria declared war on Serbia, leading to the outbreak of World War I, Japan declared its participation in the war, and proceeded to occupy China's Shandong peninsula, and take over the German concession. Subsequently, the Japanese navy occupied several German islands north of the equator. China asked Japan to leave Shandong Province but Japan refused and made the Twenty-One Demands to China. These demands, reminiscent of Japan's domination of the Korean Empire, included demands which seriously infringed on China's sovereignty but China was coerced to sign the humiliating contract.

Japan, along with the United States, Britain, France, and Italy, was a member of the Supreme Council of the Paris Peace Conference and waged a diplomatic war to establish its control of former German holdings in Shandong and several islands north of the equator. The Chinese delegation insisted that the Twenty-One Demands had been signed under coercion and were therefore invalid and claimed that Shandong province should be returned to China. However, on April 22nd, the United States, Britain, France, and Italy decided to award German holdings of Shandong to Japan.

When the March First Movement broke out in Korea, the Chinese, struck by a sense of crisis at the unfolding of Paris Peace Conference, quickly and ardently delivered the news. The March First Movement was first mentioned in the *Shanghai News* (Shēnbào), the *Peking Morning Post* (Chénbào), and the *Peking Gazette* (Jīngbào) on March 5th, 1919 under the titles of "Protest March in Seoul," "Revolution at the Funeral of the Korean King," and "The Korean People's Revolutionary Fever." The Chinese media emphasized Japan's brutal repression and showed great interest in colonial Koreans' non-violent peaceful protests.

Chinese intellectuals and students published editorials on the March First Movement, and compared it to the situation and the revolutionary movement in China. In the March 16th issue of the *Weekly Review* (Měizhōu pínglùn), the March First Movement was evaluated positively for protesters' detailed preparation and firm actions, which, according to the author, pointed to prior training and organization. On March 23rd, the top article dealing with the March First Movement contended that "[i]n conclusion, every single of the Korean people participated in the independence movement."

The *New Tide* (Xīncháo), a magazine published by Peking University students as part of a new cultural movement, featured on April 1, 1919, Fu Ssu-nien (Fù Sīnián)'s editorial "The New Lessons of Korea's Independence Movement," which highly commended the Koreans' spirit of independence and urged for the awakening of the Chinese youth. He became one of the leaders of the Tiananmen protest on May 4th, a month later, and was the first person to use the term "May Fourth Movement." In the editorial, he wrote that the March First Movement had opened up a "revolutionary new era" and offered three lessons. First, he regarded the Koreans' protest as the crystallization of justice in terms of a non-violent revolution. Second, he said that Koreans had started a revolution "persevering through impossibility," which, he thought, the Chinese should learn from the Koreans. Third, the fact that it was a pure student revolution was highly applauded. Fu Ssu-nien argued that although the independence of Korea had not been achieved, this spirit would definitely continue. He therefore criticized Chinese students who were "a new generation that are all talk and no action, and have a crooked heart."

On May 4, 1919, more than 3,000 students gathered at Tiananmen Square and on the streets and shouted slogans such as "Refuse to sign the peace treaty," "Obtain national rights and drive out the country's bandits," "Recover Shandong concessions," "Abolish Japan's Twenty-One Demands" and "Boycott Japanese products." The May Fourth Movement shook the country and spread to 22 provinces and 200 cities in two months. The "Declaration of the Peking Academia," one of the most important documents in the May Fourth Movement inspired the Chinese by stating that "the Koreans, seeking for the national independence, cried out 'Give me independence or give me death."

Around the time of the March First Movement and the May Fourth Movement, national liberation movements took place around the world, such as Gandhi's disobedience movement in India and the independence struggle led by Kemal Atatürk in Turkey. Both of the East Asian movements were struggles against Japanese imperialism but their goals were different. The March First Movement was a struggle for independence to overcome a colonial state while the May Fourth Movement of semi-colonial China was struggles to restore national power. Japan had been solidifying its position as an imperialist power throughout the First World War but the two movements against Japan damaged Japan's image in the international society and disrupted the East Asian regional order. Breaking out during the Paris Peace Conference, the two movements predicted that Japanese imperialism would face troubles realizing its ambition of permanently ruling Korea and dominating China because of the high wave of anti-Japanese sentiment.

6. Ideals of the March First Movement: Crying out for Democracy, Peace, and Non-Violence

Protesters in the March First Movement defined Japanese colonial rule as an enemy of democracy and insisted on independence based on the ideals of human equality and democracy. As a result, the movement led to the establishment of a democratic republic, the Provisional Government of the Republic of Korea. Furthermore, by adhering to non-violent demonstrations, the protesters appealed to the world that "Korea's independence is necessary for peace in the East and the world." This desperate appeal to peace which began during the March First Movement later evolved into contemporary Koreans' desperate desire to overcome national division and restore peace in the Korean peninsula.

1) The Declaration of Independence Advocates for Democracy

When Japan colonized Korea in 1910, Japan was a constitutional monarchy with a constitution and Imperial Diet. However, the Japanese constitution did not apply to colonial Korea. The Japanese military took control of Korea, and the general of the army was appointed the Governor-General of Korea.

The Governor-General seized all three powers of administration, legislation, and jurisdiction, and enforced a military dictatorship.

The declarations of independence during the March First Movement criticized the oppression of democracy by Japanese colonial power. "The February Eighth Declaration of Independence," published in Tokyo on February 8, 1919 by Korean students studying in Japan, criticized Japanese colonial rule as a "compulsory autocracy by an unjust and unequal government." The students further criticized Japan for denying Koreans' right to vote and freedom of assembly and association, the press, religion and business. They claimed that all governing bodies of colonial rule, including the administrative and judicial branches and the police, infringed on individual rights. They also accused the Japanese "conquerors" of blatant ethnic discrimination and human rights violations. They advocated Korean independence in order to regain freedom and justice that had been stolen by the compulsory dictatorship of the Japanese empire.

We hereby declare that Korea is an independent state and that the Koreans are self-governing people. We proclaim this fact to all nations to reaffirm the great truth that all humans are equal, so that our descendants may forever enjoy their rights to live as an autonomous people.

As seen from the above citation, "The Declaration of Independence" on March 1st, 1919 also justified Korean independence with democratic values such as self-government, autonomy, human equality and right to live. It also advocated the freedom of all nations and universal right of human kind by highlighting the "right of all nations to coexist and live in harmony."

The "Taehan Declaration of Independence," proclaimed by independence activists in Jilin Province, China on March 11th, 1919, criticized Japan's oppression and declared Korean democracy as follows:

Koreans, and peoples all over the world, we hereby declare the total independence of Korea! To provide full benefit to our descendants, we proclaim our freedom from the [Japanese] oppressor's maltreatment and the self-sufficiency of Korean democracy!

The Korean people's aspirations for democracy found its expression in the concept of national self-determination, which emerged at the end of World War I. Shortly after the Russian Revolution in November 1917, Vladimir Lenin proclaimed the "Declaration of the Rights of the Peoples of Russia," advocating national self-determination of more than 100 ethnic minorities in Russia. In January 1918, U.S. President Wilson introduced national self-determination as a principle of dealing with the postwar settlement in Europe. The Koreans ardently welcomed the principle of national self-determination, asserting that all the nations in the world should have the right to live freely and in happiness. It was this democratic perspective of national self-determination that led to the struggle for Korean independence.

Another "Declaration of Independence," released by the Korean National Assembly on March 17, 1919 in the Maritime Province of Siberia, criticized Japan as a public enemy of democracy. It said that all the democrats in the world must be "on our side" as the struggle for Korean independence was a fight for the universal value of democracy. In short, these declarations of independence shared the creed of democracy, positioning the Korean independence movement against Japanese militarism as a democratic struggle for freedom, justice, and world peace.

2) The Birth of the Democratic Republic

The Korean people's aspiration for democracy expressed in the declarations of Korean independence did not remain a futile dream. It resulted in the birth of the Korean democratic republic during the March First Movement, not after it, when the Provisional Government of the Republic of Korea was established in Shanghai, China on April 11, 1919.

Since 1910 when the Korean Empire fell, the Koreans repeatedly struggled to establish a democratic republic that would lead the way to independence, instead of mourning the fall of the old monarchy. Right before the fall of the Korean Empire, there had already been claims to establish a republic. An editorial on July 6, 1910 in the *New Korea* (*Sinhan minbo*), published by Koreans in the United States, declared that "[i]t has been a long time since the current government surrendered to Japan, so we are going to establish a government that will promote our welfare and represent our people's will." In 1911, Park Yongman, the editor-in-chief of the *New Korea,* suggested that all Koreans abroad make an immaterial nation-state with the constitution and administrative institutions, endowing duties and rights on each member of the nation. The Korean National Association (*Taehanin kungminhoe*), which was founded in 1912, established regional branches in the United States, Manchuria, and the Maritime Province of Siberia, and regarded itself as the highest organization representing Koreans overseas. However, the United States was geographically too far away from the Korean peninsula and thus the Korean National Association could not develop into a provisional government of Korea.

Koreans in the Maritime Province of Siberia also started a movement to establish a provisional government by organizing the Work Promotion Association (*Kwŏnŏphoe*) in December 1911. When World War I broke out, they accepted the war as an opportunity for Korean independence and immediately established the Government of the Korean Restoration Army (*Taehan kwangbokkun chŏngbu*). However, it was forced to dissolve by the Russian government, which was anxious about conflicts with Japan. Meanwhile, independence activists in China also tried to establish a provisional government. The Sinhan Revolutionary Party (*Sinhan hyŏngmyŏngdang*), which formed in Shanghai in March 1915, organized King Kojong's exile into China and the establishment of a provisional government. However, the mainstream of the independence activists aimed at building a democratic republic, not a restoration of monarchy. In July 1917 in Shanghai, 14 independence activists, including Pak Ŭnsik, Sin Ch'aeho, Kim Kyusik, and Cho Soang, released the "Declaration of Solidarity" (*Taedong dan'gyŏl sŏnŏnsŏ*), which included their plan to make a republican interim government by organizing the National Unity Conference (*Minjok taedong hoeŭi*), a meeting of Korean representatives living abroad.

Efforts to form a provisional government became more active at the time of the March First Movement. First, as freedom of association was allowed following the Russian Revolution in December 1917, the Central Assembly of the Association of Koreans in Russia (*Chŏllo hanjokhoe*), a Korean self-governing body located in the Maritime Province of Siberia, started a movement to establish a provisional government. On February 25th, 1919, four days before the March First Movement, 15 members of the Standing Committee of the Association of Koreans in Russia formed the Korean National Assembly (*Taehan kungmin ŭihoe*) in Nikolsk. Although it was called an "Assembly," in reality, it aimed to be a presidential system that would exercise three powers of legislation, administration, and jurisdiction, modeling after the Czechoslovak National Council at the end of World War I. The Korean National Assembly was officially founded on March 17th with the declaration of independence, when the independence demonstration in colonial Korea was in full swing.

In Korea, Ch'ŏndogyo members also started a movement to establish a provisional government. On March 3, 1919, the second issue of the *Korean Independence News* announced the organization of the Hansŏng Provisional Government and a provisional presidential election, which was led by Ch'ŏndoists and Confucians. They met on March 17th to discuss the procedures and methods of establishing a democratic republic, and finalized a list of government organizations and cabinet members. They planned to hold a meeting of 13 provincial representatives at Inch'ŏn Public Park on April 2nd and proclaim the establishment of the Hansŏng Provisional Government. However, this meeting could not be held due to a lack of support, and the establishment of the provisional government was postponed. On April 23rd, the representatives of the 13 provinces gathered again to hold a national convention and declare the establishment of the government, but they ended up holding just a small-scale demonstration. On April 17th, the "Declaration of the New Korean Government" was distributed in Sŏnch'ŏn, Ŭiju, and Ch'ŏlsan in North P'yŏngan Province by a joint action of independence activists in Korea, Jiandao (Kando), and the Maritime Province of Siberia. There were also provisional governments that existed on paper only. The Republic of Chosŏn (*Chosŏn min'guk*), the Civil Government of Great Korea (*Taehan min'gan chŏngbu*), the Provisional Government of Koryŏ (*Koryŏ imsi chŏngbu*), and the Republic of Great Korea (*Taehan konghwaguk*) were such "leaflet governments." All of them proclaimed themselves as a government of the people and dreamed of a democratic republic.

After undergoing all these trials and errors, colonial Koreans finally established the Provisional Government of the Republic of Korea in Shanghai on April 11, 1919. It proclaimed the "Provisional Charter of the Republic of Korea," the first article of which states that "the Republic of Korea shall be a democratic republic."

Ahn Changho, Minister for Home Affairs of the Provisional Government in Shanghai, led the integration of several provisional governments of Korea. Yi Tonghwi faction, one of the two largest factions of the Korean National Assembly in Russia, participated in the unified provisional government. Moreover, the Provisional Assembly in Shanghai adopted the personnel policy of the Hansŏng Provisional Government and elected Rhee Syngman as President and Yi Tonghwi as Prime Minister. It released the "Provisional Constitution of the Republic of Korea" and Article 2 of the constitution contained the regulation of sovereignty for the first time, stipulating that "the sovereignty of the Republic of Korea lies in the entire Korean people." This became the origin of Article 1 of the current Korean Constitution, which states that "(1) the Republic of Korea shall be a democratic republic. (2) The sovereignty of the Republic of Korea shall reside in the people, and all state authority shall emanate from the people."

3) A Path of Peace and Non-Violence

The participants of the March First Movement yearned for a democratic and peaceful world and shared a widespread belief that Korean independence would lead to the realization of peace in the East. The "February Eighth Declaration of Independence" declared that "[a]fter the establishment of a new country following the example of an advanced country of democracy based on justice and freedom, our people will contribute to world peace and human culture." The "Declaration of Independence," released by the Korean National Assembly affirmed that "peace in the East lies in the independence of Korea." The Declaration of Independence released on March 1, 1919 also claimed that "permanent peace in the East" could not be guaranteed if 20 million Koreans were suppressed by foreign force. Yŏ Unhyŏng, who resided in Shanghai during the March First Movement and participated in the Provisional Government of the Republic of Korea, went to Japan when the demonstrations subsided. There, he made it clear during a meeting with Japanese political figures that Korea's independence was a prerequisite for peace in the East.

Kang Ugyu, who threw a bomb at Governor-General Saitō at Seoul Station on September 2, 1919 insisted that he took such an action for genuine peace in the East because Japanese imperialism had disturbed the peace of the region. Sin Ch'aeho published an article entitled "The Independence of Korea and the Peace of the East" in the magazine *Ch'ŏn'go* in Beijing in 1921 and argued that "the best way to achieve peace in the East today is nothing other than the independence of Korea."

President Wilson justified the U.S. participation in World War I by saying "what we are always pursuing is peace and justice, and we fight for world peace and the liberation of the world's people." World peace thus emerged as a process and goal of the postwar transformation of the world. The spirit of the times strengthened the argument that Korea's independence was the path to world peace. As Sin Ch'aeho declared,

> The Korean problem is not simply a Korean issue, but a global issue that concerns world peace. The national self-determination that the Koreans demand is not a narrow-minded nationalism but an earnest quest for freedom.

The peace theory of the March First Movement was, in short, "there is no peace for those who are not independent." Such pacifism naturally led to emphasis on peaceful independence demonstrations. The *Korean Independence News* on March 1, 1919 contained the following request:

> If even one person acts violently or destructively, it will bring ruin upon Korea, so we must be extremely careful and prudent at all times.

During the March First Movement, which lasted for nearly three months, most demonstrations were held peacefully with reciting the Declaration of Independence, shouting *manse* and then marching on the streets waving the Korean national flag. Although there were some cases of violent struggle, the March First Movement has been remembered in the way of having placed more emphasis on nonviolence. Hwang Kihwan, dispatched to Britain by the Korean Provisional Government, insisted in a petition for Korean independence sent to the British Cabinet in 1920 that "colonial Koreans tried to appeal to international justice through non-violent peaceful demonstrations throughout the March First Movement."

The Chinese showed great interest in the non-violent nature of Koreans' independence demonstration. Chen Duxiu (Chén Dúxiù), a pioneer of the New Culture Movement, praised the March First as "opening a new era in the history of the world revolution by reflecting the will of the people and not using force." Fu Ssu-nien, a student at Peking University who led the May Fourth Movement, also emphasized that the main significance of the March First Movement lay in its being a non-violent revolution.

At the time of the March First Movement, independence movements were on the rise all over Asia. The Indian National Congress started nonviolent sit-in demonstrations on April 5, 1919. Gandhi preached that "we must not doubt that non-violent resistance has revolutionary potential as a means of protesting against the ruling group." He also argued that "nonviolence leads people to a pure democracy," highlighting its virtue of allowing even women and children to participate easily.

The March First Movement declared that Korea's independence was the only way to realize democracy and peace. The numerous declarations of independence proclaimed the end of monarchy and the advent of a democratic era in which the people would be sovereign. This hope was partially realized with the birth of the democratic Provisional Government of the Republic of Korea. The road to peace, however, was long and tortuous. Even after the March First Movement, invasions, colonial rule, and wars ensued for several decades. Amid this harsh reality, the March First Movement has been revered and remembered as a meaningful experience of peaceful resistance for liberation.

Trans. by Park Hyen-joo

By the Peasants, for the Peasants, the World of the Peasants:

The Tonghak Peasant Revolution
as a Pre-history of the March First Movement

Sung Joo-hyun

1. Introduction

The late 19th century was a turbulent period in Korean history. At home, the ruling ideology of the country, feudalistic neo-Confucianism (*sŏngnihak*), began to fall apart, while foreign powers forced the country to open its ports.

Encounters with the Western powers threw Korea into disorder and accelerated the collapse of the country's existing social structure. The peasantry also became increasingly fragmented, as Korean society transitioned to a modern industrial one. The ruling ideology of the previous era was fundamentally undermined and the search for new ideas began. The ruling caste of neo-Confucian scholars sought out new "Practical Learning" (*silhak*), while *Chŏng's Prophecies* (*Chŏnggamnok*) and Maitreya faith (*Mirŭk sinang*) became popular among the peasantry. Furthermore, hopes for a new society emerged in a range of different ways.

The opening of Korean ports in 1876 marked a historic turning point for Korean society. It was forced upon the country by Japan, but it resulted in the country's entry into the global capitalist system, which meant that the country became subject to the considerable influence of global social changes.

In particular, the economic encroachment of the Western powers and Japan shook Korean society to its root.

Under these challenging domestic and international circumstances, people from different segments of society made consistent efforts to resolve the issues impacting Korean society in their own ways. Amongst the social elites, those who called for a return to tradition and rejection of foreign influence, the so-called "Protect the Orthodox, Repel the Heterodox" faction (*Wijŏngch'-ŏksap'a*) competed with the advocates of "Enlightenment." Whereas the conservative elites sought to avoid exchanges with the West as well as Japan, preserve the caste system, and defend the existing feudalistic order undergirded by neo-Confucianism, the Enlightenment faction (*Kaehwap'a*) sought to introduce Western civilization in order to overcome social contradictions and modernize the country. Meanwhile, the subaltern people looked to Tonghak, literally meaning "Eastern learning." The tenets of Tonghak were expressed in terms such as veneration of God (*sich'ŏnju*; 侍天主) and of humanity (*sainyŏch'ŏn*; 事人如天). Tonghak also aimed at the abolition of the caste system and the rejection of foreign influence. It formed one distinct part of the spectrum of movements in Korean society that sought to modernize the country following the opening of its ports.

The present article examines Tonghak and the Tonghak Peasant Revolution in such a context. First, it considers the formation of Tonghak as a system of thought, and its characteristics as such, which came to provide the intellectual foundations of the Tonghak Peasant Revolution. Next, this article traces the course of the Tonghak Revolution to assess its significance in Korea's modern history. Lastly, it analyzes major documents released by Tonghak leaders during the early days of the revolution for further insights into its meaning as a movement.

2. The Emergence of Tonghak and Its Characteristics

The 19th century was a tumultuous period for Korean society. Political disorder caused by royal in-law family (*sedo* politics) had long consumed national power. As a result, the country's fiscal system fell into chaos and corruption

183

spread throughout the country. Such negative circumstances were further exacerbated by natural disasters, famine and epidemics. The frequent appearance of Western merchant ships in Korean waters created yet more tension. News of the looting of Beijing by the combined forces of Britain and France in 1860 further escalated a sense of crisis in the country. In these trying times, Korean peasantry looked to folk religion, Buddhist Maitreya belief, and even Catholicism for solace and some of them also rose up in revolt.

Ch'oe Chaeu was the late-born son of Ch'oe Ok, a member of the Yŏngnam School of neo-Confucianism. He had been critical of Korean society at a young age. After having lost his home due to fire, Ch'oe worked as a trader and studied martial arts and Taoism. He was angered by the disorder in the world and motivated to find ways to righteousness.

He sought wisdom through meditation and prayer but did not find what he was looking for. In autumn 1859, he returned to his hometown of Yongdam. While living in seclusion, he wrote a poem on the onset of spring and expressed his hope for new wisdom as follows: "Keep the truth for a long while for the wicked not to trespass. I will not take the path trodden by many people of this mundane world" (道氣長存邪不入 世間衆人不同歸). Immediately after founding Tonghak, he freed his two female slaves. He made one his daughter-in-law and adopted the other as his daughter. This is an example to show his critical outlook on caste-based Confucian society. His social criticism was not expressed through mere words, but through actual practices.

From June 1861, he began to focus on spreading Tonghak, appealing to people who wanted to create a new world. Tonghak gradually spread beyond its initial base of Kyŏngju and across North Kyŏngsang, Kangwŏn and as far as Kyŏnggi Province. The dissemination of Tonghak continued even after the execution of Ch'oe Chaeu on the grounds of "deluding the world and deceiving the people" (*hoksemumin*) in 1864. Between 1871 and 1893, believers of Tonghak organized a series of movements calling for restoration of Ch'oe's honour and freedom of belief. This series of events eventually culminated in the Tonghak Peasant Revolution in 1894.

The principal tenets of Tonghak can be summed up as follows: (1) the need to change the world, (2) the belief in God and the equality of all the people (3) the need for a community where all can live freely and peacefully without discrimination, and (4) anti-Western, anti-Japanese tendency for autonomy of the nation.

Ch'oe wrote a book entitled *The Hymns of Dragon Lake* (*Yongdamyusa*; 龍潭遺詞). In it, he used the following phrases to describe the world before he founded Tonghak: "the fifty-thousand years following the dawn of civilization," "the end of the world [according to Taoism]," "the eons of the past," and "the cold and heartless era when it was difficult to survive." In other words, for Ch'oe, his time was a period full of contradictions that had to be overcome. At the same time, Ch'oe described the period following his founding of Tonghak as "the dawn of a new world," a "10,000 year period of the future," "the first fortune of this kind in history." In his writing, Ch'oe prophesied that the era of disorder and contradictions would fall and be succeeded by an era of heaven on earth.

Ch'oe also coined the term "no effort, new becoming" (*muwiihwa*; 無爲而化), which means that a positive change of the world was inevitable. He used this idea to criticize imperialist incursions and the ruling class of Korean society, and claimed that the old era was giving way to the new civilization owing to Tonghak. He described Tonghak as recovering heaven's will and a progressive idea that would support the creation of a new civilization for the new era.

These principles of Tonghak were manifest in the Tonghak Peasant Revolution of 1894 and served as the source of the anti-feudal, anti-imperialist stance of the revolution. In *Tonggyŏngdaejŏn*, a Tonghak bible, Ch'oe articulated a humanist idea that emphasized the connection between all minds, including that between humanity and God, in the following phrase: "You and I have the same mind; God and humans have the same mind" (吾心卽汝心 天心卽人心). He also wrote: "God is not some being distant from humanity to be feared for the punishments he may give, but a being alive in the hearts of humans, a familiar being that teaches people the right way of speaking and acting." Hence, in his view, humanity and God were one, and this view led him to dismiss the caste system of the Chosŏn Dynasty and advocate for a modern form of equality.

Ch'oe Jaeu's idea of God existing in the hearts of human being was further expanded by his successor Ch'oe Sihyŏng. Ch'oe Sihyŏng advocated for a pantheism as follows: "God exists in all of nature, like trees and grass, as well as in humanity ⋯⋯ To serve God, one must serve other people. Hence, Tonghak theology calls for the complete abolition of the caste system." He also preached that "abusing children is forbidden because God is immanent in children as well." Such ideas were practiced by Tonghak believers and were crucial in uniting the armed peasants who participated in the Tonghak Peasant Revolution.

Literal meaning of Tonghak is "Eastern learning," which expressed its opposition to Catholicism, which was known as "Western Learning." Tonghak's anti-Westernism was incubated from Koreans' experience of Western imperialism and remained the fundamental tenet of the Tonghak movement even after Ch'oe's death. Such a stance was adopted, in particular, by those who led the movement for restoration of Ch'oe Chaeu's honour following his death. The movement began with a protest in Poŭn, Ch'ungch'ŏng Province, where tens of thousands of Tonghak adherents came together and demonstrated for some twenty days. The anti-imperialist stance was evident in the slogans and pamphlets distributed by the Tonghak forces during their revolution in 1894.

What is more, Ch'oe Chaeu taught wealthier believers to help the poor, fostering a spirit of community economics. Ch'oe Sihyŏng adhered strictly to Ch'oe Chaeu's ideas of community economics, teaching the creeds such as "mutual aid of rich and poor" (有無相資) and "radical equality of all" (大同思想). While Ch'oe Sihyŏng led Tonghak believers from 1875 to 1892, he sought to put such ideas in practice, making the bond among the believers even stronger.

Let's have a quick look at Ch'oe Sihyŏng's life. He became orphaned before he turned ten and had an unfortunate childhood. He worked as a farmhand and then as a laborer at a paper mill throughout his teenage years. His experience of working as a farmhand had a significant psychological impact on him. He would later recollect that "hearing [myself referred to as] a 'farmhand brute' was one of the most miserable experiences in my life." His difficult childhood also had a significant impact on his ideas. He was especially inspired by Ch'oe Chaeu's freeing of his two female slaves and became a loyal follower of him. Sincerely following the creeds of Tonghak, Ch'oe Sihyŏng was strongly opposed to all forms of discrimination.

Ch'oe Sihyŏng's teachings represented a new message for the peasantry, the middle class (*chungin*), and children of concubines (*sŏja*) at the time, and strongly contributed to the spread of Tonghak. Equality thought of Tonghak facilitated the mass induction of the newly emerging local class into Tonghak in the Yŏngdŏk region of North Kyŏngsang Province in 1863. The fact that Nam Kyech'ŏn from the lowest class (*ch'ŏnmin*) was appointed the leader of the Chŏlla region in 1891 also proved that equality thought was really practiced among Tonghak believers.

Ch'oe Sihyŏng expanded Ch'oe Chaeu's theory of social change known as *kaebyŏk* (開闢, opening of a new heaven and a new earth). Ch'oe Sihyŏng argued that "the destiny of the world is to return to its original state. The world shall be restored to the state of the era in which the heavens and the earth were created. All things in the world shall be put in a new place. A new heaven and a new earth will also bring forth a new people and new things." The expansion and further development of Tonghak teaching accompanied the expansion of its membership from all walks of Korean society. As a result, Tonghak's influence went beyond Kyŏngju, the city where Tonghak was founded.

3. The Tonghak Peasant Revolution

The movement expanded from its birthplace Kyŏngsang Province into Kangwŏn, Ch'ungch'ŏng, Chŏlla, and Hwanghae Provinces, spreading over half the country. However, the Korean government branded it a "heresy" and repressed it. Tonghak believers thought that the Korean government enforced the double standard with its policies of suppressing them as heretics while officially tolerating Catholicism. They thus sought for official recognition of Tonghak as a vital step to escaping oppression. From the latter half of 1892 to early 1893, Tonghak believers waged a struggle to have Ch'oe Chaeu's honor restored, which was part and parcel of their efforts to have their religion legalized. However, the Korean government responded their struggles with further repression.

Meanwhile, the Tonghak leadership, witnessing foreign intervention during the protests, declared their anti-Japanese and anti-Western stance. This declaration changed Tonghak, hitherto a religious movement, into a sociopolitical one. These protests also led to a restructuring of the Tonghak's regional organizations. Small-scale gatherings of Tonghak believers were incorporated into a new set of larger regional organizations. Such organizational capacity of Tonghak enabled it to undertake the revolution that soon followed.

The direct cause of the Tonghak Peasant Revolution was severe abuse and exploitation of local residents in Kobu County by County Governor Cho Pyŏnggap. Tonghak leaders prepared for the rebellion in winter 1893 but Cho Pyŏnggap was transferred to another region and the uprising plan was delayed. Cho, however, was soon reappointed Governor of Kobu County and the rebellion broke out. The rebels occupied Kobu and moved to Paeksan nearby. The central government appointed a new county governor, Pak Wŏnmyŏng, and dispatched an inspector, Yi Yongtae, for on-spot investigation. As Yi began to persecute and arrest those involved in the rebellion, however, Chŏn Pongjun, the leader of the rebellion, sent all of his followers back to their homes except only fifty leaders of the peasant rebel army.

Chŏn and the rebel leaders went to Mujang to meet Son Hwajung, the local Tonghak leader, who agreed to assist them. They issued a manifesto on March 20, 1894, and then occupied the county offices again. They then formed a revolutionary army led by Chŏn Pongjun and set out their rules of conduct. They fought their first battle against government forces at Chŏngŭp, Chŏlla Province, and then headed south to recruit more followers. At Changsŏng, they fought another battle and won again, after which they headed to Chŏnju. Chŏnju was home to the ancestral shrine of Yi Sŏnggye, the founder of Chosŏn, and his wife, and was thus considered the "spiritual heart" of the Chosŏn Dynasty. The Tonghak army sought for the seizure of Chŏnju as a strategic objective and ultimately succeeded on April 27, 1894.

After Chŏnju fell to the revolutionary army, the central government immediately dispatched more soldiers, in addition to requesting assistance from Qing China. While Qing forces arrived in Asan on May 7th, the Japanese government also decided to dispatch their troops to Korea on the grounds of the Treaty of Shimonoseki. As Japan had been keeping close watch of its neighboring countries and already anticipated the arrival of Qing forces, Japanese troops of 6,300 men landed at Inch'ŏn as early as on May 12. It was a thoroughly calculated move because Japan's true motive was to invade Korea rather than defeat the Tonghak army.

As Qing Chinese and Japanese forces were arriving on the peninsula, an intense battle was waged between the government and Tonghak forces at Chŏnju. The Tonghak army suffered a considerable loss at this battle, which led to internal conflicts. However, Chŏn Pongjun managed to keep them under control and concluded the Chŏnju Agreement with the government. After ceding Chŏnju to government forces, the Tonghak army retreated to the areas they had occupied and set up the Local Directorates called *Chipkangso*. The implementation of *Chipkangso* implied that the central government recognized the Tonghak forces' exercise of administrative control over the regions, albeit on municipal level. It marked a historical moment when the feudal order was dismantled and transformed by the subaltern people themselves, experimenting a new form of self-governing politics.

While Tonghak forces were undertaking self-governance on municipal level, Japanese forces refused Korea's demand to have its troops withdrawn and occupied the Kyŏngbok Palace in Seoul. They proceeded to set up a pro-Japanese reformist government headed by Kim Hongjip and began to actively intervene into the affairs of state in the country. As Japan's expansionary aims became evident, the First Sino-Japanese War erupted on July 29th. Japan won a victory over Qing Chana and took more aggressive intervention measures in Korea under the pretext of "reform."

The Tonghak army leadership, hearing the news that the Japanese forces had occupied the Kyŏngbok Palace, began preparing to fight against Japan. Chŏn Pongjun sent a circular to the Local Directorate of Muju, with the following instruction:

> The barbarians have entered the palace and insulted the king. Therefore, we are determined to kill them and fight for justice. However, the Japanese barbarians are at war with Qing China, and their spears are very sharp. If we fight them now, Chosŏn may fall into chaos. Let us wait, observe the situation, expand our forces, and then make plans.

The circular showed that the Tonghak leaders proactively planed to respond to Japanese invasion. Meanwhile, Tonghak forces in some regions began an active struggle against the Japanese. This had considerable influence on the Tonghak leaders and they began a new uprising to expel the foreign force. They sent solemn letters to the Local Directorates in Chŏlla Province and called for assembling a new force to expel the Japanese from Korea. At the same time, Ch'oe Sihyŏng's men also began to arm themselves. On September 18th, Tonghak forces mounted uprisings in Samrye of Chŏlla Province and Ch'ŏngsan of Ch'ungch'ŏng Province. They formed a united front and planned to advance to Seoul by way of Kongju. However, they ultimately succumbed to defeat against government forces backed up by Japanese military power equipped with far more advanced weaponry.

4. The Tonghak Peasant Revolution and Its Manifestoes

From January 10, 1894 to the following year, the Tonghak Peasant Revolution produced a considerable number of fascinating documents that are especially rich and valuable as historical documents. They can tell us much about the revolution's ideas as well as the perception of events at the time. This part considers documents produced during the early stages of the revolution because they most clearly demonstrate the legitimacy of the movement. Sources discussed below include documents from the Kobu Uprising, manifestoes issued in Mujang during the uprising, and the polemical statements written during the assembly at Paeksan.

The revolution started in Kobu, along with the first of their manifestoes, which highlighted the corruption of the elite, the despair of the subaltern people, and their pledge to help the people and ensure their livelihood. The rebellion is justified on the ground that "the most fundamental part of a country are its people, and in these times of crisis, we are risking our lives to save our people and thus protect our country." The contents of these documents generally point to the anti-feudal nature of the revolution with the calls to root out corruption.

In the document, the Tonghak revolutionaries expressed their objectives as follows: (1) to publicize the dreadful and desperate circumstances in which they lived; (2) to raise a righteous banner and save the people; (3) to expel corrupt officials; (4) to strengthen the country by fighting off Japan and the West; and (5) to urge everyone in the country to join their cause.

In Kobu, Chŏn Pongjun disbanded the rebel group to evade the persecution by the inspector Yi Yongt'ae who was dispatched to investigate the Kobu Uprising. Chŏn and other leaders of the rebel moved to Mujang, where they prepared to resume the rebellion. When everything was ready, they issued a manifesto to announce that they were on the move. This manifesto can be summarized as follows:

First, the manifesto concerned recognition of universal human dignity. Human dignity was considered the most important facet of deontological ethics that the writers of the declaration postulated. According to this ethics, everyone must act in accordance with their social and familial role: rulers must carry out their duties as rulers, and so must their vassals. The same applied to fathers and their sons. This resonated with Ch'oe Chaeu's observation that moral corruption in society resulted from "rulers not acting as rulers, vassals not acting as vassals, fathers not acting as fathers, and children not acting as children."

Second, the declaration targeted political corruption. The Tonghak leadership maintained a highly critical view of the bureaucrats, be they of the central government or of the municipality, and claimed that they were all plagued by corruption, which threatened the state. The Tonghak leaders thus lamented that there was no one within the government who could save the country.

Third, they spoke of the poverty-stricken people. They claimed that officials were tyrannical, depriving the people of their means of survival. Hence, the people had fallen into despair.

Fourth, they proposed policies to protect the country and help the people. They argued that even though the country was in crisis, noble-born officials had no interest in implementing policies that could help the people. No country could exist without its people, which provided the ground for Tonghak forces to seek justice. The rebels thus described themselves as "a righteous army that will save the people."

While the manifesto was deeply Confucian in tone, it also postulated universalist ideas. They appealed to the subaltern people living under the rule of corrupt and incompetent nobility by urging them to rise and save not only their country but also themselves from a crisis. Their words spread across the country and came to represent a call for a revolution.

5. Conclusions: The Historical Significance of the Tonghak Peasant Revolution

We have hitherto examined various aspects of the Tonghak Revolution, including its origins, ideological precepts, the course of dispersion, and some of the ideas that sprung from it.

The Korean government at the time sought to maintain the neo-Confucian caste system. Although some advocated for "Practical Learning" in late Chosŏn Dynasty, they were unable to overcome the dominant ideological status of the neo-Confucianism. Moreover, Social disorder and crisis caused by the Western imperialism were undermining the feudalism undergirded by such an ideology. It was a set of these circumstances under which Tonghak was founded, eventually leading to the outbreak of the Tonghak Peasant Revolution. Tonghak played an important role as a force that sought to overcome the structural crises that Korea faced in the late 19th century. As a movement that provided the basis for Korea's transition from a feudal society to a modern one, the Tonghak Peasant Revolution was a highly significant event in modern Korean history. It was a national movement, a peasant movement, and a religious revolution.

The Tonghak Revolution sought to end the discriminatory caste system. Ch'oe Chaeu's symbolic act of freeing his own slaves was vital to the appeal of Tonghak for the people. Ch'oe Sihyŏng, deeply inspired by his predecessor's acts, advanced a view that God was immanent in humanity and claimed that every human being must be respected like God, which was antithetical to the neo-Confucian notion of class hierarchy. Such egalitarian ideas proved to be highly influential in the late 19th and early 20th century Korean society.

The documents produced by the leadership of the Tonghak army during the revolution also point to a strong anti-feudal and anti-imperialist character of the movement. Tonghak sought to protect the country against imperialist foreign forces and was clearly a nationalist movement in a modern sense.

The Tonghak revolutionaries also implemented a democratic system of self-governance. The Local Directorates in the regions under Tonghak control accepted petitions and appeals from the people, replacing a system of top-down government with a modern, bottom-up one.

Finally, the Tonghak Peasants Revolution inspired not only its adherents and those who took up arms under its banner, but also the common people to become interested in politics and open their eyes to the imperialist encroachment and social crisis. It brought many into the world of modern politics and provided the basis for the emergence of a modern society. Although the movement fell short of realizing its ambitions, it inspired ranks of reformers who succeeded in abolishing the feudal order and the caste system not long after.

Trans. by Peter Ward

The March First Movement and International Relations

Nagata Akifumi

1. Introduction

The March First Movement in 1919 is one of the most significant historical events that occurred during the thirty-five years of Japanese colonial rule in Korea from 1910 to 1945. The year 2019 marked the 100th anniversary of the movement.

Japan paid keen attention to the international powers' response to its annexation of Korea and succeeded more or less in receiving approval from them. Following the annexation, which took place five years after Japan had made Korea its protectorate in 1905, Japan denominated the Korean Empire as Chosŏn and made it an extension of mainland Japan. Thus, any issue concerning Korea was to be treated as part of Japan's domestic affairs, which prevented any intervention in colonial Korea by foreign nations. However, the way that the March First Movement occurred and continued to expand afterward was inseparable from a series of international factors that Japan wanted to avoid. In this article, I will therefore inquire into the significance of the international context surrounding the March First Movement.

2. Japan's Annexation of Korea and Military Rule in Colonial Korea

After Korea was forced to sign the Korea-Japan Treaty in 1905 (the Ŭlsa Treaty), Japan launched a "reform-oriented" policy under Itō Hirobumi, the Resident-General of Korea. Most Koreans, however, believed that the greatest beneficiaries of the so-called reform were the Japanese, and thus responded by organizing militias, inciting patriotism, and launching enlightenment campaigns in hopes of restoring the sovereignty of Korea. Itō preferred granting nominal "autonomy" to the Koreans over annexation but hardliners such as an elder statesman Yamagata Aritomo, Prime Minister Katsura Tarō, Minister of Foreign Affairs Komura Jutarō, Minister of the Army Terauchi Masatake, and others argued for an immediate annexation of Korea. In spring of 1909, Itō agreed to annex Korea soon after consulting with Yamagata and Katsura, partly because the "rule of Resident-General" had failed. In October of the same year, Itō was shot and killed by An Chunggŭn in Harbin, China, shortly after which Japan rushed to annex Korea by taking advantage of the sympathy from Europe and the U.S. toward Itō's death. The Korea-Japan Annexation Treaty was eventually signed on August 22nd, 1910, and seven days later the Treaty was enforced on the 29th.[1]

After the annexation, the Residency-General was replaced by Government-General, and Terauchi Masatake was appointed the first Governor-General of Korea in addition to his post as the Minister of the Army, which he served between 1902 and 1911. After taking office as Governor-General, Terauchi implemented "military rule," under which the Japanese "military police" carried out law enforcement activities and thus interfered in the affairs of the Koreans on grounds of "public security."[2]

In December 1911, Terauchi toured the northwestern part of the Korean peninsula, where he visited Pyongyang, South P'yŏngan Province, and Sŏnch'ŏn and Sinŭiju, North P'yŏngan Province. In the following year, around 700 Korean people were arrested for an attempted assassination of Terauchi during his

---

1   See Moriyama Shigenori, *Research on the History of Modern Japan-Korea Relations: Chosŏn Colonization and International Relations* (Tokyo: University of Tokyo Press, 1987).

2   Yamabe Kentarō, *Colonial Korea Under Japanese Rule* (Tokyo: Iwanami Shoten, 1971), 21-43.

tour in the previous year, for which clues had been obtained from other suspects related to a different incident. Many of those arrested were Christians. Among them, one hundred and twenty-two were put on trial in 1912, while the rest were released due to lack of evidence. The Government-General of Korea and pro-government press such as the Korean newspaper *Daily News* (*Maeil sinbo*), the Japanese newspaper *Keijō Daily* (*Keijō nippo*), and the English newspaper *Seoul Press* suspected that American missionaries in colonial Korea, especially Protestant Presbyterian missionaries, had instigated the assassination attempt. The U.S. authorities and the Presbyterian Church denied the charges and raised a possibility that the Japanese authorities may have used torture to obtain forced confessions. In 1912, three American Presbyterian missionaries and Terauchi had a meeting, after which the Presbyterian headquarters, three U.S. senators, and the Japanese Embassy in the United States reached an agreement. A part of the agreement concerned Yun Ch'iho among those who were tried for the assassination attempt on Terauchi. The Americans insisted that Yun, who had studied in the United States and was acquainted with the three senators, and had signed the Korea-Japan Treaty of 1904 as an Assistant Secretary of Foreign Affairs, must not have been involved in the incident and asked for his fair and just treatment. This had reverberations on U.S.-Japan relations. The Kyŏngsŏng District Court later acquitted seventeen out of the one hundred and twenty-two people but sentenced the remaining one hundred and five people to prison on September 28th, 1912. In March 1913, the Kyŏngsŏng Court acquitted ninety nine out of those one hundred and five people, while maintaining the original verdict for the six of them, including Yun. The six appealed to the Supreme Court, which reversed and remanded the case to the High Court. Although their appeal was rejected by the High Court, the six were eventually released with the special pardon in 1915 upon the occasion of the enthronement of Emperor Taishō.

The aforementioned series of events came to be known as the "Case of 105 People," with which Japanese colonial authorities succeeded in dissolving the New People's Association (*Sinminhoe*), a secret association established during the time of Residency-General. The case exemplified the oppressive rule of the Government-General of Korea which sought to demonstrate their power in order for the Korean people not to resist its colonial rule. As even Yun

Ch'iho turned into a pro-Japanese "collaborator" as a result of the case, the Japanese grew confident that there would no longer be any strong resistance from the Koreans. However, Koreans' grievances against Japan gradually grew even though they found themselves deprived of means of resistance.[3]

3. World War I and Colonial Korea

Terauchi resigned from the Governor-General's post in 1916, returned to Japan, and became the Prime Minister after Ōkuma Shigenobu. The man who succeeded to the Governor-General's office after Terauchi was Hasegawa Yoshimichi. He had been among those who pressured the Korean government to sign the Korea-Japan Treaty in 1905 while he served as the commander of the Japanese Army stationed in Korea. Like Terauchi, Hasegawa was a military general from Chōshū and maintained the military rule.[4]

However, even before the annexation, a number of Korean people had been campaigning in China, Russia, and the United States to restore their national sovereignty. Yŏ Unhyŏng and Kim Kyusik in China, Yi Tongwhi in Russia, and Rhee Syngman, Park Yongman, and Ahn Changho in the U.S. led independence movements in their respective ways.[5]

World War I broke out in 1914 between the Allied Powers, which consisted of the United Kingdom, France, and Russia (Italy later joined in 1915) and the Central Powers, which included Germany and Austria-Hungary. World War I lasted longer than what many had expected due to the rapid development in weaponry such as airplanes, tanks, and submarines. Another contributing factor to the unexpected lengthy war was the emergence of the "total war." Whereas the previous forms of warfare had been characterized by a clear separation of the combat zone from the non-combat one, World War I as

---

3 Yun Kyŏngno, *A Study on the Case of 105 People and the Association of the New People* (Seoul: Ilchisa, 1990).

4 Japanese Government-General of Korea, *A History of 25 Years' Administration* (Seoul: Japanese Government General of Korea, 1935), 237-238.

5 Kang Tŏksang, "The Development of the Korean Independence Movement Abroad," *The Memoirs of Institute for Advanced Studies on Asia* 51 (1970).

a total war forced ordinary civilians on the "home front" to get involved in warfare.[6]

As World War I was at a stalemate and dragged on in Europe, the national strength of the Tsarist Russia, the "imperial latecomer," began to wane, which led to an increase in domestic social unrest. A series of mass protests culminated in the Russian Revolution in March 1917, bringing down the imperial Tsar regime. The new founded Russian Provisional Government, however, remained engaged in war as it sought recognition from the U.K., France, and the United States, aggravating public discontent. The Revolution reached a climax on November 7th as the Bolsheviks led by Vladimir Lenin overthrew the Provisional Government and seized power. The next day the Bolsheviks issued the Decree on Peace drafted by Lenin, which appealed to all warring countries and governments for a cease-fire and national self-determination without annexation or indemnities. The Bolsheviks also divulged secret treaties signed under the previous Tsar regime regarding the prize of war for the parties involved. The Bolshevik seizure of power in the wake of the Russian Revolution and the establishment of the first socialist regime in history had a significant impact on the world at the time.[7]

In March 1918, the Bolshevik regime signed the Treaty of Brest-Litovsk with Germany, with the intent to withdraw from the war sooner. As a result of the treaty, Germany could mobilize its forces on the Eastern Front to the Western Front. As Britain and France feared pressure from Germany and hated the socialist regime, they therefore began a series of military and political maneuvers to overthrow the Bolshevik regime and keep the German troops from leaving the Eastern Front. Although the British and the French forces invaded the Russian territory near the Arctic Ocean, they realized that this was not sufficient and asked both the U.S. and Japan to attack Siberia. Whereas the Terauchi regime wished to jump at the opportunity immediately, the Woodrow Wilson administration of the U.S. remained cautious. Moreover,

6   Saitō Takashi, *The International Political History of the Interwar Period* (Tokyo: Iwanami Shoten, 1978), 9-10.

7   A. J. Mayer, *Wilson vs. Lenin: Political Origins of the New Diplomacy 1917-1918* Ⅱ, trans. by Saitō Takashi and Kibata Yōichi (Tokyo: Iwanami Shoten, 1983), 3-38.

Hara Takashi of the Association of Friends of Constitutional Government (*Rikken seiyūkai*), from whom Terauchi sought substantial support, did not accept the Allies' request without U.S. approval. Meanwhile, the Czechoslovak army which had been dispatched to the Russian territories to assist the Russian armed forces against Austria-Hungary found themselves isolated because of the outbreak of Russian Revolution and the Bolshevik's decision to withdraw from the war. This turned out to be in Terauchi's favor as the U.S. government eventually requested Japan to go on a joint mission to Siberia and rescue the Czechoslovak troops. With Hara's support, the Terauchi regime officially decided in August 1918 to send troops to Vladivostok. Japan, however, broke the terms of agreement with the U.S., which limited Japan's operational area to Vladivostok alone and troop size to 7,000, by sending more than 73,000 soldiers and expanding the operational area to the entire East Siberia. The U.S. condemned Japan for violating the agreement and suspected that they had a different motive. For Japan, the issue of Czechoslovakia, which was a far off country in which they had no interest, was merely an excuse to expand their reach to the Siberian region and eliminate the socialist regime, which might have a negative effect on their emperor system. At the same time, Japan was trying to close in on the Korean independence activists operating in the Siberian region. Many of them, including Yi Tonghwi, were influenced by the socialist ideology of the Bolshevik regime and also sought the attention of the U.S. based on Wilson's idealism, which increasingly caused troubles for Japan.[8]

It was the United States that finally put an end to the impasse and decided the fate of World War I. Although the U.S. officially remained neutral after the outbreak of the war, they tended to side with Britain and France by providing them with weapons and other supplies. This caused a German U-boat to target and take down the British steamship Lusitania, which was transporting supplies and passengers between the U.S. and Britain. It resulted in the death of 1,260 Americans, exacerbating public opinion in the U.S. Although Germany believed that the exchange of supplies among the U.S., Britain and France would be

---

8   Hara Teruyuki, *The Japanese Siberian Intervention*. (Tokyo: Chikuma Shobō, 1989), 483-485.

to their disadvantage, it initially suspended its U-boat operations in response to the outrage from the United States. However, Germany soon resumed operations, as the war situation grew dire for the Central Powers. This caused the U.S. to sever its relation with Germany in February 1917 and carry out anti-German propaganda in April of the same year. President Wilson suggested an idea of establishing a postwar international political institution based on idealism and principles of national self-determination and equality among nations. Wilson could not remain indifferent to the Bolshevik's proclamation of Decree on Peace and the disclosure of the secret agreements between the Allied Powers on postwar distribution of profits, which troubled the alleged opposition between democratic Allied Powers and despotic Central Powers. As a result, Wilson delivered a speech before the members of Congress on January 8, 1918, in which he argued that the "only possible" program for world peace was the realization of the Fourteen Points. Points I through V and XIV referred to Wilson's initiative for a new international political order, and the rest contained solutions for specific issues in Europe. Point V, which reads, "the interests of the populations concerned must have equal weight with the equitable claims of the government whose title is to be determined," has been interpreted as Wilson advocating for "national self-determination."[9]

Although Wilson's Fourteen Points and Lenin's Decree on Peace were in competition with each other, they seemed to be similar. Wilson also expressed the idea of national self-determination in his subsequent speech at Mount Vernon on July 4th in 1918, arguing that his proposal was not limited to a particular region.[10]

Under these circumstances, the war came to a halt on November 11, 1918, as Germany accepted a peace treaty along the lines of the Fourteen Points. Accordingly, the U.S. government agreed to discuss the Fourteen Points with Britain and France. They, however, limited the application of Point V to only the German and Austro-Hungarian colonies and those affected directly by

---

9 Aruga Tadashi, "Wilson's Administration and America's Participation in the War," in *Iwanami Lecture on World History,* vol. 24 (Tokyo: Iwanami Shoten, 1970), 261-283.

10 Shindō Eiichi, *Introduction to Contemporary American Diplomacy* (Tokyo: Sōbunsha, 1974), 279-281.

the war, and did not allow "incomplete nations" to participate in the upcoming Paris Peace Conference. Although the notion of "incomplete nations" seemed ambiguous, it was clear that colonial Korea was one of them. "The idea of self-determination is like dynamite and causes sparks around the world by raising expectations that will never realize," warned Secretary of State Robert Lansing, who arrived in France as a member of the U.S. delegation to the Paris Peace Conference in December 1918. His warning came true in colonial Korea's March First Movement. However, the Japanese government was assured that Point V would not apply to Japan's colonies from talks between Chinda Sutemi, the Japanese Ambassador to the United Kingdom, and the British officials.[11]

4. The Outbreak of the March First Movement and Its International Impact

As these events unfolded in the international scene, colonial government-run *Daily News* first reported on the Fourteen Points. However, it was evident that the reporter feared that the speech would have adverse effect on colonial Korea, as the article criticized the U.S. as follows: "With their issue of racial discrimination against black people and the problem of the Philippines, is the U.S. truly determined to take the initiative?" Meanwhile, Korean religious leaders and those who were living abroad at the time kept up with the latest news. In the U.S., Rhee Syngman and others attempted to fly to Paris to attend the Paris Peace Conference, but were thwarted by the U.S. State Department. From Russia Yun Hae and Ko Ch'angil headed to Paris but got stranded on the way and arrived in Paris too late. Meanwhile, in Chinese territory, Yŏ Unhyŏng, leader of the Sinhan Youth Party (*Sinhan ch'ŏngnyŏn-dang*), which was formed in November 1918, dispatched Kim Kyusik to Paris as a representative. As Kim was able to enter Paris safely, the defense of the Korean proposal at the Paris Peace Conference was up to him. In colonial Korea, Christian and Chŏndoist leaders also saw that the conference was an

---

11 Saitō, *The International Political History*, 19-20, 50-51.

201

opportunity to promote Korean independence to the world. They soon decided to cooperate with each other and with the Buddhists, seeking to start a national independence movement.[12]

The Paris Peace Conference began on January 18, 1919 and former Korean emperor Kojong suddenly passed away on January 21. There were several rumors about his death: that he committed suicide to prevent the wedding of his son Yi Ŭn and Japanese Princess Nashimoto, which was scheduled to take place on January 25; that he was poisoned because he refused to write a letter to the Paris Peace Conference telling the western powers that he was satisfied with the Japanese rule in Korea, or because he had secretly been communicating with independence activists. It is not clear whether these hypotheses are true.[13]

Amid growing suspicions surrounding King Kojong's death, on February 8, 1919, Korean students studying in Tokyo issued the "February Eighth Declaration of Independence" at the Young Men's Christian Association (YMCA) building in Kanda and distributed it to the Japanese government agencies and foreign embassies in Tokyo. Yi Kwangsu, a renowned Korean novelist who was studying at Waseda University at the time, wrote a draft that emphasized the wrongdoings of Japan, the U.S., and Britain with regard to Japan's forced subordination and annexation of Korea and the injustice of the Japanese rule in Korea. The students argued in the Declaration that the Paris Peace Conference's call for national self-determination should also be applied to colonial Korea. The threats posed by China and Russia were over, which rendered the previous pretexts for Japan's annexation of Korea no longer valid. Otherwise, they added, the conflict between Korea and Japan would persist, threatening the peace in the East. The students were immediately detained by the Japanese authorities, but the news about their activities in Tokyo soon spread to Korea, inspiring Chŏndogyo and Christian leaders in Korea to take action themselves.[14]

---

12 Nagata Akifumi, *Japan's Rule over Korea and International Relations: The Korean Independence Movement and the United States, 1910-1922* (Tokyo: Heibonsha, 2005), 95-119.

13 Yi Pangja, *As It Goes* (Tokyo: Keiyusha, 1984), 29-60.

14 Kang Tŏksang, *Image of the Korean Independence Movement* (Tokyo: Aoki Shoten, 1984), 152-156.

King Kojong's funeral was set for March 3rd, 1919, and the authorities began to prepare for it. Religious circles in colonial Korea decided to declare the independence of Korea before the funeral as they wanted to take advantage of the thousands of people who would be coming to Seoul (then Kyŏngsŏng) for the funeral. They printed the Declaration of Independence and set the date for its announcement as March 1st. Those who came to be known as the "33 National Representatives," consisting of fifteen Chŏndoists, sixteen Christians, and two Buddhists, were arrested on March 1st after reciting the Declaration of Independence at a Chinese restaurant. During the interrogation by the authorities, they argued as follows: Despite the unlikelihood that national self-determination would be applied to colonial Korea, as Japan came out victorious from the war, there was a need for the Koreans to take advantage of the current domestic and international situations and do something. In other words, they presented a type of occasionalist argument advocating for direct action based on accurate understanding of the current state of affairs at the time. Meanwhile, the students, who had been rejected to join the National Representatives' recital of the Declaration of Independence at the restaurant, instead read out loud the document in front of hundreds and thousands of people who had gathered at T'apkol Park in Chongno. Although this Declaration of Independence called for Korean independence from Japan, its tone was less confrontational and more abstract than the February Eighth Declaration of Independence. Records indicate that the idea of national self-determination had been widespread among the masses after the outbreak of the March First Movement. Although we should not underestimate the influence of self-determination on colonial Korea, the Korean leaders at the time did take advantage of the domestic and international situations surrounding their country in starting the March First Movement. In other words, while investigating the historical cause of the March First Movement, one should not overemphasize the influence of national self-determination by neglecting other factors such as the actual conditions of the military rule and, above all, the growing dissatisfaction among the Korean people. The relationship between the idea of national self-determination and Colonial Korea was not decisive, as the March First Movement was overdetermined by factors that were both internal and external to Colonial Korea.[15]

None of the independence activists including the thirty three national representatives who had signed the Declaration of Independence informed foreign missionaries of their plans. Many foreign missionaries, however, had intuited that Koreans were planning something. Because of their close relationship with Korean followers of Christianity, foreign missionaries suspected that something was going to happen at King Kojong's funeral on March 3rd. Only Frank W. Schofield, a Canadian physician at the Severance Hospital of the Presbyterian Church, knew that the independence movement would take place on March 1st but he was a rare exception. On February 28th, Schofield was presented with the Declaration of Independence by one of the students he knew. Schofield wanted to stop the plan, saying that such a movement was unlikely to succeed and would ultimately be harmful for the Korean people, but the March First Movement took place regardless of his advice.[16]

5. Development of the March First Movement and International Relations

The Japanese authorities did not predict that the colonial Koreans would launch a large-scale independence movement. Therefore, when Governor-General Hasegawa Yoshimichi and others were informed of the uprising in the middle of their discussion over how to proceed with the funeral of King Kojong on March 1st, they were taken aback. After hearing reports from Korea, Prime Minister Hara Takashi wrote in his diary on March 2nd, "I think they were mainly incited by the empty principle of national self- determination but there were a few other factors." After consulting with Minister of the Army Tanaka Giichi and Hasegawa, who had temporarily returned to Japan, Hara dispatched six infantry battalions to suppress the movement.[17]

The movement started in Seoul and spread across the country. The protesters

---

15 Nagata, *Japan's Rule over Korea and International Relations,* 119-120.

16 Frank W. Schofield, "What Happened on Samil Day, March 1, 1919," in *The Feel of Korea,* ed. Jung In-hah (Seoul: Hollym Corporation, 1966), 277-279.

17 Nagata, *Japan's Rule over Korea and International Relations,* 245-249.

marched shouting "Long Live Korean independence!" and did not harm any Japanese residents. The Japanese authorities, however, used force to suppress the movement from the beginning, which aroused protesters' resistance and resulted in bloodshed. Meanwhile, on April 15th, one military police unit entered Cheam Village, which was located in south of Suwŏn, Kyŏnggi Province, gathered and locked up around thirty Korean men in a church. During this so-called Cheamri Massacre, the officers set fire to the church and killed those who were locked up inside. The following day, the U.S. Consul General in Seoul conducted an on-site inspection and the British Consul General's inspection followed. Japan's attempt to cover up the killing was not successful and it was reported around the world by the American writers who accompanied the inspection.[18]

The Japanese authorities believed that their rule in colonial Korea would be consolidated with ease following the annexation. In the wake of the March First Movement they began a "criminal hunt" to demonstrate their conviction that what contributed to the movement were "external factors" that had nothing to do with Japanese colonial rule in Korea. The Government-General of Korea and Japanese media outlets located the cause of the March First Movement in the following two U.S.-related factors: instigation by American missionaries and Wilsonian national self-determination. In keeping with this belief, the Government-General of Korea took a hard line on monitoring the activities of American missionaries and even had the military police patrol Severance Hospital, where injured protesters during the movement were treated before they were taken to prison. The U.S. Consul General in Seoul, however, had instructed the Americans, especially the American missionaries, not to get involved in political issues in colonial Korea before the movement even broke out and the missionaries did not raise objections. The Government-General nevertheless blamed the missionaries and intensified persecution of the Koreans. In response, the missionaries made "No Neutrality for Brutality" their slogan. The missionaries in colonial Korea cooperated with those in Japan in reporting on the brutality of the Japanese authorities during the March First Movement

---

18 Pak Ŭnsik, *The Blood History of the Korean Independence Movement*, vol. 1, trans. Kang Tŏksang (Tokyo: Heibonsha, 1972), 200-215.

for Christian organizations and media outlets in their home country, as well as the U.S. government, in order to put pressure on the Japanese government and the Government-General of Korea.[19]

The March First Movement garnered great attention from the Chinese including Chinese leaders such as Sun Yat-sen and Chen Duxiu. At that time, China as one of the victors of World War I attended the Paris Peace Conference and demanded the return of the German Concessions in Shandong Province and retraction of the Twenty-One Demands of 1915. However, China's demand was not accepted, as the Treaty concluded in a way that was mostly in Japan's favor. The outcome of the Treaty led to the May Fourth Movement in China, benchmarking the March First Movement. Koreans in China took this into account and tried to resist Japan in solidarity with China, to which the Chinese responded, albeit partially.[20]

Hara Takashi did not want the Korean issue to exacerbate the U.S.-Japan relations, which were crucial for the Japanese diplomacy but worsening for reasons such as Japan's involvement in China, the aforementioned trouble with the U.S. in Siberia and Japan's filing racial equality issue at the League of Nations. In additon to improvement of U.S.-Japan relations, Hara had another motive to launch a reform of the Government-General of Korea, which was dominated by Hara's rivaling "Yamagata faction." Tanaka discussed back and forth between Hara and Yamagata on who was to replace Hasegawa, who had been responsible for the March First Movement. Hara eventually found a "middle ground" and chose Saitō Makoto, a former Minister of the Navy, who had lived in the United States in his younger days. Although Saitō was reluctant to take office at first, he was eventually persuaded by Tanaka and Hara and accepted the post. A revision concerning the appointment of the Governor-General of Korea and Taiwan was also made during this period in order to make it possible for a civil officer to be appointed as Governor-General. This revision, along with Hasegawa's resignation, marked the end of the military rule, which had been in place since 1910.[21]

---

19 Nagata, *Japan's Rule over Korea and International Relations*, 196-214.

20 Kang Tŏksang, *Yŏ Unhyŏng Review*, vol. 1, *The March First Independence Movement* (Tokyo: Shinkansha, 2002), 189-219.

6. End of the March First Movement and International Relations

Saitō, who was appointed the Governor-General of Korea in September 1919, declared that he would abolish military rule in colonial Korea. He promised this new order would accompany the abolition of discrimination against Korean civil servants, transference of law enforcement duties from the military to the police, and freedom of press and publication in the Korean language. The implementation of these policies came to be referred to as the "cultural rule."[22]

Saitō wanted to improve the negative image of Japan that many other countries, especially the United States, had after Japan's brutal crackdown on the March First Movement. He approached American missionaries in colonial Korea and shared his plan to introduce "freer" policies, suggesting mutual non-interference: he would not interfere with their missionary work on the premise that they refrain from engaging in political matters in colonial Korea. When Saitō took specific measures regarding religious issues, the missionaries changed their perspective and decided not to get involved in politics. The missionaries accepted the cultural rule by the Government-General of Korea and believed that the situation in colonial Korea was improving. Their belief was shared by the U.S. Consulate General in Seoul, which reported to the State Department back home that colonial Korea was headed in a better direction with Saitō's "cultural rule" and that the chaos had been resolved. The U.S. government thus concluded that the situation in colonial Korea had settled down, and therefore returned to their "normal" state of indifference toward colonial Korea as they approved of the Japanese rule. Britain soon followed suit.[23]

---

21 Nagata, *Japan's Rule over Korea and International Relations,* 250-264.

22 The Foundation of the Memorial Society for Viscount Saitō Makoto, ed., *Bibliography of Viscount Saitō Makoto,* vol. 2 (Tokyo: The Foundation of the Memorial Society for Viscount Saitō Makoto, 1941), 372-545.

23 Nagata, *Japan's Rule over Korea and International Relations,* 289-293. Ku Dae-yeol, *Korea under Colonialism: The March First Movement and Anglo-Japanese Relations* (Seoul: The Royal Asiatic Society Korea Branch, 1985), 235-246.

7. Conclusion

Japan handled their "Korean problem," which had posed one of the most serious diplomatic challenges since the Meiji period, by creating a protectorate and pursuing annexation in an aggressive manner that nonetheless accorded with the international law. This move was made with the approval of the great powers. Japan subsequently made some concessions, including a ten-year extension of tariff rates that were favorable to Europe and the U.S., while trying to "Japanize" Korea and implement military rule to curb Koreans' resistance after the annexation.

The consulates of the great powers remained in colonial Korea even after Korea was made a protectorate of Japan while their legations withdrew. Some missionaries and businessmen stayed even after the annexation. In the late 19th century, the great powers were not opposed to Japan's rule in colonial Korea itself because Japan provided benefits for their citizens in colonial Korea. Meanwhile, the world had witnessed the outbreak of World War I, the birth of the Bolshevik regime in Russia, and Wilson's "New Diplomacy," which had a significant impact on Korea. Japan, however, responded to these events in a conventional way and therefore could not keep these disturbances at bay. Discontented under Japanese military rule, colonial Koreans started the March First Movement to gain independence in keeping with the international trend at the time.

The direct and the most significant cause of the March First Movement was the colonial Koreans' dissatisfaction with military rule. Had the international context differed, however, things could have unfolded in a different way. In that sense, it is worth pointing out that the March First Movement has been overdetermined by factors that were both internal and external to Korea.

Trans. by Suhyun Kim

On the 100th Anniversary of the March First Movement:

The "Eyes of the Present" in Recent Studies on the March First Movement

Jang Won-a

1. "The Centennial of the March First Movement" and Contemporary Understanding

2019 marked a special year for not only the field of Korean history but also Korean society in general, as it was the 100th anniversary of the March First Movement. Special programs and events were held across the nation in commemoration of the mass demonstration against the Japanese colonial authorities that took place on March 1st, 1919. The movement is commonly perceived as unprecedented in the national history of Korea and is deserving of the political act of commemoration.

Certain tendencies that surfaced during the commemorative period are noteworthy, some of which manifested in President Moon Jae-in's speech during the celebration:

> One hundred years ago today, we were one. On March 1st, 1919, the students began to distribute the Declaration of Independence at noon. As the national representatives declared independence in T'aehwagwan at 2 o'clock in the afternoon, about five thousand people gathered at T'apkol Park and read out loud the

209

proclamation together ⋯⋯ It was the ordinary people who led the independence movement such as workers, farmers, women, soldiers, rickshaw drivers, *kisaeng* (female entertainers), butchers, house servants, merchants, students, and monks. Those who were formerly royal and colonial subjects transformed into members of a republic, and embarked on a great journey toward a democratic republic. Liberation and independence from colonial rule were only the beginning of that journey. One hundred years ago today, we were not even divided into North and South.

What remains visible in this speech is the agenda of linking the past and the present by mobilizing the memory of the March First Movement that took place a hundred years ago. In fact, this commemorative project was led by the Moon regime throughout that year under the following slogan: "The people who saved their history will lead their nation." The Commission of the 100th Anniversary of the March First Movement and the Foundation of the Provisional Government of Korea, which reports directly to the president, ran a number of projects that sought to "reassess the values and the spirit of the March First Movement and the Provisional Government through the eyes of the present to envision a new future for the Republic of Korea that appeals to the people." The commission sought to establish links between the March First Movement from one hundred years ago and today's South Korea. This sentiment was made clear in the following statement issued on their website under the category of "The 100 Years of Memory." This section included phrases such as "the cry for independence and democracy that dates back to the March First Movement of 1919 and became manifest in the 2017 candlelight rallies," "the Democratic Republic of Korea: the Light of Tomorrow in the Tunnel of Yesterday," etc.[1]

Linking the past and the present had certain reverberations in a series of studies on the March First Movement that were conducted around its 100th

---

1 The commission's website—https://www.together100.go.kr/—from which the phrases and slogans are quoted, seems to be down as of March 2021. Nevertheless, their Facebook page remains active: https://www.facebook.com/together100years/. For more details on the commission's activities, see Ch'ŏn Chŏnghwan, "The Popular Politics of the 100th Anniversary of the March First Movement and Korean Nationalism Today," *Critical Review of History* 130 (2020): 8-51.

anniversary. Studies published around the 50th or 70th anniversary were regarded as watershed moments for the field. The scholars of a younger generation, however, sought to distinguish their work in their own way. They attempted to actively reflect upon a set of questions and problems as they witnessed, participated in, and experienced a series of changes that took place in Korean society in recent years. Among the most remarkable features in their work on the March First Movement were their intentions to deconstruct old, stagnant historiography, suggest new ways of interpreting history, and emphasize its specificity. Various public agencies, ranging from the Ministry of Education and the National Research Foundation of Korea to provincial and municipal governments, issued open calls for the funding of research projects related to the March First Movement. Due to these efforts, the field witnessed a number of scholarly books on the subject as well as over several dozens of papers published and presented at conferences held by various academic societies and research centers. This academic interest led to the increase of monographs on the March First Movement.

This paper will focus on the so-called "eyes of the present" or a perspective of contemporary Korean society that characterizes these studies. The new form of historiography that emerged in these studies originated from issues and problems pertinent to today's Korea. It is therefore the aim of this paper to examine the contemporary take on the March First Movement by highlighting what kind of questions were taken up for inquiry and in what ways they were addressed. This approach is premised on the acknowledgment that the recent works on the March First Movement and the vision for a future Korea that is being promoted today are mutually reinforcing one another.

The tendencies discernible in these works which constitute the aforementioned "eyes of the present" can broadly be categorized into two parts. One of them is focused on how to assess and locate the status of the Republic of Korea by looking back on a hundred years of Korean national history. Many of these works tend to be especially invested in the value of democracy, which entails an emphasis on continuity between the March First Movement and the foundation of the Provisional Government of Korea, whose political model was seen as that of a democratic republic. However, it is important to realize that "democracy" is a concept that is inclusive of a wide range of discrete elements. As such, this paper will critically examine the problems caused by implementing a linear understanding of the past hundred years of history.

The other category of these tendencies in current work on the March First Movement has to do with the recognition of a multitude of subjects who participated in the movement. Similar to the emphasis on "ordinary people" as the main actors in the movement in the aforementioned presidential speech, a focus on specific, individual narratives has been common in works on the March First Movement produced in celebration of its 100th anniversary. This phenomenon can be read as an attempt to find a more compelling alternative to the conventional conceptualization of "the mass" in the March First Movement as *minjok* (as an ethnic nation) or *minjung* (the subaltern people). New works instead highlight each individual and their narratives and the sheer diversity in them. Nevertheless, this current context in which a focus on "diversity" becomes prioritized must also be critically examined. Are the claims about diversity now considered axiomatic in the field of history so dominant that heterogeneity loses its potential and becomes flattened and normalized?

The sheer quantity of works on the March First Movement that were published around its 100th anniversary is astounding. Since it will be rather inefficient to examine every single one of them, this paper instead aims to examine the overall tendency among them. The works examined here will therefore mostly include recent monographs on the March First Movement, along with some noteworthy projects which were led by various academic institutions with certain agendas of their own around its 100th anniversary.

2. The Continuity between The March First Movement and the Democratic Republic

Attempts to interpret the movement and renew its significance through the eyes of the present are by no means novel measures in the literature on the March First Movement. It is safe to say that most historians have eagerly incorporated such an attitude, which is evident in the works produced around the 50th and the 70th anniversary of the movement. One of these is a massive seven-volume collection of seventy-six writings — 1,086 pages in total — on the March First Movement entitled *The 50th Anniversary of the March First Movement Essay Collection*, published by Dong-a Ilbo on the 50th anniversary of the movement in 1969. These scholars responded to the urgency of their time characterized by the aftermath of the April 19th Revolution and the normalization of diplomatic relations between Korea and Japan with the Korea-Japan Treaty in 1965. The contributors to this collection, some of whom witnessed the March First Movement in person and still "remembered it vividly," sought to inscribe the event into Korean national history, which was inseparable from a heightened sense of nationalism at the time and their will to overcome colonial historiography.[2] In 1989, Hankyoreh Media Company, the Korean History Society (*Han'guk yŏksa yŏn'guhoe*) and the Institute for Korean Historical Studies (*Yŏksamunje yŏn'guso*) hosted a joint academic conference on the March First Movement in commemoration of its 70th anniversary, leading to the publication of *Studies on the National Liberation Movement of March First*. In the preface, the editor points to the remarkable similarities between the movement and the June Democratic Struggle in 1987 and stresses the relevance of the challenges posed by the March First Movement to contemporary Korean society.[3] The role of the mass (*minjung*) in the March First Movement took on great importance in the book. Its writers adhered to a Marxist concept of class, which was indicative of the influence of so-called "progressive historiography" in the 1980s as well as the June Democratic Struggle of 1987.[4]

The eyes of the present are also prevalent in the work produced around 2019 in commemoration of the movement's 100th anniversary. The attempt to establish continuity between the historic movement on March 1st, 1919,

---

2   Dong-a Ilbo, ed., *The 50th Anniversary of the March First Movement Essay Collection* (Seoul: Dong-a Ilbo, 1969)

3   Hankyoreh Media Company, The Korean History Society, and the Institute for Korean Historical Studies, eds., *Studies on the National Liberation Movement of March First* (Seoul: Ch'ŏngnyŏnsa, 1989), 3.

4   The works produced around the 100th anniversary of the movement tended to highlight not only the movement itself and its historicity but also how the movement has been commemorated and written about in the past hundred years. One of the leading examples of these works is Korean History Society, *One Hundred Years since the March First Movement*, vol. 1, *Metahistory* (Seoul: Humanist, 2019).

and contemporary South Korean society was not unique to the academic discipline of history alone. This trend was also made evident in the aforementioned statement issued by the Commission of the 100th Anniversary of the March First Movement and the Foundation of the Provisional Government of Korea. Moreover, this tendency was also embodied in the spring and summer issue of the *Quarterly Changbi* (*Ch'angjakkwa pip'yŏng*), a renowned progressive publication in South Korea. The spring issue, entitled "Ongoing March First Movement," declared that it aimed to assess the March First Movement in the light of the "Candlelight Revolution" that culminated in the impeachment of the former president, Park Geun-hye. The editor of the issue claimed that the movement had been "the guiding light" for the more recent developments. Im Hyŏngt'aek, who claimed to have witnessed a possibility for reconciliation between the two ideological camps in the "Candlelight Revolution," argued that the ideological divide kicked off as soon as the March First Movement broke out. He also saw the movement as the starting point of Korean modernity. It was therefore an unfinished "revolution," merely a phase in the nation's transition to becoming a democratic republic. In Im's view, the peasant uprisings in the 19th century as well as the Tonghak Peasant Movements had led up to the March First Movement, which was a watershed moment that gave rise to later political revolutions such as the April 19th Revolution, the June Democratic Struggle, and the candlelight rallies. By analogizing the March First Movement with other political and social movements for democracy, Im contended that the task of putting an end to the ideological divide that had persisted in Korea ever since March 1, 1919, served as an important point of reference for today's society.[5]

In a similar vein, Baik Young-seo (Paek Yŏngsŏ) sought to contextualize the movement in the history of East Asia — namely that of China, Japan, and Korea — and suggested that the March First Movement was "an ongoing revolution" in the sense that the political initiatives of the March First Movement culminated in today's candlelight rallies in a gradual and accumulative manner.[6]

---

5   Im Hyŏngt'aek, "Rethinking the March First Movement in the Context of Modern Korean History," *Quarterly Changbi* 183 (2019): 15-36.

6   Baik Young-Seo (Paek Yŏngsŏ), "Interconnected East Asia and the March First Movement in

Furthermore, scholars like Yi Namju regarded the democratic republic as the ground for popular sovereignty, which was a crucial element that sustained a continuity between the March First Movement and the "Candlelight Revolution." He concluded that the only meaningful outcome of this continuity would be a political coalition between South Korea and North Korea.[7] Yi's view resonated with Paik Nak-chung (Paek Nakch'ŏng), who stated: "Although the process of modern nation-building on the Korean peninsula has been gradually moving forward, it still remains incomplete to this date." Paik stressed that the spirit of the March First Movement, which he saw as an example of a local population's active response to modernity, was based on the ideas of Tonghak and *kaebyŏk* that had manifested in the peasant movements. He identified both the March First Movement and what he termed "post-candlelight" nation-building on the Korean peninsula as a mass movement with a national cause, regarding the latter as a continuation of the former.[8]

All these writers put forth a diagnosis in which today's Korean society was failing to live up to the call for an "independent Korea" as identified during the March First Movement in its true sense. This lack appears to be a part of their eager attempt to establish a sense of historical continuity between the March First Movement and the candlelight rallies of 2016 and 2017. To a certain extent, the framework of "nation-building," which immediately sets up an analogy between the candlelight rallies and the March First Movement, seems to imply a hidden agenda for ascribing historical legitimacy to the current regime that seized power in the aftermath of the candlelight rallies and the impeachment that followed.

This tendency to make connections between these two events is evident in the book entitled *The March First Movement in the Eyes of the Candlelight Revolution*. The idea for this project was first conceived at the Segyo Institute, which later materialized into a book published by Changbi Publishers.[9] What

---

Korea: A Revolution that Continues to be Learned," *Quarterly Changbi* 183 (2019): 37-60.

7 Yi Namju, "The March First Movement, the Candlelight Revolution, and the 'Event of Truth'," *Quarterly Changbi* 183 (2019): 61-78.

8 Paik Nak-chung, "The March First Movement and Korean Nation-Building," *Quarterly Changbi* 184 (2019): 305-322.

9 Yi Kihun, ed., *The March First Movement in the Eyes of the Candlelight Revolution* (P'aju: Changbi

begs the question, however, is the phrase commonly used in not only this book but also other works that tend to assume a historical continuity between the two events: "The March First Movement vis-à-vis the Candlelight Revolution." The candlelight rallies, like the March First Movement, consisted of a wide range of individuals, each with a different set of aims and needs. One may therefore deduce that the term "vis-à-vis" in this phrase is open to multiple interpretations. The aforementioned book, *The March First Movement in the Eyes of the Candlelight Revolution*, provides interesting material in this regard. The text includes a number of interviews and roundtable discussions with not only historians but also scholars in other disciplines, which reveals the extent to which the idea of "the March First Movement vis-à-vis the Candlelight Revolution" can be interpreted differently. In other words, what ends up being stressed is a plurality of possible interpretations that the main premise of the book has enabled.

Despite this plurality, what takes on the most significance in not only this book but also other works that share its ethos is a naturalization of the continuity between the March First Movement and the establishment of democracy. The book entitled *Democracy in Korea: Hundred Years of Revolution 1919−2019*, published by the Institute of Korean Democracy (*Han'guk minjujuŭi yŏn'guso*), a research center affiliated with the Korea Democracy Foundation, is a case in point. According to this book, the history of democracy in Korea, which supposedly kicked off with the March First Movement and culminated in the Candlelight Revolution, is characterized as a hundred-year long history of continuous efforts for democracy and a long-term process of democratic revolution. It is from this context that Kim Jeong-in (Kim Chŏngin) criticized the tendency to take the notion of the nation-state for granted and define democracy in institutional terms. Instead, she identified democracy as a genealogy of people's movements from the 19th century. According to this latter view, the March First Movement, which claimed the legitimacy of Korean independence, was democratic at its heart.[10]

Publishers, 2019).

10 Kim Jeong-in (Kim Chŏngin), "Reconfiguring the Origin of Korean Democracy," in *Democracy in Korea: Hundred Years of Revolution 1919-2019*, ed. Institute of Korean Democracy, Korea Democracy

Emphases on democracy and a democratic republic are rhetorical tactics that are especially prevalent in the scholarly work on the March First Movement produced around its 100th anniversary. In her monograph entitled *The March First Movement Today: A New Understanding from a Democratic Perspective*, Kim Jeong-in argued that, from "a democratic perspective," the March First Movement was an important juncture to the extent that it signaled a divide between modernity and contemporaneity, and encouraged others to adopt this democratic perspective. In her analysis, it was voluntary participation that made a nation-wide response to and reception of the March First Movement possible. After this event, establishing a democratic nation became the dominant vision for the independence movements that followed.[11] In *1919: The First Spring in the Republic of Korea*, Pak Ch'ansŭng identified 1919 as "the year in which a new nation and its future vision emerged for the liberated, independent people of Korea." As the title "The First Spring" suggests, Pak locates the kernel of South Korea's political model of a democratic republic within the March First Movement: "It was springtime in March 1919, one hundred years ago from now, when the people, their sovereignty taken away and their land sabotaged by foreign forces, cried for freedom and independence. Every single drop of their tears and blood had made possible the democratic republic, where every individual is sovereign under the banner of democracy, freedom, and equality."[12] For Pak, the most significant outcome of the March First Movement was the establishment of the Provisional Government of Korea. According to Pak, this government was based on the political model of not just any republic but a democratic republic. Pak claims that the term democratic republic had been widely used among Korean intellectuals as early as the period of the Korean Empire, which later gave way to a consensus that the new nation ought to be a democratic republic. The establishment of the Provisional Government in Shanghai was the natural outcome of such a development.

Foundation (P'aju: Hanul, 2019).

11 Kim Jeong-in, *The March First Movement Today: A New Understanding from a Democratic Perspective* (Seoul: Ch'aekkwa Hamkke, 2019).

12 Pak Ch'ansŭng, *1919: The First Spring in the Republic of Korea* (P'aju: Tasanch'odang, 2019), 343.

This emphasis on democracy seems to illustrate that the idea with which Korean society was preoccupied the most in 2019 was being projected onto the historical movement. In fact, the literature from three or five decades earlier stressed the importance of *minjok* or *minjung* in the March First Movement, which was not irrelevant to what scholars at the time and, as a matter of fact, the rest of Korean society valued. Only this time, the term democracy has become the new keyword on which contemporary discussions of the March First Movement hinge. Moreover, it was the term democracy that was constantly stressed during government-sponsored events commemorating the March First Movement. During these events, one could easily witness political acts and speeches that sought to provide a ground for the legitimacy of not only the current regime but also the national history of South Korea and located the just origin of today's Republic of Korea in the March First movement.

In this light, one may claim that assessing the significance of the March First Movement in terms of democracy is not limited to academia alone. The discourse around democracy is an ongoing one, which is also evident in the slight differences found among not only the aforementioned writers but also in the rhetoric employed by government apparatuses, civil society organizations, and academic institutions. What they have in common, however, is a focus on a transition to democracy. One therefore cannot help but suspect that a desire for democracy in today's Korean society — which has a long history, and has not been completely fulfilled even after "democratization" — is the driving force of this attempt to foreground democracy in contemporary assessments of the March First Movement.

This tendency, therefore, calls for closer scrutiny. One must examine whether the participants of the March First Movement truly had democracy in mind when they went out to protest against the colonial authorities. The same applies to the specific cases examined in the aforementioned works that identify democracy as the cause of the March First Movement. One must thus ask whether each individual case was consistent with the March First Movement in its entirety. In other words, the important question we must ask is the following: Are the elements of democracy in the March First Movement being exaggerated in a way that distorts what actually happened on March 1, 1919? One must acknowledge that an overemphasis on "the eyes of the present" in historical analyses could lead to a misinterpretation or misrepresentation of the actual movement.

In light of this acknowledgment, several writers have pointed out that an understanding of democracy in 1919 could have been radically different from what the same term signifies in our times. Democracy and republicanism must also be carefully distinguished when considering the historical context of the March First Movement. For example, in his analysis of various declarations of independence issued around the March First Movement, Yi Kihun contends that the so-called "national representatives" of the March First Movement did seek to embody the principle of rule by representatives, which was an important facet of republicanism. There is, however, no evidence that anyone involved in the movement proposed a specific political vision for adopting a republican form of government.[13] In this regard, Kwon Boduerae (Kwŏn Potŭrae) points out that an insistence on republicanism was widespread during the movement, which implies that the matter of adopting what form of government was subject to serious debate in the 1910s. Kwon suggests an understanding of the March First Movement as a basis for a public sphere where direct action and discourse gave way to the formation of a new political consensus. In other words, Kwon sees the movement as a moment during which the population of the Korean peninsula was able to finally part ways with the monarchy that had persisted for centuries.[14] The different ideas that the people had of independence at the time reflected all kinds of wishes and desires that they projected onto it. In Kwon's words, "no dream was lucid, as it circulated only in the rumors and words of the street."[15] This comment implies that no consensus had yet emerged as to what this new nation that everyone dreamed of would actually look like. Kwon and Yi Kihun are invested in analyzing specific cases in which the adherence to the monarchy weakens, signaling the emergence of a new mode of political consciousness. They thus conclude that the adoption of a

---

13 Yi Kihun, "The March First Movement and Republicanism: Times of Overlap, Compression and a Leap Forward," *Critical Studies on Modern Korean History* 127 (2019): 90-116.

14 Kwon Boduerae (Kwŏn Potŭrae), *The Night of March First: Dreaming of Peace in a Century of Violence* (P'aju: Dolbegae, 2019), 112.

15 Kwon, *The Night of March First,* 124.

democratic republic was not a decisive matter during the March First Movement. Their analyses suggest that an overemphasis on democracy — which results from overvaluing the eyes of the present — in analyzing the March First Movement could lead to the omission of other elements that do not fit neatly into such a framework.

The series of works in which the March First Movement is examined in terms of democracy, then, begs the question of whether those fragments of the past that seem less relevant in the eyes of the present are really insignificant. It is important to realize that one must not rely on the needs of the present as the sole guideline for assessing historical facts. Narrating the modern and contemporary history of Korea in terms of democracy is a political act of claiming a certain significant historical event. One thus comes to an understanding that discussions around democracy must involve inquiries into which values and historical fragments are prioritized and omitted through the eyes of the present. As E. H. Carr points out, certain historical facts will be considered insignificant in terms of their suitability to some present purpose if the past is looked at only as a key to solving the problems of the present. It is in this vein that some scholars have criticized the schematics and linearity of the view that the March First Movement was a democratic revolution. They further point out that this view is homogenizing in that it reduces the thoughts and acts of a wide range of subjects to a single cause. As a result, a singular historical direction is imposed on a movement that consisted of heterogeneous individuals.[16]

This insight leads to another crucial question: Would the March First Movement be rendered insignificant had it not led to the establishment of the Provisional Government of Korea? Various events and projects were organized in commemoration of both the 100th anniversary of the March First Movement and the establishment of the Provisional Government. Most of these efforts tended to assume a causal relationship between the March First Movement and the establishment of the Provisional Government of Korea. According to this tendency, the past is only read as a prehistory of today's

16 Yi, *The March First Movement in the Eyes of the Candlelight Revolution*, 47.

South Korea. South Korea is proclaimed as the rightful heir of the Provisional Government, which provides historical legitimacy to the current regime. According to this rationale, the birth of the South Korean state is something that ought to be celebrated.[17] Recent studies have pointed out that political support for such a view appeared to elicit nationalist sentiments.[18] Some of these studies also postulate the dangers of distorting history for their criticism. I, however, would like to emphasize the risks involved in a linear understanding of history in terms of its suitability to the needs of the present, which in turn reinforces the idea that the present is not only inevitable but also desirable.

In fact, the memory of the March First Movement has been actively and continuously reconfigured over the years.[19] The problem of interpreting the past is directly related to the problem of social conflict and integration in the present. Representation of the past takes on a certain political orientation or belief and is therefore not divested from political and ideological interest in the present.[20] If the discursive status of the past is subject to change in accordance with the values of the present, the past can be used as a pragmatic, political means to meet the needs of certain actors.[21] The same principle applies to the historical analysis of the March First Movement: it can be used as a means to promote national integration by reminding people of how their ancestors stood against the colonial authorities together. Such an analysis will inevitably constitute a political arena. The problem is, however, that we should not gloss over historical facts that were not deemed useful for a certain purpose. We must also realize that the future, unlike schematic historical analyses, is

---

17 Yi Yongki, "Criticism of the Sanctification of the Legitimacy Theory of the Provisional Government of Korea and the Rise of 'ROK Nationalism'," *Critical Review of History* 128 (2019): 326-352.

18 For insights into the political controversies surrounding the "national foundation" of South Korea — popularly known as the "history wars" — see the writings of Hong Sŏngnyul, Yi Yonggi, and Im Chongmyŏng, published in a special section entitled "National Legitimacy and the Trap of the 'History Wars'" in the 128th issue of *Critical Review of History.*

19 O Cheyŏn, "Democratic Movements in South Korea and the Memory of the March First Movement," in Yi, *The March First Movement in the Eyes of the Candlelight Revolution.*

20 Pak Sanguk, "Historical Politics and Its Function Mechanism," *Journal of North-East Asian Cultures* 56 (2018): 233-248.

21 Edgar Wolfrum, *Geschichtspolitik in der Bundesrepublik Deutschland: Der Weg zur bundesrepublikanischen Erinnerung 1948-1990* (Darmstadt, Germany: Wissenschaftliche Buchgesellschaft, 1999), quoted in Pak, "Historical Politics and Its Function Mecanism," 243-244.

not predetermined by a framework or scheme that seeks to fulfill the needs of the present. The aforementioned studies on the March First Movement force us to face the challenges involved in implementing the eyes of the present.

3. An Emphasis on the "Multiplicity of Subjects" and Its Trajectories

The question "Who led the March First Movement?" is a classic one in the field of Korean history, and scholars have often emphasized "the eyes of the present" as they grappled with this concern. *Minjok* (the ethnic nation) was claimed as the main actor of the March First Movement in the series of studies sponsored by Dong-a Ilbo around 1969. *Minjung* (the subaltern people), however, took on greater importance in *Studies on the March First National Liberation Movement,* which, published in 1989, described the movement as a "national liberation movement" that enabled the active political participation of subaltern people. The difference between these perspectives originates from the different social and political climate that gave rise to each. The former reflected the heightened sense of nationalism in the 1960s when the Korean society was swept by nationalist protests against the Korea-Japan Treaty. The influence of the Marxist concepts of class struggle and "history from below" is evident in the latter, which took place against the backdrop of the June Uprising in 1987 and the foundation of Hankyoreh Media Company.

The works produced around 2019 reflect on and criticize the aforementioned works that highlighted the role of *minjok* and *minjung* in the March First Movement, which is indicative of the trends in the field of modern Korean history. This change is evident in the following excerpt from *One Hundred Years since the March First Movement*, a five-volume collaboration of thirty-nine writers published by the Korean History Society:

> As a new era dawns, the field of history is being fueled with a new vitality. Scholars are bringing a diverse range of novel ideas to the table. A new historiography is in formation in the field of modern Korean history. For a long time, the main actors of modern Korean history have been what we call *minjok* or *minjung* ..... In 2019, we are about to witness a new historiography that allows us to

see *minjok* or *minjung* not as a homogenous mass but as a wide spectrum of dynamic, transgressive subjects, and seek out and resuscitate those excluded from history, such as people with disabilities and sexual minorities. ····· Public historians are still too caught up in a nationalist view of history. However, nothing is axiomatic in the new historiography. As binaries fall apart and a vast grey zone emerges, existing historiography becomes subject to reflections and criticisms, engendering new, diverse representations of history.[22]

The engendering of "new, diverse representations of history" is the new imperative in studies of modern Korean history, and the March First Movement was one of its main targets for such a task. Instead of adhering to a fixed, stagnant narrative of the movement, excavation of other diversified narratives was demanded. However, such rhetoric begs the question of whether the existing literature actually was dreary and stagnant. The basis for historical research on the March First Movement was mostly established around its 50th anniversary, which responded to the felt necessity of nationalist historiography at the time. The historical inquiries into the March First Movement in themselves amounted to a direct attempt to represent *minjok, which* persisted even in the face of colonialism. Furthermore, the "vitality" of the late 1980s was exemplified by a "history from below" or *minjungsa* ("history of the subaltern people") model that was prevalent in the works produced around the 70th anniversary of the movement. A younger generation of scholars, however, saw these approaches as outmoded and stagnant, and therefore needed to be overcome.

What, then, was the nature of this "vitality" that emerging scholars were after around the 100th anniversary of the March First Movement? It seems like the answer is already outlined in the excerpt above: they sought the vitality of the movement in the diversity of a "wide spectrum of dynamic, transgressive subjects" that are not "a homogenous mass" and the lives of "those excluded from history, such as people with disabilities and sexual minorities." However, such a pursuit begs the following question: What notion(s) other than *minjok* or *minjung* were the contributors of *One Hundred Years since the March First*

---

22 Korean History Society, "Summary: In Pursuit of a New Historiography on the 100th Anniversary of the March First Movement," in *One Hundred Years since the March First Movement,* 1: 5-9.

Movement proposing to characterize the main actors of the March First Movement? Im Kyŏngsŏk, who grapples with this question in his review of the book, suggests the following:

> The contributors did not address the problem [of who the main actors of the March First Movement were]. None of the recent papers have examined this issue, let alone alluded to it in any way. However, there must be a rationale for such absence, and I'd like to refer to their own writing for clues. In the preface to the third volume, they claim that they have left out a conventional framework that hinges on the binary of oppression and resistance in dealing with matters of power and politics. Instead, they went after, for example, narratives told by a multitude of witnesses, and tried to adopt the method of "political history" instead of a "history of movements." The debate around the question of who the main actors of the March First Movement were, which has been ongoing for the past several decades, seems to have lost its appeal for these writers. This is unfortunate from my perspective, as I see this as an aversion to a debate that has been ongoing for a significant amount of time.[23]

Although Im criticizes that the contributors of *One Hundred Years since the March First Movement* have avoided the question of agency in regard to the March First Movement, I believe that while they have not given a definite answer, they have not completely avoided the question either. The contributors, in one way or another, attempt to analyze certain actors in the movement, and the list of social groups that are highlighted in their writings is long. Whereas some emphasize generational and regional differences in the movement or the role of students and young people dreaming of revolution, others more closely examine those who were regarded as "witnesses," ranging from Confucians, oppressors, and missionaries to influential figures who migrated from other regions to Seoul. While some of these writers highlight "residents of Seoul from all walks of life," others have incorporated into their analyses "class difference." In addition, they have examined those who mourned

---

23 Im Kyŏngsŏk, "On Our Books: A Review of *One Hundred Years since the March First Movement*," *Korean History Society Webzine*, May 19, 2019, http://www.koreanhistory.org/7202.

for or felt tired of the movement instead of participating in it at the time.

It seems plausible to deduce that their answer to the aforementioned question is that one must not look for a particular group as the leaders of the movement. By deviating from existing literature that set up a binary between "oppression and resistance," they seek to examine the individual narratives of those who were involved in the movement from multiple points of view and allow rich and diverse interpretations. In other words, they refuse the notion of a collective subjectivity based on homogeneity in favor of a diverse range of heterogeneous subjects, around which a new history of the movement can be written. Consequently, concepts such as "diversity," "plurality," and "multiplicity" were emphasized. As the contributors have stated:

> We attempted to represent the March First Movement by implementing a wide range of different perspectives and subjects. The existing literature on the March First Movement has tended to highlight those who participated directly in the movement and the legal documents about them. However, in our writings, we shifted our focus to various witnesses ····· [By incorporating their perspectives] we were able to examine the movement from different angles. Furthermore, we sought to represent the movement in terms of generational difference and solidarity.

Criticism of collective subjectivity based on homogeneity and an emphasis on "the multiplicity of subjects" were common in studies on the March First Movement around its 100th anniversary. In *1919: The First Spring in the Republic of Korea*, Pak Ch'ansŭng writes about various people, ranging from Koreans living abroad, students studying abroad, religious leaders, the thirty-three national representatives, student groups, and workers. He emphasizes the fact that the "heroes of the March First Movement" were everyone who, regardless of their gender, age, etc., inhabited the Korean peninsula at the time. He also notes that each of the regions where protests corresponding to the March First Movement had taken place had a different set of needs and therefore had organizers and participants of their own. What he emphasizes above all is the fact that the organizers of the movement were all commoners. Pak sees this pattern as a sign that the Korean society was transitioning from a caste-based society to an egalitarian one.

In *The Night of March First: Dreaming of Peace in a Century of Violence*, Kwon Boduerae uses a number of different terms to describe the main actors of the March First Movement. One of the terms that she uses frequently is *taejung* (the mass), which consists of multiple layers. Kwon argues that a number of people across the country who proclaimed themselves to be national representatives and vanguards of the movement had different motives, and that there was no mastermind behind them. One of the specific groups that Kwon analyzes concerns urban laborers and women from all walks of life. Each of the people involved in the March First Movement had a different idea about the movement, which consisted of various expectations and wishes that could not be satisfied under a single cause. Kwon points out that there were even Japanese people who participated in the protests, which testifies to the multiplicity of the subjects involved in the March First Movement.

Analyzing specific individuals or groups involved in the March First Movement instead of conflating all of them in the concept of *minjok* or *minjung* is a prevalent tendency in the works produced around the 100th anniversary. Likewise, Cho Hansŏng specifies who the organizers, operators, and executors of the movement were in his *Tales of Protest*.[24] In fact, the field of history has witnessed progress with regard to an emphasis on the specificities of the movement and scrutinizing these in a meticulous manner. The March First Movement Database, created by the National Institute of Korean History, also set up specific categories for participants of the movement such as "general participants," Ch'ŏndoists, Christians, Taejongists, Buddhists, Confucians, merchants, workers, students, teachers, civil workers, etc. The database also specifies different ways through which the movement unfolded, including what kind of media was used, how it became oppressed, how it was carried out, etc., which will serve as a great resource for further research.[25]

Kim Jeong-in states that her aim was to deviate from interpreting the March First Movement in terms of *minjok* by focusing on democracy and the contemporary notion of selfhood. In other words, Kim went as far as to break the collective subjectivity of the March First Movement into various "I"s:

24 Cho Hansŏng, *Tales of Protest* (Seoul: Saenggak Chŏngwŏn, 2019).

25 The web address of the database is as follows: https://db.history.or.kr/samil.

To reconstruct the history of the March First Movement from the perspective of democracy, one must individualize and contemporize this history. The March First Movement has always been regarded as nationalist at its heart, that is, an event of the past that made today's South Korea. It was a monumental event that took place a hundred years ago. However, upon closer examination, one may discover a myriad of contemporary "I"s in the movement.[26]

This multiplicity of subjects emerged as an important topic through its emphasis on diversity, which also implies a form of reading history through the eyes of the present. In contemporary South Korean society where social conflict, bigotry, discrimination, and exclusion are becoming ever more intensified, diversity has come to represent an ideal that ought to be respected. This concept has also been proposed as a driving force for corporations and the government to grow more competent.

There have also been a series of protests, including those against the implementation of state-issued history textbooks and the candlelight rallies as early as 2015, which have shaped the experiential landscape of the scholars who have been producing work on the 100th anniversary of the March First Movement. During the protests against the implementation of government-issued history textbooks, the notion of diversity provided the ground on which people refused the conformist idea of "a correct history textbook." Such an anachronistic agenda became severely criticized by not only historians and educators but also practitioners in other fields. The candlelight rallies, which were attended by people from a wide spectrum of different needs and wishes, also left a huge impact on individual scholars. In those days, they did not run into each other at conferences but on the streets. Perhaps they were trying to locate the diversity and multiplicity of slogans, banners, and political orientations they saw in the March First Movement.

Still, not all of them have denied the notion of collective subjectivity, as some of the writings in the aforementioned compilation published by the Korean History Societ addressed it. Ki Yuchŏng, for example, discusses the notion

---

26 Kim Jeong-in, *The March First Movement Today*, 5.

of *kunjung* (the mob) in the streets. Unfortunately, however, Ki's focus is on the 1920s, and the matter of subjectivity in the March First Movement is not examined. Hŏ Yŏngnan highlights the organizing and the network within the movement, where solidarity among discrete groups and individuals was foregrounded. By doing so, Hŏ is able to distinguish between two different notions of *minjung* — an attempt that can be traced back to the call for a "new history of *minjung*." One version refers to *minjung* as a homogenous mass, and the other, which was the focal point for Hŏ, is a form of collective subjectivity characterized by multiplicity and heterogeneity.[27] Hŏ claims that the latter was the main driving force of the March First Movement. Others have also suggested in some interviews that a view like Hŏ's, which tries to show the different dreams, ideals, and limits of discrete individuals that are difficult to subsume under any given collective subjectivity, is continuous of *minjung* history.[28] However, unlike this suggestion, the term *minjung* is not widely shared by other scholars. Rather, *minjung* seems to have been avoided precisely because of the strong political implications that the term evokes.

I would like to raise two questions in regard to the emphasis on diversity in these works. One of these has to do with the avoidance of the terms *minjok* and *minjung*, both of which were advanced in earlier studies on the March First Movement. Certainly, there is a clear sense of continuity among the works produced around the 50th, 70th, and 100th anniversary. However, as Im Kyŏngsŏk has pointed out, the Korean History Society's recent compilation has never clearly suggested, explained, or reflected on what grounded the writers' choice in regard to their suggested notion of a multiplicity of subjects and terms that had been advanced in earlier studies such as *minjok* and *minjung*. In this respect, this compilation stands in stark contrast to works produced around the 70th anniversary, which sought to appropriate the earlier notion of *minjok* while proposing a new set of lenses. After grappling with the task of expanding the scope of their predecessors as well as continuing the spirit of their inquiries, they came away with the notion of *minjung*, in which "the

---

27 The History of the Minjung Group at the Institute for Korean Historical Studies, *Reiterating the History of Minjung* (Seoul: Yŏksabip'yŏngsa, 2013).

28 Yi, *The March First Movement in the Eyes of the Candlelight Revolution*, 47.

contradictions of the nation and class were conflated."[29] However, recent works on the March First Movement simply put forth the idea of diversity, which reflects the recent trend in the field in which the notion of homogeneous collective subjectivity is losing currency, without assessing the work of their predecessors.

The next question addresses the idea of a multiplicity of subjects and how it is supported by recent works on the March First Movement. As quoted above, the contributors to the Korean History Society's compilation claim that they aim to discover "a wide spectrum of dynamic, transgressive subjects, and to seek out and resuscitate those excluded from history, such as people with disabilities and sexual minorities." However, none of the pieces included in this compilation actually examines a specific group of minorities, with the only exception of women. Their proposal to highlight the role of "those excluded from history" thus remains nominal. For those who claim to have focused on the role of women, their biggest accomplishment is merely proving that some of the participants of the March First Movement turned out to be biological women. This conclusion only reminds readers of the need for further studies on women's participation in the March First Movement. In this respect, what especially holds true is So Hyŏnsuk's criticism that women's history can no longer be regarded as "supplementary history." We instead need to go as far as to identify the changes in gender norms and representation of women that were brought about by women's participation in the March First Movement.[30] To answer the question, "Who were the women that participated in the March First Movement, specifically?" Kwon examines specific cases of female students, courtesan-entertainers, housewives, Christian women, female bar owners, female butchers, etc., and emphasizes the differences among them.[31] Such an approach is based on the awareness that women, like other categories of subjects, should not merely be counted as one among many different subjects.

29 Korean History Society and Institute for Korean Historical Studies, *Studies on the National Liberation Movement of March First*, 27-36.

30 So Hyŏnsuk, "The March First Movement and Women as Political Subjects," in *One Hundred Years Since the March First Movement*, vol. 5 (Seoul: Humanist, 2019), 161-186.

31 Kwon, *The Night of March First*, 387-389.

All this amounts to the fact that mere claims of diversity are not enough, as they seem indistinguishable from the tokenistic approach to "the women's March First Movement" in 1969. One must closely examine what has changed from regarding the March First Movement as a nationalist movement during Japanese colonial rule that propounded the nation as a form of totality and various categories of such totality. Although an emphasis on diversity originates from an awareness that a conventional framework enabled by the notions of *minjok* or *minjung* fails to capture certain elements of history, discussions of diversity in recent work seem too premature and schematic. The multiplicity of subjects is treated in a somewhat isolated manner in individual writings in the aforementioned compilation. Furthermore, in contrast to the claims made in the compilation, some of the contributions do propound a notion of collective subjectivity. It seems like the issue of multiplicity of subjects exists as isolated instances in individual writings included in the compilation, instead of adhering to a shared ethos or a core subject of research for some joint project.

The above criticism leads to a suspicion about whether the emphasis on a multiplicity of subjects, which corresponds to a contemporary ethics of diversity, really amounts to a new set of norms in recent works. This question is not irrelevant to the aforementioned shared experience — the various protests against the implementation of state-issued history textbooks — where the emphasis on diversity was perceived as synonymous with a "correct view on history."[32] Against the notion of "correct history textbooks" issued by the government, scholars and activists propounded diversity as the moral imperative of their time. Here, the problem of historiography becomes an ethical one, which is a matter of "should" rather than "is." However, is this association between "correctness" and diversity to be taken for granted? In regard to recent studies on the March First Movement, the notion of diversity remains an empty signifier in need of specifics and particularities, and no consensus seems to have been reached or serious inquiry accomplished. This leads us to question whether

[32] Chŏng Yŏnguk, "The Self Identification of 'Having a Correct Perception of History' by 'Progressive' Korean History Academia during the 1980s-1990s," *Critical Studies on Modern Korean History* 37 (2016): 55-92.

this emphasis on diversity has become axiomatic in a way that took after the aforementioned "correct view on history" or so-called "political correctness" in the field of historical inquiry. It is important to remember that political correctness is sometimes criticized for amounting to "a systematic avoidance of an actual encounter with the other"[33] or "a prescriptive, evasive measure that reduces the probability of forming actual relations with those whose bodies are inscribed with the histories of discrimination and oppression."[34] Democracy is something specific. It cannot be accomplished by empty gestures toward the excluded without accounting for specific, particular individuals.[35]

To secure a multiplicity of subjects and secure their place in the history of the March First Movement, one must engage in serious debates with existing frameworks instead of avoiding them or waving the banner of diversity in a monotonous manner. "The new vitality" cannot be obtained by merely supplementing certain individuals without challenging the conventional framework of historiography used to assess the March First Movement. The attempts to reveal a multiplicity of subjects in the March First Movement, through which diversity could be incorporated into the field, deserve positive assessment. However, the mere reciting of a slogan or reliance on a rhetoric of inclusion alone are not enough. One must take a step further and be willing to extensively discuss what kind of historiographical significance is at stake in an emphasis on a multiplicity of subjects.

One must also raise the question whether it is actually possible to fill in the "void" of the March First Movement, which has been suggested in the Korean History Society's compilation by including sexual minorities or people with disabilities. Without a doubt, the call for incorporating women, sexual minorities, and people with disabilities into serious debates is an urgent one in the present, which also applies to the field of Korean history.[36] Still, we

---

33 Pok Tohun, "Political Correctness or Hate Speech? No, thanks! On a Critique of 'Political Correctness' by Slavoj Žižek," *Inmunhak Yŏn'gu* 56 (2019): 41-75.

34 Fujii Takeshi, "Does Political Correctness Hold Sway over the Public?" *Munhak3*, June 26, 2017.

35 For further discussion in this regard, see Wendy Brown, *Regulating Aversion: Tolerance in the Age of Identity and Empire* (Princeton, NJ: Princeton University Press, 2006).

36 Mun Min'gi et al., "The Current State of and Future Challenges for Disability Studies in Korea," *Critical Studies on Modern Korean History* 42 (2019): 565-612; Kim Taehyŏn, "Claiming Genealogical

must first ask whether we can find their voices or traces in the archive of the March First Movement in a way that is available to us in the present moment. We must also ask whether we can locate new clues for historical interpretation by reading the power hierarchy evident in surviving documents against the grain. These questions do not amount to an imperative to "write only what we can write about" or adhere strictly to verifiable facts. The impossibility of historical interpretation does not entail setting aside the incomprehensible. On the contrary, it entails a reminder that the incomprehensible has always been there, and that historiography itself is predicated on what cannot be written about.

The notion that an emphasis on diversity has become the "correct" answer can be found in arguments that other local movements affiliated with the March First Movement must be examined from different perspectives.[37] Cho Tonggŏl's 1970 study on said movements in Kangwŏn Province, which raised the problem of "the local" in the March First Movement, initiated a trend has been perceived as characteristic of studies on the March First Movement around its 100th anniversary. These works, of which the Association for Korean Historical Studies' (Han'guksa yŏn'guhoe) compilation is a leading example, attempt to criticize and decentralize a form of historiography that privileges the "center." These works instead emphasize regions that have previously lacked scholarly attention, such as the northern provinces, and examine protests affiliated with the March First Movement that took place all over the country. However, an emphasis on diversity functions like a norm in these studies as well, as all of them failed to suggest a new finding on what had caused these protests across various regions and how they differed from one another. Hŏ Yŏngnan aptly points out that the accretion of these studies on "local" March First Movements ironically ends up reinforcing the image of "a singular March

Membership Known as History by Sexual Minorities in Korea," in *One Step Further for Korean History*, ed. The Organization Of Korean Historians (Seoul: P'urŭn Yŏksa, 2018).

37 Chŏng Yonguk, "Current Trends in Historical Studies of the March First Movement, and Where It Is Apparently Headed," *Quarterly Review of Korean History* 110 (2018): 269-304; To Myŏnhoe, "Reflections on and Suggestions in Regard to the Debate over What Caused the March First Movement," in The Organization Of Korean Historians, *One Hundred Years since the March First Movement*, 1: 145-178.

First Movement."[38] Han Kyumu suggests that the new challenge for these studies involves a complete reexamination of and reading between the lines of the available documents, instead of perpetuating existing narratives.[39] In this respect, the studies conducted by the National Institute of Korean History, which incorporated the March First Movement Database, seem promising in their take on the "local" characteristics and significance of the movement, despite the fact that they are still in the early phase.[40]

4. Challenges for Future Research

In this section, I intend to provide a brief summary of this article and seek future directions for research on the March First Movement.

The studies on the March First Movement conducted around its 100th anniversary were characterized by recent attempts to commemorate the movement and establish a sense of continuity between the past and the present in various social sectors. The eyes of the present functioned as an important factor in the historical analyses of the March First Movement, since the movement has been assessed as a historical threshold that gave rise to the "democratic republic of Korea." Although government apparatuses, civil organizations, and academic institutions have each suggested a different take on what "democracy" means, they all share an emphasis on "a transition to democracy" in their analyses. We must, however, warn ourselves against an understanding of history as a linear development that yields to the inevitability of the present. Such

---

38 Hŏ Yŏngnan, "Networks, Organizations, and the Plural Solidarity of the March First Movement," in The Organization Of Korean Historians, *One Hundred Years Since the March First Movement*, 5: 215.

39 Han Kyumu, "Protests Led by Religious Figures in Jeolla Province," in The Association for Korean Historical Studies, *The Historical Significance of the March First Movement and its Local Manifestations*, 262-293.

40 Yŏm Pokkyu, "The Progress and Characteristics of the March First Movement in Urban Areas," *Korean Cultural Studies* 84 (2019): 85-129; Yi Songsun, "The Spread and Regional Trends of the March First Movement in Rural Areas," *Korean Cultural Studies* 84 (2019): 131-177; Chŏng Pyŏnguk, "Reconstructing the Historical Narrative of the Protest in Suan of Hwanghae Province in March 1919," *Korean Cultural Studies* 84 (2019): 179-220; Ch'oe Usŏk, "How the 'Manse' Protests Spread in the Gyeonggi·Incheon Area," *Quarterly Review of Korean History* 113 (2019): 47-84.

a view excludes historical facts and desires from the past that do not fit neatly into such a framework.

Responding to present needs also became necessary in the field of history, which gave rise to an emphasis on diversity in recent works on the March First Movement. One of the important contributions of these works is their attempt to highlight the multiplicity of subjects in the March First Movement. They carefully examine the particularities of each actor instead of relying on previously suggested notions of collective subjectivity such as *minjung* or *minjok*. However, these efforts are also not free from criticism that their emphasis on diversity seems nominal at best, which, ironically, can be seen as a normative move that lives up to a "correct" historical perspective. In order to reflect on this current state in which an emphasis on diversity seems rather normative or exists in isolation from one work to another, we must engage in serious debates. We not only need to discuss notions of collective subjectivity in earlier literature on the March First Movement but also critically examine the idea of a multiplicity of subjects.

Perhaps these multiple subjects that have been highlighted in recent studies are also reflective of the different needs, visions, and orientations of scholars and researchers in 2019, which reveals a need for self-reflection. In this respect, suggesting directions for further research on the March First Movement amounts to imagining different futures for us and actualizing them. Such an effort would also keep the entire "100th anniversary" project going instead of only treating it as a one-time event. Our most important task is to critically reflect on the eyes of the present and directly engage with the premises of the existing literature on the March First Movement. This challenge lies in seeking ways to continue discussions and assess an appropriate scope for research that has expanded quantitatively in recent work. The future generation of scholars will also rely on their eyes of the present to interpret the March First Movement. I therefore hope that we will be able to provide more opportunities to read between the lines or make new discoveries from the voids of history.

Trans. by Jang Han-gil

Cultural Metamorphosis

Two Tales of Admiral Yi Sunsin:

Comparative Research on Yi Sunsin Narratives in South and North Korea

Jang Kyung-nam

1. Introduction

Admiral Yi Sunsin is one of the most commonly depicted historical characters in Korean fiction, not only in literary fiction books, but also films, plays, TV shows, comics and the like. In this regard, he transcends genres and can be found in works for young and old. In history, Yi is thought of as the hero who won many important battles during the Imjin War (1592−1598)[1] and helped overcome a crisis that the Chosŏn Dynasty faced. His reputation is thus partially the product of the historical record, but arguably his depiction in fiction has done even more to cement his reputation as a hero.

Literature on Yi began to appear immediately following the end of the Imjin War. Admiral Yi's activities in the war were recorded in various historical documents, and among them was his nephew Yi Pun's (李芬) volume of writing entitled *Record of Activities* (*Haengnok*; 行錄), which became an important source for later literary depictions of Admiral Yi. In the late 17th and early

---

1 The name usually given to the Japanese invasions of Korea in the years 1592-1598. In the Sexagenary cycle (六十干支), the year 1592 is known as "Imjin" according to the modern Korean pronunciation of the Chinese characters "Im" (壬), which connotes water, and "Jin" (辰), which connotes dragon.

237

18th centuries, the classical novel *Record of Imjin* (*Imjillok*; 壬辰錄) offered the first fictional depiction of the Admiral. With the original author unknown, *Record of Imjin* exists in various versions, which offer a slightly different portrayal of Admiral Yi from one another. Their difference also casts decisive doubt on the notion that, even during the Chosŏn Dynasty, there was a unitary narrative about Admiral Yi. But it was not before the late 19th century when Korean intellectuals grappled with imperial encroachment and the need to modernize that large numbers of literary works portraying Admiral Yi began to appear. In 1908, Sin Ch'aeho penned a series called *The Biography of Yi Sunsin* for the *Korea Daily News* (*Taehan maeilsinbo*), and this presaged the start of many fictional works that dealt with the topic. In the 1920s, during the Japanese colonial period, with the growing popularity of printed novels, Admiral Yi would become an important character for this medium then new on the Korean peninsula. Yi Kwangsu and Pak T'aewŏn, both of whom were major figures in the Korean literary fiction of the era, wrote about him, as Admiral Yi was widely seen as a hero to be emulated in the struggle to liberate the country from Japanese colonial rule. The heroic portrayal of Admiral Yi as the savior of the country was thus far from irrelevant to the historical context of the time.

Following the division of Korea into North and South in 1945, the two emergent states developed their own distinct literary cultures and consequent depictions of Yi. Writers on both sides of the peninsula base their depictions of Yi in the historical record, but they depict him very differently. Even in South Korean fiction, different authors writing in different times have taken different approaches to their work depicting Admiral Yi.[2]

I will present a brief overview of some of the well-known literary works on Admiral Yi, listed and categorized as follows:

Category 1
Authors Unknown, *Record of Imjin* (『壬辰錄』).

---

2   Jang Kyung-nam, "Periodizing the Fictional Depictions of Admiral Yi Sunsin," *Journal of Korean Literary History* 35 (2007): 1-13.

Category 2

Sin Ch'aeho, *The Biography of Yi Sunsin* (*Isunsinjŏn*), *Korea Daily News* (*Taehan maeilsinbo*), June 15 – October 24, 1908.

Pak Ŭnsik, *The Biography of Yi Sunsin* (*Isunsinjŏn*), Samirin sŏgwan, 1923.

Category 3

Chang Tobin, *The Biography of Yi Sunsin* (*Isunsinjŏn*), Koryŏgwan, 1925.

Choe Ch'ansik, *The Record of Yi Sunsin* (*Isunsin Silgi*), Pangmun sŏgwan, 1925.

Kang Ŭiyŏng, *The Record of Ch'ungmugong Yi Sunsin* (*Ch'ungmugong Yisunsin Silgi*), Yŏngch'angsŏgwan, 1925.

Unknown author, *The Biography of Yi Sunsin* (*Isunsinjŏn*), Hoedongsŏgwan, 1927.

Category 4

Yi Kwangsu, *Yi Sunsin*, Dong-a Ilbo, July 16, 1931 – April 3, 1932.[3]

Category 5

Pak T'aewŏn, *General Yi Sunsin: A Historical Novel* (*Yŏksasosŏl Yisunsin Changgun*), Ahyŏp, 1948.

Category 6

Pak Sŏngbu, *Yi Sunsin: A Novel* (*Sosŏl Yisunsin*), 2 vols., Haengnim Ch'ulp'an, 1994.

Kim T'akhwan, *The Immortal* (*Pulmyŏl*), 4 vols., Miraejisŏng, 1998.[4]

Kim Hoon (Kim Hun), *Song of the Sword* (*K'arŭi Norae*), 2 vols., Saenggaŭi Namu, 2001

Category 7

Pak T'aewŏn, *The Story of Admiral Yi Sunsin* (*Yisunsin Changgun Iyagi*), National Publishing House, 1955.

Kim Hyŏn'gu, *Admiral Yi Sunsin* (*Yisunsin Changgun*), Munye Ch'ulp'ansa, 1990.

---

3 This work was published by different publishers in Munsŏngsŏrim (1932), Sanmunsa (1936), Yŏngchangsŏgwan (1948), Usinsa (1991), Ilshin Book Publishers (1995), Green Grapes (under the title "The Immortal Renowned General Yi Sunsin" in 2004), Dana Plan (2004), and Changhyŏn Culture Company (2004).

4 This work was published in eight parts in 2004 under the title *Immortality Yi Sunsin*.

Category 8

Pak T'aewŏn, *Imjin Patriotic War* (*Imjin Choguk Chŏnjaeng*), National Publishing House, 1960.

Pak Chonghwa, *Imjin War* (*Imjinwaeran*), *Chosun Ilbo*, September 13, 1954 – April 18, 1957.[5]

Kim Sŏnghwan, *Imjin War* (*Imjinwaeran*), 2 vols., Ŏmun'gak, 1985.[6]

Hong Sŏngwŏn, *The Moon and the Sword* (*Talgwa K'al*), 5 vols., Hanyang, 1993.

Record of Imjin is a historical fiction about the Imjin War. Many editions of it exist and their content varies from one edition to another. Some of them do not even include stories about Admiral Yi. This shows he was represented in many different ways at the time. The second category of works listed above is composed of the works of Sin Ch'aeho and Pak Ŭnsik, which provide us a glimpse into the views of Korean intellectuals during the years of the so-called "Patriotic Enlightenment" period (*aegukkyemonggi*). The third category contains works published during the period when print novels emerged, which thus reflect commercial publishing trends from that time. *The Record of Ch'ungmugong Yi Sunsin,* in particular, drew mostly from Yi Pun's *Record of Activities*. The fourth is made up of Yi Kwangsu's fictional work of Admiral Yi, which was serialized at first and then compiled into a single volume. This work has been made available in the 1990s and in print since then. The fifth category includes a novel that Pak T'aewŏn wrote before he left for North Korea. It is centered on Admiral Yi's military exploits during the Imjin War rather than an overall account of his life.

During the 1960s and 1970s, a number of biographical works appeared. The 1970s, in particular, was a time when the Park Chung-hee regime sought to turn Admiral Yi into a kind of holy hero, which was deeply political in its motive. By characterizing the 1970s as a period of national crisis akin to the Imjin War, Park Chung-hee attempted to cast himself as a savior of the

---

5 This work was published as a book by Ŭlyu Culture Company (1958), and again in 2004 by Talgung.

6 The book was published in 1990 in seven volumes by Haengnim, and under a new title *The Seven Year War* in 2012 by Sanch'ŏnjae.

nation by analogizing himself to Admiral Yi, who had been instrumental in overcoming the crisis of war.[7] Hence, narratives of Yi Sunsin propounded at the time often sought as much to give legitimacy to Park Chung-hee's military regime. Only one biography of Admiral Yi was published in the 1980s, during which the dictatorship of General Chun Doo-hwan ruled South Korea following the death of Park Chung-hee in 1979, and faced unrelenting demands for democratization. People's heightened desire for democracy and democratization also led many to question and revise the image of a hero that had been constructed by the Park regime.

Since the 1990s, Admiral Yi again became the subject of literary work. Although biographical works remained the mainstream, novels were also released. The sixth category includes a wide range of different literary genres. Pak Sŏngbu's work marks itself as a "novel" in the title, but is closer to a biographical work. Kim T'akhwan and Kim Hoon's works present very different portrayals of Admiral Yi. Rather than emphasizing Yi's heroic attributes, they bring his human side to the fore, which underlines their intention to move beyond the conventional representation of Yi. The work of the two Kims are now regarded as representative of the South Korean literature depicting Yi Sunsin.

The seventh category consists of fictions on Yi Sunsin published in North Korea since the division of Korea. Pak T'aewŏn's historical novel, *The Story of Admiral Yi Sunsin*, was written before Pak went to the North and was first published in 1948, which went to press again in 1955 with Pak in the North. Even though they were published under the same title, these are actually two distinct works. The 1948 novel is structured around the major battles that Admiral Yi fought, while the 1955 work covers the entirety of Yi's life based on the historical records. Kim Hyŏn'gu's novel takes a similar approach, focusing on the overall account of Yi's life with the addition of fictional characters created by the author to further expand and enrich the narrative.

The eighth are stories that do not focus on Yi directly, but are set during the Imjin War. These stories depict the war with Yi as a character within it. Pak T'aewŏn's *Imjin Patriotic War* is perhaps the most important in its

---

7   Yun Chinhyŏn, "A Study on an Aspect of Discursive Struggle in Historical Drama," *Journal of Korean Literary History* 26 (2004): 37.

portrayal of both the war and the character of Yi, which has been widely praised by critics as the pinnacle of such literature.[8] While Pak Chonghwa's *Imjin War* was serialized in 946 installments in the newspaper *Chosun Ilbo*, with stories of Yi Sunsin taking up about 15%.[9] As both works were published immediately following the Korean War, they serve as important materials for comparatively analyzing the ways in which the Imjin War has been understood in North and South Korea. Kim Sŏnghwan and Hong Sŏngwŏn's novels also cover the Imjin War with Admiral Yi as a part of it, but their focus is less on the single character of Yi than on the overall account of the war.

The present article compares the two Koreas' depictions of Yi following the division of the peninsula in 1945. Up to division, there were a considerable number of fictional portrayals of Yi, but immediately following division, there was a lull in such work especially in the North since 1955, with Yi only reemerging in 1990 with Kim Hyŏn'gu's novel. This novel was published after Pyongyang had begun to push a new ideology of Korean ethnocentrism in the late 1980s, built upon the established *Juche* ideology. At the same time, Admiral Yi reemerged in South Korean fiction soon after, as the country was democratized. In the latter half of the 1990s, Kim T'akhwan's novel *The Immortal* prompted a decisive break from the conventional representation of Yi. As division has ossified, new forms of representation of Yi have emerged on the two sides of the peninsula, and the differences in these can tell us much about the respective cultures of the two Koreas. Among these literary work that have emerged starting in the 1990s, this article examine Kim T'akhwan's *The Immortal* and Kim Hyŏn'gu's *Admiral Yi Sunsin*.

2. Narrative Structure

Yi Pun's *Record of Activities* (行錄) forms the basis of stories written about

---

8   Pang Minho, "Introduction to Pak T'aewŏn's Imjin Patriotic War," in *Imjin Patriotic War* (Seoul: Kip'ŭnsaem, 2006), 319.

9   Ko Sŏkho, "National Awakening in Wŏlt'an's Historical Novel *Imjin War*: Yi Sunsin's Love of People and King Sŏnjo's Incompetence," *Yi Sunsin Studies* 5 (2005): 204.

Yi Sunsin before the division of the Korean peninsula. Yi Pun's *Record* provides an overall account of Yi Sunsin's life and thus is useful for those seeking to create a narrative of Yi Sunsin. Although this was probably due to the conventional scope of Korean classical fiction that narrated a comprehensive account of a protagonist's life from their cradle to their grave, it also pertained to a belief that Yi's heroism was inseparable from his personal life. Conversely, unlike the conventional literary treatment of Admiral Yi before the division, neither *The Immortal* nor *Admiral Yi Sunsin* seeks to provide a thorough biography of Yi. Rather, as narratives, both are structured around a particular period in his life.

1) *Admiral Yi Sunsin*: Narrative of an Undying, Godlike Hero

Kim Hyŏn'gu's *Admiral Yi Sunsin* was released by North Korea's Literature & Arts Publishing House (*Munye ch'ulp'ansa*) in 1990. It is a full-length novel composed of six chapters and 522 pages. In this work, Kim introduces a fictional character, Sŏ Punnyŏ, to add further flavor to the story of Admiral Yi's naval battles, which form a large part of the narrative. In addition to Sŏ Punnyŏ and another fictional character Changsoe, the people of Chosŏn also play a remarkable part in the narrative as well. That is to say, Kim presents Admiral Yi's victories not as his individual feat but as a form of collaborative effort made by other characters and the masses. Furthermore, Kim juxtaposes the narrative of Sŏ Punnyŏ with that of Yi to augment his message on structural level as well.

The Yi Sunsin part of the novel begins with his appointment as Commander of the Chŏlla Province Left Naval District in 1591, and spans Yi's construction of the "turtle ships" (*kŏbuksŏn*) to prepare for potential Japan's invasion; battles at Okp'o, Hansando, and Pusanp'o; Japan's political maneuvering that led to his imprisonment; being made to serve in war as a commoner in exchange of his acquittal (*paegŭi chonggun*, literally meaning "military service in white clothes"); his rise to the position of Commander-in-chief of Chosŏn Naval Force; and the Battle of Myŏngryang. The narrative of Yi Sunsin in the novel is based on the history surrounding the events of his life from just before the start of the Imjin War up to the Battle of Myŏngryang.

By comparison, the Sŏ Punnyŏ narrative is entirely fictional. Her narrative begins with the love story between Sŏ and Changsoe, another fictional character. As it unfolds, the reader discovers that Sŏ's father, Sŏ Ch'ŏmji, lost his arm while fighting off Japanese invaders in 1555, and how his daughter follows in her father's footsteps and disguises herself as a man in order to fight in the Imjin War, during which Sŏ Punnyŏ performs a series of spectacular feats. Like a phoenix, Sŏ escapes death on the battlefield numerous times and manages to return home and marry her lover. In the climax, she leads the way to victory at the Battle of Myŏngryang.

Kim's novel actually begins with the love story between Sŏ and Changsoe, not with Admiral Yi. While this structural choice in part functions as a "hook," it also implies that the author establishes Sŏ as a character of equal importance to Yi Sunsin in the story. In fact, Sŏ is a character who embodies the common people, whose actions that Kim considered crucial to Yi's victories are portrayed in detail in the battle scenes.

The naval battles depicted in Kim's novel are the Okp'o, Hansando and Myŏngryang battles. In each of the battles, Kim meticulously keeps track of the contributions made by the fishermen of P'ungdŏkkol, a village near where all these battles take place, in addition to those by other fictional characters such as Changsoe, Tolman, and Sŏ Punnyŏ, whose skill and prowess in war are unmatched. The story reaches the climax at the Battle of Myŏngryang, where the role of the P'ungdŏkkol fishermen is maximized. Immediately preceding the battle, a P'ungdŏkkol village elder named Pak Ch'ŏnse appears before Yi, who has just been reinstated to fight the battle, and promises to assist him by mobilizing some 100 fishing boats in the battle. As Yi's predecessor, Wŏn Kyun, has lost a number of battles, Yi is decisively lacking in ships, and therefore accepts Pak Chŏnse's suggestion. With the help of the P'ungdŏkkol fishermen, Yi manages to win the battle.

The final scene of the novel seeks to emphasize the role of the masses in the ultimate victory:

> Yi Sunsin with sword in hand, and fiery passion, pushed forward the battle against the enemy ships. As the saying goes, if your general is a great strategist and is brave, soldiers fight well, and this was proven a thousand times over.

Under his direction, it was as if soldiers knew of no fear, cowardice or pettiness.

Adjutant General Yi Wan, invigilator Song Hŭirip, and bannerman Tolman all fought with great valor.

Amidst the fires of war, Tol Man sounded a drum, Yi Wan conducted proceedings with his battlefield standard while they all sought to rout the Japanese invaders as one.

Changsoe of "twin battleship" jumped aboard enemy ships wielding his sword, and on every occasion, the Japanese invaders would cry out and die.

This spectacle was to be seen on many an enemy ship. The dead bodies and ships of the enemy were consigned to a watery grave in the straits of Uldolmok, and they fell into the netherworld of defeat.

The record left shows that the heads of some 5,000 invading bastards rolled, including that of General Matashi and Kuroshima, some 30 enemy ships rode fire to destruction, and many more were damaged.[10]

This final scene thus highlights the combined effort of the people and military leadership in the victory. Yi is portrayed as a military leader with strategic brilliance and bravery, which does not differ from that of other works. What makes Kim's novel unique is that it highlights not only Yi's heroism but also that of ordinary soldiers like Changsoe, Tolman, and Sŏ.

What sets Kim's work from other novels of Yi Sunsin further is that the story concludes with the Battle of Myŏngryang. The Battle of Noryang, at which Yi would meet his death, is only implied in the narrative. Perhaps this is because the author wanted to maintain the image of Yi Sunsin as an undying god of war. Kim's novel ends with the following passage:

Soldiers' shouts reach the sky and their wielding spears, swords and flags are resplendent under the sun. The sound of drums reverberates on the sea. Now only the final drum of victory at Noryang is yet to sound.

The image of the ever-victorious, patriotic Admiral Yi Sunsin in helmet and armor, among the soldiers, holding his sword, looks like an undying god dazzling

10 Kim Hyŏn'gu, *Admiral Yi Sunsin* (Pyongyang: Munye ch'ulp'ansa, 1990), 519-520. Subsequent citations and quotes from this book include only the page numbers after quotations.

in the morning sunlight. (522)

Admiral Yi rejects Japanese General Konishi's entreaties and urges his troops forward to the final battle to wipe out their enemies. The soldiers obey Yi's order and prepare for battle. The author is engrossed in the role of the masses, but he cannot ignore Admiral Yi's heroism entirely, and ends by christening him a hero in the lofty terms given above: ever-victorious, patriotic, undying, dazzling in the morning sunlight.

2) *The Immortal:* Narrative of an Immortal Human

Kim T'akhwan's *The Immortal* was published in four volumes in 1998.[11] It does not cover the entirety of Yi's life, but begins in 1587 when he was the Governor of Chosŏn Navy and ends with the Battle of Noryang on November 18, 1598. The bulk of the narrative is concentrated on Yi's military exploits and seeks to cast doubt on some of the ideas commonly held about the admiral.

The author seeks to create a new image of Yi Sunsin by not only depicting the battles but also describing the political circumstances under which Yi finds himself and his interpersonal relationships. It is those relationships through which the narrative unfolds. The author seeks to make sense of the admiral's situation by bringing in more characters from the period, which can be read as an attempt to depict the human side of Yi in and through these relationships.

The final scene of the novel presents an all-together different view of Yi Sunsin to other narratives. The author raises doubts about whether Yi Sunsin died in battle, as was widely thought to be the case. He suggests that there has been a power struggle between Yi Sunsin and King Sŏnjo, through his own reading of a large number of historical sources. In the author's reading, Sŏnjo is a calculating and clever monarch. He ferments factional struggle to

---

11 This article makes use of the four-volume version of Immortality. Compared to the eight-volume version, the four-volume version is more focused on the individual of Yi Sunsin, and the story offers a new and different depiction of the admiral.

maintain his hold on the thrown and remove all who could potentially threaten his grip on power. It is not just the Japanese invaders whom he fears, but also Admiral Yi. Despite having been imprisoned and made to serve again as a commoner, Yi continuously adds to his record of achievements, and his reputation keeps rising as the war reached its end. Seeing this, Sŏnjo demotes the man who recommended Yi, Minister Yu Sŏngryong, and sends an official named Yun Tusu to Admiral Yi to inform him that he would be held accountable for his actions during the war once it is over. This would mean death for Yi.[12]

Here, King Sŏnjo is portrayed as one of Yi Sunsin's greatest antagonists. He goes so far as to dispatch agents undercover to monitor Yi's every move. And the better Yi does in battle, the more hostile their relationship becomes. The king does not even trust his own son, Prince Kwanghae, let alone his other retainers, all of who merely strive to win the war. The Prince seeks out Hŏ Kyun, a high official, to discuss how victory could be secured, after which Hŏ consults with Admiral Yi about what policies should be put in place. The man who recommended Yi, Prime Minister Yu Sŏngryong, also does his part. Yet, the king trusts none of them, and resorts to threatening his son and his other retainers.

"The crown prince is right. But the vassals have advised me to give Yi Sunsin a chance. They were hoping for a miracle. Yi's reappointment as the Commander-in-chief of the Navy was to not only show the people the mercy of the crown but also root out future trouble."

"Trouble, Your Majesty?"

"Yi must also know. When the war is over, he will surely suffer death by beheading. No general who has committed treason can live. He will revolt before the war is finished. It will be too late by the time he does. Keep that in mind."

"Yes, Your Majesty!"

Prince Kwanghae's face stiffened. King Sŏnjo's voice was colder and sharper than usual. The appointment of Yi to Commander-in-chief of Navy was a carefully

---

12 Ch'oe Yŏngho, "Historical Fact and Literary Imagination: Yi Sunsin in South Korean Literature," *Yi Sunsin Studies* 1 (2003): 106.

calculated move, both legitimate and practical. It was fitting for his father, who excelled in handling politics in such a way. The important thing was not the law itself, but the person who executed that law.[13]

The above is from the conversation between the king and the crown prince about whether to restore Yi Sunsin to command following Wŏn Kyun's defeat. In the novel, Prince Kwanghae is portrayed as a capable leader who has led a provisional government on Korean peninsula while Sŏnjo was in exile and is popular among young and emerging nobles. Whereas Kwanghae will be able to consolidate such a status of his once the war is over, Sŏnjo's reputation will be damaged. As such, Kwanghae has to be either checked or embraced. The king tells him what will happen to Yi afterwards, because he has already sensed that the prince and Yi Sunsin were secretly working together, and attempted to bring pressure to bear on Kwanghae. The author is implying that what drove Yi to death was none other than Sŏnjo's political maneuver to keep in check an officialdom that was more powerful than the crown.

In the novel, Yi Sunsin at the Battle of Noryang is depicted as follows:

Song Hŭirip, who had stayed up for much of the night playing the drum, watched Yi Sunsin out of the corner of his eyes hold his sword high and give out his battle cry.

"W-What? Admiral!"

He almost dropped the drumstick. And the next thing he knew, Yi Sunsin had discarded his gold armor and helmet, and was encouraging the troops dressed in his red army uniform. That golden armor was bulletproof; it had been made by blacksmiths under the direction of Chŏng Sajun after an arrow pieced Yi's shoulder at the Battle of Sach'ŏn in May 1592. Inside the armor was lined with strong, thick layers of fabric that could withstand a direct hit by a bullet.

"Put them back on, Admiral. The Japanese fleet is nearly upon us."

Song shouted while picking up the armor and helmet that had been discarded on the deck. Yi ignored him and continued to issue orders. (4: 366)

---

13 Kim T'akhwan, *Immortality*, vol. 4 (Seoul: Mirae Chisŏng, 1998), 197. Subsequent citations and quotes from this book include only the volume number and page numbers after quotations.

The author uses this scene to lend weight to the view that Yi Sunsin was looking to die at the battle. The author is seeking to define the circumstances of the battle in a different way to other narratives. Yi's actions are presented within the political context. The admiral anticipates that he will be sacrificed to political turf wars after the battle is over and seeks death in battle.

Let's have a look at the novel's epilogue:

> Despite the flood of questions that surged forth, Yi Tŏkhyŏng stopped asking, as he suddenly realized that he shouldn't be asking too many questions.
>
> "Your Excellency! Ten days ago, during the battle near Kwanŭmp'o, the Japanese naval force lost well over ten-thousand men, whereas our navy lost less than 30. Among the dead, however, are Commander-in-chief Yi Sunsin, Adjutant General Yi Yŏngnam, and Captain Yi Ŏnryang, that is, all of whom were among the most brilliant military leaders of Chosŏn's naval forces."
>
> "Those words ····· Are you insinuating that Commander Yi intentionally chose death?"
>
> "No one chooses death over life. However, one may use death to achieve immortality, as to take revenge against one's fate ····· No one can be killed twice."
>
> "But·····"
>
> Kwŏn Chun turned his head and looked directly into Yi Tŏkhyŏng's eyes.
>
> "If the commander had survived the war, do you think he'd still be safe by now, let alone yourself, under these circumstances? Do you think Minister Yu Sŏngryong would have been guaranteed with quiet and comfortable life in his old age? His Majesty did not believe that we had won, and that is why you came from so far away to see with your own eyes. Is it not?" (4: 372−373)

Following the end of the war, Yi Tŏkhyŏng sent a detailed report to the king about the death of Yi Sunsin and the retreat of Japanese forces, but Sŏnjo didn't believe the reports and demanded that Yi Tŏkhyŏng double check on what exactly happened to Admiral Yi and report again. Yi went all the way to Namhae Island to meet the admiral's close aide, Kwŏn Chun, who was in charge of administration of the navy. While Yi Sunsin had died after being struck by an enemy bullet, he chose his own death to remain an immortal god of war rather than falling prey to politics. The author thus presents the life of Yi not as an epic narrative of a hero but as that of a human being who dreamed of immortality.

3. The Depiction of Characters

Whereas both novels are set in the Imjin War period and avoid narrating the entirety of Yi's life, they differ in their portrayal of him: while one emphasizes his heroism, the other brings his human side to the fore. These differences are also evident in the way characters are constructed more generally in each novel. *Admiral Yi Sunsin* makes liberal use of fictional characters to demonstrate Yi's heroism, while *The Immortal* shows Yi's human side by detailing the relationships he had with actual historical characters.

1) The Creation of Fictional Characters in *Admiral Yi Sunsin*

In *Admiral Yi Sunsin*, fictional characters, all of whom are of peasantry, are more prominent than actual historical characters. This implies the author's intention to depict him as a hero of the masses who fight alongside the peasantry. The narrative is mostly set in a fishing village called P'ungdŏkkol, which is located near the naval headquarters in Chŏlla Province. Yi Sunsin is portrayed as a down-to-earth figure who goes through thick and thin with the villagers and overcome the crisis of war together. These fishermen villagers are known for their bravery in fighting off a pack of bandits known as Black Turban, who move around the coast in the province and raid villages.

The author describes their accomplishment in detail. On their way back home from work, the fishermen run into a pirate ship. Whereas the young among them suggest that they leave the pirate to local naval forces, Pak Ch'ŏnse, the village elder, decides to stop them and has the fishermen work together with a patrol boat to take down the pirate ship. Having suffered damage from bandits and pirates before, the fishermen had their own self-made bow and arrows and spears on borad to help navy patrol boats fight off pirates. Yi Sunsin witnesses this scene himself on his way back to the headquarters. When Song Hŭirip reports that the local fishermen assisted in fighting off the pirates,

Yi is surprised, and later devotes himself to protecting the lives of the P'ungdŏkkol villagers. Such a fictional account alludes to how the narrative will unfold later. The P'ungdŏkkol fishermen represent the masses in the novel, which the author utilizes to show how the ordinary people were instrumental in Yi Sunsin's victories. In a way, the author chooses to emphasize the fishermen's fighting spirit and Yi Sunsin's devotion to the local population as the main factors of their motivation to fight in war.

In other words, Yi Sunsin's heroism owes much to those without names from the peasantry. The author gives them names by recreating them into specific, fictional characters such as Sŏ Ch'ŏmji and his daughter Sŏ Punnyŏ, as well as the village elder Pak Ch'ŏnse, soldier Changsoe, the former castle gatekeeper and current oarsman Tolman, and Okchi, a carpenter who works on building turtle ships.

The main character of the book is in many regards Sŏ Punnyŏ, as she takes up the largest portion of the narrative. She is born to a lowborn woman and Sŏ Ch'ŏmji, who, originally of the free class of commoners (*yangmin*), was relegated to the status of the slavery following his marriage to a slave woman. However, he is recognized for his prowess in battle against the Japanese during the Japanese Invasion of 1555 (*Ŭlmyo waeran*) and is given his freedom. Having lost his one arm during the battle against the pirate ships of the "barbarian islanders," which refer to the Japanese invaders, Sŏ Ch'ŏmji has been serving as a gatekeeper since then. He keeps the bow and the sword he has used during the war as family treasures. His bronze bow has been used by his son in battle with the Japanese at Karaip'o in 1587, but his son died during the battle. As such, he harbors a deep grudge against the Japanese and watched over the gate of the Left Naval Headquarters, determined to protect the country against them. When his daughter Sŏ Punnyŏ decides to join the fight against the Japanese by disguising herself as a man, he passes on the bronze bow to her and helps her fight under Yi Sunsin's command. At one point, Sŏ Ch'ŏmji learns that his daughter went missing-in-action, and, during his final moment after the battle against the Japanese at Kŭmsan, he pleads not to inform her daughter of his death before the war is over, have they find her alive. When Pak Ch'ŏnse reports to Yi Sunsin about Sŏ's death, he relays his final words and regards highly his patriotism.

As if following her father's footsteps, Sŏ Punnyŏ gradually transitions from being a diver (*haenyŏ*) to a competent warrior after meeting Changsoe, who has saved her when she got almost drowned out in the sea. Later, when Changsoe sets sail for battle and returns with only one eye, she decides to join the war by disguising herself as a man and fights in a number of battles. At a victory celebration, her disguise is uncovered and is imprisoned. However, news of her heroism reaches the admiral, who has her freed, and thanks to his help she is also able to marry her lover during the war. The couple plays a pivotal role in the following battle at Myŏngryang. The travails of their love story make for an unrealistic narrative, with them brought together, separated and then reunited by the war. At the same time, however, it provides the readers with a concrete and direct portrayal of what the life of ordinary people might have been like during this period.[14]

Sŏ is portrayed mostly as a warrior, and her lover Changsoe is also treated in a similar way. In particular, alongside Tolman, he performs great feats at the Battle of Okp'o. Born to a fisherman, he harbors a grudge against the Japanese after they killed his father. He joins the naval command at an age of seventeen during the war to take revenge of his father, is captured during his reconnaissance mission, and loses one eye. However, he breaks out of captivity and delivers to Admiral Yi crucial information on the state of the enemy forces that he learned during captivity, which proves vital to victory. Tolman, who used to work as a gatekeeper under Sŏ Ch'ŏmji before joining the navy, assists Changsoe on the same reconnaissance mission. The intel they gather and bring back proves pivotal for victory at the Battle of Okp'o.

Another very important character in this narrative is Pak Ch'ŏnse, a village elder in P'ungdŏkkol. He acts as the village leader, and facilitates cooperation between the villagers and the local naval forces under Yi's command. As a close friend of Sŏ Ch'ŏmji, he helps Sŏ Punnyŏ when she finds herself in trouble and assists her as she fights a number of battles. Although he is well over 60, he is a seasoned warrior, having joined a militia and fought alongside

---

14 Ch'oe Yŏngho, "North Korean Novels of Yi Sunsin: An Analysis of Kim Hyŏn'gu's *Admiral Yi Sunsin*," *Yi Sunsin Studies* 6 (2006): 49.

Sŏ Ch'ŏmji during the Japanese invasion at Yŏngam. Pak Ch'ŏnse is portrayed as an enthusiastic man who runs to the naval commandry when the people of P'ungdŏkkol are hit by pirates and asks for weapons so that he can hit back at them. He also mobilizes the villagers and supply the materials that Admiral Yi needs to construct turtle ships.

The Battle of Myŏngryang is where Pak Ch'ŏnse shines the most. Pak appears before Yi on the brink of the battle and provides him the most crucial assistance as follows:

"In fact, there was nothing left after the Battle of Ch'ilchŏndo, and now the enemy has the total control of the sea. Unless there were some volunteer recruits from somewhere·····"

The admiral's honest thoughts flowed out naturally.

"You must come up with a way to win the battle on your own. What will become of you if you put your faith in others and wait····· Recall how General Ŭlchi Mundŏk back in the Koguryŏ dynasty defeat the Sui dynasty's forces or General Kang Kamch'an during the Koryŏ dynasty beat the Khitans with such a small troop?"

He spoke half under his breath, his head swaying from side to side, deep in thought.

General Ŭlchi Mundŏk that he spoke of had installed a temporary bridge in a river and then removed it as the enemy crossed, plunging them into it, while General Kang Kamch'an succeeded in wiping out a force of 100,000 Khitans at Kaesŏng by cutting off their supplies.

It seemed to Admiral Yi Sunsin that Pak wasn't unaware of the stories of these two generals. It is sure that Pak remarked on the two cases to help the admiral come up with a strategy.

What a considerate man Pak Ch'ŏnse was·····" (492−495).

As shown above, Pak is there when Yi needs him, offering encouragement and assistance. And he ultimately mobilizes 100 boats, and leads to a victory. In so doing, he brings together the people of the village with the admiral, which is crucial for Yi Sunsin's military success.

Instead of keeping separate the upper caste of Chosŏn society and the peasantry, the author seeks provide a realistic and comprehensive account by portraying the complicated interactions between them: While Admiral Yi represents the upper caste, fictional characters such as Sŏ and Changsoe represents the peasantry, and Sŏ Ch'ŏmji and Pak Ch'ŏnse serve as a bridge between them.[15] The key to Yi Sunsin's rise to a national hero is found not only in his individual attributes but also in the ordinary people with whom he interacted. As such, Yi emerges as a hero of the masses, not a hero above or separate from them.

2) The Utilization of Historical Figures in *The Immortal*

The supporting cast of characters employed in *The Immortal* are actual historical figures. They can be divided into the following three categories: (1) military leaders who directly participate in the battles alongside Yi Sunsin, including Wŏn Kyun, Yi Ŏkki, Kwon Yul and other military leaders; (2) the royalty and the officialdom, whose members inadvertently see everything in political terms even amidst the crisis of war. Aside from the king himself and the crown prince, they also include figures such as Yu Sŏngryong, Yun Tusu, Yi Tŏkhyŏng, Chŏng T'ak, etc.; and (3) artists and other professionals who, along with the masses, seek to overcome the death and sorrows of war, such as a famous calligrapher Han Sŏkpong, poet Yi Tal, writer Hŏ Kyun, and court physician Hŏ Chun and his friend Ch'oe Chunghwa.[16] The author also invents female characters who play the role of lover for some of the protagonists in the novel: Wŏn Kyun's lover "the treasured Jurchen dancer Muok," Yi Sunsin's lover "Pak Ch'ohŭi, who had been dragged off to Taema island and had returned by a miracle," and Hŏ Kyun's lover Chŏnghyang, who "by his side sought out the path of a Taoist poetry master as a *kisaeng*." These relationships in which the admiral is nestled are the basis of the character of Yi that the author constructs.

All of the members of this supporting cast play a role, but the most important among them is Wŏn Kyun. As Yi's competitor, he maintains a definite presence

---

15 Ch'oe, "North Korean Novels of Yi Sunsin," 50.

16 Kim T'akhwan, "Author's Note," in *Immortality*, 1: 3.

throughout the book. As Yi describes:

> There had been a high peak in front of me. It took me some seventeen years to climb it. And at last I have. But the moment I surmounted that peak there was a bigger and greater peak blocking the path ahead. And that peak was said to have not been passed by anyone. In fact, it was so high that not even a seagull had been able to fly over it. I, I ⋯⋯ I am not certain. Can I make it over such a peak, before my life is over? General Wŏn Kyun has to surpass me now, like I have before. Haha, that's just how life goes. I won't let him, though. If he does, I will be back where I was seventeen years ago. I cannot go back, I don't have it in me. I will fall into despair. Reconciliation, huh? Well⋯ What a lovely word. But it's for simpletons who know nothing of how this world work. Do you think true reconciliation is possible in our lives? We struggle in eternity to crush one another, that's life. General Wŏn and I know this all too well. We've passed the age where we can whine or smile at each other. That's the way things go. Just as the river only flows in one direction, so do our meetings, our fights, our sardonic laughs, our jealousies, to the end. Until one of us finally ceases to exist. (3: 61−62).

When Yi Sunsin is appointed to Commander-in-chief of Navy, Yi throws a banquet for everyone in the navy to celebrate his promotion, which Wŏn Kyun does not attend. Yi sees Wŏn as an obstacle to overcome, and someone who he has labored to surpass up to that point. As a result of these efforts, Yi ascends to the top of a chain of command in Chosŏn Navy.

However, Yi loses his position as a result of a Japanese plot that framed him as a traitor, is imprisoned, and is made to serve as a commoner upon acquittal. Although Wŏn Kyun takes Yi's place and commands the naval forces, he opts for a reckless tactic during the battle with the Japanese fleet, which costs him his life. Upon hearing the news, Yi delivers the following soliloquy:

> He always shone. With confidence, he did things that I would have considered shameful for myself. In 1598, when he lost so many ships and asked for my help, he didn't beg. Rather, he reproached me for not having provided assistance

more quickly. When he lost at Port Changmun and was demoted to Provincial Commander of Ch'ungch'ŏng, he was not discouraged. He frankly acknowledged his mistakes and kept requesting that he be given another chance. He was a calm and frank military leader.

Compared to him, I had a long and dark shadow, that I often got lost in⋯⋯ Ah, I am far too weak.

My men call me undefeated, upright, flawless, and wise, and the people hail me as a hero. But I know that I am just a man. If I do not keep justifying what I am, I cannot go on, I drink heavily to forget my shadow, I fire off arrows to look good, I keep an ear on the petty fights at court, I care too much about my career, shed tears a lot, and fear much.

But I will not deny it. I do not want to live out the rest of my life as an ordinary man. The large and ugly shadow I have created, the devious fate I have willed, the hypocrisies of the world I have exploited. ⋯⋯ My men and the people are innocent. If someone is to be punished for such sins, it is of course me.

How will the heavens punish me for deceiving the world like this? (4: 150−151).

Yi's confession reveals his realization that everything that he did to surpass Wŏn had cast a heavy shadow, that his reputation as a virtuous and wise military leader had become to him an empty facade. And with such a realization, he confesses to being a mere human being, "far too weak." His confession reveals his human side, which conforms to the image of Yi that the author seeks to create. The debt of his self-deception is repaid only in death.

This image of Yi deviates to an extensive degree from the conventional representation of Yi Sunsin, which the author bolsters by bringing actual historical figures in the novel. He exercises creative license and invents the silent tension between the king and crown prince, Yu Sŏngryong's worries, the arguments between Hŏ Kyun and the crown prince, Hŏ Kyun's dreams of revolution, and much else. The author enriches the narrative with supporting characters who nonetheless are based on actual historical figures such as Han Sŏkpong, Hŏ Chun and Hŏ Kyun, all of whom are described in detail, in addition to those who are invented, such as Yi Sunsin's lover Pak Chohŭi, who suffers a tragic death in the novel. The way he gives life to a large cast of historical figures and fictional characters further speaks to the richness of the narrative.

3) The Anguish of a Person and the People's Hero

In South Korea, one can trace a line from Yi Kwangsu's portrayal of Yi Sunsin as sacred hero to the appeals made by Park Chung-hee in the 1960s and 1970s to Admiral Yi's heroism. Yet, such an image of the man was based on biographies written about him, not fictional narratives, because he was considered too sacred for fictionalization. This view was reexamined after Park died. As a result, the image of Yi Sunsin that emerged in the late 1990s was no longer that of a sacred hero. The gravity of his portrayls had lightened up a little in the South Korean society that had undergone the seismic change of democratization. There came out a number of literature that entertained the speculations of his suicide and seclusion, among others. In cultural and artistic work depicting Yu Sunsin, his human side came to the fore, which is no less due to the change in Korean society's understanding of masculinity. Tough patriarchs were no longer the object of respect. Increasingly it was soft, pure, handsome, muscular, and fashionable metrosexuals who were in vogue. At the same time, this trend also triggered a nostalgia for images of strong men, leading to the appearance of heroic historical men in popular culture. Although Yi Sunsin was no exception to this, he began to be portrayed in different light.

Kim T'akhwan's *The Immortal* was the first to cast doubt on the depiction of Yi Sunsin as a sacred hero. Although his narrative is centered on Yi's major activities as a military leader, it seeks to raise doubts about the commonly held view of Yi Sunsin. He is depicted as someone who strives to surpass General Wŏn Kyun, which reveals Yi's image of an upstanding and wise man as meaningless. The Yi Sunsin the author sought to create is an anguished man who confesses his weaknesses.[17]

By comparison, the understanding and assessment of Yi Sunsin in North

---

17 This characterization can also be seen in Kim Hun's *The Song of the Knife* (Saenggak ŭi Namu, 2001). Kim Hun also presents an image of Yi Sunsin as a man of anguish and loneliness.

Korea developed and changed considerably in accordance with the priorities of the regime. Up to 1967, he was considered the country's greatest war hero. However, no discussion on Yi Sunsin exists between May 1967 and the late 1980s, during which North Korea witnessed the consolidation of *Juche* ideology, and Kim Il-sung's cult of personality would not have allowed for other national heroes. With the emergence of North Korean ethnocentrism in the late 1980s, however, things changed. Kim Il-sung sought to revive what he called "authentic nationalism" to overcome the worldwide crisis of communism and maintain his regime. In such a context, it is easy to understand why renowned national heroes like Yi Sunsin were suddenly summoned again.[18] Interestingly, the portayal of Yi Sunsin in the 1990s evolved in a number of different directions beyond the uniform representation of him in the 1950s and 1960s.

Kim Hyŏn'gu's novel thus reflects the North Korean historiography at the time, where Yi was summoned as a patriotic hero who was willing to go through thick and thin with the masses. This sets Kim's novel apart from other previous work. It is difficult, however, to see Kim Hyŏn'gu's work unrelated to Kim Jong-il's notion of *Juche* literature.

The literary theory espoused by Kim Jong-il put the popular masses at the center of narratives about society and history. The key text in defining this theory was his *On Juche Literature*, which describes the masses as the key agents of history and insists on portraying them as a driving force of social development and progress with emphasis on their autonomy and creative capacity. As Kim Jong-il put it:

At one time, *Admiral Yi Sunsin* was performed at the National Theatre. The play depicted the victories in the sea battles fought during the Imjin Patriotic War as having been won thanks to the admiral alone. Of course, it is true that Yi, as a patriotic and renowned admiral, performed great exploits in the battles. But as the saying goes, a general by himself is no general. Had the people not fought courageously for the motherland with him, then he would not have emerged victorious. It was the people that played the decisive role in the Imjin Patriotic

---

18 Kwŏn Chunsŏk, "Perception and Assessment of Yi Sunsin Seen through North Korean Historical Perception," master's thesis, Yonsei University, 2006, 45-84.

War, as they dedicated their lives without hesitation to defend their dear motherland from foreign aggressors. Any work that grapples with history must portray in bold relief the idea that history and society are created and developed not by great or outstanding individuals but by the people.[19]

Here, Kim Jong-il offers a comparative account of what he considers to be an ideal work of historical fiction. More specifically, he insists that historical literary narratives of the Imjin War must be written under the assumption that without the popular masses, there would have been no victory. The writer must emphasize, according to Kim, that it was not a handful of great individuals but the masses who create history and prompt social development. Kim Hyŏn'gu's depiction of the people in his novel follows such principles.

4. Conclusion

Yi Sunsin has served as a subject matter for literary treatment on both sides of the Korean peninsula. In the South, Yi was the object of a quasi-deification under Park Chung-hee, but with the death of Park, Yi fell out of the spotlight until the 1990s. As Korean society in the 1980s underwent democratization, the figure of Yi Sunsin was not of great interest to Korean novelists or biography writers. In North Korea, Yi was initially heralded as the greatest of war heroes until 1967, after which the cult of Kim Il-sung did not allow room for other heroes.

In the face of worldwide crisis of communism in the late 1980s and early 1990s, the North Korean regime turned to ethnocentrism, which called for national heroes from Korean history like Yi Sunsin again. In South Korea, changed understanding of masculinity that undermined images of an authoritative patriarch and tough macho proliferated and coexisted with a nostalgia for stereotypes of the older notion of masculinity.

The narrative structure of Kim Hyŏn'gu's novel reflects the North Korean

---

19 Kim Jong-il, *On Juche Literature* (Pyongyang: Workers' Party of Korea Press, 1992), 89-90.

ideology at the time: a hero who represents the will of the people. Although Yi Sunsin is the protagonist, those who play a pivotal role in the plot and ensure Yi's victory are the commoners. Conversely, the South Korean novel *The Immortal* emphasizes the human frailties of the admiral, how he is embedded within social relations, and the anguish that these relations cause him. This narrative moves beyond the myths constructed around Yi and offers a new view of him that is all too human.

Both narratives are about heroes. The South Korean novel focuses on Yi less as a war hero than a mere human being. In *The Immortal*, Yi is a man in competition with Wŏn Kyun. He is not a wise and upright general but a mere human. Whereas the author of *The Immortal* tries to create a portrait of a frail human being, the North Korean narrative epitomized by *Admiral Yi Sunsin* is still very much a portrait of a war hero. This portrait, of course, comes with a North Korean twist: Admiral Yi is a popular hero, fighting alongside the peasantry of traditional Korean society. In the North, a hero of the masses, is the authentic model of a hero. Whereas the South Korean portrayal of Yi Sunsin follows the modernist trope of a tortured individual, the North Korean narrative presents him as a heroic figure who, alongside the masses, overcomes whatever hardship he faces in the end.

The present article has demonstrated that the two Koreas present very different depictions of Admiral Yi Sunsin. In both, Yi remains a war hero, but their understanding of heroism differ radically from each other, which reflects the difference between their social values: Whereas the North prioritize the collective good over the individual, the South cherishes freedom and dignity of the individual.

Trans. by Peter Ward

Fetishism and the Encounter between Two Religions

Bhang Won-il & David W. Kim

1. Introduction

The 2008 film *Fetish* tells the story of the daughter of a shaman who deceives the devout Protestant family into which she has married.[1] Following the death of her husband, the protagonist becomes close to the young couple who lives next door. She is envious of the wife Julie and begins to imitate her as she attempts to seduce the husband. In this story about the destructiveness of desire and temptation, viewers are led to understand that the title refers to sexual fetishization. The title, however, actually refers to a small bell that the protagonist's mother gives to her when she gets married. The fetishes themselves hint at the destiny of shamans whose calling is like a curse that they cannot escape. But what is the origin of these kinds of fetishes that are so alien to the modern viewers? They can actually be traced back to the work of Protestant missionaries who came to the Korean peninsula in the late 19th and early 20th centuries. They used the term "fetish" to describe the symbols of folk religion and shamanic items.

---

[1]   Fetish is a 2008 independent film by Sohn Soo-pum, a Korean-American filmmaker, that starred Song Hye-kyo, Arno Frisch, and Athena Currey.

Fetishism is a term loaded with an extremely complex set of meanings and refers to a network of customs. The word was first coined by French Enlightenment thinker Charles de Brosses in 1760. The term has since been used in many different academic disciplines and as an idea associated with considerable vitality in numerous areas of contemporary culture. The complexity of this concept is evident in the numerous ways in which it has been translated into Korean.[2]

The historical development of the concept of the fetish will be touched upon in this article, but it is not the central topic. This article will instead primarily focus on the concept as it appeared in documents left by Protestant missionaries operating on the Korean Peninsula in the late 19th and early 20th centuries. How and in what context did they use the term fetishism? Why did Protestant missionaries use this term when referring to Korean religious practices at the time?

The present article therefore begins with a brief historical overview of the concept of fetishism, which had first emerged from European encounters with Western African religion and developed different meanings within religious studies, economics, and psychology. Despite such changes, the underlying implications remained intact: a perception of the other as inferior and a focus upon the reversed material value placed upon a specific object.

These two aspects of fetishism can also be found in the use of the word by missionaries in Korea, for whom the use of the term fetishism undergirded their writing about foreign cultures. It demonstrates how the West perceived the non-European "other" and reflects the academic discourse of the time. Further, this earlier use of fetishism includes meanings that are potentially obscure to readers today. The documents left by missionaries referred to the religion of the other as fetishism. If we examine these texts more closely, the following three features can be deduced. First, the missionaries understood the objects that were used for familial worship to be receptacles of material

---

2   Whereas economists opt for the term "*mulsinsungbae*," "*chumulsungbae*" is widely used in todays' religious studies, replacing the previously used terms such as "*paemullon*" and "*sŏmulsungbae*." In psychology, the translated terms of preference include "*isŏngmurae*," "*chŏlp'yŏnŭmnanjŭng*," and "*p'et'isijŭm*," a transliteration of the English word fetishism, which also refers to a specific genre of pornography in South Korea.

value. Second, the objects of shamanic worship were generally understood as fetishes. In fact, burning these objects constituted climactic moments in the tropes of conversion into Christianity. Third, there were missionaries who used the term without negative intentions and simply used it as an academic description of what they saw. This last group sought to explain shamanism as a religious practice through the concept of fetishism.

In the following, I will offer a brief outline of and reflect on the history of the concept of fetishism before examining the three ways it was used by missionaries in Korea.

2. Fetishism: The History of the Concept

1) Emergence

The concept of the fetish first emerged in the space of encounter and transition between different cultures on the West African Coast during the 16th and 17th centuries.[3] West Africa was a contact zone where the Portuguese established their colonial posts and engaged in commerce and the slave trade from the late 15th century onward. Portuguese merchants described the religious objects and practices of the West Africans as "*feitiço*" (objects or acts that are part of witchcraft). This term was pidginized into "fetisso"[4] and appeared for the first time in English in 1613.[5]

From the 17th century onward, Christian merchants from Northern Europe used fetishism in a derogatory manner to indicate the worship of idols in particular. They used the following terms to describe what they saw: "the idolater who believes in the native religion hangs a leather pouch around their neck, called a fetish." Fetishism became synonymous with idol worship. This was the same logic that Protestants had used to criticize Catholicism. Max Muller explains the thoughts of the Protestant merchants as follows:

---

3   William Pietz, "The Problem of the Fetish, I," *RES: Anthropology and Aesthetics* 9 (1985): 5.

4   Pietz, "The Problem of the Fetish, IIIa: Bosman's Guinea and the Enlightenment Theory of Fetishism," *RES: Anthropology and Aesthetics* 16 (1988): 108.

5   Samuel Purchas, *Pilgrimage*, VI.xv.651, quoted in Sebeok, "Fetish," 116.

Why did the Portuguese navigators, who were Christians, but Christians in that metamorphic state which marks the popular Roman Catholicism of the last century — why did they recognize at once what they saw among the negroes of the Gold Coast, as feitiços? The answer is clear. Because they themselves were perfectly familiar with feitiço, an amulet or talisman; and probably all carried with them some beads, or crosses, or images, that had been blessed by their priests before they started for their voyage. They themselves were fetish-worshipers in a certain sense.[6]

West Africans functioned as the other for Europeans in a way that is similar to how Catholics were the other for Protestants. During the Reformation in Europe, Catholics were othered as "idolators," and the same logic was transposed onto West Africans. This history explains how fetishism began to have derogatory connotations.

The work of Dutch merchant Willem Bosman brought West African religious practices to the attention of European scholars.[7] He claimed that fetishism emerged from "the perversion of the true principle of social order: interest."[8] Such concerns in economic value was indeed prominent in early discussions of fetishism. The concept was further theorized by French Enlightenment scholar de Brosses in his book *Du culte des dieux fétiches* published in 1760. As can be seen in the following quotation, he expanded and generalized the use of the term from its limited prior application in a West African context. He presented fetishism as a rudimentary form of religion, which subsequently led to discussions of the origins of religion.

I ask permission to use this term habitually, and though in the proper signification it refers in particular to the religion of the negroes of Africa only, I give notice beforehand that I mean to use it with reference also to any other nation paying worship to animals, or to inanimate things which are changed

---

6   F. Max Müller, *Lectures on the Origin and Growth of Religion*, 3rd ed. (London: Longmans, Green, 1901[1878]), 63; Pietz, "The Problem of the Fetish, IIIa," 108.

7   Pietz, "The Problem of the Fetish, I," 5.

8   Pietz, "The Problem of the Fetish, IIIa," 121.

into gods, even when these objects are less gods, in the proper sense of the word, than things endowed with a certain divine virtue, such as oracles, amulets, or protecting talismans. For it is certain that all these forms of thought have one and the same origin, which belongs to one general religion, formerly spread over the whole earth; which must be examined by itself, constituting, as it does, a separate class among the various religions of the heathen world.[9]

Hence, fetishism emerged within a colonial context amidst the encounters of different economic systems. It represented an assessment of the unique value that West Africans placed upon specific objects. The value system of the observer was, however, different from the value system in the culture they observed. The former did not understand the latter, which gave rise to a theory that positioned the transference of value in confused terms.

2) Fetishism in Religious Studies

Fetishism developed into a universal theory in the philosophy of Auguste Comte. Comte argued that humanity proceeded through three stages of progress: theological, metaphysical, and positivist. He further divided the theological into fetishist, polytheistic, and monotheistic.[10] Fetishism was postulated as a system of thought characterized and bound by discrete and specfic objects, and when these concrete objects became abstract, the religion passed into the state of polytheism.[11] Comte's formula exerted considerable influence and became received wisdom. Indeed, fetishism became synonymous with primitive religion.

In the late 19th century, the academic study of religion emerged, and scholars began to propose new theories about the origin of religion. At this point, fetishism was considered an old fashioned theory, an impediment to be overcome. For instance, in 1869, John Ferguson McLennan proposed the theory of "totemism," which he defined as the combination of fetishism and exogamy.[12]

---

9 Müller, *Lectures on the Origin and Growth of Religion*, 61.

10 Peter Melville Logan, *Victorian Fetishism: Intellectuals and Primitives* (Albany, NY: State University of New York Press, 2009), 31.

11 Logan, *Victorian Fetishism*, 36-37.

He utilized fetishism as a theoretical construct of the basic form of religion, while proposing his new theory of totemism. In the 1870s, Edward Burnett Tylor proposed the theory of animism, which too included fetishism. According to Tylor, fetishsm was constituted by beliefs that souls acted on physical objects.[13]

Multiple forms of religious study developed and gradually the theory of fetishism was pushed aside for being old fashioned. Early religious scholars, who asserted that the religious forms they were interested in were the most primitive, attacked the idea that fetishism was the most primitive. For instance, Max Müller, a major religious scholar of the time, included a chapter in a volume in 1878 entitled "Is fetishism the original form of religion?" in which he constantly asserted the contrary.[14]

Going into the 20th century, fetishism lost almost all of its attractiveness as a theory about the origins of religion. Already in 1894, Robertson Smith observed: "fetishism is just a popular term, it has no precise meaning····· it merely connotes something that is very barbarous and contemptible."[15] Nowadays, fetishism is not used in the context of evolutionary theory, but rather denotes a basic form of religious culture. For instance, Gerard van der Leeuw claimed that awe with respect to objects that had allegedly been filled with energy were commonly associated with the feelings of children, primitive religion, and ancient religion.[16]

3) Fetishism in Economics and Psychology

Fetishism was conceptually given a new life by Karl Marx and Sigmund Freud. It is their ideas that dominate our current understanding of the concept. This section thus primarily examines their respective interpretations of fetishism.

---

12 John Ferguson McLennan, "The Worship of Plants and Animals," *Fortnightly Review* 6 (1869): 422-23.

13 Edward B. Tylor, *Primitive Culture: Researches into the Development of Mythology, Philosophy, Religion, Art, and Custom*, vol. 2 (London: John Murray, 1871), 132-133.

14 See Lecture 2 of Müller, *Lectures on the Origin and Growth of Religion.*

15 W. Robertson Smith, *Lectures on the Religion of the Semites*, 2nd ed. (London: Adam & Charles Black, 1894[1889]), 209.

16 G. van der Leeuw, *Religion in Essence and Manifestation* (Princeton, NJ: Princeton University Press, 1986), 37.

In Marx's system of thought, fetishism was a key term for understanding the properties of commodities within capitalism. The value of commodities was divorced from the actual character of the labor that produced them. Commodity value was rather decided by social relations and endowed with a fictive set of relations with other commodities. According to Marx, under capitalism the products of human labor are endowed with a life of their own within the world of commodities and have an independent position relative to other things and between people. In this regard, the commodity was identical to the life that objects were given within fetishistic religious practices.[17] Marx thus termed the value given to commodities within the context of human relations under the capitalist mode of production "fetishism," which was a value separate from the intrinsic value that such objects had in relation to other objects. His concept was informed by a close reading of the literature on Western African religious practice.[18] Hence, he deliberately made use of a concept that had thus far been utilized to explain allegedly primitive religious practices of "barbarians" to understand modern capitalism – which is an important reversal of conventional wisdom. A centerpiece of the rhetoric that othered and dehumanized "barbarians" had thus been repurposed by Marx in order to elucidate the core of the society of which he himself was a member.[19]

Sigmond Freud, the famed psychoanalyst, focused on the sexual desire with which objects could be endowed. He offered the following explanation of sexual fetishism:

> Fetish is not a substitute for any chance penis, but for a particular and quite special penis that had been extremely important in early childhood but had been later lost. That is to say, it should normally have been given up, but the fetish is precisely designed to preserve it from extinction. To put it plainly: the fetish is a substitute for woman's (mother's) penis that the little boy once believed

---

17 Karl Marx, *Capital*, trans. Samuel Moore & Edward Aveling, vol. 1 (Ware: Wordsworth Editions Ltd, 2013), 118-132.

18 W. J. T. Mitchell, *Iconology : Image, Text, Ideology* (Chicago: University of Chicago Press, 1986), 186.

19 Mitchell, *Iconology*, 205-206.

in and — for reasons familiar to us — does not want to give up.[20]

Freudian psychology posited the male castration complex: During childhood, boys were shocked by their sexual organs and those of their mother because they thought their mother had been castrated. Fetishism arose in the imagination of boys to substitute for the lost sexual organs of their mother. In popular psychology, however, the psyhoanalytic notion of fetishism as substitute for women's missing phallus became simplified into an object that had been endowed with a kind of sexual value. The concept of fetishism in art and cultural criticism, as well as in the pornography industry, can be seen as an extension of this simplified notion. In general usage, fetishism refers to a voyeuristic sexual obsession with specific body parts like legs and items such as stockings, shoes, and underwear.

3. The Fetishism of Missionaries in the Field

Let us now examine how missionaries used the concept of fetishism in the transitional space that was Korea in the late 19th and early 20th centuries. Fetishism was a commonly used word to describe the culture of the "other" at the time. The reinterpretations of the concept in economics and psychology that are well known to us now were not available to missionaries at the time. They rather used the concept in a religious context. This is not say, however, that they were making use of contemporary ideas in religious studies. By the early 20th century, the idea of fetishism was already out of use in the field of religious studies. It was perceived as a contemptuous term in the same way that superstition, worship of idols, and heresy were.[21] But it is worth remembering that the concept was widely used in Victorian documents. One cannot explain the language of an era with reference to academic literature

20 Sigmund Freud, *The Standard Edition of the Complete Psychological Works of Sigmund Freud*, vol. 21 (London: Hogarth Press and the Institute of Psycho-Analysis, 1953), 152-153.

21 Tomoko Masuzawa, "Troubles with Materiality: The Ghost of Fetishism in the Nineteenth Century," in *Religion: Beyond a Concept*, ed. Hent de Vries (Fordham University Press, 2008), 648.

alone, and the term clearly had a distinct popular meaning. Protestant missionaries considerably expanded in number in the late 19th and early 20th centuries, and the term fetishism was widely used to describe religious practices witnessed in the field. The way the term was used by missionaries shows us yet another way that the idea had permeated popular discourse. According to an analysis of the records of Protestant missionaries active in Indonesia at a similar time by Webb Keane, the missionaries thought of fetishism as identical to idol worship. They viewed it as inappropriate worship or a fear of inferior objects and thus concluded that it threatened human dignity.[22] Let us now have a detailed look at how such tendencies manifested in Korea.

1) Inversion of Material Value

As we saw above, the core issue regarding fetishism is how material value is assessed. The values imparted to physical objects that are held to be sacred in one group may appear unintelligible to outsiders. When these outsiders assess what they see as "inversion," they see the value bestowed upon such objects as fetishistic. In a similar manner, Westerners who visited Korea in the late 19th and early 20th centuries, during the so-called "open ports" period, expressed skepticism about the religious objects of Koreans, and even expressed derision. They considered such objects to be an indication of fetishism among Koreans during the time.

In the first case we examine, the term "fetish" is not used. The views of the Western authors that I will discuss nonetheless exhibit such a logic. The text discussed below was written by William G. Gilmore, an Englishman who lived in Korea from 1886 to 1889 and worked as a teacher at Yukyŏng Institute, one of the early modern educational institution in Korea. Following his return to Britain from Korea, he published a book about his experience in 1894. The following is an excerpt from that book:

The main building will generally be found dark, but when opened, the figure

---

22 Webb Keane, *Christian Moderns: Freedom and Fetish in the Mission Encounter* (Berkeley, UC: University of California Press, 2007), 225.

of the deified warrior, in red and gilt, with glaring eyes and impossible mustache, may be seen, seated in defiant attitude on his throne. In close proximity to each other may be seen the strangest objects — gifts of worshipers. Here an ancient sword of native make keeps guard while a Waterbury clock ticks the seconds as if in derision. In one shrine I saw before the god a solitary rubber boot, much the worse for wear, which the donor had perhaps picked up from the ash-heap of some foreign resident of the capital, or which had been discarded by a disgruntled hunter.[23]

Here, Gilmore provides his account of the following two objects: The first seems to be Tongmyo, a grave built to honor Guān Yǔ, a Chinese general from the Three Kingdoms Period, in the vicinity of Tongdaemun, which corresponds to Gilmore's description of a shrine erected to a warrior god. The sword and clock at the shrine clearly caught Gilmore's eye. The second object concerns a rubber boot found at another shrine. The fact that a new and unfamiliar object would be given such value as to be placed on an altar demonstrates the flexibility of Korean folk beliefs. In the eyes of a Westerner, however, this practice appeared identical to a Bushman's veneration of a Coca-Cola bottle, something that is inappropriately placed in a lofty position. A rubber boot clearly was not of much economic value, which, for Gilmore, indicated an instance of inversion. Although he was not a Protestant missionary, the writings of the German journalist Siegfried Genthe, who visited Korea in 1901, present a similar view. Here again Genthe does not mention fetishism, but when analyzing the economic value of Korean folk religious symbols, he arrives at conclusions with such implications:

Up and down the branches within reach hung all kinds of rags, pieces of paper, and similar pieces of junk. This superstitious wanderer offered up old straw shoes as a holy offering, they also hung solemnly blessed objects on this humble shrine. Yet, the spirits they feared did seem to be that important to them. Because what could only be called presents to sooth these spirits were

---

23 George W. Gilmore, *Korea from Its Capital* (Philadelphia: Presbyterian Board of Publication and Sabbath-School Work, 1892), 192.

basically worthless······A [new] pair of straw shoes cost 8 won, with a dollar worth 2,500 won, so a pair of straw shoes would only cost two-thirds of a penny. How much would an old pair of straw shoes fetch? I speculate, but surely this was enough for [their] god.[24]

The records of missionaries who wrote about shamanism align with such views. Horace N. Allen, the first missionary to operate in Korea, attacked Korean shamans for allegedly exploiting the beliefs of their followers for economic gain.[25] The view of shamans as effectively being con artists became a commonly shared belief by missionaries who were critical of Korean traditions. They believed that the Korean shamanistic customs distorted the economic values.

Mattie Wilcox Noble's diary also has similarly critical views of shaman symbols in economic terms. Mattie Wilcox Noble moved to Korea after marrying William Arthur Noble and lived on the peninsula from 1892 until 1934. She worked as a Methodist Episcopal missionary in Seoul, Pyongyang, and in Kyŏnggi Province. She left a thorough record of her forty-two years in the country working as a missionary, and was emotionally forthright to an extent that one rarely sees in official records. In her journal entry from April 8, 1897, written during her sixth year on the Korean peninsula, she recounts a visit to a Korean family and her interest in their objects of worship. She describes these objects as "offerings to the spirits," implying their fetishistic feature:

At another home, I found many fetish still in the house. One was two small bags of rice hanging on a wall, which had been put as an offering to the spirit of life, when their baby was born. They promised to take it down & use the rice. Then there was a long shelf on which were two covered baskets & an earthen crock. I wished to investigate them & see what had been offered to the spirits at various times. The woman of the house seemed afraid to touch them, but when we told her that no harm would befall her from showing them to us & that with offerings to the spirits she could not serve God, she brought them

24 Siegfried Genthe, *Korea: Reiseschilderungen*, trans. Kwŏn Yŏngkyŏng (Seoul: Ch'aekkwa Hamkke, 2005), 109-110.

25 Horace N. Allen, "Some Korean Customs: Mootang," *The Korean Repository* 3 (1896): 163-65.

down & open them. They seemed to be covered with the dust of years. One basket contained some coarse linen folded up & laid there as an offering to the spirits; it also contained a dressed waist of the old woman's 35 yrs. before, at the time of her wedding, laid there also a long skirt. The other also contained old clothes laid in the basket yrs. before as offerings to the various spirits. The crock contained old cooked rice & bread which had decayed long ago & kept there on the shelf to appease the spirits.[26]

Noble directly witnessed a Korean family worshiping Chowang, the kitchen god, and T'ŏju, the house spirit. She did not merely encourage them to avoid doing so, but requested that they show her their objects of worship. These included a bag of rice, basket, clay jar, hemp cloth, old clothes, cooked rice, and rice cake. Although she does not express it directly, Noble implies that the objects prized by the Korean household were insignificant. Bestowing special value upon insignificant everyday objects was behavior in keeping with the classical meaning of fetishism.

2) The Destruction of Fetishes: Religious Conversion Ceremonies

Protestant missionaries called the objects used in folk religious ceremonies and by shamans "fetishes." Interestingly, when Koreans converted to Protestantism, they had to destroy such items. But why? This act can be seen as demonstrating that the convert had turned their back upon old things, but the need to destroy specific objects also paradoxically represents a recognition of their value. Destroying and burning "fetishes" is the most dramatic moment in conversion stories of Koreans, and was frequently included in reports about conversions.[27]

W. G. Cram, a Methodist missionary who was active in Korea from 1902 to 1922, wrote the following account about a conversion of a shaman. A particular

26 Mattie Wilcox Noble, *The Journals of Mattie Wilcox Noble 1892-1934* (Seoul: Institute for Korean Church History, 1993), 65.

27 Sung-Deuk Oak, "Healing and Exorcism: Christian Encounters with Shamanism in Early Modern Korea," *Asian Ethnology* 69-1 (2010): 103-105; Laurel Kendall, *Shamans, Nostalgias, and the IMF: South Korean Popular Religion in Motion* (Honolulu, HI: University of Hawai'i Press, 2009), 5.

shaman decided to convert to Christianity, whereupon a Korean Christian leader demanded that the shaman destroy the objects they used in shamanist rituals. The reason being: "·····for in Korea when one believes in Christ all articles, vessels, clothes or anything whatever that has been used in heathen worship are destroyed as were the books in Ephesus (4:22−24): You were taught to put away your former way of life, your old self, corrupt and deluded by its lusts, and to be renewed in the spirit of your minds, and to clothe yourselves with the new self."[28] Cram wrote that by burning these objects the shaman expressed that they had left their former self behind.

E. A. Lewis, a Methodist missionary active in Korea from 1891 to 1929, provided an account of her more active involvement. She even entitled one of her reports from 1906 "A Holocaust of Fetishes."

> At Chang Chai Nai I met with the women in class, visited with them several neighboring villages, and helped make way with more fetishes. This time quite a crowd gathered to see the performance. Martha, the wife of Pak the patriarch. took the lead; she called for a gourd, took down a double bag from the wall, emptied the rice into it, and handed it back, saying "This is enough for your evening meal;" then she went out to a corner of the yard and pulled down a little straw roof which covered a crock half filled with barley chaff (the rats had eaten the grain). This she emptied in the fire place and proceeded to take down a stick, half covered with a dirty fringe, which was put with the chaff and the whole burned.[29]

Lewis moved across the southern part of Kyŏnggi as she took out and destroyed "fetishes" from the houses of believers. An altar for the Tŏju could usually be found in the area near earthenware jars outside the house, where people placed a pot filled with rice and covered with straw that served as a physical vessel for the house spirit. These altars were destroyed and burnt in the yards of converts. Lewis would sing hymns while accompanying Korean

---

28 W. G. Cram, "Rescued after Years of Bondage," *The Korea Methodist* 1-11 (September, 1905): 149.

29 E. A. Lewis, "A Holocaust of Fetishes," *The Korea Mission Field* 2-7 (May, 1906): 134-135.

Christian leaders undertaking such tasks. Lewis described the burning of "fetishes" as "performance" or "ceremony," which implied that she understood these acts of destruction as ritual. As the title of her report on such activities implies, this act represented a burnt offering to God, a holocaust in its literal sense.

Annie Laurie Adams Baird's novel, *Daybreak in Korea: A Tale of Transformation in the Far East*, combines all of the elements we have thus far seen. After marrying William Baird, the founder of Soongsil University, she arrived on the Korean peninsula in 1891 and lived in Pyongyang until her death in 1916. She was dedicated to education and wrote numerous books. *Daybreak in Korea* was a novel about missionary work written for an English-speaking audience. The book tells the story of a woman, Pobae, who is burdened by the chains of traditional Korean society, finds happiness, and helps influence those around her in a positive way following her encounter with Christianity. The antagonist in the novel is a shaman called Sim Ssi, who tries to cast Pobae into hell. The story reaches a climax when Sim Ssi repents and converts to Christianity, during which "fetishes" play a significant part.

In the first half of the story, an episode is recounted in which Sim Ssi visits the home of a missionary. After the visit, the narrator informs the reader: "When Sim Ssi reached home after her visit to the missionary's, she took the label off the tomato can and pasted it on the wall for an ornament."[30] In other words, the shaman character is presented as offering up a new Western item she had obtained. The story thus reproduces observations made by Westerners as discussed above. This part of the narrative reflects the view that "fetishes" are items chosen as objects of worship that have little economic value.

In the climatic part of the narrative, Sim Ssi's conversion is accomplished through the destruction of her "fetishes." Her own conversion is anticipated by what happens to one of her colleagues, Ko P'ansu, who successfully converted before her by destroying the drum that he had previously used for ritual.[31] Sim Ssi's conversion involves the complete and thorough destruction of the physical environment in which she previously operated as a shaman.

---

30 Annie Laurie Adams Baird, *Daybreak in Korea: A Tale of Transformation in the Far East* (New York: Young People's Missionary Movement of the United States and Canada, 1909), 69.

31 Baird, *Daybreak in Korea*, 92-93.

"Half-way measures were not possible to one of her nature, and having parted company with Satan, Sim Ssi's first act was to repudiate him wholly and entirely. From every nook and corner of her house and yard she brought out a host of wretched fetiches, some of recent date, many that had been festering in their places for years. Among the lot were old wornout straw shoes, pieces of rag rotten with filth, scraps of paper written over with prayers and incantations, human bones, images made of straw, pieces of gourds and broken dishes, and spirit-garments of silk and gauze, made and stuck away in dark Corners in the hope that the spirits would find them and be pleased."[32]

The story of Sim Ssi's conversion is a fictionalization of Lewis's "A Holocaust of Fetishes." She is portrayed as piling up all the objects she had previously used in shamanist worship and burning them. In the mean time, onlookers also bring out "fetishes" they had previously forgotten to discard and add them to the fire. They then sing hymns while watching the fire burn. Baird gives an inventory of all the "fetishes" burnt. It is difficult to ascertain whether such items were actually used by shamans at the time, but the list is quite exhaustive, and some of these items were indeed used for such purposes. What is important here, however, is that the longer the list, the more worthless many of these items appear to be, and the more justified their destruction is. These are items imbued with the "sins" of the past, and their destruction, which serves as a metaphor for ritual of redemption, is a perfect plot device for creating a dramatic effect of the conversion scene.

3) Academic Writings on Fetishism

Most missionaries loathed "fetishes" and wanted them to be destroyed. There were, however, at least some missionaries who sought to maintain a neutral perspective on the matter by describing the obejcts and practices associated with "fetishes" in academic terms. In the early 20th century, George Heber Jones was known as an authority on Korean "fetishes."[33] He described

32 Baird, *Daybreak in Korea*, 99-100.
33 Homer B. Hulbert, *The Passing of Korea* (London: Page & company, 1906), 412.

275

such objects without derision as being symbols of Korean folk worship.

Jones's first recorded observations about "fetishes" date to 1895. He wrote that "spirits are represented by fetiches — a bundle of straw, a paper of rice, a gourd, an old pot or a cast off shoe hung in a conspicuous place to stand for a supernatural conception."[34] In another writing from 1901, he argues that fetishism is a characteristic of Korean folk worship:

> Most of these spiritual beings are represented to the eye by some material object or fetich, thus making fetichism an important feature of Korean Shamanism. The fetich, whatever it may be, is regarded as clothed with a certain sanctity and to it the Korean pays his worship. Spirit and fetich become so identified in the mind of the devotee that it is hard to determine which has the greater ascendancy, but it is certain that the fetiches, however decayed and filthy they may become from age, are still very sacred and the Korean dreads to show them violence.[35]

Jones's views were widely accepted by his missionary colleagues. He argued that any object could be chosen as a "fetish," and that there was an arbitrary relationship between symbol and symbolic object chosen. Jones pointed out that this symbolic power could be so strong to an extent that the symbol and the symbolized were perceived as identical to one another in the mind of the believer. It was this identification that sustained the sacred quality of symbolic object. If he had taken a critical view of the fetishism he described, he could have written about the arbitrariness of the choice of objects, or the confusion about what was actually being worshipped. He, however, neither took such an approach nor sought to expose the fear that Koreans had of their objects of worship.

Jones sought to apply Tylor's concept of animism to Korean shamanism.[36]

---

34 Anonymous [attributed to George Heber Jones], "Obstacles Encountered by Korean Christians," *The Korean Repository* 2-4 (April, 1895): 147.

35 George Heber Jones, "The Spirit Worship of the Korea," *Transactions of the Korean Branch of the Royal Asiatic Society* 2 (1901): 41; George Heber Jones, *Korea: The Land, People, and Customs* (New York: Eaton & Mains, 1907), 49.

36 Bhang Won-il, "The Early Protesant Missionaries' Understanding for Korean Religion," doctoral thesis, Seoul National University, 2011, 168-175.

Hence, he took the view that fetishism was subsumed under a broader concept of animism. Therefore, his usage of the term fetishism did not imply the conflation of Korean shamanism with fetishism. Rather, it was for locating one aspect of Korean shamanism that had to do with physical objects.

Homer Bezaleel Hulbert frequently used the same terminology in the manner of Jones when he referred to Korean traditions as "fetishism."[37] He not only included shamanism, but also ancestral worship that was part of Confucianism, which he called "fetishism of ancestors."[38] Fetishism thus had become a term that could describe all physical religious symbols in Korean religious practice.

After 1910, however, the term "fetishism" was less often used, and critical remarks became more common. For instance, J. Robert Moose in 1911 made the following comment: "Our village religion is truly and simply religion, not some particular system of religion. It cannot be called Confucianism, it is not Buddhism, neither is it fetishism pure and simple."[39] Here Moose appears to have been influenced by the most up-to-date theoretical assessment of fetishism in religious studies at the time, rather than the older notions of fetishism.

4. Conclusion

Fetishism derived from the cultural encounter between the Catholic merchants from Portugal and the West Africans. Dutch Protestant merchants added derogatory connotations of idolatry and inversion of values that they saw in these practices. Fetishism then developed as a universal concept for describing primitive religion. In the late 19th century, however, as theories about the origins and subsequent evolution of religion developed within the field of religious studies, fetishism was discarded as a concept. It was re-introduced by Marx as a means to understand what he perceived to be the irrational core of Western capitalism's commodity economy. Freud also used the term to analyze the sexual value bestowed upon objects that acted as replacements

---

[37] Homer B. Hulbert, "Korean Survivals," *Transactions of the Korean Branch of the Royal Asiatic Society* 1 (1900): 35.

[38] Hulbert, *The Passing of Korea*, 404.

[39] J. Robert Moose, *Village Life in Korea* (Nashville, TN: M. E. Church, 1911), 190.

for the missing phallus. Hence a new understanding of fetishism was born.

The modern space of Korea of the late 19th century was characterized by encounters between Christian missionaries and shamanism. The result of this interaction was a largely negative language that was critical of the alleged fetishism of religious household objects and those of shamans. A lack of understanding of the other's system of symbols resulted in critical views of objects that appeared to lack economic value. Contempt for such objects of worship resulted in them being the subject of attack and destruction. The burning of fetishes by shamans was often a radical scene in conversion stories.

Religious studies scholars have, however, reassessed the idea of fetishism. The concept formed the basis for the first modern theory of religion. As such, it was the first to allow for an explanation of the emergence of religion that does not take God as its central concern. In other words, it contributed to the shift away from the understanding of religion in terms of the relationship between people and god by foregrounding the relationship between people and things as being the start of religious history.[40]

During the encounter between Christianity and Korean shamanism, the physical aspects of worship caught the attention of the Western observers, which led them to address fetishism. If such aspects of Korean shamanism — its attachment to particular physical objects — can be recognized in terms of cultural specificity rather than, for example, inversion, they cease to be the subject of criticism. Obviously, in Christianity, there is a conflict between the spiritual and the material, with a hostility to materialism and secularism. Hence, it was difficult for Christians to fairly evaluate the status of the material in religion. In fact, association with the material in religion have been criticized as "prosperity gospel," which is often believed to have been influenced by result of shamanism. A reconsideration of fetishism, however, will include a proper understanding of shamanism, the materiality of religion, and the place of "prosperity theology" within Christianity.

Trans. by Peter Ward

---

40 William Pietz, "Fetishism and Materialism," *Fetishism as Cultural Discourse* (Ithaca, NY: Cornell University Press, 1993), 138-139.

Korean Studies
Abroad

Interview with Professor Yeounsuk Lee

(Hitotsubashi University, Japan)

Q: I'm very happy to see you, Professor Lee. I'm looking forward to your advice for our fellow junior researchers in and out of South Korea, as you have been playing a crucial role in the field of Korean Studies in Japan for a long time. I'd like to start by asking you some personal questions. How did you come to study abroad in Japan, and what were some differences and similarities that you observed there in regard to the ways of engaging with humanities studies?

A: Yes, thank you. Thank you for having me over for this interview. I'm not sure if I am the right person to ask for any advice for young and emerging scholars. To answer the first part of your question, looking back now, how I came to study abroad in Japan had been a result of a series of coincidences, one after another, as is with probably most of our significant life events.

My bachelor's degree was in Korean Language and Literature, which didn't bear much relevance to having to study abroad in Japan. At the time, in the 1970s, I had neither been given any opportunity to study Japanese language nor personally motivated to do so. Student protests were everywhere, so I didn't really pay too much attention to academic training itself. However, I had a group of colleagues and senior students around me who were serious about discourses on society, nation, and intellectual history, to which I myself had also been introduced. It was probably under their influence that I wrote a bachelor's thesis on one of Ch'oe Inhun's novels in terms of what had been

281

labeled as "division literature" (*pundan munhak*). It was a shabby attempt, but a decisive moment nonetheless, as I began to consider the problem of Korean modernity and the division in a more serious manner afterwards. This was also when I realized that the presence of Japan would be crucial if one were to engage seriously with such subjects.

So I was thinking at the time that it wouldn't be a bad idea to study abroad in Japan. And then, when the opportunity arose, I jumped at it. It was a reckless decision. I didn't even know any Hiragana at the time! (*laughter*)

In regard to the second part of your question, it's not easy for me to say whether there is a clear difference between how humanities studies is done in Korea and Japan. More than anything, I only finished a bachelor program in Korea, with which I hadn't been seriously and fully engaged. So I would say my knowledge in regard to the field of humanities in Korea was limited when I first came to Japan. It was only after I began studying abroad in Japan that I became interested in how humanities studies was carried out in Korea and started comparing it to how it was done in Japan.

I'd like to warn you that any talk of differences between the field of humanities in Korea and Japan is often easily reduced to the subject of "national character" of the two countries. The spirit of humanistic inquiry, however, lies in challenging what is taken for granted or regarded as even axiomatic, and revealing a new, multifaceted view on people and society. So one must be aware of the reductive tendency that I just mentioned.

Although I have been conducting research and teaching for many years in Japan, I still feel uncertain when it comes to talking about the said difference. However, one thing I can point out about the humanities in Japan is the generational gap between the older, more established scholars and the young and emerging scholars. Those who were born in the 1930s, which is to say that they have witnessed Japan's defeat during World War II and went to college right before Japan's rapid economic development, tend to manifest historical and social concerns and relevant insights in their work. I suppose the same would apply for the Korean scholars as well. These scholars tend to be meticulous in their studies, and avoid jumping quickly to a decisive, simple conclusion about anything. This has left a profound impression. I am not sure if this analogy would work, but their work seems far more inductive than deductive. In a way, they exhibit craftsmanship in their humanities studies.

I tend to make confident statements, both in academic work and everyday life, which, I suppose, has to do with my personality. However, unfortunately, I haven't run into that many Japanese scholars who are like that.

Also, there is a discernible difference in terms of research approach and attitude between those who were born in the 1950s and went through the period of widespread student protests in the 1970s — which ended with a sense of loss and despair — and those who went to graduate school after the bubble period. But I'd like to finish this up, as it would get too long and take too much time for our interview.

Q: I'm guessing that the understanding of Korean literature, language, and culture in Japan wasn't that profound back when you studied abroad, which probably could have led to some biases as well. Would you be able to provide a brief overview of how the field of Korean Studies in Japan has developed or changed in the past decades?

A: I began graduate school in 1982. Relatively speaking, there weren't that many Korean students studying abroad in Japan back then. Also, their policies in regard to foreigners were pretty backward, the best example of which included having to provide your fingerprint for your alien registration card. In regard to the field of Korean Studies in Japan at the time, however, things were quite different. The postwar spirit of critical reflection of not only the Japanese society but also Japan's colonial rule in Korea was very much alive in the field of Korean Studies in postwar Japan, combined with innocent enthusiasm for academic work. This is embodied in the work of historian Kajimura Hideki. Aside from the field of history, there were great scholars in the field of Korean language and literature. Also, the field of Korean Studies has benefited from the profound work of *zainichi* Korean scholars, most of which were produced under unfavorable circumstances.

With the rapid economic growth in South Korea and the democratization around the 1980s, the overall attitude toward South Korea in Japan has changed significantly. This change in attitude, however, also had to do with the call for "internationalization" in Japan. One of the goals for the Nakasone regime at the time was to attract up to 100,000 international students. The motive behind proclaiming this goal was the decline in economically productive population, which resulted as the period of rapid economic growth came to an end and the birth rate dropped.

Q: You founded the Center for Korean Studies at Hitotsubashi University, which, I believe, is inseparable from your interest in training future generations of scholars as well as your experience of studying abroad in Japan earlier. Would you be able to share the trajectories that led to the foundation of the Center and some of the activities that are going on there?

A: There was a sense of crisis as the diplomatic relation between South Korea and Japan was getting ever more exacerbated. Of course, it has been hostile most of the time, but in the past there was some sense of implicit agreement by which they were trying to keep a balance even as they tried to keep each other in check. After the 2011 Tōhoku earthquake, however, the political maneuvering in regard to the territorial dispute or the problem of Japan's imperial past got rather belligerent.

The Japanese society's overall attitude toward Korea is twofold. On one hand, people are genuinely fascinated by Korean TV dramas and K-pop, which play a huge role in their daily life. On the other hand, conservative politicians incite antagonism.

With this in mind, the main academic approach of the Center is twofold as well. One has to do with serious humanistic inquiry for historical analysis and reconciliation; the other concerns the Korean Studies with the focus on the culture and sensibility.

Q: I suppose doing Korean Studies in Japan would feel very different from, say, doing Korean Studies in North America or Europe, or even from doing other types of regional studies within Japan, especially because of the tension between Korea and Japan as well as the historical circumstances that shape the relation between the two countries. Do you believe there is a certain vision for academic exchange that transcends the national boundary, an outlook for a future that is more "global"?

A: The field of Korean Studies in Japan is different from that of other regions in terms of the legacy and historical memory with which it must wrestle. The history of violence between the two countries has left behind wounds that still haven't healed completely to this date, and the politicians today exploit them to instigate further conflict. If the *raison d'être* of the humanities has to do with enrichment of human life through the means of intellectual inquiry, then this is the right time for the Korean Studies in Japan to exhibit what the field is truly capable of. The field has accrued some great scholarly achievements, and the work of its practitioners are solid and meticulous. Inheriting their legacy with an open outlook for the future of humanities studies, I believe, would contribute to the hope and the possibility of realizing the common intellect.

Q: Although the Center is based in Japan, it has also been actively engaging with anglophone and sinophone institutions abroad. Is there anything that has particularly struck you about them?

A: True. The Center for Korean Studies at Hitotsubashi University has been making scholarly exchanges and building friendships not only with scholars in Japan but also scholars in other regions. I was able to see the world at large through the scholars that I met, which helped me give up some of the things that I have been very stubborn about in my research. I learned to be humble, both personally and work-wise. The Korean Studies differs depending on the social and historical context of each region. Learning and acknowledging each other's differences would help elevate the field to the horizon of universality.

Q: I believe that the field of Korean Studies in Japan is inseparable from the literature, thought, and history of *zainichi* Koreans. Are there any intersections between their accomplishments and the field of Korean Studies, and what would be the significance of such intersections?

A: As I mentioned earlier, the work of *zainichi* Koreans served as the bedrock of the Korean Studies in Japan. They are, in a sense, in-between beings, both in Korea and Japan. Although the role of the in-between has

285

been pivotal in the general history of humankind, they have also been subject to marginalization. Therefore, it is necessary to provide an environment where *zainichi* Koreans can thrive, for which research grants and other forms of support in and from Korea are also in need.

The problem of language, in particular, also needs to be considered. You must understand that the primary language for most *zainichi* Koreans is in fact Japanese, deconstructing the myth of the unity between one's language and nationality that can ostracize them. For instance, we shouldn't blame them for not being able to speak their ethnic language. I am eagerly looking forward to the work by the emerging *zainichi* Korean scholars.

Q: When we were organizing events for international exchange in South Korea among Korean Studies scholars across the world, the Center for Korean Studies at Hitotsubashi University played a pivotal role. I am sure that there were some moments when you, as an "outsider," have experienced inconvenience or discomfort as you were working with a number of universities and research centers in South Korea. What advice would you give so that these events will no longer be planned as merely one-time-only?

A: I am pretty sure that you always learn from the process of trial-and-error as you organize these events. One thing, I'd like to see them carried out under a subject that is broader in scope. If the event is one-time-only, then most of the time you simply end up with just questions. I wish that keeping constant academic exchange could lead to an opportunity where people can wrestle with such questions, develop their thoughts, and share them.

Q: Your book, *The Ideology of Kokugo* (University of Hawai'i Press, 2010), has become a classic in the context of Japanese intellectual history. At the same time, I believe that it has exerted a profound influence on the field of Korean Studies as well. I remember reading a striking passage from one of your writings where you said you "became a linguistic orphan" after coming to Japan. Would you be able to share more about the kernel of your thought, and, perhaps, about plans for future work?

A: I'd say that *The Ideology of Kokugo* was born out of my desire to become free from the chains of modernity as well as that of Japan. One of the reasons why this work has been received well in the Japanese society is because I managed to penetrate through the binary problem of interiority and exteriority in studies on Japanese modernity by taking up the issue of language. At the time, the existing work on the Japanese modernity tended to assume either the position outside of Japan or the inside of Japan. Another has to do with my attempt at "deterritorialization" by traversing different fields such as linguistics and intellectual history. To undertake such work, you need to sharpen your logic and argumentation and make them as transparent as possible. In the course of this project, I was able to learn a lot and grow.

At the same time, I have always wanted to do work on affect, which could not only sustain human life but also devour it. It is our affective capacity that enables us to fall in love with or harbor hatred toward one another. I've only begun to touch the surface in this area, but my interest in ethno-aesthetics or humanistic inquiry that tackles both intellect and affect has to do with that wish. Also, it is for the sake of my personal well-being. (*laughter*)

Q: This would be the last question. Was there something that you have stressed the most when teaching international students, including those from South Korea, of Korean Studies in Japan, especially at Hitotsubashi? Also, would you like to say something to a new generation of Korean Studies scholars who wrestle with the question of what it means to do Korean Studies between Korea and Japan?

A: Japan is a well-organized society. It's orderly. Once you figure out their "social grammar," you would be able to get along pretty well here. But it does feel pretty closed-off, which can be frustrating.

For scholars to sustain their work, their daily life matters. So my advice in terms of the everyday would be that you would need to filter out the things that are deliberately provocative, instigated by the politicians or the mass media to promote anti-Korea or anti-Japan sentiments. This lesson comes from my own experience, that you can simply choose not to engage with the bad, nasty people. University is a safe place, so take comfort, learn with an open mind, and make good friends there. Be humble, but also take confidence, and be merry with your academic endeavors. I'm pretty sure all this will turn out to be fruitful.

Trans. by Jang Han-gil

Interview with Professor Jooyeon Rhee

(The Pennsylvania State University, U.S.)

Q: Hello, nice to meet you. I'd like for you to think of this as a less formal opportunity to share the current status of the field of Korean Studies overseas and advise on how to navigate one's way in academia, with and for emerging Korean Studies scholars both within and outside of South Korea. I'd like to begin by asking personal questions. How did you first get into Korean Studies? Would you be able to give a brief overview of your background and trajectories?

A: I was not aware of the existence of Korean Studies when I started my BA in Canada back in the mid-1990s. I got my BA in Art History focusing on Western art, and it was some years after I got my BA when I began to see the presence of Area Studies. I enjoyed the university education there in terms of the faculty's and students' serious approach to the subjects they studied and the mutual respect existed among them. Despite the liberal and respectful atmosphere of the study environment, however, I met a number of challenges that discouraged me from pursuing further professional goals. The biggest challenge was the feeling of marginalization at the everyday level that was largely shaped by the near absence of anything about Korea. Finding employment opportunities in the art industry was especially challenging because of the prevailing biased view that someone with an Asian face suits the "Asian art" industry but nothing else. My conflicting relationship with work and life in Canada was quite intense and I decided to give myself a break from my academic work.

When I reflect on that time now, rather than the challenge to find a professional position, my individual crisis over my racial identity was a much bigger factor that directed my intellectual inquiry of art to the East v. West. After working for some years in the visual art industry, I decided to go back to school with a new interest, that is, exploring art and literature in the triad relationship between Euro-America, Japan, and Korea. Naturally, historical understanding of Euro-American imperialism and Japanese colonialism as well as Enlightenment philosophy and aesthetics were my primary interests, and ironically enough it was through this study I started reading Japanese literature seriously. I began comparative and cross-cultural studies of literature and visual culture in my graduate years from the mid-2000s. It was only towards the end of my PhD study when I interacted with researchers in "Korean Studies," mostly in the United States. In addition to the learning opportunities provided by these researchers, I think my previous studies of Western art, philosophy, and aesthetics were quite useful for my research since they became a fairly good ground for my cross-cultural, cross-regional or transnational research on Korean literature and culture.

Q: It seems like the size of or the circumstances surrounding the Korean Studies departments in overseas institutions were not favorable compared to nowadays. I suppose it differs from one institution to another, but I wonder how things were with Korean Studies in North America back then — like twenty years ago? — what it was like when situated on the inside of the field as well as when looking at it from the outside.

A: The Canadian academia of Asian Studies was concentrated on Chinese studies and Japanese studies in the mid-1990s. My alma mater, York University, did not have a BA program for Asian Studies. It only had a certificate program in which students could take some courses on China, Japan, and Korea. Courses on Korea were extremely limited. There were a couple of courses in modern Korean history and Korean literature. When *hallyu* gained global cultural currency from the late 1990s, we began to see a substantial increase in the number of students in Korean language courses.

As far as Toronto and its vicinity were concerned, there was only one university, University of Toronto, where students could take courses offered in multiple disciplines, namely, history, literature, sociology, and anthropology. The East Asian library at University of Toronto was a great resource for those who were pursuing studies about Korea, and I think the availability of academic resources was at a somewhat satisfactory level due to support from the Korean funding agencies from the mid-2000s. You cannot really compare the scope of the material support Chinese studies and Japanese studies have been receiving from China and Japan to that of Korean studies, but Korea's strategic investment in the Korean Studies program was not visible until the mid-2000s.

When I was in a PhD program, my coursework was concentrated on modernist philosophy and aesthetics, and there were virtually no courses on Korea at the graduate level. The situation in other universities was little better, I think, but overall, at the graduate level, you just had to learn how to find things on your own and narrow down your research focus. So I didn't particularly feel that I was disadvantaged except for the purchasing of materials in Korean through distributors. It took a lot of effort to get materials at times, and just like many other graduate students, I had very little resources to support study materials and research-related travel. The number of graduate students in Korean Studies was also quite small as well, but my interaction with these students, who received their undergraduate and graduate degrees in Korea, was tremendously helpful for me to widen the scope of my research at the time in terms of their generous sharing of their insights on Korean Studies and previous experiences of disciplinary trainings and study trends.

Q: Is there any considerable change that you notice in the field of Korean Studies, especially Korean literature, in North America?

A: From around 2010, the position of Korean Studies in North America changed dramatically. When I was finishing my PhD, I was able to teach language courses in many different places beyond universities such as cultural centres, the Korean embassy, etc. College students in Korean language classes have increased significantly over the last decade in North America. At Pennsylvania State University, out of three major Asian languages (i.e., Chinese,

Japanese, and Korean), Korean is the only language that has seen continuing growth in terms of enrollment. And this trend is also seen in many universities across North America and is becoming a driving force behind the creation of positions in other disciplines.

However, just like most universities in North America, a researcher like myself is the only tenure track faculty in the Asian studies department and is expected to teach courses beyond literature. I have never been able to offer courses on literature of colonial Korea, for example. For the first seven years after the graduation, I taught courses on literature, film, popular culture, and history. Despite this limitation, and many thanks to established scholars of Korean literature, the presence of Korean literature became somewhat visible. More universities offer Korean literature courses, and Korean literature is represented well at MLA, for example. It also must be noted that translators of Korean literature have been playing a vital role in making Korean literature visible over the last two decades or so as their works have helped a number of Korean writers garner interest from the general public in recent years. The availability of translated literary and other cultural works has been impactful force to receive interest in Korean literature from students and the general public.

Besides the aforementioned factors, several factors helped students' exposure to various aspects of Korean culture beyond K-pop these days. The first factor is the global social network that enables audiences in North America to access Korean cultural forms quickly. The much-developed content of web materials in English are also helpful. It is quite amazing to see that many BA students write about Korean literature, especially contemporary literature, covering various topics such as diaspora, gender, family, colonial history, etc.

Second, there has been a steady increase of researchers of Korean literature as well. These scholars have been marking their presence known by teaching, researching, and publishing Korean literature in academic journals beyond the Korean Studies cluster, eventually reaching wider audiences. Last, comparative and transnational research in Korean literature in recent years has generated some notable scholarly dialogues between "Koreanists" and scholars of area studies.

Q: What is Korean Studies like at Penn State University? Would you be able to share, for example, the disciplinary structure or some of the topics that are taught? How does it fare in terms of student enrollment and the level of their engagement in the field?

A: The history of Korean program at Penn State University is impressive. It was only five or six years ago when Korean was established as a minor while Chinese and Japanese Major programs had long been established. I sense that the university felt the necessity to expand the program by hiring a Korean specialist beyond language not too long ago. When I came to Penn State in Fall 2019, most Korea-related courses were language-related. Currently, we have about 250 students who take Korean language courses and about 70 students who are minoring in Korean language. The student enrollment in my content courses, namely modern Korean history, modern Korean literature, and Korean film and popular culture, usually reach a maximum of 49 students each.

Students' subjects of interest in Korea are very diverse, starting with language, history, literature, religion, film, popular culture, art, and even martial arts. I try to accommodate students' diverse interests as much as possible, and I think language courses can also reflect the diversity in their upper-level courses as well.

In fact, effective in Summer 2021, the Korean minor will be elevated to a Korean major, which will see a significant increase of content courses taught in Korean language. I cannot offer more courses than what I have been teaching, but I have been organizing academic talks by researchers in North America who deliver lectures on various fields of their expertise so that faculty and students at Penn State get to know about current research trends in Korean studies. I just established the Penn State Institute for Korean Studies, which supports and promotes Korea-related research, and I am hoping that we can create another tenure track position in Korean history, which is essential to enhance research and teaching here at Penn State.

Q: It's great to know that people are getting more and more interested in Korean Studies, which is also accompanied by substantial support for the field. I also feel like there is a slight gap in terms of topics in which Korean scholars in South Korea and the Korean Studies scholars in North America are interested. Since you are situated in between, I'd like to ask you about how you feel about such a gap, and whether you think that there are some topics or questions to which Korean Studies scholars in South Korea ought to pay more attention.

A: I think senior scholars who are much more experienced than I am can answer these questions better, but based on my relatively short experience and observation of Korean Studies, there are a few differences between Korea and North America in terms of the scholarly approach to Korean Studies, topical interests and periodical focus. These differences do not come from individual scholars' interests only. Rather, they come from different disciplinary trainings, availabilities, and the history of Korean Studies itself in both regions. Nonetheless, as far as my field is concerned, I see that scholars of modern Korean literature and culture who are researching in Korea seem to be very interested in learning about theories and study trends through interacting with scholars in North America whereas scholars in North America seem to have much broader interests in terms of the objects of their studies such as speculative fiction, *manhwa*, webtoons, the "bang" culture, new social media, etc. This difference is also rooted in the disciplinary boundary, which is still rigid in Korea, I think. Interdisciplinarity is a loaded term, but scholars and institutes in North America have been serious about deconstructing disciplinary boundaries to critique the Euro-America centrism and to lay common grounds to solve big questions that require intellectual investment of more than one discipline. I also notice that many scholars in North America pay attention to gender dynamics, sexual identity and politics, and racial/ethnic relations in Korea. Gender studies and women's studies have long played a significant role in critical research in human relations in North America whereas these studies have yet to gain stable intellectual and institutional supports in Korea for various reasons.

Race/ethnic relations is another area that scholars in Korea may want to explore more actively. Considering how the number of refugees, migrant workers, and foreign wives has increased significantly in the last two decades or so, and how the academic investment in Korean diasporas in various parts of the world became highly visible by now, studies of these changes in humanities and social sciences in Korea have yet to make themselves more visible.

I also notice that Korea-based scholars' participation in major North American conferences on Asia have been increasing in recent years and this is a very positive development because these venues provide opportunities to learn about research trends and approaches of others. I would like to encourage these scholars to think also about participating in theme-based conferences rather than region-focused ones in and beyond North America because these venues host many innovative panels and papers that may help us to develop research ideas and methods and share mutual interests.

Q: You have been based in Israel before coming to Penn State. A lot of Korean Studies scholars in South Korea are unfamiliar with the state of Korean Studies in Israel and the Middle East in general. Would you be able to share some of that?

A: I taught at The Hebrew University of Jerusalem for six years. I cannot comment so much about Korean studies in the Middle East, but based on my preliminary research that was conducted a few years ago, Korea is definitely gaining a strong presence in many countries in the Middle East such as Egypt, Jordan, Saudi Arabia, Iran, and Turkey, especially with its appeal of music and TV dramas. Israel is quite different from the rest of the Middle East as you probably know already. But its strong support of humanities-oriented research and teaching, as well as people's curiosity about Asia, were grounding forces behind the study of Korea. A significant turn in Israeli Universities' interest in Korea, however, came with the popularity of *hallyu*: TV dramas in the beginning and other forms of Korean culture more recently.

Both Arabic and Jewish communities put a lot of emphasis on family-oriented life and family values, and the representation of Korean familial relationship, although lacking realistic elements in many cases in popular cultural products, appeals to them. In addition, the somewhat exaggerated and intense expressions of emotions by people for their communities and countries in Korean popular cultural products have been one of the major factors for Israeli students' fascination with Korea as well. I also think that these young (and older) Israelis' view of Korea is something like a self-reflected mirror in terms of their empathy towards Korea's history of "suffering" derived from colonialism and wars with neighbouring countries since premodern times. I do not wish to generalize sentiment, especially one's sentiment towards history and nation, which is, more often than not, ideologically constructed. However, it appears that the "shared" history is an important factor that bridges Koreans with Israelis.

Many young people in Israel are frustrated with the political climate, more specifically, the right-wing politics that has been heavily influenced by powerful religious groups. They are attracted to dynamism, creativity, and passion expressed in Korean popular culture, and some seem to value Korea's democratization process that has no direct relationship with religion. I must emphasize that most students who are interested in Korean popular culture are young women who are highly discontent with the hypermasculine, militaristic culture of Israel. They seem to believe that Korean society has achieved gender equality to some extent, and this belief is formed by their exposure to "soft masculinity" represented in Korean popular culture. When it comes to Palestinian students, consuming Korean culture and learning about Korea are the manifestation of their desire to obtain mobility because their socioeconomic and gender positions in Israel are precarious while they feel familiarity with the traditional values reflected in Korean popular culture. At any rate, the number of students and researchers in Korean studies in Israel has been steadily growing in the last decade. The Hebrew University of Jerusalem has a Korean Studies major program, and two other major universities in Israel, namely Tel Aviv University and Haifa University, offer some courses on Korean history, religion, and language. I foresee that students and researchers will be in a good position to contribute their scholarship to Korean Studies, first due to their linguistic ability — most of them publish their works in English — and second due to their solid training that has been obtained in Israel, North America, and Korea.

Q: It's great to know that the number of people taking interest in Korea all over the world is rising. At the same time, I fear that there might be a gap between the image of Korea that people have, which is mediated

mostly by the Korean pop cultural representations, and what it's actually like in Korea. As an educator, you must be thinking a lot about how to respond to their interest while trying to have them get a more comprehensive picture of Korea. How do you strike a balance between the two?

A: Those who teach about Korean history, society and culture for foreign students are deeply aware of the gap between the media representation of Korea and the socio-economic and political reality of Korea(s). Thus it is important for us to help these students to learn about critically. My attempts to provide students with tools to understand Korea critically is not much different from others. The first is to make them conscious of historical contexts of things they learn either through providing historical texts or cultural texts that require historical understanding. If the latter is the case, I would spend some time lecturing about the historical context. The second is to include scholarly texts that deal with social issues in contemporary Korea such as class and gender inequality, misogyny, xenophobia, poverty, refugees, etc. that can be useful when analyzing various forms of Korean popular culture. The third is to make them to conduct research and write an essay on a certain topic that must contain critical angles. This requires some time since I need to design several steps that enable them to build their research and writing skills. Last, and as an extension of class discussions, I ask students share their opinions and research in written forms via learning management systems so that they learn from their peers. Besides these components, asking students questions that require a comparative analysis is a good practice, giving them opportunities to reflect on their own societies and cultures in the form of group discussions, debates, and presentations. Most students do possess critical thinking abilities. We just need to provide some tools for them to articulate their thoughts and ideas.

Q: Would you be able to share some of the research subjects that you have worked or are currently working on, and plans for future projects?

A: I have been working on literature and culture of colonial Korea. I explored the gendered imagination of nation and colonial modernity by focusing on

New Fiction, domestic fiction, and crime fiction in my first book, *The Novel in Transition: Gender and Literature in Early Colonial Korea* (Cornell University Press, 2019). I am currently working on my second book project on crime and detective fiction that aims to further explore cultural responses to modernity by examining narratives of crime including detective fiction penned by both Korean and Japanese writers. In the current project, I am interested in the domestication of the Western literary genre, detective fiction in particular, in the colonial cultural environment and its capacity to unpack the imagination of colonial modernity through the handling of socially deviant behaviours such as murders and 'uncontrollable' female sexuality. The 'fantasy-like' descriptions of crime and detection do not mean that the genre has no space to deal with social issues. It is just that it approaches the reality in different ways in terms of the attempt to depict the socio-economic backgrounds and motivations of crimes and psychology of criminals that more often than not are grounded on the confluence of the past and the present social lives. If my previous investigation of *sin sosŏl* (New Fiction) was to probe the literary imagination of the positivity of the enlightenment and civilization discourse, the current work is to show flaws of the discourse that manifest in the forms of murders, violence and misogyny. I just initiated a new research on the representation of food in contemporary literature and visual media and it will take some time for me to sharpen the focus of this research though I will be exploring these works from gender perspective.

Q. A while back, one Korean Studies scholar in North America told me about the difficulty involved in sharing and discussing the content of Korean Studies outside of the field of Korean Studies, with even the practitioners of Japanese Studies or Chinese Studies within the same field of East Asian Studies. There must be several reasons for this. Do you have any thoughts on this?

A: The challenge of sharing research on Korea is rooted in the cultural hegemony that has been formed since the Cold War period, I think. As most of us are aware, it is not an easy task to undo the hegemony because it was constructed by multiple forces including international politics and economy.

The number of researchers and publications on Korea has been lower than that of those on China and Japan, in particular. In this research environment, Korean Studies has not been visible enough at least to researchers of Area Studies or of multiple disciplines beyond history, literature, and religion. There has been an improvement in this area in the last two decades or so, mainly due to the Korean government's material investment in Korean Studies as well as the popularization of Korean culture that took off with the mass consumption of *hallyu* products. Another challenge lies in the narrow scope of research in terms of the geographical, periodic, and thematic focuses. Recently, I've been witnessing a fairly good amount of cross-regional and cross-cultural research that link Korea to the history and culture of neighbouring countries or the global communities such as the exploration of the problem of colonial intimacy in the Japanese literary sphere, the status of former Ming soldiers and Japanese samurais in Chosŏn Korea, the transnational approach to the study of the Imjin War, and the multi-national research cluster on the study of Korean diaspora, for example. I am also aware of your research, Youngshil, for your investigation of the intellectual history in East Asia, comparing Korean, Japanese, and Chinese intellectuals and their works in the early twentieth century. These kinds of research will appeal to researchers of China, Japan, Russia, North America, etc.

However, I don't think the researchers of Korean Studies, regardless of their geographical locations, should be conscious of research trends or appeal to other fields and areas of research too much. Accumulation and dissemination of research takes time, and the content and scope of research expand gradually. It seems to me that the steady increase of researchers in Korean Studies as well as the widening scope of their research are a natural progression that came out of their exposure to previous research. Further, the foundational research that scholars in Korea have been carrying out is tremendously important for researchers overseas. I have a lack of knowledge as to what this process has been like, but my impression is that their digitalization and translations of historical sources are crucial for future researchers, for example.

Q: I hope that the field of Korean Studies could contribute to the academia in general, going beyond the national boundaries of South Korea or simply

"delivering information" about Korea to the Western academia. This, however, is not an easy task. I'd like to know your thoughts on this.

A: I do not agree that Korean Studies is circulated only within Korea or that it only provides "information," although I understand that Koreanists have the sense of pressure to contribute their works to expand the intellectual engagement with other researchers across regional and cultural boundaries. As I mentioned earlier, we see a wider sharing of the Korea-focused research beyond Koreanists in recent years. The pressure, it seems, is an epistemological one that affirms Koreanists' understanding of Area Studies as a periphery vis-à-vis Euro-American academia. As many scholars have pointed out, a regional collectivity is desirable to make Korean Studies' contribution to knowledge production about Asia more visible. Academic collaborations with scholars in Asian countries could be one way to make that happen, and a more active scholarly exchange between scholars of Korean studies in Korea and other parts of the world in the form of conferences, workshops, or seminars could be another way. Materialization of the research that comes out of these kinds of collaboration will take time, and at times the language barrier can pose a great challenge as well. But in the long run, these would become effective and constructive academic platforms. I would also like to point out that the urgency to make Korean Studies visible should not pressure researchers of Korean history and literature, who have been trained in Korea in their native language as well as *hanmun,* to publish their works in English. This is a waste of time and energy that can be better invested to nourish their research.

Another way to enhance the intellectual dialogues across multiple disciplines and regions is to establish Korea-focused, peer-reviewed journals, or journals that are dedicated to Asian humanities and social sciences. These will make emerging scholars and their scholarship visible in the field and quicken the process of making their works available for researchers and students, shortening the workflow, so to speak. I hope that *Metamorphosis* series books which Soongsil University is now attempting can become a critical space for scholars and students in their deeper engagement with Korean history and culture.

Q: There have been numerous attempts at the so-called "internationalization" of Korean Studies, especially the projects funded by projects such as BKs (Brain Korea) or HKs (Humanities Korea) in the past decade. However, there have been critical views, as many of the events organized by them have been one-time only, rather than providing a space for sustained scholarly exchange. Would you be able to give any advice in terms of research or policy-making for the "internationalization of Korean Studies"?

A: I know less about the nature of HK or BK projects and their broader impacts on the agenda of "internationalizing" Korean Studies than those who are involved in them directly in Korea. So I will abstain from commenting on these. Instead, I will reflect on my experience of participating in these projects as a guest lecturer and a presenter at conferences and symposiums. I was grateful for these opportunities where I could present my work and interact with established and emerging scholars. But most of these were "one-time only" events without plans for further scholarly interactions. As far as I remember, no publication plans were laid out either. It would be good to plan long-term academic exchanges between scholars in Korea and other parts of the world under a specific theme or topic that could materialize in the form of publication. Instead of hosting conferences and symposiums that cover so many topics and disciplines such as "globalizing Korean Studies," setting up a topic specific to the research cluster with long-term goals will be more productive both in terms of publication as well as providing venues for younger and emerging scholars.

I would also like to add that a more inclusive and expanded approach to Korean Studies is necessary. Policy makers and institutional leaders seem to focus on spreading knowledge on Korean history and culture globally. However, there has been ongoing scholarship of Chinese/Japanese/European/American history, philosophy, and culture within Korea. There are many research fields established and developed in Korea that do not comfortably fit into the "official" or "established" field of Korean Studies. Scholars who have been working on Korean reception of Irish literature, American literature, or Korea-Europe/Korea-Latin culture, for example, can expand their intellectual dialogue with people in translation studies, comparative literature, or even American studies. In my knowledge, scholars in China and Japan have been actively engaging in these fields by establishing relationships with major journals or institutes in North America and Europe. We should also support these fields to nourish the scholarship that aims to understand others and other cultures. Fundamentally, however, we need to reconceptualize the "globalization" or "internationalization" of Korean Studies. What does it mean by "globalization of Korean Studies"? Who is globalizing what? Who is included in and excluded from this process? More importantly, how do we make this process intellectually stimulating and productive?

Q: Although the number of opportunities for physical interactions among scholars dwindled due to the COVID-19 crisis, it seems like people are more motivated in terms of trying to overcome physical distance. Would you be able to share some good examples of such an attempt? Do you have any suggestions for turning this crisis into a new opportunity, for instance by utilizing the online platform for exchange among Korean Studies scholars across the globe?

A: I am a member of three study groups that regularly occur online. One group includes scholars from Korea, Japan, China, and North America. It is challenging to carry out the group project due to linguistic barriers and time differences. However, I foresee that materialization of this group's work will occur gradually. To most people in this group, sharing their knowledge is a priority, and it has been highly satisfying. The second one is an international workshop that I am co-directing. Compared to the first one that focuses on a very specific period and topic, or more specifically, certain world literary/cinema genres, the second one is quite broad but thematically specific. I read works produced by historians, anthropologists, sociologists, literature and media scholars, and health and environment studies. Being in this group widens the scope of my knowledge about the theme, and getting to know about studies in different disciplines reshapes my research direction in constructive ways. The third group is on the understanding of archives in which we read the ideological formation and reading of archival materials, flexible approaches to "reading" archives and the discipline of archival studies, and actual applications of these approaches to book monographs and journal articles. This perhaps is a bit distant from what I do, but highly inspirational in terms of how these readings expand my usage of archives and archival imaginations of colonial culture. Out of these three, the last two are extremely well organized, and this is very important to have all the members feel included and valued. In sum, as long as the study group, workshops, or even conferences have clear thematic/topical focuses, the current learning and research barrier can be overcome to some extent, I think. The current environment definitely limits us in many ways but it also has become a moment of realization that we can be connected more easily than before as far as sharing research is concerned.

Q: This is the last question. Do you have any advice for the young and emerging Korean Studies scholars who are dreaming of embarking on a journey to the bigger world?

A: This is the most difficult question of all. At any rate, I hope you understand that my "advice" is limited since you are hearing one person's observation. I hope you will hear more productive and constructive advice from many other scholars in the future. First, whether these young scholars are in Korea or overseas, I strongly recommend that they obtain linguistic abilities such as reading knowledge in classical and modern Chinese, Slavic languages, European languages, or even Arabic. There are texts written in the Middle East about Korea that virtually no researchers work on until now, for example. These will enrich Korean Studies for its widened global connections. Second, I know that many graduate students in Korean universities participate in international conferences and workshops. Even though they may feel that they have yet to mature their linguistic abilities, I also recommend that they make active engagement with study groups and professional associations overseas.

Culture Review

Korea, the Land of the Living Dead: The Biopolitics of the Korean Zombie Apocalypse

Shin Seung-hwan

One of Korean cinema's strengths over the past two decades or so has been the inventive use of genre cinema. Markedly, "genre auteur" has often been used to describe prominent figures in Korean cinema, such as Bong Joon-ho, Park Chan-wook, Kim Jee-woon, and Ryu Seung-wan, who all have led the renaissance of Korean cinema. What is particularly remarkable about its genre experimentation is the distinctive way in which it orchestrates political and social issues and genre imagination. Bong's *The Host* (*Koemul*, 2006), for instance, begins as a sci-fi creature film; however, it soon diverges from the genre's conventions as the monster fades into the background and our attention is drawn to deeper social issues — imbalanced international relationships, a flawed power-knowledge relation (suppression of local knowledge), a corrupt or incapable bureaucracy, and a pervasive materialistic culture — which suggests that the real monster is, in fact, our society which is more monstrous than the monster itself. On the other hand, Park uses the revenge narrative to comment on a condition in which socially acceptable forms of action for justice are unavailable and consequently individuals — especially, those vulnerable to crisis — are often helplessly driven to extreme measures, such as the individual use of force, to realize justice.

More recently, Korean cinema's genre imagination has found new territory:

307

the zombie film. The surge of Korean zombie cinema arguably began with Yeon Sang-ho (Yŏn Sangho).[1] His *Train to Busan* (*Pusanhaeng*, 2016) was a tour de force. It was the first film of the year to surpass the ten-million admission mark in Korea. Released about a month later, his animated film *Seoul Station* (*Sŏulryŏk*, 2016), a prequel to *Train to Busan*, created a sensation in the overseas film festival circuit, including the 2016 Edinburgh International Film Festival. Yeon's triumph both at home and abroad then quickly instigated a series of new investments in the zombie theme: *Rampant* (*Ch'anggwŏl*, Kim Sŏnghun, 2018), *The Odd Family: Zombie on Sale* (*Kimyohan Kajok*, Yi Minjae, 2019), *Kingdom* (*K'ingdŏm*, Kim Sŏnghun and Pak Inje, 2019−2020; a Netflix series), *Peninsula* (*Pando*, Yeon, 2020), *Alive* (*Saraitta*, Cho Irhyŏng, 2020), and *Sweet Home* (*Sŭwit'ŭ hom*, Yi Ŭngbok, 2020; a Netflix series). Within this trend there are noteworthy attempts to rework the zombie film by interweaving it with other genres like historical drama (*Rampant* and *Kingdom*), comedy (*The Odd Family*), and science fiction (*Peninsula* and *Sweet Home*). Korean cinema, in other words, has become a major laboratory for new possibilities for the zombie film. This new development invites the question: Why would Korean society need the zombie narrative? What historical and aesthetic validity does the film genre have for Korean society?

As noted above, one of the major fortes in Korean cinema today is the creative fusion of genre sensibility and social criticism. Here, however, we need to reckon with some challenging questions. Genre cinema is neither the only nor the best means of social criticism. Instead, it has long been subject to doubts about its conservative propensity as it often ends with reaffirming

---

1   Korean zombie film was not unprecedented. Its history goes back to *A Monstrous Corpse* (*Koesi*, Kang Pŏmgu, 1980), allegedly the first Korean zombie film. Then, in tandem with the growing interest in genre film and perhaps encouraged by the revival of the zombie film after the global success of such films as *28 Days Later* (Danny Boyle, 2002), *Dawn of the Dead* (Zack Snyder, 2004; a remake of George A. Romero's 1978 *Dawn of the Dead*), *Land of the Dead* (George Romero, 2005), and TV dramas such as AMC's *The Walking Dead* (2010-) and HBO's *Game of Thrones* (2011-2019), Korean filmmakers started to return to the zombie narrative in the new millennium. Examples include *Dark Forest* (*Chukŭmŭi sup*, Kim Chŏngmin, 2006), and *The Neighbor Zombie* (*Iutchip chombi*, 2009; a six-part anthology film by O Yŏngdu, Ryu Hun, Hong Yŏnggŭn, and Chang Yunjŏng), *A Brave New World* (*Mŏtchin sinsegye*, Yim P'ilsŏng, 2012; a short in an omnibus film *Doomsday Book* [*Illyu myŏlmang pogosŏ*]), and *Ambulance on the Death Zone* (*Aembyullŏnsŭ*, Kim Kok and Kim Sun, 2012; the final entry in another quartet anthology film *Horror Stories* [*Musŏun iyagi*]). Still, few would deny Yeon's standing as the main catalyst of the recent rise of Korean zombie cinema.

or reinforcing the established norms. Why then do filmmakers frequently turn to genre imagination for social criticism, even at the cost of perceptual and ideological adequacy? If genre language is not just an inferior form of political commentary, then what special validity does genre cinema have for critical intervention in our society?

It would be pointless to assume that there are subversive qualities inherent in and essential to genre cinema. Genre cinema's critical cogency instead requires careful positioning or historicizing. In dialectical use, as Fredric Jameson noted in exploring how marginalized genres such as romance serve as a vehicle for the return of the repressed[2], genre cinema can become a proper alternative to the ruling modes of storytelling. For instance, when realism loses much of its ability to embrace historical heterogeneities as it understands principles like verisimilitude in a prescriptive way, or when modernism, giving in to schematic understanding, turns notions like heterogeneity into a de-historicized tenet, counter-historical experiences often seek new outlets in denigrated forms of representation such as romance, fairy-tale, and fantasy. Genre language, in other words, can work as a strategically valid means to act counter to our time and thereby to act on our time, or make legible things that neither realist rigor nor modernist sensibility is able to represent, at a certain historical juncture.

With regard to zombie movies, particularly recent ones such as *28 Days Later* (Danny Boyle, 2002), *Dawn of the Dead* (Zack Snyder, 2004), *Land of the Dead* (George Romero, 2005), *World War Z* (Marc Forster, 2013), *The Night Eats the World* (Dominique Rocher, 2018) and TV dramas such as *Dead Set* (Zeppotron, 2008), *The Walking Dead* (AMC, 2010-) and *Game of Thrones* (HBO, 2011–2019), much of their appeal stems from their special ability to tap into the anxiety of the total annihilation of human civilization. In other words, the angst of a large-scale catastrophe finds a forceful expression in the imagery of a zombie apocalypse. Zombification is, in Peter Dendle's words, "the logical conclusion of human reductionism."[3] It is the final verdict on

---

2 Fredric Jameson, *The Political Unconscious: Narrative as a Socially Symbolic Act* (Ithaca: Cornell University Press, 1982), 103-107, 193.

3 Peter Dendle, "The Zombie as Barometer of Cultural Anxiety," in *Monsters and the Monstrous:*

the degeneration of humans to automatons deprived of all human qualities such as consciousness, spirit, and emotion, except for the insatiable hunger for human flesh. The zombie is thus often symptomatically read as a metaphor for the biopolitics of our society where humans are not just reduced to functionality but also frequently find their lives ruled by the pathological need for continual growth and the logic of endless competition and survivalism. Zombie land is a world where people are haunted by the feeling that they have become little more than "monads of self-interest in perpetual and feverish struggle with one another."[4] In zombie society, human qualities such as sympathy and compassion are nothing but signs of weakness; or more horrendously, they only hasten the demise of the human species as they make humans more vulnerable to zombie attacks. In this milieu, survivalism becomes the *raison d'être*, and takes on an extreme form as humans are repeatedly pushed into a situation in which they are obligated to exterminate their zombie-turned neighbors, families, friends, and lovers.

This observation of zombie tropes, to my mind, has far-reaching resonance in Korean society that has been shocked and traumatized by a series of unsettling events, both at home and in neighboring nations in the recent past: the 1997 IMF crisis, the 2008 global financial collapse, the 2011 Fukushima nuclear disaster, the 2014 Sewŏl Ferry accident, and a string of pathogenic outbreaks such as BSE (or mad cow disease), SARS, MERS and COVID.[5] This interpretation is not simply a reflectionist perspective. The zombie narrative often invites us to self-reflection, particularly as the distinction between human and zombie often becomes blurred. A painful irony in zombie films is that the more human and compassionate the people are, the more vulnerable they become to the zombie's attack. On the other hand, the more soulless people are, the more likely they will stay alive longer. A paradox at the core of the zombie narrative

---

Myths and Metaphors of Enduring Evil, ed. Niall Scott (New York: Rodopi, 2007), 48.

4   Dendle, "The Zombie as Barometer of Cultural Anxiety," 50.

5   For more information about the blend of the zombie narrative and social criticism, and specifically the ways in which Korean cinema draws upon zombie tropes to comment on social issues within Korea's context, see Keith B. Wagner, "Train to Busan (2016): Globalization, Korean Zombies, and a Man-Made Neoliberal Order," in *Rediscovering Korean Cinema*, ed. Sangjoon Lee (Ann Arbor: University of Michigan Press, 2019), 515-532.

is that humans can remain human through inhuman survivalism; they stay human by becoming a wolf to others. The zombie apocalypse is thus often marked by an alternation between empathy and antipathy toward the zombies. In a zombifying world, human society quickly collapses, not just because of the zombies' endless attacks, but more importantly because of the inability of humans to work together.[6] As repeatedly suggested in many celebrated zombie films, humans are as much of a threat to life as zombies.[7] Indeed, less of their narrative attention goes to human-zombie conflicts than to those among the humans themselves.

Likewise, in Korean zombie films, the zombie is not so much antithetical to the human, but the zombie rather often feels like a mirror reflecting the zombie-like aspects of our own society. Consider Yongsŏk, the CEO of a bus company in *Train to Busan*, for example. As a figuration of amoral survivalism, he shows no hesitation or remorse about endangering others' lives for his own self-interest, which makes him analogous to a cannibalistic zombie. Notably, this zombie-like man becomes one of the longest-surviving characters. In contrast, a character like Sanghwa, a working-class deliveryman, falls victim to Yongsŏk's animalistic actions and eventually sacrifices himself for the other passengers. In the Netflix series *Kingdom* set in the post-Imjin War era Chosŏn Dynasty, the zombified King, the cause of a national zombie outbreak, is kept alive for the royal in-law family's wicked scheme to rule the court. What is truly horrifying in these cases is not the zombies but rather the humans, who appear inhumane or more monstrous than the zombies. Thus, the narrative and optical tensions in these zombie narratives frequently emerge from the double movement of identification (familiarity) and disidentification (unfamiliarity), instead of relying on the simple rejection of the zombie as anti-human. Noteworthy in this sense is the character Chonggil in *Train to Busan*, an elderly woman who is sickened by the unscrupulous actions of the survivors in her train car. She opens the door to the adjacent car where her zombified sister is

---

6   Barry Keith Grant, "Taking Back the Night of the Living Dead: George Romero, Feminism, and the Horror Film," in *The Dread of Difference: Gender and the Horror Film*, ed. Barry Keith Grant (Austin: Texas University Press, 1996), 207.

7   Grant, "Taking Back the Night of the Living Dead," 202.

walking amid a horde of zombies. Her decision, registering both her deep contempt for the animalistic survivors in her car and her irrepressible attachment to her sister, brings our attention to an ironic aspect of a zombifying society: becoming a zombie as the last way to stay human.

The zombie narrative also has its own merit by offering a critical reading of our everyday spaces: to name just a few titles, the farmhouse in George A. Romero's *Night of the Living Dead* (1968) questions insular domesticity, the shopping mall in his follow-up *Dawn of the Dead* (1978) examines consumer capitalism, the deserted London streets in *28 Days Later* envision post-apocalyptic urban civilization, and the images of the countryside, empty small towns, and ruined buildings in *The Walking Dead* function as the setting for the birth of a new civilization. In Korea's case, *Alive* comes to mind. One of the overriding sentiments in zombie films is claustrophobia. In *Alive*, the feeling of confinement not only arises from constant zombie attacks, but equally from spatial aspects; that is, the apartment complex where the two main characters, Chunu and Yubin, remain trapped until the last moment. As the dominant form of housing in Korea, the apartment constitutes a central component in the fabric of Korea's urban landscape. Apartment culture is, moreover, multi-layered. Its demographic density does not necessarily mean more contact. Households in the apartment complex are concealed and separate. The interactions with neighbors are usually kept to a minimum. Consequently, domestic spaces in the apartment are modern caves that have been cut off from one another. The apartment complex is, in brief, a microcosm of society atomized by isolation. This reality is especially true for millennials who often prefer to be left alone and communicate online. Chunu is an online gamer who spends much of his time gaming in his room instead of venturing out in search of social contact. His dark room is illuminated with the colorful lights of a computer gaming setup. Quarantining from the zombie outbreak, he video-logs his incarcerated life and emotional journey. It is thus fair to say that this post-apocalyptic condition is not that different from his everyday life. It is even rather fortunate he does not go outdoors; thanks to that, he saves himself from the fast spread of the zombie epidemic. Yet the situation quickly turns as food runs out, the Internet connection is cut off, and the virtual world crumbles down along with the real world. He struggles with his sense of utmost loneliness and eventually concludes that the only escape from this reversed Kafkaesque milieu is ending his life. Here, the claustrophobic aspects of the apartment complex, combined with zombie apocalypticism, gain special aesthetic validity for themes such as social anomie, urban isolation, and the search for a new form of social connection.

The anxiety of isolation in zombie cinema also brings us to another central thematic strain in the genre — the impetus to extend our cognitive and spiritual reach. Built on the growing division of labor and social stratification, our modern society has been marked by the erosion of intercommunal and intersubjective connections. The zombie narrative often highlights this issue through rampant amoral survivalism. In horror films, intercommunal and intersubjective awareness is eventually restored — although unfortunately, it often becomes the horror to be escaped at the end — through supernatural events of interaction across different spaces and times. In zombie apocalypse films, however, it is often the rapid spread of a pathogenic infection that makes palpable the hidden or forgotten networks in our deeply fractured society. When the far-reaching effects of an event in one place are observable in other areas within a short span of time, the concealed structure of social relations becomes more recognizable. To return to *Train to Busan*, Sŏgu, a self-absorbed fund manager insulated in his own financial world, appears disassociated from the perceptual and emotional connections with the rest of society and remains clueless, or uncaring, of the effects his actions may have on the lives of others. Hence, he is not so far from self-centered characters like Yongsŏk at the start. As the story unfolds, however, he transforms into a self-sacrificing father. A pivotal moment in his metamorphosis is when he learns that the cause of the zombie epidemic, now threatening him and his own family, stems from a chemical leak at a biotech plant he helped recover from financial troubles with dishonest stock trades. Here the zombie narrative turns into an opportunity for serious self-reflection.

The theme of wide-scale contagion and cross-contamination, pushed to extreme velocity during the zombie apocalypse, invites us to imagine new collective identities. The zombie apocalypse repeatedly dramatizes people's struggles under conditions where humans become wolves to each other and there is a desperate search for a new people or a new civilization in the midst of the zombified masses. Conversely, the surge of the zombie apocalypse attests

313

to an escalation of our struggles with the historical condition in which humans often prove incapable of recognizing or empathizing with each other and increasingly grow hostile to one another instead.

The BTS Phenomenon and Digital Cultures

Lee Kee-woong

1. Serendipity: A Rhizomatic Emergence of a Pop Star

A special session titled "The Present and the Future Outlook of BTS Syndrome" was held during the Korean Association for the Study of Popular Music (hereafter KASPM)'s biannual conference in December 2018, which was organized in swift response to an unprecedented event where BTS rose to the No. 1 on the Billboard 200 for the first time as Korean artists. The conference was filled with people and their enthusiasm, and the heated debates continued in the comment sections of the online news articles on the following day. The KASPM conference had never attracted this much attention from the general public since its establishment in 2005.

As a facilitator of the very session in question, it was not difficult for me to guess that, aside from the members of the KASPM, most of the audience in the conference room was ARMY. Indeed, my intuition was confirmed when the floor was open for questions and one audience member rose from her seat to criticize the presenters for "not having understood fully the profound worldview of BTS." Similar criticisms were found in the online comments on the following day, to no one's surprise. Whenever a news or editorial was published on the Internet, they were met by a flood of such ARMY comments almost without exception. I have never seen any popular stars whose fans were this eager to engage with anything related to them. Perhaps, there was a reason that ARMY had been claimed as "a fandom that has the most to say about their artists."[1]

The success of BTS has been often attributed to their fandom and the proliferation of digital media. Digital media, to which interactivity is inherent, has demonstrated that the exchange between and desires of ordinary individuals could be channeled into a power that could transform the world. The rise of BTS to global stardom was partially enabled by "the power from below," as the group had previously been underfunded, lacking the marketing and promotional aid from the mainstream music industry. Therefore, the case of BTS is telling in regard to the successes and failures of their K-pop predecessors in the U.S. market. Whereas those who sought to carve up their niche in the U.S. market through mainstream music outlets — such as BoA, Rain, Se7en, or Wonder Girls — had failed, the success of BTS or Psy relied mostly on the spontaneous "online buzz." There was a difference between the two in regard to whether their popularity could endure: While the success of Psy who does not have a solid overseas fanbase has been a one-time thing, the popularity of BTS endures especially with the fervent support from ARMY.

All this testifies to the gap between needs or taste of the mass and the U.S. mainstream music industry. A case in point was one American radio station program where its DJ scoffed at an ARMY member's request for a BTS song, to which he replied, "We only play real music."[2] Contrary to the belief of the mainstream music industry, however, a lot of American listeners opened up to the non-English songs — with lyrics in Korean — sung by a "manufactured boy band" from East Asia, which culminated in sweeping five Billboard No. 1s. The aforementioned "power from below" ruptures the existing order and enables unexpected occurrences, and thereby reinforces the rhizomatic nature of the world.[3] In this regard, BTS suggests an illuminating example of what it means to create popular music for empowered audience in the

---

1 Yi Chihaeng, *BTS and ARMY Culture* (Seoul: Communication Books, 2019), 47.

2 Yi, *BTS and ARMY Culture*, 59.

3 See Yi Chiyŏng, *Revolution of Art: BTS Meets Deleuze* (Seoul: Paresia, 2018).

hyper-connected space of digital media. Although the claim that the success of BTS amounts to "a fundamental and sweeping change on a global scale" seems a bit premature, it certainly has shaken the existing order.[4] This paper examines the changes in popular music by inquiring into its nature, aesthetic judgment, and the meaning of pop star.

2. Epiphany: ARMY as a Global Subculture

It is well known that ARMY has played a major role in the success of BTS in the U.S. market, which has been regarded as almost impenetrable for Korean musicians.[5] Since the mid-20th century, studies on fandom tended to emphasize the active agency of the fans.[6] By coining the notion of participatory culture, Henry Jenkins sought to identify fans as cultural producers, which brought about a paradigmatic change in the studies on fandom. The "idol fandom" in South Korea, however, pushed this phenomenon further by engendering "managerial fandom," where fans are actively and strategically involved in every aspect — ranging from planning, fostering, and promoting — of the business of producing their idols.[7]

In this respect, ARMY is a "managerial fandom," which used to be locally specific to South Korea, on a global scale. Non-Korean fans were able to experience an intimate and horizontal relationship with their music star that has hitherto

---

4 Yi, *Revolution of Art*, 8.

5 For details, see Hong Sŏkkyŏng, *On the Road of BTS* (Seoul: Across, 2020). The detailed accounts of ARMY in the U.S. are posted on the Korean blog named "Blssyr": https://blessingyear.tistory.com/entry/%EC%8A%A4%ED%80%98%EC%96%B4-%EB%B0%A9%ED%83%84%EC%86%8C%EB%85%84%EB%8B%A8-%EB%AF%B8%EA%B5%AD%ED%8C%AC%EB%93%A4%EC%9D%80-%EC%96%B4%EB%8A%90-%EC%A0%95%EB%8F%84%EB%A1%9C-%EC%BD%94%EC%96%B4%ED%95%A0%EA%B9%8C.

6 See John Fiske, "The Cutlural Economy of Fandom," in *The Adoring Audience: Fan Culture and Popular Media*, ed. Lisa A. Lewis (New York: Routledge, 1992); Henry Jenkins, *Textual Poachers: Television Fans and Participatory Culture* (New York: Routledge, 1992); and Kim Sujŏng and Kim Sua, "Beyond the Hermeneutic Paradigm and Toward Performative Paradigm: Debates in Fandom Studies," *Korean Journal of Broadcasting and Telecommunication Studies* 29, no. 4 (2015): 33-81.

7 See Chŏng Minu and Yi Nayŏng, "Fans Managing Stars, Industry Managing Fans: Characteristics and Implications of the Cultural Practice of '2nd Generation' Idol Fandom," *Media, Gender & Culture* 12 (2009): 191-240; and Sin Yunhŭi, *Fandom 3.0* (Seoul: Pukchŏnŏllijŭm, 2019).

been unavailable, where their star was no longer a distant figure for worship and respect but a companion and a project in which they could get involved. The members of ARMY have built strong mutual affection and solidarity as they worked hard towards the common goal: the global stardom of their beloved idols. Of course, there are conflicts between Korean and non-Korean ARMY around the issues of "special treatment" and cultural difference, which tend to escalate rather often. Nevertheless, for the BTS fans, ARMY is more than just a fan club, as its significance lies in forging a community where they could identify and communicate with their idols as well as with one another.[8]

In this sense, ARMY is also an affective community, serving subcultural and religious roles.[9] The narrative of redemption can easily be analogized in the confessions from the fans about how their life changed after their encounter with BTS, after which they claimed that they were able to live a fuller life. Perhaps it is this near-religious zeal that underlies the unusually strong loyalty and devotion that ARMY has for BTS. This also leads to the subcultural nature of ARMY: the members of ARMY share an identity of "outsider" ostracized in the mainstream culture, which serves as a firm ground for their mutual affection and solidarity with one another. The subcultural nature of ARMY is manifest in their activities as well, as they reinforce their collectivity and sense of belonging by developing their own narrative and lingo; sporting common symbolic items such as "ARMY Bomb," a light stick, T-shirts, and logo; engaging in everyday interaction among themselves via social network; and organizing various activities ranging from fan donation and translation to publishing white papers.[10]

Since the popularity of BTS derives from the ardent support from their

---

8   Hong, *On the Road of BTS*, 174-175.

9   In regard to the religious aspect of a fan community, see Jennifer Otter Bickerdike, *The Secular Religion of Fandom: Pop Culture Pilgrim* (London: Sage, 2015) and Sun Young Lee, "Practicing K-pop: A New Religion called BTS and ARMY," paper presented at BTS: A Global Interdisciplinary Conference, Kingston University, London, January 4, 2020.

10   The BTS fans relate themselves to a wide range of different narratives--from the personal and the historical to a series of participatory transmedia fictions called "BTS Universe." They also have coined various neologisms such as "rabbit hole" (their introduction to the BTS fandom), "I purple you" (an expression of trust in and love for one another), "I-lovelies" (an affectionate way of referring to overseas BTS fans), etc.

fans, the public reception of BTS is divisive. Despite the status of BTS as global superstars, those outside of the BTS fandom are mostly oblivious to their songs, names of individual BTS members, and what they look like. This stands in stark contrast to Psy's "Gangnam Style": Although BTS would be deemed more successful than Psy in the U.S. market, "Gangnam Style" is a song that almost everyone in the world could recognize and sing along with. At the same time, this contrast reveals the distinct nature of BTS's success grounded on digitized culture. What sets BTS apart from other subcultural phenomena in the past is the sheer size of their fan base. Although precise statistics has not been provided yet, the number of ARMY members has been suggested by numerous studies to be ranging from 29 million to 46 million, which is sufficient enough to exert substantial influence over the market.[11] What stands out is the fact that "Life Goes On," with its lyrics written mostly in Korean, has been able to rank 1st in Billboard Hot 100, owing to the support from the fans of BTS in the U.S., whose number is only a fraction of that of the entire ARMY across the globe. This is a telling account that it does not take that big of a number of fans to produce a hit song.

Some have argued that BTS has become mainstream based on their success in the U.S. market.[12] However, a different picture emerges when one takes into account the fact that BTS and ARMY are one: Some overseas BTS fans feel as though BTS is not taken seriously in the mainstream media, and others doubt the possibility that BTS will ever rise to mainstream stardom, leading to an opinion that they are better off not being part of the mainstream culture.[13]

---

11 Hong, *On the Road of BTS*, 163. See also Yi Chiyŏng, *Revolution of Art*.

12 Dam-young Hong, "How K-pop is becoming mainstream on U.S. talk shows: BTS paved the way, more effort needed to overcome language barrier," *Korea Herald*, March 27, 2020, http://www.koreaherald.com/view.php?ud=20200326000961; and Kim Kyŏnguk, "K-Pop is Mainstream in the World Music: Series of Huge Successes, Exporting Idol System," *Hankyoreh*, September 16, 2020, http://www.hani.co.kr/arti/culture/culture_general/962322.html.

13 See Kang In'gyu, "Is BTS Mainstream in the U.S. Market? Fortunately Not," *Ohmynews*, October 13, 2020, http://www.ohmynews.com/NWS_Web/Series/series_premium_pg.aspx?CNTN_CD=A00026 83380; Tram Anh Ton Nu, "Why Some Fans Are Glad BTS Does Not Have Mainstream Popularity," *Showbiz CheatSheet* (Asheville, NC), July 26, 2020, https://www.cheatsheet.com/entertainment/why-some-fans-are-glad-bts-does-not-have-mainstream-popularity.html/. Bloggers such as Sarah C and Courtney Lazore criticize how the Western mainstream media promotes deliberate misunderstandings of and biases toward BTS.
    See Sarah C, "The Curious Case Of BTS: How Journalism Mistakes Production For Manufacture,"

The overall sentiment that ARMY has toward the mainstream culture can be described as discomfort, if not antagonism.[14] In this respect, the rise of BTS to mainstream stardom might pose a threat to the very identity of ARMY.

At the same time, one might argue that the question of whether BTS is mainstream or not is an inappropriate one, given the undeniable fact that they already are global superstars. However, the significance of the question lies in the following grounds: (1) BTS, a group made up of non-Anglophone Asian members, has emerged from the peripheries of the mainstream music industry, and (2) the meaning of mainstream in popular music is being challenged in the era of digital media. The changing media environment, ever-more refining algorithms of music recommendation, content overload, and accelerated pace of the so-called "music cycle" have all contributed to the decline of the monoculture on national as well as international level. Gone are the stars like Michael Jackson or Cho Yong-pil (Cho Yongp'il) who used to provide a sense of shared temporality, nationally or internationally. Such changes call for the need to redefine the notion of "popular" in popular music. Popular music is no longer a one-size-fits-all type of music for "everyone" or an indifferent mass. Whereas popular music in the past relied on a clear-cut distinction between the mainstream and the "indie" or the subcultural, now the notion of mainstream is being dismantled and popular music being subdivided into various subgenres. What the success of BTS implies is the changing environment

April 29, 2019, https://medium.com/@selizabethcraven/the-curious-case-of-bts-how-journalism-mistak es-production-for-manufacture-73721c270088; and Courtney Lazore, "How mainstream media is still failing BTS: The album didn't flop, and we're not 'little girls,'" July 28, 2020, https://medium.com/@courtn eylazore/how-mainstream-media-is-still-failing-bts-the-album-didnt-flop-and-we-re-not-little-girls-27 938c2abc8c.

Music critic Kim Yŏngdae notes how such tendencies are also commonplace in South Korean media. See Ha Sŏngt'ae, "South Korean Media was Obsessed with Psy, But Belittles BTS's Success. Why? BTS Overturns 'Success Formula,' and ARMY Becomes System," *Gobal News*, December 5, 2020, http://www.gobalnews.com/news/articleView.html?idxno=31413.

14 The following post on Quora is very telling: "Why do you think that BTS would never reach the mainstream popularity of One Direction? Is it because 1D was more talented, or what are the other reasons?" *Quora*, February 28, 2020, https://www.quora.com/Why-do-you-think-that-BTS-would-never-reach-the-mainstream-popularity-of-One-Direction-Is-it-because-1D-was-more-talented-or-wh at-are-the-other-re. Greenwood, on the other hand, criticizes ARMY for being way too defensive. See Douglas Greenwood, "Pop Is Not A Dirty Word: How BTS and Brockhampton Are Giving the Boyband an Essential 2018 Re-up," *NME*, August 22, 2018, https://www.nme.com/blogs/nme-blogs/b rockhampton-bts-boyband-2018-2369479.

of popular music where the popularity of subgenres like K-pop are now able to outrun those who are regarded as "mainstream" these days.

3. Idol: From Artwork to Total Production

The development of popular music is inseparable from the evolution of media. For instance, the music industry in its modern sense could not have emerged without the invention of music recording technology. The emergence of digital media also brought about revolutionary changes to popular music. Although physical performance came to take on less significance in the era of music records, it was restored as music videos became widely accessible, during which people began to pay more attention to visual elements of music such as cinematography of the music video, choreography, look, etc. Bang Si-Hyuk (Pang Sihyŏk), the mastermind behind BTS, coined the term "total production," which refers to a form of digital entertainment that spans from the sonic to the visual, to describe the distinct feature of K-pop.[15] Popular music also developed into a form of multimedia entertainment that is irreducible to the record or sound media alone, as information about popular music artists and their work became widely accessible. BTS is exemplary when it comes to popular music artists who utilize the aforementioned feature of digital media. Aside from their public appearance as popular music artists, BTS members fulfill the needs of their fans through communicating with them via social network, live-streaming their V-logs, and providing an ample amount of "fan service" material.[16]

In this sense, BTS fits the description of "post-album" pop.[17] Whereas the main "job" of popular music artists in the past was producing an album, for

15 Kristine Kwak, "Big Hit Chief Bang Si-Hyuk, Mastermind Behind BTS, Talks Music, Fans and New Ventures," *Variety*, September 4, 2019, https://variety.com/2019/biz/news/bts-big-hit-bang-si-hyuk -talks-music-fans-1203322755/

16 Yi Chŏngyŏn, "When It Comes to Special Fan Service, BTS Never Rests," *Dong-A Ilbo*, August 20, 2019, https://www.donga.com/news/Entertainment/article/all/20190819/97025751/4.

17 Keith Jopling, "Preparing for the Post-Album Music Industry," *Midiaresearch* (blog), March 14, 2019, https://www.midiaresearch.com/blog/preparing-for-the-post-album-music-industry.

BTS album production is only one among many channels through which they communicate with their fans. What stands out in BTS's prioritization of interactions with their fans is a sense of intimacy: BTS publicize each member's personality, thoughts, state of mind, how they get along with one another, and how they are doing on a consistent basis on social network. In doing so, their fans feel as if they are part of the team, developing trust in and empathy toward their idols that turn into a sense of loyalty, to which the quality of their music is irrelevant. What this phenomenon implies is that in the digital era, the mandate of the entertainment industry, which is to create good music, has transitioned into the insistence on forming affective relationship with the audience.

Such an approach implemented by BTS, arguably the biggest pop group for the "digital natives," often runs into conflict with the conventional attitude toward what popular music ought to be. I sometimes hear from popular music scholars and critics that BTS is "more about dance than music," or that their music is "conventional." Alexis Petridis, a chief critic for the *Guardian*, has expressed similar sentiments when he assessed that the music of BTS is "commonplace" in the review of *Love Yourself 轉 Tear*.[18] Their message can be summarized as follows: In terms of music, BTS is nothing extraordinary, and their popularity relies on "attractions" such as dance, music videos, and their looks. The underlying prediction is that their popularity will be short-lived, as it is gained by stimulating pubescent excitement in "little girls" who are unable to tell apart good music and bad music.

It is not difficult to discern sexism as well as racism in these assessments. The subject of my examination here, however, is the aestheticism on which their claims are based. Matthew Bannister has demonstrated the process in which the middle-class white men in the West have genealogized, theorized, and canonized genres of popular music such as punk, post-punk, and indie rock by appropriating the terminology of Western high art.[19] Music albums

---

18 Alexis Petridis, "BTS: Love Yourself: Tear Review – K-pop's Biggest Band Keep Ploughing on," *Guardian*, May 18, 2018, https://www.theguardian.com/music/2018/may/18/bts-love-yourself-tear-revie w-k-pop.

19 See Matthew Bannister, "'Loaded': Indie Guitar Rock, Canonism, White Masculinities," *Popular Music* 25, no. 1 (2006): 77-95.

were perceived as works of art in this process of consecration, leading to a discourse that ascribed absolute value to music in recorded form. Critics of popular music came to adopt the aesthetic criteria developed in the discourse of Western high art such as originality, autonomy, and purity. The hierarchy of credibility for popular music artists has been established in a way that excludes "manufactured pop bands" like BTS since its inception.

The way that ARMY and BTS have responded to this is intriguing. Instead of seeking recognition in this hegemony, they decided to build their own discourse. Members of ARMY began writing and publishing books on BTS as early as 2018, leading to a 2020 international academic conference organized by ARMY in London and foundation of *The Rhizomatic Revolution Review* — commonly known as the *R3Journal* or R3 — in the same year.[20] All this can be seen as efforts to intervene the elitist popular music discourse dominated by middle-class white men "from below," as the R3Journal refuses the hierarchical relationship between academic knowledge and "fan knowledge" and seeks to embrace value of the latter. The transition of power that is anti-elitist is accelerated by not only digitalization but also the emergence of the mass who are equipped more knowledge on the popular music star they adore and challenge the notion of academic expertise, like the one member of ARMY who reprimanded the panels at the KASPM conference.[21]

4. Boys with "Luv": BTS Talks to ARMY

There would be a wide range of reasons as to why one is obsessed with BTS or joins ARMY: their good looks, great music, fantastic performance, etc. What sets them apart from fans of other K-pop artists is their frequent emphasis on the sense of comfort and "healing" that, they claim, the band provides. The space of social networks is filled with confessions from their

---

20 Kim Hyojŏng, "ARMY Scholars Across the Globe Hold Conference in London, Discusses BTS," *Yonhap News*, January 12, 2020, https://www.yna.co.kr/view/AKR20200112008100005. Examples of such authors include Yi Chiyŏng and Yi Chihaeng. Although Hong Sŏkkyŏng claims that she is not a member of ARMY, her book is based on a great number of interviews with ARMY members.

21 Kim Sangbae, *Knowledge and Power Transition* (P'aju: Hanul Akademi, 2010).

fans about how their lives have dramatically changed with their first encounters with the message "Love Yourself" from the band. Communication and empathy are crucial elements for the strong bond between BTS and their fans, as the fans are moved by how their idols constantly express gratitude toward them and send honest messages, to and with which the fans could relate and identify.

These virtues stand in stark contrast to the "rock 'n' roll" attitude, which has been idealized in Western popular music since the mid-20th century. Although the era of excess, characterized by "sex, drugs, and rock 'n' roll" is long over, the Western audience still expects transgressive, rebellious attitude against the social norm from their popular music artists. In this combination of avant-garde aesthetics and the Romanticist ideals, the popular music artist is perceived as an agent of negation, an aloof figure who is free from the secular standards and public opinions. The unequal relationship between the artist and the audience — the artist being the object of adoration and the audience mere followers — relies on the supposed superiority and extraordinariness of the artist. Society, then, provides a different set of moral criteria for these artists, granting them the right to defy the social norms to a certain degree. In this light, the qualities that characterize BTS — innocence, modesty, and integrity — are seen as bland, unexciting, and conservative, which places them as a mere aura-less entertainer for the mass.

The global popularity of BTS shows how a substantial number of people in the West have been also ready to welcome a popular music artist who is innocent, down-to-earth, and not alienated from the mass. While it is certainly true that not everyone in the West is attracted to the figure of a rebellious artist and the aesthetics of subversion, which explains the long tradition of manufactured boy bands in the West, they have not hitherto been given any space to make their voice heard.[22] What seems particularly interesting about the BTS syndrome is that the ranks of middle-class intellectuals, celebrities,

---

22 One of the first "manufactured boy bands" in the West is The Monkees, formed in 1966 for an American TV show. They were followed by The Partridge Family in the 1970s and New Kids on the Block in the 1980s. The golden age of manufactured boy bands started in the 1990s with the appearance of Backstreet Boys and Take That, followed by Westlife and One Direction in the 2000s. Although their biggest appeal was being clean-cut and wholesome, this image was essentially fabricated for profit and often turned out to be incompatible with the real personalities of boy band members. The initial appeal of such one-dimensional character did not last long, either.

and the so-called "influencers" — who would less likely have expressed interest in this type of music — have joined the fandom. The fact that most of these figures are women reflects the feminist aspect of the BTS syndrome. What captures their attention the most, however, is authenticity. As the status of BTS has been built on the long-term exchange between themselves and their fans, people come to believe in the authenticity of their message such as "Love Yourself" rather than dismissing it as hypocrisy or reputation-building with commercial aims.

A number of critics explain the significance of the messages in BTS songs — about providing comfort and encouragement — in terms of social competition in the neoliberal world, where a majority of its members are bound to be losers and have no one other than themselves to hold responsible for their failure. To these individuals who are prone to despair and self-contempt, the message of "Love Yourself" would indeed be empowering. However, this is nothing novel or unprecedented, as it has been used as a self-development mantra that is often deployed in the production of neoliberal subjects.[23] Therefore, what truly matters is not the message but its medium — the speaker of the message and the manner in which the message is delivered. It appears that BTS's consistent effort to lower themselves in service of their fans makes them the least egoistic superstars in history. It would be safe to claim that the explosive power latent in the message of their songs derives from such an attitude. Perhaps BTS is suggesting an only viable way in which a popular music star could communicate with the mass in the digital era, where the hegemony of the mainstream music industry weakens and the elitist aestheticians lose their authority.

Trans. by Jang Han-gil

---

[23] Lee Moonsung, "Decoding the Neoliberal Subjectivity in Self-helping Adult Learners," *International Journal of Lifelong Education* 36, no. 1-2 (2016): 151.

Book Review

Nation–Empire: Ideology and Rural Youth Mobilization in Japan and Its Colonies. By Sayaka Chatani

(Ithaca, NY: Cornell University Press, 2018. 347 pp.)

Ko Sun-ho

Nation-Empire opens with a line from the notebook of a young colonial Taiwanese man named Xu Chongfa: "I am turning into a passive person working at the institute. I have to become a volunteer soldier next year!" (1) Xu was not an outlier. Hundreds of thousands of colonial Taiwanese and Korean men applied to the volunteer soldier program during the Asia Pacific War years from 1937 to 1945. In consideration of this fact, the text asks the reader to reflect on the following: "How did young men in the colonies become passionate about their colonizer's nationalism?" Why did these men "embrace a presumably imposed ideology and express willingness to fight for a cause so irrelevant to their immediate interests?" (2)

What makes Chatani's response to these questions impressive is her comparative, transnational approach. In examining the relationship of the rural youth with *seinendan*, state-led village youth associations, she explores three different villages in the Japanese empire — one in the Japanese archipelago, one in Taiwan, and one on the Korean peninsula. It is now quite common to speak about the necessity of transnational approaches, yet it is still difficult for scholars of the Japanese empire to write a transnational history given the many linguistic and archival barriers. With her language skills in Japanese,

Chinese, and Korean, Chatani not only utilizes secondary works written in all three languages but also primary sources and oral interviews with two Taiwanese people and one Korean.

The value of this research can be found in Chatani's attempt to move beyond a top-down history on these associations and instead conduct a bottom-up analysis of mobilized youth. This approach yields a productive focus on the hopes, joys, grievances, and anxieties of these particular subjects.[1] In examining these emotions, Chatani uses the term "social mobility complex" (15) as a mechanism through which the rural youth from the "middling class"[2] pursued upward social mobility in intertwined, local social relations. Among these social relations, Chatani pays special attention to the geographical entities of the rural and the urban. Regardless of ethnic difference and local variances in the Japanese empire, the antagonism of the rural youth against the urban elite pushed success-seeking young men to adopt the war mobilization's rhetoric of agrarianism as a chance to express their pride and moral superiority. In this way, rural youth in the colonies as well as in the metropole internalized imperial ideologies for nation-empire building while pursuing their own mobility. Similarly, Chatani explains the generational tensions in rural society as another important factor for the rural youth to embrace war mobilization as a chance to form their identity as new modern subjects for the village and the empire.

Although Chatani's research is innovative in her analysis of local relations, the ethnic differences among the rural youth and the colonial grievances against the colonizer deserve more attention. Doing so would better convey the complexity of the colonial countryside. The text allows ample space for elaboration, particularly if we consider that Chatani's analysis of colonial Korea relies on a single case study of Kim Yŏnghan from Ch'ungch'ŏng Province.

---

1   There has been some research on the seinendan (ch'ŏngnyŏndan in Korean) against the background of colonial Korea. As one author, however, admits, these works do not reveal the thoughts and responses of individual participants as much as the Government-General of Korea's policy on youth. Hŏ Su, "The Organization and Activities of the Youth Associations in the War Era," *Kuksagwan Nonch'ong* 88 (March 2000): 204.

2   Chatani uses this term loosely. She writes, "Those in the middling class cultivated a sufficiently large area of land and secured a relatively stable source of income. They were wealthy enough to send their sons to at least six years of elementary school and often the additional two-year upper-level program. But they were not affluent enough to be able to pursue higher education in cities" (15).

Kim summarizes his experience with the Japanese settlers in a confirmative sentence: "The Japanese lived well with us" (199). Yet the social interactions between the Koreans and Japanese were far more textured than suggested by Kim's account. Kim also expresses hostility toward Korean Marxist historians by saying that "They don't know the real situation of the countryside" (18). Although Korean scholars of rural history have stressed ethnic antagonism and colonial exploitation, scholars such as Yun Haedong, Kim Yŏnghŭi, Yi Yonggi, and Chŏng Pyŏnguk have furthered a more nuanced understanding of the countryside through analyses of personal diaries and oral interviews. With the accumulation of more works on specific rural villagers, historians will be able to understand to a far greater degree the diverse motivations and experiences of rural residents who participated in wartime mobilization.

During the last few years, youth and children have emerged as important social categories in English-language scholarship on historical studies of Korea.[3] With its research scope beyond Korea, Nation-Empire is a welcome addition to this academic discussion on youth in Korean history. The book is particularly useful for scholars drawn to the subject of youth in the context of the countryside, war mobilization, colonialism, and empire.

---

[3] For instance, Charles Kim, *Youth for Nation: Culture and Protest in Cold War South Korea* (Honolulu: University of Hawai'i Press, 2017); Yoon Sun Yang, *From Domestic Women to Sensitive Young Men: Translating the Individual in Early Colonial Korea* (Cambridge: Harvard University Asia Center, 2017); Dafna Zur, *Figuring Korean Futures: Children's Literature in Modern Korea* (Stanford: Stanford University Press, 2017).

The Intimacies of Conflict:
Cultural Memory and the Korean War.
By Daniel Kim

(New York, NY: New York University Press, 2020. 336 pp.)

Joo Young Lee

Over the last 20 years, scholars of race and ethnicity in the United States have published numerous monographs on the Korean War and its legacies. Recent examples include Yuh (2002), Cho (2008), Kim (2010), Oh (2015), Park (2016), Baik (2019), and Graves (2020). These studies have shed light on critical issues relevant to the causes and effects of the Korean War on a global scale, including U.S. imperialism and militarism, the politics of the Cold War, war brides, transnational and transracial adoption, and racial conflict and solidarity experience by members of the Korean diaspora in the United States.

Daniel Kim's *The Intimacies of Conflict: Cultural Memory and the Korean War* expands on such scholarship by taking a comparative racial and transnational approach to cinematic, literary, and photographic representations of the Korean War produced in the United States and South Korea from the 1950s to the present. Although scholars have long argued that race is vitally important for understanding U.S.-Korea relations, Kim's work is the first book-length study in English that analyzes cultural artifacts through the lens of interracial relationships in the context of American and Korean foreign policy and domestic politics.

Kim begins with an analysis of American cinematic, journalistic, and photographic representations of Korean civilians, Asian Americans, and their interracial interactions, highlighting ways that these depictions are driven by two hegemonic ideologies: "humanitarian Orientalism" and "military Orientalism." Kim defines humanitarian Orientalism as a sentimental "mode of warfare" that identifies Korean civilians as "objects of care" for the United States, the paternalistic savior of Korea (11). Through the lens of humanitarian Orientalism, the deaths of Korean civilians are a "tragic but necessary consequence of war" since it is hard to distinguish innocent civilians from communist enemies (51). These modes of portrayal are evident in American films such as *The Steel Helmet* (1951), *One Minute to Zero* (1952), and *Battle Hymn* (1957), as well as in articles published by *Life* magazine in the 1950s.

Meanwhile, military Orientalism transforms racial minorities into a "transnational military labor force" and casts Asians and Asian Americans as "model collaborator[s]" supporting U.S. imperialism (25 and 83). In the context of racial integration in the United States, marginalized people of color earned the "right to be treated as fully American" by means of their military service (35). For instance, Japanese Americans, who had previously been imprisoned in internment camps during World War II, joined U.S. forces in their pursuit of loyalty to the United States as exemplified in films such as *Go for Broke!* (1951). Their military service granted them model-minority status in postwar America. In outlets such as the *Atlanta Daily World*, the Black press also used similar rhetoric to highlight Black soldiers' upward mobility but ignored the high mortality rates of both enemy soldiers and civilians during the Korean War.

Building on this framework, Kim then turns his attention to an examination of counter-hegemonic literary projects by Korean American, African American, Latinx, Chinese American, and Korean authors. For example, Chang-rae Lee's *The Surrendered* (2008) and Susan Choi's *The Foreign Student* (1998) prioritize the devastation caused by U.S.-centric accounts of the Korean War. Such novels undermine the concept of humanitarian Orientalism by asserting imperialism, colonialism, and racism embedded in U.S. interventions and certifying the Korean War as a "foundational trauma" for much of the "immigrant generation" of Korean Americans (264). In contrast to Hollywood movies that celebrate multiculturalism and the victory of the U.S. military during the Korean War, Toni Morrison's *Home* (2012), Rolando Hinojosa's *Rites and Witnesses* (1982), and Ha Jin's *War Trash* (2004) archive the traumas endured by people of color and avoid sanctifying the deaths of Korean civilians at the hands of soldiers of color as "martyrs to [the] divine cause" of the Cold War (239–240). Nevertheless, these literary works do not properly provide reparations or apology to the innocent victims of the war.

For Kim, Hwang Sok-young's *The Guest* (2000) provides the most panoptical vision of the Korean War by highlighting overlapping ideologies of Japanese colonialism, the Korean War, and U.S. imperialism and racism. It tells the story of Korean brothers haunted by the memory of the Korean War even after emigrating to the United States. The brothers' violence, which originated in their elite social status in colonial Korea, led to their unforgivable complicity in U.S. imperialism and their internalization of racial hierarchies, as reflected in their killing of innocent neighbors during the Korea War and their discrimination against African Americans in the United States.

Kim's innovative cultural criticism of literary, cinematic, and photographic representations of the Korean War through the lens of interracial interactions is an invaluable asset that advances current transpacific studies and critical race studies in the United States and Korea. His theoretical frames such as "humanitarian Orientalism" and "military Orientalism" are useful for analyzing the uncharted territory of race and mixed-race studies in Korean culture and for exploring interracial relations among Koreans and people of color as a part of the afterlife of the Korean War and the U.S. militarization of Korea. In addition to providing valuable scholarship, Kim's work is an exciting sign of a shift toward transnational approaches in the field of American studies that aligns with the emergence of critical race theory in Korean studies.

Framed by War: Korean Children and Women at the Crossroads of U.S. Empire. By Susie Woo

(New York: New York University Press, 2019. xvi, 325 pp.)

Na Sil Heo

"A second-generation Korean American, I did not live through the Korean War, but I am tied to the migration of peoples who moved because of it" (xiii). As revealed in this statement, Susie Woo is one of Korean American scholars who are contributing to the growing literature on sociocultural studies of the Korean War, transnational adoption, and the U.S. empire. Building on critical work on transnational adoption, including those by Eleana J. Kim and Arissa H. Oh, Woo centralizes Korean children and women who became transnational migrants during and after the Korean War. Divided into three parts – Imagined Family Frames, International Cold War Families, and Erasing Empire – containing two chapters each, Woo charts the ways in which various figures of the Korean child were constructed and circulated in American media and how they contributed to the elision of U.S. imperial ambitions, violence, and presence in Korea during and after the Korean War. Weaving nuanced textual and visual analysis of racial, gender, and sexual representations of Korean children and women as found in U.S. and Korean government documents and newspapers, orphanage records, popular U.S. magazines, and photographs, *Framed by War* argues that American imaginaries of Korean children and obscuring of Korean women were crucial in the workings of U.S. empire.

As she states, "It made sense to work out the tensions of empire via children" (8).

If Korean children often appeared alongside American GIs during the war, Woo argues that the postwar period was characterized by images of unaccompanied Korean children who could be adopted by American families, which served as a symbol of racial democracy and humanitarianism in a racially contentious time of the Cold War. As Woo points out, this was a project of racial liberalism during the Cold War, where Communists were rendered the enemy and perpetrator of violence against the racialized, gendered, and infantilized subject of the Korean War orphan. By circulating and adopting "Korean" children and not mixed-race children into dominantly white American families, the U.S. empire rendered Korea an object of U.S. military rescue and humanitarianism, which helped to justify its continued military and political presence in South Korea.

One question that arose in my reading was Woo's use of the term, "scripts," to describe the dominant narratives about U.S. liberalism that influenced the lives of both Americans and Koreans involved in the war and the liberal projects of humanitarianism and racial democracy. Yet, the authors of the "scripts" remain unclear throughout the book. Where did the "ready-made scripts" originate from? (60) What does this term do for the author and readers that other possible terms, such as "dominant narratives," cannot do? Essentially, script-writing, and not simply scripts, is a question of power. From the performers' perspective, however, script by nature can be played and performed in multiple ways, at times veering from the original intent of the script's author. It can also be completely ignored or abandoned. More theoretical engagement with the term would be helpful in understanding the multiple power relations during this time.

What may be most fascinating about Woo's work for Korean Studies scholars is her brief but important attention to how this very logic that was useful for Americans was at times problematic for the South Korean government. Although Korea did experience mass death and destruction during the Korean War, the South Korean government also sought to present itself as an autonomous nation that was well on its way to economic development and even an equal partner in a global fight against Communism. In her second chapter, "U.S.

Aid Campaigns and the Korean Children's Choir," we learn about the American-Korean Foundation's Korean Children's Choir that toured the United States in 1954 and served as a symbol of democratic and economic possibilities of Korea. What this chapter suggests is that the two states had different goals in regard to representations of the Korean child. Although the book's main object of critique is the U.S. empire and its violence that was masked through selective prominence and erasure of Korean children and women, the book opens up the question of how Koreans themselves sought to envision the "Korean" child during the Cold War. There is much work to be done to understand how and what kinds of images and narratives of children the Koreans created and mobilized for domestic and international political purposes.

Ultimately, Woo demonstrates how the history of the Korean War is a deeply personal, intimate one that is not forgotten by the children who were directly and indirectly wounded and reinvigorated by an unending war. It is a story that reminds us that histories of Korea and the United States continue to be intertwined till our present moment. This book will be of interest not only to students and scholars of the Cold War, American studies, empire, childhood, and adoption studies, but also to scholars of Korean Studies who could examine similar and new issues from Korean perspectives.

Korean Skilled Workers: Toward a Labor Aristocracy.
By Hyung–A Kim

(Seattle: University of Washington Press, 2020. xviii, 212 pp.)

James Flynn

Hyung-A Kim makes an important contribution to the field of Korean labor history, which continues to suffer from a thin historiographical corpus. English-speaking scholars of Korea interested in its labor and working-class history still face a very limited selection from which they might build a framework for understanding the subject, despite groundbreaking studies by Hagen Koo, Namhee Lee, and Hwasook Nam. Prior to their additions Korean workers were often misunderstood as nothing more than passive inputs into the industrialization projects of the authoritarian Park Chung-hee (1961–1979) and Chun Doo-hwan (1980–1981) Administrations. Kim situates *Korean Skilled Workers* between these earlier works on the role of the Korean developmental state in the so-called "economic miracle" and the relatively more recent studies by Koo, Lee, and Nam focusing on working-class subject formation and the labor movement.

Far from the assumed submissiveness of Korean workers, Kim begins by noting that highly skilled heavy and chemical industrial (HCI) workers in large conglomerates (*chaebŏl*) have become known in the popular media and the right-wing press in particular as a militant labor aristocracy (1). Refraining from a critique of these labels, Kim accepts them as more or less valid and instead asks *how* HCI workers became so "militant" and "aristocratic." To that end, the study follows the same cohort of industrial workers across several decades to examine their subjective transformation and the accompanying changes in their social status.

The first chapter, "The Creation of Industrial Warriors" examines how her cohort of highly skilled HCI workers came into being in the early 1970s through mass training programs instituted by the developmental state as it commenced its drive toward heavy and chemical industrialization. Upon completion of their training, these workers could expect to find relatively well compensated employment in the rapidly expanding manufacturing sector, as long as they reciprocated with ideological commitment to national development and conformity to the state-constructed role of "industrial warrior" (39–40). Workers disrupt this arrangement in Chapter 2, where their pent-up frustrations with expectations of obedience, insufficient wage growth, and draconian labor laws explode in the Great Labor Struggle of 1987. Through this and subsequent struggles, HCI workers, especially those working in *chaebŏl*, like Hyundai Heavy Industries, create a new image of themselves as "Goliat warriors" allied with radical students and intellectuals in their fight for industrial democracy against violent state repression. However, Chapter 2 features the breakdown of this alliance as HCI workers withdraw from the wider class struggle to defend their individual gains made at the factory-level through "enterprise unionism" (57–60). In contrast to Chapter 1, where the state constructs worker identity, Chapter 2 emphasizes that workers' self-action not only disrupted their image as dutiful "industrial warriors," but also undermined the expectation among their radical allies that they would serve as a revolutionary vanguard.

Beginning from Chapter 3, "Counterrevolution," the emergence of a distinct labor aristocracy among HCI workers becomes more discernable. Here Kim analyzes the measures chaebŏl take to reassert managerial authority in the workplace and reorient workers toward the company through the Corporate Culture Movement in the early 1990s. Although firms like Kia resorted to coercive surveillance of militant unionists that succeeded in frightening many of the rank-and-file (85), Kim argues that a combination of labor flexibility reforms and concessions granting increased compensation and benefits to unionized workers were far more effective at fostering cooperative worker-management relations (90).

In Chapters 4 and 5, further labor flexibility reforms and economic restructuring taken in the wake of the 1997 Asian Financial Crisis and IMF intervention produce a new class of precarious, underpaid "nonregular workers" (*pijŏnggyujik*) against which the "labor aristocracy" becomes defined. At this time, changes to the labor law made it easier for industrial firms to conduct layoffs for the purpose of restructuring (92–93), and Kim captures well the sense of anger and helplessness that fell over unionists as they failed to stop mass firings, which deliberately included union activists (96–98). Enlarged through the takeover of bankrupt firms, *chaebŏl* take the lead in economic recovery, and those unionized workers lucky enough to remain with these firms in the following decade reap the benefits of wage increases over and above the rate of inflation (120–124). Yet, much of the chaebŏl led growth in the 2000s is attributed to the abuse of nonregular workers, hired on a temporary basis, paid far less, and provided far fewer benefits than regular unionized employees (125–128). Far from defending this marginalized class of workers, Kim sees HCI unionists as a "tyrannical labor aristocracy" actively contributing to the increased hiring and "exploitation" of nonregular workers through exclusionary practices (see Chapter 5).

At times, Kim employs a vocabulary closely resembles polemic. She describes HCI workers and unionists as "tyrannical" and "militant," finding them guilty of declining competitiveness in the Korean economy exacerbating nonregular workers marginalization (143). Insistence on these polemical terms unfortunately risks muddling her empirical work. Though she expresses sympathy with rank-and-file HCI unionists justifiably struggling for improvements in their conditions and pay, she repeatedly accuses them of wielding a tyranny over their nonregular counterparts (Chapter 5). On the one hand, Kim rightly points out that HCI unions have not acted as strong advocates for nonregular workers. On the other hand, the claimed link between HCI union "militancy" and "exploitation" of nonregular workers is not clearly drawn out and forgets that multiple institutional and legal constraints mitigate union ability to advocate for nonregular workers. Further, Kim's conception of union militancy is also left undefined. Confoundingly, she even finds to be militant unions that adopt non-strike agreements and whose members voice support for cooperative labor-management relations (132). Kim also conflates actions taken by union officers with sentiments of workers in general. Where she does include voices of the rank-and-file, they often refute her claims over worker self-identification as labor aristocracy (128–134) and attitudes toward nonregular workers (133). Clearly the emergence of labor aristocracy and the abuse of nonregular workers are complicated issues that deserve more complex consideration. Kim provides historical antecedents to some of the injustices and contradictions continuing to plague industrial society in Korea, but it is clear that much work remains to be done in the field of Korean labor history.

Bibliography

Interconnected East Asia and the March First Movement in Korea:
A Revolution that Continues to Be Learned

Baik Young-seo

An Hoenam. "A Tumultuous History." In *An Outline of Modern Korean Novels*. Vol. 24. Seoul: Tonga Publishing, 1995.

The Association For Korean Historical Studies and The Institute for Korean Historical Studies, eds. *Studies on the March First National Liberation Movement*. P'aju: Ch'ŏngnyŏnsa, 1989. [한국역사연구회·역사문제연구소 편, 『3·1 민족해방운동 연구』, 파주: 청년사, 1989]

Baik Ji-woon (Paek Chiun). "Toward a Transformation of Civilization and the Reconstruction of the World: Civilization Discourses of Kaizō Right after World War I." *The Journal of Korean Studies* 173 (2016): 135-159. [백지운, 「문명의 전환과 세계의 개조-1차대전 직후 『카이조오』의 문명론」, 『동방학지』, 2016]

Baik Young-seo (Paek Yŏngsŏ). *A Study of China's Modern University Culture*. Seoul: Ilchogak, 1994. [백영서, 『중국현대대학문화연구』, 서울: 일조각, 1994]

_____. *Rethinking East Asian History from Core Locations*. P'aju: Changbi Publishers, 2013. [백영서, 『핵심현장에서 동아시아를 다시 묻다』, 파주: 창비, 2013]

_____. "Democracy and the National Congress Movements in the Modern History of China." *Journal of Humanities* 84, no. 10 (2002): 161-180. [백영서, 「중국현대사에서의 민주주의와 국민회의운동」, 『인문과학』 84(10), 2002]

_____. "East Asia on the Move in 1919: The Revolutionary Movements of March First and May Fourth." *Concepts and Communication* 23 (2019): 5-37. [백영서, 「역동하는 동아시아의 1919: 혁명의 기점으로서의 3·1운동과 5·4운동」, 『개념과소통』 23, 2019]

Ch'a Sŭnggi. "Thoughts in a Wasteland: World War I and Colonial Korea, or Regarding 'Absence-awareness'." *Literature and Society* 106 (2014): 406-431. [차승기, 「폐허의 사상: '세계 전쟁'과 식민지 조선, 혹은 '부재 의식'에 대하여」, 『문학과사회』 106, 2014]

Chang Ilsun. "Changing the Other and with the Other." In *I Had Not Realized, Thou Wast I*, edited by Kim Ingnok, 113-118. Seoul: Sigol Saenghwal, 2012. [장일순, 「상대를 변화시키며 함께」, 김익록 편, 『나는 미처 몰랐네 그대가 나였다는 것을』, 서울: 시골생활, 2012]

Chang Sŏngman. "Religion and the March First Movement." In Pak and Ryu, *Inquiries on March First, 1919*, 189-212. [장석만, 「종교와 3·1운동」, 박헌호·류준필 편, 『1919년 3월 1일에 묻다』]

Cho Kyŏngdal. *The Populace and Utopia*. Translated by Hŏ Yŏngnan. Koyang: Yŏksa bip'yŏngsa, 2009. [조경달, 『민중과 유토피아』, 허영란 역, 고양: 역사비평사, 2009]

_____. "Dogmas and Practices of Buddhist Society in Colonial Korea." In *War, Disasters, and Popular Religions in Modern East Asia*, edited by Takeuchi Husasi, 243-264. Tokyo: Yujisha, 2014. [趙景達,「植民地朝鮮における佛法研究會の教理と活動」, 武内房司 編,『戰爭・災害と近代東アジアの民衆宗教』, 東京: 有志社, 2014]

_____. "The Siberian Expedition and the Rice Riots." *History Geography Education* 880 (2018): 4-9.

Cho Sŏnghwan. *The Birth of Korean Modernity: From Reform to the Great Opening*. Seoul: Mosinŭn Saramdŭl, 2018. [조성환,『한국 근대의 탄생: 개화에서 개벽으로』, 서울: 모시는사람들, 2018]

Ch'oe Suil. *Studies on Kaebyŏk*. Seoul: Somyong Publishing, 2008. [최수일,『'개벽' 연구』, 서울: 소명출판, 2008]

Ch'ŏn Chŏnghwan. "Rumors, Gossip, Newspapers, and Appeals: The Media at the Time of the March First Movement and the People's National Subjecthood." In Pak and Ryu, *Inquiries on March First, 1919*, 247-288. [천정환,「소문(所聞)・방문(訪問)・신문(新聞)・격문(檄文): 3・1운동 시기의 미디어와 주체성」, 박헌호・류준필 편,『1919년 3월 1일에 묻다』]

Chŏng Yonguk. "Current Trends in Historical Studies of the March First Movement, and Where It Is Headed." *Quarterly Review of Korean History* 110 (2018): 269-304. [정용욱,「3・1운동사 연구의 최근 동향과 방향성」,『역사와현실』110, 2018]

Conrad, Sebastian and Dominic Sachsenmaier. *Competing Visions of World Order: Global Moments and Movements, 1880s-1930s*. London: Palgrave Macmillan, 2007.

Dong-a Ilbo. *Collection of Dong-a Ilbo Editorials Seized under the Japanese Colonial Rule of Korea*. Seoul: Dong-a Ilbo, 1978. [동아일보,『일제하 동아일보 압수 논설집』, 서울: 동아일보사, 1978]

Fu Ssu-nien. "The New Lessons of Korea's Independence Movement." *New Tide* 1, no.4, April 1919. [傅斯年,「朝鮮獨立運動中之新教訓」,『新潮』1(4), 1919. 4]

Han Sŭnghun. "How the Meaning of the March First Movement in 'World History' Was Incompletely Established and Then Stuck." *Quarterly Review of Korean History* 108 (2018): 209-243. [한승훈,「3・1운동의 세계사적 의의와 불완전한 정립과 균열」,『역사와현실』108, 2018]

Hŏ Su. "The Dissemination of Post-World War I Reconstruction Discourse and Korean Intellectuals." In Pak and Ryu, *Inquiries on March First, 1919*, 141-160. [허수,「제1차 세계대전 종전 후 개조론의 확산과 한국 지식인」, 박헌호・류준필 편,『1919년 3월 1일에 묻다』]

_____. "The Theory of Peace in Korea in the Early 20th Century." *Critical Review of History* 106 (2014): 37-68.

Hŏ Yŏngnan. "A 'Cultural Historical Turn' in the Study of the Early Modern History of Korea: The Popularization of History, Colonial Modernity, and the Historicization of the World of Experience." *Korean Cultural Studies* 53 (2010): 65-100. [허영란,「한국 근대사 연구의 '문화사적 전환'-역사 대중화, 식민지 근대성, 경험세계의 역사화」,『민족문화연구』53, 2010]

Im Hyŏngt'aek. "East Asia in 1919, the March First Movement and May Fourth Movement: An Introduction to Methodologies in Reading East Asian Modernity." In Pak and Ryu,

Inquiries on March First, 1919, 23-52. [임형택, 「1919년 동아시아 3·1운동과 5·4운동: 동아시아 근대 읽기의 방법론적 서설」, 박헌호·류준필 편, 『1919년 3월 1일에 묻다』]

_____. "Another Way to Consider the History of Korean Literature: The Minjung Movement, Public Sphere and Justice." *The Study of Korean Classical Literature* 54 (2018): 5-24. [임형택, 「한국문학사를 사고하는 하나의 길: 민중운동·공론장·정의」, 『한국고전문학연구』 54, 2018]

Irie Akira. *War and Peace in the 20th Century*. Translated by Cho Chin'gu and Yi Chongguk. Koyang: Yŏnam Publishers, 2016. [이리에 아키라(入江昭), 『20세기의 전쟁과 평화』, 조진구·이종국 역, 고양: 연암서가, 2016]

Kim Chinho. "March First Movement Day and the T'aegŭkki Demonstrations: The Forgotten Memories of the Populace." In Yi, *The March First Movement in the Eyes of the Candlelight Revolution*, 175-200. [김진호, 「3·1절과 '태극기 집회': 읽어버린 민중의 기억」, 이기훈 편, 『촛불의 눈으로 3·1운동을 보다』]

Kim Hŭnggyu. *Beyond the Privileging of the Modern*. P'aju: Changbi Publishers, 2013. [김흥규, 『근대화의 특권화를 넘어서』, 파주: 창비, 2013]

Kim Jeong-in (Kim Chŏngin). "The Politicalness and Scholarliness of the March First Movement and Provisional Government Legitimacy Awareness." *Seoul and History* 99 (2018): 206-242. [김정인, 「3·1운동과 임시정부 법통성 인식의 정치성과 학문성」, 『서울과역사』 99, 2018]

_____. *The March First Movement Today: A New Understanding from a Democratic Perspective*. Seoul: CUM Libro, 2019. [김정인, 『오늘과 마주한 3·1운동』, 서울: 책과함께, 2019]

Kim Yŏngbŏm. "Violence during the March First Movement and its Implications." *Korean Studies Quarterly* 41, no. 4 (2018): 67-104. [김영범, 「3·1운동에서의 폭력과 그 함의」, 『정신문화연구』 41(4), 2018]

Kong Im-soon (Kong Imsun). "Historical Memory and the Betrayal of the March First Movement, and Ideological Politics about Its Succession." *Korean Modern Literature Studies* 24 (2011): 197-236. [공임순, 「3·1운동의 역사적 기억과 배반, 그리고 계승을 둘러싼 이념정치: 3·1운동의 보편(주의)적 지평과 과소/과잉의 대표성」, 『한국근대문학연구』 24, 2011]

Kwon Boduerae (Kwŏn Podŭrae). "The Transformation of 'Revolution' in 1910 Korea." *Concept and Communication* 15 (2015): 47-82. [권보드래, 「1910년대의 '혁명': 3·1운동 전야의 개념과 용법을 중심으로」, 『개념과소통』 15, 2015]

_____. "The Utopianism of Manse: The Restoration of Sovereignty and the Idea of a New World during the March First Movement." *The Journal of Korean Studies* 38 (2015): 193-226. [권보드래, 「'만세'의 유토피아: 3·1운동에 있어 복국(復國)과 신세계」, 『한국학연구』 38, 2015]

_____. "The Night of the March First Movement." In *'Modern' Experiences of East Asia*, edited by Pak Kyŏngsŏk, 82-109. P'aju: Hanul, 2018. [권보드래, 「3·1운동의 밤」, 박경석 편, 『동아시아의 '근대' 체감』. 파주: 한울, 2018]

Kwŏn T'aeŏk. "'The Civilization' Project of Japan and Koreans' Perception in the 1910s: How the March First Movement Could Become Nationwide." *Korean Culture* 61 (2013): 327-360. [권태억, 「1910년대 일제의 '문명화' 통치와 한국인들의 인식: 3·1운동의 '거족성' 원인 규명을 위한 하나의 시론」. 『한국문화』 61, 2013]

Kwon Heon-ik (Kwŏn Hŏnik). "Interview: 'Peace Studies' That Need to Reconsider the World

Historical Significance of 1919." *Hankyoreh*, September 19, 2018. https://www.hani.co.kr/ar
ti/culture/book/862031.html. [권헌익, 「인터뷰: 1919년의 세계사적 의미를 되새기는 평화
연구 필요」, 『한겨레신문사』, 2018.9.10]

Matsuo Takayoshi. "The Taishō Democracy Era and the March First Independence Movement."
In *The March First Movement and the World Historical Significance of 1919*, edited
by North East Asian History Foundation, 125-172. Seoul: North East Asian History
Foundation, 2010. [마쓰오 다카요시, 「다이쇼 데모크라시와 3·1독립 운동」, 동북아역사재단
편, 『3·1운동과 1919년의 세계사적 의의』, 서울: 동북아역사재단, 2010]

Min Tugi. *The Chinese Republican Revolution*. P'aju: Chisiksanŏpsa, 1999. [민두기, 『중국의
공화혁명』, 파주: 지식산업사, 1999]

Miyajima Hiroshi. "Nationalism and Civilizationism: Toward a New Understanding of the
March First Movement." In Pak and Ryu, *Inquiries on March First, 1919*, 53-67. [미야지마
히로시, 「민족주의와 문명주의: 3·1운동에 대한 새로운 이해를 위하여」, 박헌호·류준필
편, 『1919년 3월 1일에 묻다』]

National Institute of Korean History. *Anthology of Historical Documents on the Korean
Independence Movement*. Vol. 13. Kwach'ŏn: National Institute of Korean History, 1990.
[국사편찬위원회, 『한국민족독립운동사자료집 13』, 과천: 국사편찬위원회, 1990]

Pak Hŏnho and Ryu Chunp'il, eds. *Inquiries on March First, 1919*. Seoul: Sungkyunkwan
University Press, 2009. [박헌호·류준필 편, 『1919년 3월 1일에 묻다』, 서울: 성균관대학교출
판부, 2009]

Pae Sŏngjun. "The Aspect of Rural Uprisings during the March First Movement." In Pak
and Ryu, *Inquiries on March First, 1919*, 289-313. [배성준, 「3·1운동의 농민봉기적 양상」,
박헌호·류준필 편, 『1919년 3월 1일에 묻다』]

Paik Nak-chung (Paek Nakch'ŏng). *Studies on the Transformation in the Division System*.
P'aju: Changbi Publishers, 1994. [백낙청, 『분단체제 변혁의 공부길』, 파주: 창작과비평사,
1994]

_____. "The Double Project of Modernity." *New Left Review* 95 (2015): 65-79.

_____. *The Great Shift in Civilization and the Great Opening*. Seoul: Mosinŭn Saramdŭl, 2016.
[백낙청, 『문명의 대전환과 후천개벽』, 서울: 모시는사람들, 2016]

_____. "South Korea's Candlelight Revolution and the Future of the Korean Peninsula." *The
Asia-Pacific Journal: Japan Focus* 16, Issue 23 no. 3 (2018): https://apjjf.org/2018/23/Paik.html.

_____. "What to Do after Catching a Glimpse of the Heaven." *Changbi Weekly Commentary*,
December 27, 2018. [백낙청, 「하늘을 본 뒤에 무엇을 할까」, 창비주간논평, 2018. 12. 27]

_____. "The March First Movement and Korean Nation-Building." *Quarterly Changbi* 183
(2019): 305-322. [백낙청, 「3·1과 한반도식 나라 만들기」, 『창작과비평』 183, 2019]

Paik Nak-chung et al. *Examining the Great Shifts of Civilization*. P'aju: Changbi Publishers,
2018. [백낙청 외, 『문명의 대전환을 공부하다』, 파주: 창비, 2018]

Ryu Sihyŏn. "Memories of the March First Movement in the 1920s: Time, Place, and
'Nation/Masses'." *Quarterly Review of Korean History* 74 (2009): 175-202. [류시현, 「1920년
대 삼일운동에 관한 기억: 시간, 장소, 그리고 '민족/민중'」, 『역사와현실』 74, 2009]

Song Chiye. "Translation of 'Self-Determination' and the Feb. 8th Independence Movement."
The Review of Korean and Asian Political Thoughts 11, no.1 (2012): 179-209. [송지예,

「민족자결'의 수용과 2.8 독립운동」, 『한국동양정치사상사연구』 11(1), 2012]

Song Hogŭn et al. *The Programs and Challenges of Civil Society*. Seoul: Minŭmsa, 2016. [송호근 외, 『시민사회의 기획과 도전』, 서울: 민음사, 2016]

"Whether the Solution of the Problem Will Be Determined by Ourselves or by Others." *Kaebyŏk*, March 1923. [「문제의 해결은 자결(自決)이냐 타결(他決)이냐」, 『개벽』, 1923. 3]

Yi Chŏngŭn. *A Study on the Demonstrations in the Rural Regions during the March First Movement*. Seoul: Kukhak Charyowŏn, 2009. [이정은, 『3·1독립운동의 지방시위에 관한 연구』, 서울: 국학자료원, 2009]

Yi Chunsik. "'Movement' or 'Revolution'?: Rethinking the March First Revolution." Paper presented at The March First Revolution 95th Anniversary Academic Conference, The Center for Historical Truth and Justice, Seoul, 26 February 2014.

Yi Kihun. "The Growth of Republican Discourse during the Japanese Imperial Period: With 'National Representation' as a Core Concept." Paper presented at The Notion of 'Republic' and Its Development in Modern Korea and East Asia Conference, Institute of International Affairs, Seoul National University, 30 November 2008. [이기훈, 「일제 시기 공화담론의 확장: '(민족)대표'의 관념을 중심으로」, 『근대 한국과 동아시아에서 공화(Republic)의 담론과 진화』, 서울대 국제학연구소 학술대회 자료집, 2008. 11. 30]

_____. "The March First Movement and the Flag." In Yi, *The March First Movement in the Eyes of the Candlelight Revolution*, 77-104. P'aju: Changbi Publishers, 2019. [이기훈, [3·1 운동과 깃발」, 이기훈 편, 『촛불의 눈으로 3·1운동을 보다』]

Yi Kihun, ed. *The March First Movement in the Eyes of the Candlelight Revolution*. P'aju: Changbi Publishers, 2019. [이기훈 편, 『촛불의 눈으로 3·1운동을 보다』, 파주: 창비, 2019]

Yi Namju. "The March First Movement, the Candlelight Revolution, and 'the Event of Truth'." *Quarterly Changbi* 47, no.1 (2019): 61-78. [이남주, 「3·1운동, 촛불혁명 그리고 '진리사건'」, 『창작과비평』 47(1), 2019]

Yi T'aehun. "Attitudes and Perceptions about the First World War by Members of the Colonial Korean Society during the 1910s and 1920s." *The Review of Korean History* 105 (2012): 187-227. [이태훈, 「1910-20년대 초 제1차 세계대전의 소개양상과 논의 지형」, 『사학연구』 105, 2012]

Yŏm Sangsŏp. "A Plea to Everyone in the Whole Nation." In *The Complete Works of Yŏm Sangsŏp's Essays*. Vol. 1, *1918-1928*, edited by Han Kihyŏng and Yi Hyeryŏng, 47-50. Seoul: Somyong Publishers, 2013. [염상섭, 「조야의 제공에서 호소함」, 한기형, 이혜령 편, 『염상섭 문장 전집 1: 1918-1928』, 서울: 소명출판, 2013]

Yu Yongt'ae. "China's Vision for Democracy in the 20th Century." *Green Review*, January and February 2018. [유용태, 「20세기 중국의 민주주의 구상」, 『녹색평론』, 2018. 1-2월호]

Manifesto: From a Desired Reality to Its Advent

Kwon Boduerae

Ch'ae Mansik. "On the Day of March First." In *The Collected Works of Ch'ae Mansik*. Vol.

10, 472-473. P'aju: Changbi Publishers, 1987. [채만식, 「기미 3·1날」, 『채만식전집 10』, 파주: 창작과비평사, 1987]

Ch'oe Chŏngun. *The Sociology of May*. P'aju: Maybooks, 2012. [최정운, 『오월의 사회과학』, 파주: 오월의봄, 2012]

Ch'ŏn Chŏnghwan. "Rumors, Gossip, Newspapers, and Appeals: The Media at the Time of the March First Movement and the People's National Subjecthood." In *Inquiries on March First, 1919*, edited by Pak Hŏnho and Ryu Chunp'il, 247-288, Seoul: Sungkyunkwan University Press, 2009. [천정환, 「소문(所聞)·방문(訪問)·신문(新聞)·격문(檄文): 3·1운동 시기의 미디어와 주체성」, 박헌호·류준필 편, 『1919년 3월 1일에 묻다』, 서울: 성균관대학교출판부, 2009]

Cho Hangnae. "An Account of the Taehan Declaration of Independence's Time Period of Presentation." In *Collected Writings on the History of the Korean Independence Movement*, 513-536. Seoul: T'amgudang, 1992. [조항래, 「대한독립선언의 발표시기 경위」, 『한민족독립운동사논총』, 서울: 탐구당, 1992]

_____. "The Context and Ideology of The Korean Declaration of Revolution." *Journal of Studies on Korean National Movement* 10 (1994): 221-229. [조항래, 「조선 혁명선언의 배경과 이념」, 『한국민족운동사연구』 10, 1994. 12]

Cho Tonggŏl. *The Collected Writings of 'Usa' Cho Tonggŏl*. Vol. 6. Seoul: Yŏksa konggan, 2010. [조동걸, 『우사 조동걸 저술전집 6』. 서울: 역사공간, 2010]

The Compilation Committee for the History of the Independence Movement. *The History of Independence Movements*. Vol. 3, *The March First Movement (2)*. Seoul: Financial Committee for Persons of Distinguished Service to Independence, 1971. [독립운동사편찬위원회, 『독립운동사 3: 3·1운동 (하)』, 서울: 독립유공자사업기금운용위원회, 1971]

The Compilation Committee for the History of the Independence Movement, ed. *Collected Sources on the History of the Independence Movement*. Vol. 5. Seoul: Financial Committee for Persons of Distinguished Service to Independence, 1971. [독립운동사편찬위원회, 『독립운동사자료집 5: 3·1 운동 재판기록』, 서울: 독립유공자사업기금운영위원회, 1971]

"Declaration of Independence of the Czechoslovak Nation by Its Provisional Government." Wikisource. Accessed June 14, 2021. https://en.wikisource.org/wiki/Declaration_of_Independence_of_the_Czechoslovak_Nation

"Declaration of Independence." Documents on Irish Foreign Policy. Accessed June 14, 2021. https://www.difp.ie/docs/1919/Declaration-of-independence/1.htm

Dubois, Laurent. *A Colony of Citizens: Revolution and Slave Emancipation in the French Caribbean, 1787-1804*. Chapel Hill, NC: University of North Carolina Press, 2012.

"Estonian Declaration of Independence (the Manifesto to the Peoples of Estonia)." Wikipedia. Accessed June 14, 2021. https://en.wikipedia.org/wiki/Estonian_Declaration_of_Independence.

"Finnish Declaration of Independence." Wikipedia. Accessed June 14, 2021. https://en.wikipedia.org/wiki/Finnish_Declaration_of_Independence#Text_of_Finland's_Declaration_of_Independence.

"The Interrogation Record of Ch'ae Sunbyŏng." In National Institute of Korean History, *Sourcebook on the History of the Korean Independence Movement*, 14: 225-228. [「채순병

신문조서」, 국사편찬위원회 편, 『한민족독립운동사자료집 14』]

"The Interrogation Record of Kang Kidŏk." In National Institute of Korean History, *Sourcebook on the History of the Korean Independence Movement*, 11: 81-89. [「강기덕 신문조서」, 국사편찬위원회 편, 『한민족독립운동사자료집 11』]

"The Interrogation Record of Kim Hochun." In National Institute of Korean History, *Sourcebook on the History of the Korean Independence Movement*, 13: 128-134. [「김호준 신문조서」, 국사편찬위원회 편, 『한민족독립운동사자료집 13』]

"The Interrogation Record of Kim Paekp'yŏng." In National Institute of Korean History, *Sourcebook on the History of the Korean Independence Movement*, 17: 243-246. [「김백평 신문조서」, 국사편찬위원회 편, 『한민족독립운동사자료집 17』]

"The Interrogation Record of Pak Noyŏng." In National Institute of Korean History, *Sourcebook on the History of the Korean Independence Movement*, 16: 300-308. [「박노영 신문조서」, 국사편찬위원회 편, 『한민족독립운동사자료집 16』]

"The Interrogation Record of Yang Chaesun." In National Institute of Korean History, *Sourcebook on the History of the Korean Independence Movement*, 13: 126-132. [「양재순 신문조서」, 국사편찬위원회 편, 『한민족독립운동사자료집 13』]

"The Interrogation Record of Yi Kyuyŏng." In National Institute of Korean History, *Sourcebook on the History of the Korean Independence Movement*, 17: 153-156. [「이규영 신문조서」, 국사편찬위원회 편, 『한민족독립운동사자료집 17』]

"The Interrogation Record of Yun Iksŏn." In National Institute of Korean History, *Sourcebook on the History of the Korean Independence Movement*, 13: 3-6. [「윤익선 신문조서」, 국사편찬위원회 편, 『한민족독립운동사자료집 13』]

James, C. L. R. *The Black Jacobins: Toussaint L'Ouverture and the San Domingo Revolution*, 2nd ed. New York: Vintage Books, 1989.

Kang Tŏksang. *Materials on Modern History*. Vol. 25, *Chōsen(1): The March First Movement(1)*. Tokyo: Misuzu Shobō, 1966. [姜德相 編, 『現代史資料 25: 朝鮮 (一) 三・一 運動 (一)』, 東京: みすず書房. 1966]

Kim Chinho, Pak Ijun, and Pak Ch'ŏlgyu. *The March First Movement Within Korea: The Southern Region*. Vol. 2. Ch'ŏnan: History of the Korean Independence Movement Research Center, The Independence Hall of Korea, 2009. [김진호・박이준・박철규, 『국내 3・1운동 2』, 독립기념관 한국독립운동사연구소, 2009]

Kim Jeong-in (Kim Chŏngin) and Yi Chŏngŭn. *The March First Movement Within Korea: The Central and Northern Regions*. Vol. 1. Ch'ŏnan: History of the Korean Independence Movement Research Center, The Independence Hall of Korea, 2009. [김정인・이정은, 『국내 3・1운동 1』, 천안: 독립기념관 한국독립운동사연구소, 2009]

"The Korean Declaration of Independence." Translated by Kim Han-kyo. In *Sources of Korean Tradition*, Vol. 1. Edited by Ch'oe Yŏng-ho, Peter H. Lee, and Wm. Theodore de Bary, 337-339. New York: Columbia University Press, 2000.

Masaryk, Jan Garrigue. "Our People Is Free and Independent!" In *The Spirit of Thomas G. Masaryk (1850-1937): An Anthology*, edited by George J. Kovtun, 191-204. New York: Palgrave Macmillan, 1990.

National Institute of Korean History, ed. *Sourcebook on the History of the Korean Independence*

Movement. Vol. 11. Kwach'ŏn: National Institute of Korean History, 1990. [국사편찬위원회
편, 『한민족독립운동사자료집 11』, 과천: 국사편찬위원회, 1990]

National Institute of Korean History, ed. *Sourcebook on the History of the Korean Independence Movement.* Vol. 13. Kwach'ŏn: National Institute of Korean History, 1990. [국사편찬위원회
편, 『한민족독립운동사자료집 13』, 과천: 국사편찬위원회, 1990]

National Institute of Korean History, ed. *Sourcebook on the History of the Korean Independence Movement.* Vol. 14. Kwach'ŏn: National Institute of Korean History, 1991. [국사편찬위원회
편, 『한민족독립운동사자료집 14』, 과천: 국사편찬위원회, 1991]

National Institute of Korean History, ed. *Sourcebook on the History of the Korean Independence Movement.* Vol. 16. Kwach'ŏn: National Institute of Korean History, 1993. [국사편찬위원회
편, 『한민족독립운동사자료집 16』, 과천: 국사편찬위원회, 1993]

National Institute of Korean History, ed. *Sourcebook on the History of the Korean Independence Movement.* Vol. 17. Kwach'ŏn: National Institute of Korean History, 1994. [국사편찬위원회
편, 『한민족독립운동사자료집 17』, 과천: 국사편찬위원회, 1994]

Nosek, Vladimir. *Independent Bohemia: An Account of the Czechoslovak Strategy for Liberty.* London: J. M. Dent & Sons Ltd., 1918.

Pak Ch'ansŭng. *The Activities of the Press.* Ch'ŏnan: History of the Korean Independence Movement Research Center, The Independence Hall of Korea, 2009. [박찬승, 『언론운동』, 천안: 독립기념관 한국독립운동사연구소, 2009]

Pergler, Charles. "An Experiment in Progressive Government: The Czechoslovak Republic." *The Annals of the American Academy of Political and Social Science* 84 (July 1919): 58-63.

Yi Hŭisŭng. "The March First Movement That I Experienced." In *Collected Essays to Commemorate the 50th Anniversary of the March First Movement,* 400-405. Seoul: Dong-a Ilbo, 1969. [이희승, 「내가 겪은 3·1운동」, 『3·1운동 50주년 기념논집』, 서울: 동아일보사, 1969]

Yi Yongnak. *A Historical Record of the March First Movement.* Seoul: 3·1 tongjihoe, 1969. [이용락, 『3·1운동 실록』, 서울: 3·1동지회, 1969]

Yun Soyŏng, ed. and trans. *Collected Articles on the Korean Independence Movement in Japanese Newspapers.* Ch'ŏnan: History of the Korean Independence Movement Research Center, The Independence Hall of Korea, 2009. [윤소영 편역, 『일본신문 한국독립운동기사집』, 천안: 독립기념관 한국독립운동사연구소, 2009]

The March First Movement and Decolonization

Hong Jong-wook

Chosŏn Ilbo [『朝鮮日報』]
Dong-a Ilbo [『東亞日報』]

Ashcroft, Bill, Gareth Griffiths, and Helen Tiffin. *Post-Colonial Studies: The Key Concepts.* New York: Routledge, 2000.

"Bulletin: Establish a Planning Board in the Headquarter." *Chōsen* 296. January 1940. [「彙報: 本府に企劃部設置さる」, 『朝鮮』 296, 1940. 1]

Chiang Kai-shek. "Chiang Kai-shek's Memorial Week Speech in Refutation of the Konoe Statement (1938.12.26.)." In *Top Secret Anti-Japanese Government Criticism on the East Asian New Order*, edited and translated by Tōa Kenkyūjo, 1-20. Tokyo: Tōa kenkyūjo, 1941. [蔣介石, 「蔣介石の近衛聖明反駁の紀念週演説」, 東亞研究所 編譯, 『抗日政權の東亞新秩序批判』, 東京: 東亞研究所, 1941]

"Chŏnguhoe's New Organization, Holding a Lecture, Writing a Declaration." *Chosŏn Ilbo*, November 17, 1926.

Cho Sŏnggu. *Korea's Nationalist Movements and Soejima Michimasa*. Tokyo: Kenbun Shuppan, 1998. [趙聖九, 『朝鮮民族運動と副島道正』, 東京: 研文出版, 1998]

"Decolonization." United Nations. Accessed October 31, 2018. http://www.un.org/en/decoloniz ation/ga_resolutions.html

Duus, Peter. "Imperialism without Colonies: The Vision of a Greater East Asia Co-Prosperity Sphere." *Diplomacy and Statecraft* 7, no. 1 (1996): 54-72.

"Establish a Planning Board in the Government-General." *Chosŏn* 296, 1940. [「本府に企劃部設置さる」, 『朝鮮』 296, 1940]

Gandhi, Mahatma. "Speech at Public, Bombai (June 16, 1918)." In *The Collected Works of Mahatma Gandhi*. Vol. 17. Gandhi Sevagram Ashram. https://www.gandhiashramsevagra m.org/gandhi-literature/mahatma-gandhi-collected-works-volume-17.pdf

General Headquarter of Japanese Army of Korea. "The State of the Korean Ideological Movement in the Second Half of 1938." In *Complete Collection of Materials on Ideological Movements under Japanese Colonialism*. Vol. 3, edited by The Organization Of Korean Historians, 5-198. Seoul: Koryŏsŏrim, 1992. [朝鮮軍参謀部, 「昭和十三年後半期朝鮮思想運動概況 (1939.2)」, 한국역사연구회 편, 『일제하 사회운동사 자료총서 3』, 서울: 고려서림, 1992]

Haithcox, John Patrick, *Communism and Nationalism in India: M. N. Roy and Comintern Policy, 1920-1939*. New Jersey: Princeton University Press, 1971.

Hobsbawm, Eric. *The Age of Empire: 1875-1914*. New York: Pantheon Books, 1987.

Hong Jong-wook (Hong Chonguk). *Wartime Korean Converts: Integration and Cracks in the Colonial Empire*. Tokyo: Yūshisha, 2011. [洪宗郁, 『戦時期朝鮮の転向者たち: 帝国/植民地の統合と亀裂』, 東京: 有志舎, 2011]

_____. "Thought Crime Control and Yamato Juku in Wartime Korea." *The Study of Korean Culture and Society* 16 (2017): 43-67. [洪宗郁, 「戦時期朝鮮における思想犯統制と大和塾」, 『韓国朝鮮文化研究』 16, 2017]

Kang Tŏksang, ed. *Materials on Modern History*. Vol. 25, *Chōsen(1): The March First Movement(1)*. Tokyo: Misuzu Shobō, 1966. [姜德相 編, 『現代史資料 25: 朝鮮 (一) 三・一 運動 (一)』, 東京: みすず書房. 1966]

_____. *Materials on Modern History*. Vol. 26, *Chōsen(2): The March First Movement (2)*. Tokyo: Misuzu Shobō, 1967. [姜德相 編, 『現代史資料 26: 朝鮮 (二) 三・一 運動 (二)』, 東京: みすず書房. 1967]

Kang Tongchin. *Japan's Policy for Korean Invasion*. Seoul: Hangilsa, 1980. [강동진, 『일제의 한국침략정책』, 서울: 한길사, 1980]

"Keijō Minjō Ihō (Kōkei 26490, 1919.10.18)." In *Chōsen(1): The March First Movement(1)*, edited by Kang Tŏksang, 522-523. Vol. 25 of *Materials on Modern History*. Tokyo: Misuzu Shobō, 1966. [「京城民情彙報」(高警 第26490號, 1919. 10. 18), 姜德相 編, 『現代史資料 25: 朝鮮 (一) 三・一 運動 (一)』, 東京: みすず書房. 1966]

Kennedy, Dane. *Decolonization: A Very Short Introduction*. Oxford: Oxford University Press, 2016.

Kim Myŏngsik. "A Review of the Fluctuations in Korean Economic Wealth." *Tonggwang*, July 1931. [김명식, 「조선 부(富) 증감에 관한 검토」, 『동광』 23, 1931. 7]

_____. "On the National Problem: An Answer to Mr. To Yuho in Berlin." *Samch'ŏlli*, February 1932. [김명식, 「민족문제에 대하야 - 백림(伯林)에 계신 도유호(都有浩)씨에게 답함」, 『삼천리』 4(3), 1932. 2]

_____. "On the Plan to Reconstruct National Associations: Is it Disunification? Betrayal?" *Criticism*, March 1932. [김명식, 「민족단체 재건 계획에 대하야: 분열이냐? 배반이냐?」, 『비판』 2(3), 1932. 3]

_____. "The Problem of Korea's Manufacturing Industry." *Sindonga*, February 1935. [김명식, 「조선공업문제」, 『신동아』 5(3), 1935. 2]

_____. "Continental Expansion and Koreans." *Chogwang*, April 1939. [김명식, 「대륙진출과 조선인」, 『조광』 5(4), 1939. 4]

_____. "On the Problem of Controlling Korea's Economy." *Chogwang*, October 1939. [김명식, 「조선 경제의 통제 문제」, 『조광』 5(10), 1939. 10]

_____. "The Specific Process of Realizing the Unity of Japanese and Korean Peoples." *Mining Industry of Korea*, January 1940. [김명식, 「내선일체의 구체적 실현과정」, 『鑛業朝鮮』 5(1), 1940.1]

Kim Tongmyŏng. *Rule, Resistance, and Collaboration: Japanese Imperialism and Korean Political Movements in Colonial Korea*. Seoul: Kyŏngin Munhwasa, 2006. [김동명, 『지배와 저항, 그리고 협력: 식민지 조선에서의 일본제국주의와 조선인의 정치운동』, 서울: 경인문화사, 2006]

_____. *Rule and Collaboration: Japanese Imperialism and Political Participation in Colonial Korea*. Seoul: Yŏksagonggan, 2018. [김동명, 『지배와 협력: 일본제국주의와 식민지 조선에서의 정치 참여』, 서울: 역사공간, 2018]

Kim Yunsik. *Yŏm Sangsŏp Studies*. Seoul: Seoul National University Press, 1987. [김윤식, 『염상섭 연구』, 서울: 서울대학교출판부, 1987]

Matsuda Toshihiko. *The Problem of Political Rights and Koreans in Korea under Japanese Rule*. Translated by Kim Indŏk. Seoul: Kukhak Charyowŏn, 2004. [마쓰다 도시히코(松田利彦), 김인덕 역, 『일제시기 참정권 문제와 조선인』, 서울: 국학자료원, 2004]

Matsumoto Sachiko. "The Formation of a National Liberation Theory in the Early Comintern: Focusing on the Lenin-Roy Controversy at the Second Comintern Convention." *The Historical Science Society of Japan* 355 (1969): 1-15. [松元幸子, 「初期コミンテルンにおける民族解放理論の形成―コミンテルン第2回大会におけるレーニン・ロイ論争を中心に」, 『歴史学研究』 355, 1969]

_____. "M. N. Roy's Political Thought in the 1930s: Focusing on Its Decolonization Theory." *Shiron* 43 (1990): 31-50. [松元幸子, 「一九三〇年代におけるM・N・ロイの政治思想－その

植民地脱化論を軸にして」,『史論』43, 1990]

Miyata Setsuko. *Korean People and Japanization Policy*. Tokyo: Miraisha, 1985. [宮田節子, 『朝鮮民衆と皇民化政策』, 東京: 未來社, 1985]

Mizuno Naoki. "A Propaganda Film Subverting Ethnic Hierarchy? Suicide Squad at the Watchtower and Colonial Korea." *Cross-Currents* 5 (2012): 63-87.

Murakami Katsuhiko. "Yanaihara Tadao's Colonial Theory and Policy." In *Iawanami Lecture, Modern Japan and the Colonies,* edited by Ōe Shinobu et al., 205-238. Tokyo: Iwanami Shoten, 1993. [村上勝彦, [矢内原忠雄における植民論と植民政策」, 大江志乃夫(ほか) 編, 『岩波講座 近代日本と植民地』4, 東京: 岩波書店, 1993]

Nagata Akifumi. *Japan's Rule Over Korea and International Relations: The Korean Independence Movement and the United States, 1910-1922*. Tokyo: Heibonsha, 2005. [長田彰文,『日本の朝鮮統治と国際関係－朝鮮独立運動とアメリカ, 1910~1922』, 東京: 平凡社, 2005]

Nakajima Taichi. "M. N. Roy's Decolonization Theory: A Perspective on the Method of World Economy." *Hikone Ronsō* 134/135 (1969): 74-90. [中嶋太一,「M. N.ロイの植民地脱化論について－世界経済論の方法への一視角」,『彦根論叢』134/135, 1969]

"National Experience and Knowledge (2): Political Society and Movements." *Dong-a Ilbo*, January 3, 1924.

Nozawa Yutaka. "For Progress in Studies of Asia's Modern History." In *Drastic Changes in Asia*. Vol. 1, edited by Nozawa Yutaka, 280-290. Tokyo: Azekura Shobō, 1978. [野沢豊, 「アジア近現代史研究の前進のために(上)」, 野沢豊 編,『アジアの変革 (上)』, 東京: 校倉書房, 1978]

Sakai Tetsuya. "Empire and Regionalism: Interwar Japan's Theory of International Order." *The Historical Science Society of Japan* 794 (2004): 84-92. [酒井哲哉,「帝国と地域主義: 戦間期日本の国際秩序論」,『歴史学研究』794, 2004]

"The So-Called Problem of Count Soejima's Speech (2): The Ruler's Tactics of the Disturbance Maneuver." *Chosŏn Ilbo*, December 5, 1925.

Soejima Michimasa. "On the Ruling of Korea." In *Jōhōisan*. Vol. 12, edited by Chōsen Jōhō Iinkai, Seoul: The Japanese Government General of Korea, 1923. [副島道正,「朝鮮統治に就て」, 朝鮮情報委員會 編,『情報彙纂 12卷』, 京城: 朝鮮總督府, 1923]

_____. "The Fundamentals of Korean Rule." In *Anthology of Articles on the Issue of Governing Korea*. Vol. 1, edited by Yi Chongsik, 98-103. Seoul: Chikazawa Shoten. 1929. [副島道正, 「朝鮮統治の根本義」, 井本幾次郎 編,『朝鮮統治問題論文集: 第1集』, 京城: 近澤書店, 1929]

Song Chinu. "Major Currents in the World and Korea's Future (5)·(6)." *Dong-a Ilbo,* September 1-2, 1925.

The Staff Section of Chōsen Military. "The State of the Korean Ideological Movement in the Second Half of 1938 (March 1939)." In *Complete Collection of Materials on Ideological Movements of Korean under Japanese Rule.* Vol. 3, edited by The Organization Of Korean Historians, Seoul: Koryŏsŏrim, 1992. [朝鮮軍參謀部,「昭和十三年後半期朝鮮思想運動概況(1939. 2)」, 한국역사연구회 편,『일제하사회운동사자료총서: 3권』, 서울: 고려서림, 1992]

"Strengthen Leadership Over the Populace, and Bring About a 'Moral Korea': First Instruction to the Three Thousand Officials of Governor-General Koiso." *Maeil Sinbo* (Seoul), June

19, 1942. [「民衆에 對한 指導力强化, 道義朝鮮을 顯現하라」, 小磯總督 三千廳員에 初訓示」, 『每日新報』, 1942. 6. 19]

"United Nations and Decolonization." United Nations. Accessed October 31, 2018. https://www. un.org/dppa/decolonization/en/about.

Yamanouchi Yasushi. "Methodological Introduction: Total War and System Integration." In *Total War and Modernization*, edited by Yamanouchi Yasushi, Victor Koschman, Narita Ryūichi, 9-56. Tokyo: Kashiwa Shobō, 1995. [山之内靖, 「方法的序論: 総力戦とシステム統合」, 山之内靖・ヴィク.ターコシュマン・成田龍一 編, 『総力戦と現代化』, 柏書房, 1995]

Yanagita Kunio. "The Development of the League of Nations." *The League of Nations* 2, no. 3 (1922): 18-23.

Yanaihara Tadao. "Policy to Govern Korea." *Chūōkōron*, June 1926. [矢内原忠雄, 「朝鮮統治方策」, 『中央公論』, 1926. 6]

____. "Whereabouts of the China Problem." *Chūōkōron*, March 1937. [矢内原忠雄, 「支那問題の所在」, 『中央公論』 52(2), 1937. 2]

Yi Hyŏngsik. "'A Broker of Empire,' Abe Mitsuie and Cultural Rule." *Critical Studies on Modern Korean History* 37 (2017): 433-480. [이형식, 「'제국의 브로커' 아베 미쓰이에(阿部充家)와 문화통치」, 『역사문제연구』 37, 2017]

____. "Abe Mitsuie's Political Career in Korea in the Mid and Late 1920s." *Korean Cultural Studies* 78 (2018): 155-194. [이형식, 「1920년대 중후반 아베 미쓰이에(阿部充家)의 조선에서의 정치 행보」, 『민족문화연구』 78, 2018]

Yonetani Masafumi. "Social Thought in Japan During the Wartime Period." *Shisō*, December 1997. [米谷匡史, 「戦時期日本の社会思想: 現代化と戦時変革」, 『思想』 882, 1997. 12]

____. *Ajia/Nihon*. Tokyo: Iawanami Shoten, 2006. [米谷匡史, 『アジア/日本』, 東京: 岩波書店, 2006]

National Self-Determination of Colonial Peoples and World Democracy

Youn Young-shil

Daily News (*Maeil sinbo*, 每日申報)
New Korea (*Sinhan minbo*, 新韓民報)
Revue Diplomatique (*Gaikō jihō*, 外交時報)

Agamben, Giorgio. *Means without End: Notes on Politics*. Translated by Vincenzo Binetti and Cesare Casarino, Minneapolis, MN: University of Minnesota Press, 2000.

Ambrosius, Lloyd E. *Wilsonian Statecraft: Theory and Practice of Liberal Internationalism during World War I*. London: SK Books, 1991.

Arendt, Hannah. *The Origin of Totalitarianism*. New York: Harcourt Brace & Company, 1973.

Badiou, Alain. "The Democratic Emblem" In *Democracy in What State?* edited by Georgio Agamben et al., 6-15. New York: Columbia University Press, 2010.

Balibar, Etienne. "Is There a 'Neo-Racism?'" In *Race, Nation, Class: Ambiguous Identities*, translated by Chris Turner, 17-28. London: Verso, 1991.

Bluntschli, J. C. *The Theory of the State*. Translated by D. G. Ritchie, P. E. Matheson, and R. Lodge, Oxford: The Clarendon Press, 1885.

Butler, Judith and Gayatri Spivak. *Who Sings Nation-State? Language, Politics, Belonging*. Chicago: Seagull Books, 2007.

Chakrabarty, Dipesh. *Provincializing Europe*. Princeton, NJ: Princeton University Press, 2000.

Chin T'aewŏn. "Right to Have Rights." Webzin Minyŏn, June 2013. Accessed June 11, 2021. http://rikszine.korea.ac.kr/front/article/humanList.minyeon?selectArticle_id=384 [진태원, 「권리들을 가질 권리」, 웹진민연 26, 2013. 6.]

Ching, Leo T. S. *Becoming Japanese: Colonial Taiwan and the Politics of Identity Formation*. Berkeley, CA: University of California Press, 2001.

Ch'oe Wŏn. "The Issues of the Division of Korea and Its Reunification Seen from the Perspective of the Politics of Human Rights." *Humanities for Unification* 61 (2015): 119-151. [최원, 「인권의 정치의 관점에서 본 분단과 통일」, 『통일인문학』 61, 2015]

Chŏn Sangsuk. "Reorganization of International Relations after World War I and the Understanding of Korean National Leaders." *Journal of Korean Political and Diplomatic History* 26 (2004): 313-350. [전상숙, 「제1차 세계대전 이후 국제질서의 재편과 민족 지도자들의 대외 인식」, 『한국정치외교사논총』 26, 2004]

_____. "Paris Peace Conference and the Issue of Independence of the People of a Small and Weak Power." *Journal of Korean Modern and Contemporary History* 50 (2009): 7-36. [전상숙, 「파리강화회의와 약소민족의 독립문제」, 『한국근현대사연구』 50, 2009]

Fitzgerald, Scott F. *The Great Gatsby*, London: Harper Press, 2010.

Foucault, Michel. *The Birth of Biopolitics: Lectures at the College de France, 1978-79*. Translated by Graham Burchell. New York: Palgrave Macmillan, 2008.

Fujitani, Takashi. *Race for Empire: Koreans as Japanese and Japanese as Americans during World War II*. Los Angeles: University of California Press, 2013.

Hardt, Michael and Antonio Negri. *Empire*. Cambridge, MA: Harvard University Press, 2000.

Hussain, Nasser. *The Jurisprudence of Emergency: Colonialism and the Rule of Law*. Ann Arbor, MI: University of Michigan Press, 2003.

Hwang Tongha. "'Wars of National Self-Defence': The German Social Democratic Party and Rosa Luxemburg." *Marxism 21* 11, no. 3 (2014): 12-39. [황동하, 「제1차 세계대전기 독일 사회민주당의 '방어전쟁'과 로자 룩셈부르크」, 『마르크스주의연구』 11-3, 2014]

Kim Chunsŏk. "The Lessons of the First World War and Implications for International Relations of East Asia." *Critical Review of History* 108 (2014): 154-187. [김준석, 「1차세계대전의 교훈과 동아시아 국제정치」, 『역사비평』 108, 2014]

Kim Sungpae and Kim Myŏngsŏp. "The Versailles Peace System's 'Universal Nomos' and the Different Dreams of Korea and Japan." *Korean Journal of International Relations* 52, no. 2 (2012): 37-68. [김숭배·김명섭, 「베르사유 평화체제의 '보편적 표준'과 한국과 일본의 이몽(異夢): 민족자결원칙과 국제연맹규약을 중심으로」, 『국제정치논총』 52(2), 2012]

Kim Tohyŏng. "The March First Movement and Koreans' Activities and Responses in America." *Journal of Korean Modern and Contemporary History* 50 (2009): 73-101. [김도형, 「3·1운동기 미주 한인사회의 동향과 대응」, 『한국근현대사연구』 50, 2009]

_____. "A Survey on the Related Materials for the Petition to the Mandate." *Journal of Korean Modern and Contemporary History* 68 (2014): 104-139. [김도형, 「안창호의 위임통치청원 관련 자료 검토」, 『한국근현대사연구』 68, 2014]

Lambert, Henry. *Pax Economica.* New York: John C. Rankin Company, 1917.

_____. "National Self-Determination." *The North American Review* 207, no. 749 (1918): 541-548.

Lenin, Vladimir. *The Right of Nations to Self-Determination.* Moscow: Foreign Languages Publishing House, 1947.

_____. *Imperialism: the Highest Stage of Capitalism.* New Delhi: General Press, 2021, Kindle.

Manela, Erez. *The Wilsonian Moment: Self-Determination and the International Origins of Anticolonial Nationalism.* Oxford: Oxford University Press, 2007.

Mignolo, Walter D. *Local Histories/Global Designs: Coloniality, Subaltern Knowledges, and Border Thinking.* Princeton, NJ: Princeton University Press, 2000.

Nagata Akifumi. *Japan's Rule of Korea and International Relations: The Korean Independence Movement and the United States 1910-1922.* Translated by Pak Hwanmu. Seoul: Ilchogak, 2008. [나가타 아키후미, 박현무 역, 『일본의 조선통치와 국제관계: 조선독립운동과 미국 1910-1922』, 서울: 일조각, 2008]

Narita Ryūichi. *Taishō Democracy.* Translated by Yi Kyusu. Seoul: Ŏmunhaksa, 2012. [나리타 류이치(成田龍一), 이규수 역, 『다이쇼 데모크라시』, 서울: 어문학사, 2012]

O Yŏngsŏp. "Disputes over the Petition for Mandate in the Early Stages of the Provisional Government of the Republic of Korea." *Journal of Korean Independence Movement Studies* 41 (2012): 81-156. [오영섭, 「대한민국임시정부 초기 위임통치 청원논쟁」, 『한국독립운동사연구』 41, 2012]

Pak Hyŏnsuk. "Paradox of Wilsonian Peace." *Daegusahak* 98 (2010): 177-212. [박현숙, 「윌슨 평화주의의 모순: 1차 세계대전의 참전결정과 베르사유 평화 회담을 중심으로」, 『대구사학』 98, 2010]

_____. "Woodrow Wilson's Self-Determination and World Peace." *The Korean Journal of American History* 33 (2011): 149-190. [박현숙, 「윌슨의 민족 자결주의와 세계 평화」, 『미국사 연구』 33, 2011]

Rancière, Jacques. *The Names of History.* Translated by Hassan Melehy. Minneapolis, MN: University of Minnesota Press, 1994.

_____. "Who is the Subject of the Rights of Man?" *South Atlantic Quarterly* 103 (2004): 297-310.

_____. *On the Shores of Politics.* Translated by Liz Heron. New York: Verso, 2007.

_____. *Hatred of Democracy.* Translated by Steve Corcoran. New York: Verso, 2009.

_____. *Dissensus: On Politics and Aesthetics.* Translated by Steven Corcoran. London: Bloomsbury Publishing, 2015.

Rhee Syngman. *Neutrality as Influenced by the United States.* Translated by Chŏng Insŏp. Seoul: Nanam Press: 2000. [이승만, 정인섭 역, 『이승만의 전시중립론: 미국의 영향을 받은 중립』, 서울: 나남출판, 2000]

Said, Edward W. *Culture and Imperialism.* London: Chatto & Windus, 1993.

Sakai, Naoki. *Translation & Subjectivity: On 'Japan' and Cultural Nationalism.* Minneapolis: University of Minnesota Press, 1997.

Smith, Adam. *An Inquiry into the Nature and Causes of the Wealth of Nations.* Edited by

Edwin M. Cannan. Chicago: University of Chicago Press, 1976.

Smith, Tony. *Why Wilson Matters: The Origin of American Liberal Internationalism and Its Crisis Today*. Princeton: Princeton University Press, 2017.

Song Chiye. "Translation of 'Self-Determination' and the Feb. 8th Independence Movement." *The Review of Korean and Asian Political Thoughts* 11, no.1 (2012): 179-209. [송지예, 「'민족자결'의 수용과 2.8 독립운동」, 『한국동양정치사상사연구』 11(1), 2012]

Song Kue-jin. "The Introduction of the Concept of 'Nation' into Korean Society and the Adaptation of Its Usage." *International Journal of Korean History* 13 (2009): 125-151.

Svirsky, Marcelo et al. *Agamben and Colonialism*. Edinburgh: Edinburg University Press, 2012.

Throntveit, Trygve. *Power without Victory: Woodrow Wilson and the American Internationalist Experiment*. Chicago: University of Chicago Press, 2017.

Tooze, Adam. *The Deluge: The Great War, America and the Remaking of the Global Order 1916-1931*. New York: Viking, 2014.

Yamamuro Shin'ichi et al. *World War I: The Starting Point of Contemporary*. Tokyo: Iwanami Shoten, 2014. [山室信一 外, 『世界戦争:現代の起点 第一次世界大戦』 第1巻, 東京:岩波書店, 2014]

Yi Sŭngil. *Legislative Policy of the Government-General of Colonial Korea*. Seoul: Yŏksabip'yŏngsa, 2008. [이승일, 『조선총독부 법제 정책』, 서울: 역사비평사, 2008]

Yonetani Masafumi. *Asia/Japan*. Translated by Cho Ŭnmi. Seoul: Greenbee, 2010 [요네타니 마사후미(米谷匡史), 조은미 역, 『아시아/일본: 사이에서 근대의 폭력을 생각한다』, 서울: 그린비, 2010]

Young, Robert J. C. *Postcolonialism: A Historical Introduction*. New York: Blackwell, 2001.

Yi Kwangsu's March First Movement:
Colonial Violence and the "Civilizing Mission"

Kong Im-soon

Césaire, Aimé. *Discourse on Colonialism*. Translated by Robert D. G. Kelley. New York: Monthly Review Press, 2000.

Ch'ae Yŏngguk. "Trends in the Independence Army before and after the 1920 Hunchun Incident." *Korean Independence Movement History Research* 5 (1991): 273-294. [채영국, 「1920년 '훈춘사건' 전후 독립군의 동향」, 『한국독립운동사연구』 5, 1991]

Cho Tonggŏl. "The Truth about the Kando Massacre in 1920." *History Critique* 45 (1998): 47-57. [조동걸, 「1920년 간도참변의 실상」, 『역사비평』 45, 1998]

Ch'oe Kiyŏng. *The National Intellect and the Cultural Movement during the Colonial Period*. P'aju: Hanul, 2003. [최기영, 『식민지시기 민족지성과 문화운동』, 파주: 한울, 2003]

Ferry, Luc. *Homo Aestheticus: The Invention of Taste in the Democratic Age*. Translated by Robert De Loaiza. Chicago: University of Chicago Press, 1992.

Han Mansu. *Permitted Sedition*. Seoul: Somyong Publishing, 2015. [한만수, 『허용된 불온』, 파주: 소명출판, 2015]

Kim Chonguk. "The Anti-Japanese Editorials of Yi Kwangsu Prior to His Conversion." *Square* 160 (1986): 222-243. [김종욱, 「변절 이전에 쓴 춘원의 항일 논설들」, 『광장』 160, 1986]

Kim Chuhyŏn. "Unearthing and Understanding Yi Kwangsu's Editorials in the Shanghai 'The Independence Newspaper'." *Korean Language and Literature* 176 (2016): 575-626. [김주현, 「상해 『독립신문』에 실린 이광수의 논설 발굴과 그 의미」, 『국어국문학』 176, 2016]

Kim Sayŏp, ed. *The Independent Newspaper: Yi Kwangsu's Patriotic Writing.* Seoul: Munhak Saenghwalsa, 1988. [김사엽 편, 『독립신문: 이광수의 애국의 글』, 서울: 문학생활사, 1988]

Kim Tongin. "A Research on Yi Kwangsu (6)," *Samch'ŏlli*, June 1935. [김동인, 「춘원연구 (6)」, 『삼천리』, 1935.6.]

Kim Wŏnmo. *Yi Kwangsu's Theory of Liberation: The Independence Newspaper.* Seoul: Dankook University Press, 2009. [김원모, 『춘원의 광복론: 독립신문』, 서울: 단국대학교출판부, 2009]

Kong Im-soon (Kong Imsun). "Remembering and Forgetting the Battle of Ch'ŏngsalli." *Korean Language and Literature in International Context* 76 (2018): 55-98. [공임순, 「청산리 전투'를 둘러싼 기억과 망각술: '청산리 전투'에 대한 이범석의 자기서사와 항(반)일=반공의 회로」, 『국제어문』 76, 2018]

Ōsaka Asahi Shinbun Research Team, ed. *Articles about Korea in the Ōsaka Asahi Shinbun.* Vol. 1. Ch'ŏnan: History of the Korean Independence Movement Research Center, The Independence Hall of Korea, 2016. [대판조일신문조사부, 『대판조일신문 한국관계 기사집 1』, 천안: 독립기념관 한국독립운동사연구소, 2016]

Pak Chonghwa. "A Record of My Youth." In *With the Moon, with the Clouds, and with Ideas*, 113-115. Seoul: Mimun Publishers, 1965. [박종화, 「나의 청춘기」, 『달과 구름과 사상과』, 서울: 미문출판사, 1965]

____. "Unpublished Diary, August 1-September 9." In *The Life and Literature of Pak Chonghwa*, edited by Yun Pyŏngno, 54-56. Seoul: Korean Studies Service, 2001. [박종화, 「미공개 월탄 박종화 일기초(抄), 윤병로 편, 『박종화의 삶과 문학』, 서울: 한국학술정보, 2001]

Shin, Michael D. "Interior Landscapes: Yi Kwangsu's 'The Heartless' and the Origins of Modern Literature." In *Colonial Modernity in Korea*, edited by Gi-wook Shin and Michael Robinson, 248-287. Cambridge: Harvard University Press, 1999.

Sŏ Jungsŏk. *Sinhŭng Military School and Exiles.* Seoul: Yŏksabip'yŏngsa, 2001. [서중석, 『신흥무 관학교와 망명자들』, 서울: 역사비평사, 2001]

Yun Ch'iho. *Yun Ch'iho's English Diary.* Vol. 19. Kwach'ŏn: National Institute of Korean History, 1969. http://db.history.go.kr/item/level.do?itemId=sa&levelId=sa_031_0010_0110_0180&types=o.

Yi Kwangsu. "The Kando Massacre and the Future of the Independence Movement." *Independent*, December 18, 1920. [이광수, 「간도사변과 독립운동 장래의 방침」, 『독립신문』, 1920.12.18.]

____. "The Sound of the Wind." *Independent*, December 18, 1920. [이광수, 「바람의 소리」, 『독립신문』, 1920.12.18.]

____. "My Confession." In *The Complete Works of Yi Kwangsu.* Vol. 7, 219-288. Seoul: Usinsa, 1979. [이광수, 「나의 고백」, 『이광수전집 7』, 서울: 우신사, 1979]

____. "The Troublesome Path of Half a Life." In *The Complete Works of Yi Kwangsu.* Vol.

8, 445-456. Seoul: Usinsa, 1979. [이광수, 「다난한 반생의 도정」, 『이광수전집 8』, 서울: 우신사, 1979]

____. "Preface to My Confession." In *The Complete Works of Yi Kwangsu*. Vol. 10, 539-540. Seoul: Usinsa, 1979. [이광수, 「나의 고백」 서문, 『이광수전집 10』, 서울: 우신사, 1979]

____. "National Reconstruction." In *The Complete Works of Yi Kwangsu*, 10: 116-147. [이광수, 「민족개조론」, 『이광수전집 10』, 서울: 우신사, 1979]

____. "Letter of Suggestions." *The Modern Bibliography Review* (2013): 391-403. [이광수, 「건의서」, 『근대서지』, 2013]

The March First Movement and International Relations

Nagata Akifumi

Aruga Tadashi. "Wilson's Administration and America's Participation in the War." In *Iwanami Lecture on World History*. Vol. 24, 256-302, Tokyo: Iwanami Shoten, 1970. [有賀貞, 「ウィルソン政権とアメリカの参戦」, 『岩波講座 世界歴史 24』, 東京: 岩波書店, 1970]

The Foundation of the Memorial Society for Viscount Saitō Makoto. *Biography of Viscount Saitō Makoto*. Vol. 2, Tokyo: The Foundation of the Memorial Society for Viscount Saitō Makoto, 1941. [斎藤子爵記念会 編, 『子爵斎藤実伝 2』, 東京: 斎藤子爵記念会, 1941]

Japanese Government General of Korea. *A History of 25 Years' Administration*. Seoul: Japanese Government General of Korea, 1935. [朝鮮総督府, 『施政二五年史』, 京城: 朝鮮総督府, 1935]

Hara Teruyuki. *The Japanese Siberian Intervention*. Tokyo: Chikuma Shobō, 1989. [原暉之, 『シベリア出兵』, 東京: 筑摩書房, 1989]

Kang Tŏksang. "The Development of the Korean Independence Movement Abroad." *The Memoirs of Institute for Advanced Studies on Asia* 51 (1970) [姜徳相, 「海外における朝鮮独立運動の発展」, 『東洋文化研究所紀要』 51, 1970]

____. *Image of the Korean Independence Movement*. Tokyo: Aoki Shoten, 1984. [姜徳相, 『朝鮮独立運動の群像』, 東京: 青木書店, 1984]

____. *Yŏ Unhyŏng Review*. Vol. 1, *The March First Independence Movement*, Tokyo: Shinkansha, 2002. [姜徳相, 『呂運亨評伝 1: 朝鮮三・一独立運動』, 東京: 新幹社, 2002]

Ku Dae-yeol. *Korea under Colonialism: The March First Movement and Anglo-Japanese Relations*. Seoul: The Royal Asiatic Society Korea Branch, 1985.

Mayer, A. J. *Wilson vs. Lenin: Political Origins of the New Diplomacy 1917-1918*. Translated by Saitō Takashi and Kibata Yōichi. Tokyo: Iwanami Shoten, 1983. [A・J・メイア, 斉藤孝・木畑洋一 訳, 『ウィルソン対レーニン 2』, 東京: 岩波書店, 1983]

Moriyama Shigenori. *Research on the History of Modern Japan: Korea Relations: Colonization of Korea and International Relations*. Tokyo: University of Tokyo Press, 1987. [森山茂徳, 『近代日韓関係史研究: 朝鮮植民地化と国際関係』, 東京: 東京大学出版会, 1987]

Nagata Akifumi. *Japan's Rule over Korea and International Relations: The Korean Independence Movement and the United States, 1910-1922*. Tokyo: Heibonsha, 2005. [長田彰文, 『日本の

朝鮮統治と国際関係－朝鮮独立運動とアメリカ, 1910~1922』, 東京: 平凡社, 2005]

Pak Ŭnsik. *The Blood History of the Korean Independence Movement.* Vol. 1, translated by Kang Tŏksang. Tokyo: Heibonsha, 1972. [朴殷植, 姜徳相 訳注, 『朝鮮独立運動の血史 1』, 東京: 平凡社, 1972]

Saitō Takashi. *The International Political History of the Interwar Period.* Tokyo: Iwanami Shoten, 1978. [斉藤孝, 『戦間期国際政治史』, 東京: 岩波書店, 1978]

Schofield, Frank W. "What Happened on Samil Day, March 1, 1919." In *The Feel of Korea,* edited by Jung In-hah, 277-279. Seoul: Hollym Corporation, 1966.

Shindō Eiichi. *Introduction to Contemporary American Diplomacy.* Tokyo: Sōbunsha, 1974. [進藤栄一, 『現代アメリカ外交序説』, 東京: 創文社, 1974]

Yamabe Kentarō. *Colonial Korea Under Japanese Rule.* Tokyo: Iwanami Shoten, 1971. [山辺健太郎, 『日本統治下の朝鮮』, 東京: 岩波書店, 1971]

Yi Pangja. *As It Goes.* Tokyo: Keiyusha, 1984. [李方子, 『流れのままに』, 東京: 啓佑社, 1984]

Yun Kyŏngno. *A Study on the Case of 105 People and Shinminhoe.* Seoul: Ilchisa, 1990. [윤경로, 『105인 사건과 신민회 연구』, 서울: 일지사, 1990]

On the 100th Anniversary of the March First Movement:
The "Eyes of the Present" in Recent Studies on the March First Movement

Jang Won-a

The Association for Korean Historical Studies, ed. *The Historical Significance of the March First Movement and Its Local Manifestations.* Seoul: Kyŏngin Munhwasa, 2019. [한국사연구회, 『3·1운동의 역사적 의의와 지역적 전개』, 서울: 경인문화사, 2019]

Baik Young-seo (Paek Yŏngsŏ). "Interconnected East Asia and the March First Movement in Korea: A Revolution that Continues to Be Learned." *Quarterly Changbi* 183 (2019): 37-60. [백영서, 「연동하는 동아시아와 3·1 운동: 계속 학습되는 혁명」, 『창작과비평』 183, 2019]

Brown, Wendy. *Regulating Aversion: Tolerance in the Age of Identity and Empire.* Princeton, NJ: Princeton University Press, 2006.

Carr, Edward Hallet. *What is History?* New York: Vintage, 1967.

Cho Hansŏng. *Tales of Protest.* Seoul: Saenggak Chŏngwŏn, 2019. [조한성, 『만세열전』, 서울: 생각정원, 2019]

Ch'oe Usŏk. "How the 'Manse' Protests Spread in the Gyeonggi·Incheon Area." *Quarterly Review of Korean History* 113 (2019): 47-84. [최우석, 「경기·인천 지역 만세시위의 확산 양상」, 『역사와현실』 113, 2019]

Ch'ŏn Chŏnghwan. "The Popular Politics of the 100th Anniversary of the March First Movement and Korean Nationalism Today." *Critical Review of History* 130 (2020): 8-51.

Chŏng Pyŏnguk. "Reconstructing the Historical Narrative of the Protest in Suan of Hwanghae Province in March 1919." *Korean Cultural Studies* 84 (2019): 179-220. [정병욱, 「1919년 3월 황해도 수안 만세시위의 재구성」, 『민족문화연구』 84, 2019]

Chŏng Yonguk. "The Self Identification of 'Having a Correct Perception of History' by 'Progressive' Korean History Academia during the 1980s-1990s." *Critical Studies on Modern Korean History* 37 (2016): 55-92. [정용욱, 「8, 90년대 '진보적' 한국사학계의 '올바른 역사인식'이라는 자기규정」, 『역사문제연구』 37, 2016]

____. "Current Trends in Historical Studies of the March First Movement, and Where It Is Apparently Headed." *Quarterly Review of Korean History* 110 (2018): 269-304. [정용욱, 「3・1운동사 연구의 최근 동향과 방향성」, 『역사와 현실』 110, 2018]

Dong-a Ilbo, ed. *The 50th Anniversary of the March First Movement Essay Collection.* Seoul: Dong-a Ilbo, 1969. [동아일보사, 『3・1운동 50주년 기념논집』, 동아일보사, 1969]

Fujii Takeshi. "Does Political Correctness Hold Sway over the Public?" *Munhak 3*, June 26, 2017. [후지이 다케시, 「정치적 올바름, 광장을 다스리다?」, 『문학 3』 2, 창비, 2017]

Hankyoreh Media Company, Korean History Society, and Institute for Korean Historical Studies, eds. *Studies on the National Liberation Movement of March First.* Seoul: Ch'ŏngnyŏnsa, 1989. [한겨레・한국역사연구회・역사문제연구소, 『3・1민족해방운동연구』, 서울: 청년사, 1989]

Han Kyumu. "Protests Led by Religious Figures in Jeolla Province." In The Association for Korean Historical Studies, *The Historical Significance of the March First Movement and its Local Manifestations*, 262-293. [한규무, 「종교계 중심의 전라도 만세시위」, 한국사연구회 편, 『3・1운동의 역사적 의의와 지역적 전개』, 서울: 경인문화사, 2019]]

The History of Minjung Group at The Institute for Korean Historical Studies. *Reiterating the History of Minjung.* Seoul: Yŏksabip'yŏngsa, 2013. [역사문제연구소 민중사반, 『민중사를 다시 말한다』, 역사비평사, 2013]

Hŏ Yŏngnan. "Networks, Organizations, and the Plural Solidarity of the March First Movement." In The Organization Of Korean Historians, *One Hundred Years Since the March First Movement*, 3: 191-228. [허영란, 「3・1운동의 네트워크와 조직, 다원적 연대」, 한국역사연구회 편, 『3・1운동 100년 3』, 서울: 휴머니스트, 2019]

Im Hyŏngt'aek. "Rethinking the March First Movement in the Context of Modern Korean History." *Quarterly Changbi* 183 (2019): 15-36. [임형택, 「3・1운동, 한국 근현대에서 다시 묻다」, 『창작과비평』 183, 2019]

Im Kyŏngsŏk. "On Our Books: A Review of *One Hundred Years since the March First Movement*." Korean History Society Webzine. May 19, 2019. http://www.koreanhistory.org/7202. [임경석, 「우리 책을 말한다: 3・1운동 100주년 기념총서 서평 『3・1 운동 100주년』」, 한국역사연구회웹진, 2019.5.19]

Kim Jeong-in (Kim Chŏngin). "Reconfiguring the Origin of Korean Democracy." In *Democracy in Korea: Hundred Years of Revolution 1919-2019*, edited by Institute of Korean Democracy, Korea Democracy Foundation, 19-52. P'aju: Hanul, 2019. [김정인, 「한국 민주주의 기원의 재구성」, 『한국 민주주의, 100년의 혁명 1919~2019』, 민주화운동기념사업회 한국민주주의연구소 편, 서울: 한울, 2019]

____. *The March First Movement Today: A New Understanding from a Democratic Perspective.* Seoul: Ch'aekkwa Hamkke, 2019. [김정인, 『오늘과 마주한 3・1 운동』, 책과함께, 서울: 2019]

Kim Taehyŏn. "Claiming Genealogical Membership Known as History by Sexual Minorities in Korea." In *One Step Further for Korean History*, edited by The Organization Of Korean Historians, 92-98. Seoul: P'urŭn Yŏksa, 2018. [김대현, 「한국의 성소수자에게 역사라는 이름의 계보적 성원권을」, 한국역사연구회 편, 『한국사, 한 걸음 더』, 서울: 푸른역사, 2018]

Korean History Society, ed. *One Hundred Years since the March First Movement*. Vol. 1, *Metahistory*. Seoul: Humanist, 2019. [한국역사연구회 편, 『3·1운동 100년 1: 메타역사』, 서울: 휴머니스트, 2019]

Kwon Boduerae (Kwŏn Podŭrae). *The Night of March First: Dreaming of Peace in a Century of Violence*. P'aju: Tolbegae, 2019. [권보드래, 『3월 1일의 밤: 폭력의 세기에 꾸는 평화의 꿈』, 파주: 돌베개, 2019]

Mun Min'gi et al. "The Current State of and Future Challenges for Disability Studies in Korea." *Critical Studies on Modern Korean History* 42 (2019): 565-612. [문민기 외, 「한국장애사의 현황과 과제」, 『역사문제연구』 42, 2019]

O Cheyŏn. "Democratic Movements in South Korea and the Memory of the March First Movement." in Yi, *The March First Movement in the Eyes of the Candlelight Revolution*, 105-144. [이기훈 편, 『촛불의 눈으로 3·1운동을 보다』, 파주: 창비, 2019]

The Organization of Korean Historians, ed. *One Hundred Years since the March First Movement*. Vol. 1-5. Seoul: Humanist, 2019. [한국역사연구회, 『3·1운동 100년』 1-5, 서울: 휴머니스트, 2019]

Paik Nak-chung (Paek Nakch'ŏng). "The March First Movement and Korean Nation-Building." *Quarterly Changbi* 184 (2019): 305-322. [백낙청, 「3·1과 한반도식 나라 만들기」, 『창작과비평』 183, 2019]

Pak Ch'ansŭng. *1919: The First Spring in the Republic of Korea*. P'aju: Tasanch'odang, 2019. [박찬승, 『1919: 대한민국의 첫 번째 봄』, 파주: 다산초당, 2019]

Pak Sanguk. "Historical Politics and Its Function Mechanism." *Journal of North-East Asian Cultures* 56 (2018): 233-248. [박상욱, 「역사정책: '현재'에서 재현되는 '과거'의 '작용 메커니즘'」, 『동북아문화연구』 56, 2018.]

Pok Tohun. "Political Correctness or Hate Speech? No, thanks! On a Critique of 'Political Correctness' by Slavoj Žižek." *Inmunhak Yŏn'gu* 56 (2019): 41-75. [복도훈, 「정치적 올바름입니까, 혐오입니까? 아뇨, 괜찮아요! 슬라보예 지젝의 '정치적 올바름' 비판을 중심으로」, 『인문학연구』 56, 2019]

So Hyŏnsuk. "The March First Movement and Women as Political Subjects." In The Organization of Korean Historians, *One Hundred Years since the March First Movement*, 5: 161-186. [소현숙, 「3·1운동과 정치 주체로서의 여성」, 한국역사연구회 편, 『3·1운동 100년 5』, 서울: 휴머니스트, 2019]

To Myŏnhoe. "Reflections on and Suggestions in Regard to the Debate over What Caused the March First Movement." In The Organization Of Korean Historians, *One Hundred Years since the March First Movement*, 1: 145-178. [도면회, 「3·1운동 원인론에 대한 관한 성찰과 제언」, 한국역사연구회 편, 『3·1운동 100년 5』, 서울: 휴머니스트, 2019]

Yi Kihun. "The March First Movement and Republicanism: Times of Overlap, Compression and A Leap Forward." *Critical Studies on Modern Korean History* 127 (2019): 90-116. [이기훈, 「3·1 운동과 공화주의 – 중첩, 응축, 비약」, 『역사비평』 127, 2019]

Yi Kihun, ed. *The March First Movement in the Eyes of the Candlelight Revolution*. P'aju:

Changbi Publishers, 2019. [이기훈 편, 『촛불의 눈으로 3·1운동을 보다』, 파주: 창비, 2019]

Yi Namju. "The March First Movement, the Candlelight Revolution, and the 'Event of Truth'." *Quarterly Changbi* 183 (2019): 61-78. [이남주, 「3·1운동, 촛불혁명, 그리고 '진리사건'」, 『창작과비평』 183, 2019]

Yi Songsun. "The Spread and Regional Trends of the March First Movement in Rural Areas." *Korean Cultural Studies* 84 (2019): 131-177. [이송순, 「농촌 지역 3·1운동 확산과 공간적, 형태별 특성」, 『민족문화연구』 84, 2019]

Yi Yonggi. "Criticism of the Sanctification of the Legitimacy Theory of the Provisional Government of Korea and the Rise of 'ROK Nationalism.'" *Critical Review of History* 128 (2019): 326-352. [이용기, 「임정법통론의 신성화와 '대한민국 민족주의'」, 『역사비평』 128, 2019]

Yŏm Pokkyu. "The Progress and Characteristics of the March First Movement in Urban Areas." *Korean Cultural Studies* 84 (2019): 85-129. [염복규, 「도시 지역에서 3·1운동의 전개와 특징」, 『민족문화연구』 84, 2019]

Two Tales of Admiral Yi Sunsin:
Comparative Research on Yi Sunsin Narratives in South and North Korea

Jang Kyung-nam

Ch'oe Yŏngho. "Historical Fact and Literary Imagination: Yi Sunsin in South Korean Literature." *Yi Sunsin Studies* 1 (2003): 100-113. [최영호, 「역사적 사실과 문학적 상상력: 한국문학 속에 나타난 이순신」, 『이순신연구논총』 1, 2003]

____. "North Korean Novels of Yi Sunsin: An Analysis of Kim Hyŏn'gu's Admiral Yi Sunsin." *Yi Sunsin Studies* 6 (2006): 40-63. [최영호, 「북한의 이순신 소설 연구 – 김현구의 『리순신 장군』을 중심으로」, 『이순신연구논총』 6, 2006]

Jang Kyung-nam (Chang Kyŏngnam). "Periodizing the Fictional Depictions of Admiral Yi Sunsin." *Journal of Korean Literary History* 35 (2007): 339-372. [장경남, 「이순신의 소설적 형상화에 대한 통시적 연구」, 『민족문학사연구』 35, 2007]

Kim Hyŏn'gu. *Admiral Yi Sunsin.* Pyongyang: Munye Ch'ulp'ansa, 1990. [김현구, 『리순신 장군』, 평양: 문예출판사, 1990]

Kim Jong-il (Kim Chŏngil). *On Juche Literature.* Pyongyang: Workers' Party of Korea Press, 1992. [김정일, 『주체문학론』, 평양: 조선로동당출판사, 1992]

Kim Hun. *The Song of the Knife.* Seoul: Saenggak ŭi Namu, 2001. [김훈, 『칼의 노래』, 서울: 생각의나무, 2001]

Kim T'akhwan. *The Immortal.* Vol. 1-4. Seoul: Mirae Chisŏng, 1998. [김탁환, 『불멸』 1-4, 서울: 미래지성, 1998]

Ko Sŏkho. "National Awakening in Wŏlt'an's Historical Novel Imjin War: Yi Sunsin's Love of People and King Sŏnjo's Incompetence." *Yi Sunsin Studies* 5 (2005): 200-229. [고석호, 「월탄 역사소설 『임진왜란』의 민족 각성: 이순신의 애민주의와 무능한 지도자 선조」, 『이순신 연구논총』 5, 2005]

Kwŏn Chunsŏk. "Perception and Assessment of Yi Sunsin Seen through North Korean Historical

Perception." Master's thesis, Yonsei University, 2006. [권준석, 『북한의 역사 인식을 통해 본 이순신 인식과 평가』, 연세대학교 석사논문, 2006]

Pang Minho. "Introduction to Pak T'aewŏn's Imjin Patriotic War." In *Imjin Patriotic War*, by Pak T'aewŏn, 311-331. Seoul: Kip'ŭnsaem, 2006. [방민호, 「박태원의 『임진조국전쟁』론」, 박태원, 『임진조국전쟁』, 서울: 깊은샘, 2006]

Yun Chinhyŏn. "A Study on an Aspect of Discursive Struggle in Historical Drama." *Journal of Korean Literary History* 26 (2004): 34-62 [윤진현, 「1970년대 역사 소재극에 나타난 담론투쟁 양상: 이재현의 『성웅 이순신』과 김지하의 『구리 이순신』을 중심으로」, 『민족문학사연구』 26 (2004)]

Fetishism and the Encounter between Two Religions

Bhang Won-il & David W. Kim

Allen, Horace N. "Some Korean Customs: Mootang." *The Korean Repository*, April 1896.

Baird, Annie Laurie Adams. *Daybreak in Korea: A Tale of Transformation in the Far East*. New York: Young People's Missionary Movement of the United States and Canada, 1909.

Bhang Won-il (Bang Wonil). "The Early Protesant Missionaries' Understanding for Korean Religion." PhD dissertation, Seoul National University, 2011. [방원일, 「초기 개신교 선교사의 한국 종교 이해」, 서울대학교대학원 박사학위논문, 2011]

Cram, W. G. "Rescued after Years of Bondage." *The Korea Methodist*, September 1905.

Freud, Sigmund. *The Standard Edition of the Complete Psychological Works of Sigmund Freud*. London: Hogarth Press and the Institute of Psycho-Analysis, 1953.

Genthe, Siegfried. *Korea: Reiseschilderungen*. München: Iudicium, 2005.

Gilmore, George W. *Korea from its Capital*. Philadelphia: Presbyterian Board of Publication and Sabbath-School Work, 1892.

Hulbert, Homer B. "Korean Survivals." *Transactions of the Korean Branch of the Royal Asiatic Society* 1 (1900): 25-50.

_____. *The Passing of Korea*. London: Page & Company, 1906.

Jones, George Heber. "The Spirit Worship of the Korea." *Transactions of the Korean Branch of the Royal Asiatic Society* 2 (1901): 37-58.

_____. *Korea: The Land, People, and Customs*. New York: Eaton & Mains, 1907.

Kendall, Laurel. *Shamans, Nostalgias, and the IMF: South Korean Popular Religion in Motion*. Honolulu: University of Hawai'i Press, 2009.

Lewis, E. A. "A Holocaust of Fetishes." *The Korea Mission Field*. May 1906.

Logan, Peter Melville. *Victorian Fetishism: Intellectuals and Primitives*. Albany: State University of New York Press, 2009.

Marx, Karl. *Capital*. Vol. 1. Translated by Kim Yŏngmin. Seoul: Iron'gwa Silch'ŏn, 1987. [칼 마르크스, 김영민 역, 『자본 I-1』, 서울: 이론과 실천, 1987]

Masuzawa, Tomoko. "Troubles with Materiality: The Ghost of Fetishism in the Nineteenth Century." In *Religion: Beyond a Concept*, edited by Hent de Vries, 647-667. New York:

Fordham University Press, 2008.

McLennan, John Ferguson. "The Worship of Plants and Animals." *Fortnightly Review* 6 (1869): 407-427.

Mitchell, W. J. Thomas. *Iconology: Image, Text, Ideology*. Chicago: University of Chicago Press, 1986.

Moose, J. Robert. *Village Life in Korea*. Nashville, TN: Publishing House of the M. E. Church, 1911.

Müller, F. Max. *Lectures on the Origin and Growth of Religion*. 3rd ed. London: Longmans, Green, 1901.

Noble, Wilcox Mattie. *The Journals of Mattie Wilcox Noble 1892-1934*. Seoul: Institute for Korean Church History, 1993.

Oak Sung-deuk. "Healing and Exorcism: Christian Encounters with Shamanism in Early Modern Korea." *Asian Ethnology* 69, no. 1 (2010): 99-132.

"Obstacles Encountered by Korean Christians." *The Korean Repository*, April 1895.

Pietz, William. "Fetishism and Materialism." In *Fetishism as Cultural Discourse*, edited by Emily Apter and William Pietz, 119-151. Ithaca, N.Y.: Cornell University Press, 1993.

Sebeok, Thomas A. "Fetish." In *A Sign Is Just a Sign*, 116-127. Bloomington: Indiana University Press, 1991.

Smith, W. Robertson. *Lectures on the Religion of the Semites*. 2nd ed. London: Adam & Charles Black, 1894.

Tylor, Edward B. *Primitive Culture: Researches into the Development of Mythology, Philosophy, Religion, Art, and Custom*. London: John Murray, 1871.

Van der Leeuw, G. *Religion in Essence and Manifestation*. Princeton, N.J.: Princeton University Press, 1986.

Korea, the Land of the Living Dead:
The Biopolitics of the Korean Zombie Apocalypse

Shin Seung-hwan

Dendle, Peter. "The Zombie as Barometer of Cultural Anxiety." In *Monsters and the Monstrous: Myths and Metaphors of Enduring Evil*, edited by Niall Scott, 45-57. Amsterdam and New York: Rodopi, 2007.

Grant, Barry Keith. "Taking Back the Night of the Living Dead: George Romero, Feminism, and the Horror Film." *In The Dread of Difference: Gender and the Horror Film*, edited by Barry Keith Grant, 200-212. Austin: Texas University Press. 1996.

Jameson, Fredric. *The Political Unconscious: Narrative as a Socially Symbolic Act*. Ithaca: Cornell University Press, 1982.

Wagner, Keith B. "Train to Busan (2016): Globalization, Korean Zombies, and a Man-Made Neoliberal Order." In *Rediscovering Korean Cinema*, edited by Sangjoon Lee, 515-532. Ann Arbor: University of Michigan Press, 2019.

The BTS Phenomenon and Digital Cultures
Lee Kee-woong

Bannister, Matthew. "'Loaded': Indie Guitar Rock, Canonism, White Masculinities." *Popular Music* 25, no.1 (2006): 77-95.

Bickerdike, Jennifer Otter. *The Secular Religion of Fandom: Pop Culture Pilgrim.* London: Sage, 2015.

Chŏng Minu and Yi Nayŏng. "Fans Managing Stars, Industry Managing Fans: Characteristics and Implications of the Cultural Practice of '2nd Generation' Idol Fandom." *Media, Gender & Culture* 12 (2009): 191-240. [정민우·이나영, 「스타를 관리하는 팬덤, 팬덤을 관리하는 산업: '2세대' 아이돌 팬덤의 문화실천의 특징 및 함의」, 『미디어, 젠더 & 문화』 12, 2009]

Fiske, John. "The Cultural Economy of Fandom." In *The Adoring Audience: Fan Culture and Popular Media*, edited by Lisa A. Lewis, 30-49. New York: Routledge, 1992.

Greenwood, Douglas. "Pop Is Not A Dirty Word: How BTS and Brockhampton Are Giving the Boyband an Essential 2018 Re-up." *NME* (blog), August 22, 2018. https://www.nme.com/blogs/nme-blogs/brockhampton-bts-boyband-2018-2369479.

Ha Sŏngt'ae. "South Korean Media was Obsessed with Psy, But Belittles BTS's Success. Why? BTS Overturns 'Success Formula' and ARMY Becomes System." *Kobal News* (Seoul), December 5, 2020. http://www.gobalnews.com/news/articleView.html?idxno=31413. [하성태, 「'싸이'에 열광했던 한국언론, BTS 성과 '평가절하' 왜?: '성공 공식' 뒤집은 BTS, 하나의 시스템이 된 '아미'」, 『고발뉴스』, 2020. 12. 5]

Hong Dam-young. "How K-pop is becoming mainstream on U.S. talk shows: BTS paved the way, more effort needed to overcome language barrier." *Korea Herald* (Seoul), March 27, 2020. http://www.koreaherald.com/view.php?ud=20200326000961.

Hong Sŏkkyŏng. *On the Road of BTS.* Seoul: Across, 2020. [홍석경, 『BTS 길 위에서』, 서울: 어크로스, 2020]

Jenkins, Henry. *Textual Poachers: Television Fans and Participatory Culture.* New York: Routledge, 1992.

Jopling, Keith. "Preparing for the Post-Album Music Industry." *Midiaresearch* (blog), March 14, 2019. https://www.midiaresearch.com/blog/preparing-for-the-post-album-music-industry.

Kang In'gyu. "Is BTS Mainstream in the U.S. Market? Fortunately Not." *Ohmynews*, October 13, 2020. http://www.ohmynews.com/NWS_Web/Series/series_premium_pg.aspx?CNTN_CD=A0002683380. [강인규, 「방탄소년단이 미국 음악시장 주류? 다행히도 정반대다」, 『오마이뉴스』 2020. 10. 13]

Kim Hyochŏng. "'ARMY' Scholars Across the Globe Hold Conference in London, Discusses BTS." *Yonhap News*, January 12, 2020. https://www.yna.co.kr/view/AKR20200112008100005. [김효정, 「전 세계 '학자 아미'들 BTS를 논하다: 런던서 글로벌 학회」, 『연합뉴스』, 2020. 1. 12]

Kim Kyŏnguk. "K-Pop is Mainstream in the World Music: Series of Huge Successes, Exporting Idol System." *Hankyoreh*, September 16, 2020. http://www.hani.co.kr/arti/culture/culture_

general/962322.html. [김경욱, 「대기록 행진·아이돌 시스템 수출: K팝, 세계대중음악 주류」, 『한겨레』, 2020. 9. 16]

Kim Sangbae. *Information Revolution and Power Transition*. P'aju: Hanul Academy, 2010. [김상배, 『정보혁명과 권력변환』, 파주: 한울 아카데미, 2010]

Kim Sujŏng and Kim Sua. "Beyond the Semiotic Paradigm and Toward Performative Paradigm: Debates in Fandom Studies." *Korean Journal of Broadcasting and Telecommunication Studies* 29, no. 4 (2015): 33-81. [김수정·김수아, 「해독 패러다임을 넘어 수행 패러다임으로: 팬덤 연구의 현황과 쟁점」, 『한국방송학보』 29(4), 2015]

Kwak, Kristine. "Big Hit Chief Bang Si-Hyuk, Mastermind Behind BTS, Talks Music, Fans and New Ventures." *Variety* (New York), September 4, 2019. https://variety.com/2019/biz/news/bts-big-hit-bang-si-hyuk-talks-music-fans-1203322755/.

Lee, Moonsung. "Decoding the Neoliberal Subjectivity in Self-helping Adult Learners." *International Journal of Lifelong Education* 36, no. 1-2 (2016): 1-19.

Lee, Sun Young. "Practicing K-pop: A New Religion Called BTS and ARMY." Paper presented at BTS A Global Interdisciplinary Conference, Kingston University, London, January 4, 2020.

Nu, Tram Anh Ton. "Why Some Fans Are Glad BTS Does Not Have Mainstream Popularity." *Showbiz CheatSheet* (Asheville, NC), July 26, 2020. https://www.cheatsheet.com/entertainment/why-some-fans-are-glad-bts-does-not-have-mainstream-popularity.html/.

Petridis, Alexis. "BTS: Love Yourself: Tear Review – K-pop's Biggest Band Keep Ploughing on." *Guardian* (New York), May 18, 2018. https://www.theguardian.com/music/2018/may/18/bts-love-yourself-tear-review-k-pop.

Sin Yunhŭi. *Fandom 3.0*. Seoul: Bookjournalism, 2019. [신윤희, 『팬덤 3.0』, 서울: 북저널리즘, 2019]

Yi Chihaeng. *BTS and ARMY Culture*. Seoul: Communication Books, 2019. [이지행, 『BTS와 아미 컬처』, 서울: 커뮤니케이션북스, 2019]

Yi Chiyŏng. "BTS ARMY Evolves into Community with No Borders." *Hankook Ilbo*, September 9, 2020. https://www.hankookilbo.com/News/Read/A2020090709320000045?did=NS&dtype=2. [이지영, [BTS 아미, 팬덤 넘어 국경 없는 공동체로 진화중」, 『한국일보』, 2020. 9. 9]

_____. *Revolution of Art: BTS Meets Deleuze*. Seoul: Paresia, 2018. [이지영, 『예술혁명: BTS 들뢰즈를 만나다』, 서울: 파레시아, 2018]

Yi Chŏngyŏn. "When It Comes to Special Fan Service, BTS Never Rests." *Dong-a Ilbo*, August 20, 2019. https://www.donga.com/news/Entertainment/article/all/-20190819/97025751/4. [이정연, 「떡밥도 특별, BTS의 팬 서비스엔 쉼표가 없다」, 『동아일보』, 2019. 8. 20]

Nation-Empire: Ideology and Rural Youth Mobilization in Japan and Its Colonies
Ko Sun-ho

Hŏ Su. "The Organization and Activities of the Youth Associations in the War Era." *Kuksagwan nonch'ong* 88 (2000): 163-204. [허수, 「전시체제기 청년단의 조직과 활동」, 『국사관논총』

88, 2000.3]

Kim, Charles. *Youth for Nation: Culture and Protest in Cold War South Korea.* Honolulu: University of Hawai'i Press, 2017.

Yang, Yoon Sun. *From Domestic Women to Sensitive Young Men: Translating the Individual in Early Colonial Korea.* Boston: Harvard University Asia Center, 2017.

Zur, Dafna. *Figuring Korean Futures: Children's Literature in Modern Korea.* Redwood, CA: Stanford University Press, 2017.

The Intimacies of Conflict: Cultural Memory and the Korean War

Joo Young Lee

Baik, Crystal. *Reencounters: On the Korean War and Diasporic Memory Critique.* Philadelphia, PA: Temple University Press, 2019.

Cho, Grace. *Haunting the Korean Diaspora: Shame, Secrecy, and the Forgotten War.* Minneapolis, MN: University of Minnesota Press, 2008.

Graves, Kori A. *A War Born Family: African American Adoption in the Wake of the Korean War.* New York: New York University Press, 2020.

Kim, Eleana. *Adopted Territory: Transnational Korean Adoptees and the Politics of Belonging.* Durham, NC: Duke University Press, 2010.

Oh, Arissa. *To Save the Children of Korea: The Cold War Origins of International Adoption.* Stanford, CA: Stanford University Press, 2015.

Park, Josephine. *Cold War Friendships: Korea, Vietnam, and Asian American Literature.* New York: Oxford University Press, 2016.

Yuh, Ji-Yeon. *Beyond the Shadow of Camptown: Korean Military Brides in America.* New York: New York University Press, 2002.

Index

369